TESTIMONY

Robertson was the guitarist and principal songwriter in the Band.
He has produced many movie soundtracks for Martin Scorsese
and others, and continues to record as a solo artist. His most
recent record, *How to Become Clairvoyant*, came out in 2011.

TESTIMONY

ROBBIE ROBERTSON

WILLIAM HEINEMANN: LONDON

1 3 5 7 9 10 8 6 4 2

William Heinemann
20 Vauxhall Bridge Road
London SW1V 2SA

William Heinemann is part of the Penguin Random House group of companies
whose addresses can be found at global.penguinrandomhouse.com.

Penguin
Random House
UK

First published in Great Britain by William Heinemann in 2016
(First published in the United States by Crown, an imprint of the Crown Publishing Group,
a division of Penguin Random House LLC, New York, in 2016)

www.penguin.co.uk

A CIP catalogue record for this book is available from the British Library.

ISBN 9781785151064 (Hardback)
ISBN 9781785151071 (Trade Paperback)

Printed and bound in Great Britain by Clays Ltd, St Ives Plc

I was introduced to serious storytelling at a young age, on the Six Nations Indian Reserve. The oral history, the legends, the fables, and the great holy mystery of life. My mother, who was Mohawk and Cayuga, was born and raised there. Whether it was traditional music, or story-songs like Lefty Frizzell's "The Long Black Veil," or sacred mythologies told to us by the elders, what I heard on the reserve had a powerful impact on me. At the age of nine I told my mother that I wanted to be a storyteller when I grew up. She smiled and said, "I think you will."

So these are my stories; this is my voice, my song—

And this is what I remember.

ONE

*Stared out that train window
into the darkness,*

till I near went stone blind.

I patted out a rhythm on my knee and smiled to myself. Sounded like a song from the very place I was headed.

I was spellbound, gazing out the train window at silhouettes of passing towns, a blur of nocturnal landscapes streaming by. Only the lights were changing. Small-town shadows stirring quietly, city neon coloring the night sky, one scene blending into another. I'd been awake for many hours, but I was too wound up to sleep, too nervous. No, too buzzed! Me and that train were headed to the holy land of rock 'n' roll, to the fountainhead, where the music I loved grew right out of the ground. This was a southbound train.

Spring, 1960, sixteen years old. I was traveling from Toronto, Ontario, to Fayetteville, Arkansas, toward my chance to try out for a job playing with Ronnie Hawkins and the Hawks, the most wicked rock 'n' roll band around. Ronnie was a big rockabilly recording artist, an amazing showman with a fresh, Frankie Laine–type voice. The Hawks were a powerhouse band with perfect casting: they looked as authentic as they sounded—sideburns, slicked-back hair, Memphis cool, one part country gentlemen, three parts southern wild men.

I kept staring out that passenger-car window in wonderment. I'd never been this far from home before. Every time the train whistle blew, a chill ran through me. I tried to close my eyes but couldn't sleep. This was all too new, too unimaginable, too dreamlike, because, it occurred to me, people from my background didn't hardly know how to dream.

I REMEMBER the exact day it all turned around for me. I had just stepped out the side door of St. Theresa's Catholic grade school when it hit me: a vicious combination of driving wind, burning ice needles to the face, and blinding snow. You couldn't see more than a few feet in front of you.

The public school lay between my school and my house, and it was plainly understood that you took your life in your hands with the kids who went there if you cut through that school yard. But in this storm I had to risk it. The sleet was pushing me to the ground every few steps. So I set myself on a direct line for enemy territory, hoping none of those tough older kids could possibly be out in this blizzard; I thought, *Even Eskimos don't go out in this.*

But then I spotted a figure in the distance. I was already halfway across the school yard, no turning around now. As I got closer, I saw that the guy was big, and he was coming toward me. My heart was pounding from wading through the snow and being pushed back by the wind, and now from fear. He stumbled toward me, shielding his face with his scarf, like a mask. *Oh man, what does he want?* But when I reached him he merely stuck out his hand, holding a paper flyer, and gestured for me to take it. I blinked. Then I took the paper, stuffed it in my pocket, and kept moving.

By the time I reached the side door of my house I looked like a zombie who had just crossed the Arctic Circle. My mother was there to greet me, saying, "Goodness, get in here, you must be frozen!" While hanging up my coat, she pulled the flyer out of my pocket and read it aloud. "'Music Lessons: Accordion, Violin, Spanish and Hawaiian guitar.' Oh, are you interested in taking lessons?"

I shook the snow from my hair. "Sure, *anything* if it means I never have to walk through a blizzard like this again." I was already drawn to music and now wondered if maybe it could help me find a way out of this frozen hellscape. "But not accordion," I added. "Lawrence Welk and all . . ."

She laughed—"Okay, big dreamer"—and handed me a hot chocolate.

This was a turning point. I just didn't know it yet.

AS THE TRAIN idled at the Buffalo border crossing from Canada into the States, an immigration officer walking through the carriage asked me where I was going. It was a tricky moment: if I mentioned anything about a job, he'd turn me back. I was trembling inside, but with a straight face I told him I was going to visit my brother and his family in Arkansas. He glanced at my birth certificate, then looked me dead in the eye. I just about swallowed my gum. After a pause he said, "Have a good trip," and walked on.

As the train pulled away from the station and we crossed into the U.S., a wave of sadness came over me as I remembered what I'd had to do to get the money to make my way south. Ronnie was looking to replace the guitarist or the bassist in his band, and he had told me, "Come on down here and we'll see if it works out." This was my chance to convince him I was his man, so I thought it best not to ask him for any train money; nor did I want to bother my mother, who'd given me a rough time about quitting school.

In the end there was only one thing to do: I had to sell my prized 1958 Fender Stratocaster with the original classic sunburst body. She was a real beauty. I'd worked so hard to get her, saving up for months. But now I had to do whatever it took to get to Arkansas. I was on a mission, but leaving that beloved Strat behind cut deep.

The first time I saw Ronnie and the Hawks perform, it was a revelation. I was only fifteen and Ronnie was playing the Dixie Arena in the west end of Toronto; the band I was in, the Suedes, was opening. We'd been playing around Toronto for a few months, and opening for Ronnie Hawkins was the biggest thing we'd ever done. After that night, I would look at music in a whole different light.

We had a strong lineup of players in our own group. Our drummer then was Pete "the Bear" De Remigis. He had a unique rolling-and-tumbling feel to his playing and hummed along unconsciously while he played, like a human kazoo. Pete Traynor, or "Thumper," played bass. I'd known him since I was thirteen, when we played together in the Rhythm Chords, the first band I ever hooked up with. We called him Thumper because of the way he manhandled the instrument. Pete would play and stare at you steadily, hardly ever looking at his hands. It made for a strange and powerful musical connection. Sometimes it got so intense I had to look away.

Scott "Magoo" Cushnie, our piano man, was twenty-one, and he had more musical training than the rest of us, as well as a sharp sense of humor and a fascinating inventory of slang words that he never shied from busting out. Some of them he invented and some could be attributed to his devotion to the popular, off-the-wall Bob and Ray radio show. I played lead guitar and sometimes sang, but for the Dixie Arena gig we had Johnny Rhythm on vocals. Johnny was part street hustler, part show-bar rock 'n' roll impersonator, but the guy could sing like a bird. That night we played pretty good, and from the stage we could see Ronnie and his boys checking us out, which made us all reach a little higher.

But when the Hawk took the stage the whole atmosphere changed. The audience, which had been lingering around chatting, now crowded the front of the stage. Suddenly you could taste something raw and authentic in the air. The band was all dressed in black and red outfits. When they exploded into their first song, "Wild Little Willie," the Hawk prowled the stage like a caged animal. He soared over Will "Pop" Jones's piano, growling a primitive war cry and miming a cranking motion behind Will's back like an organ-grinder winding up his monkey. Will was oblivious—he was living inside the music, chewing gum to the rhythm, sweat flying, eyes crossed, head thrown back, hands pumping those ivories. Jimmy Ray "Luke" Paulman's Gretsch "Country Gentleman" guitar with its flat-wound strings poured on the rhythm. When Luke fired into a solo the Hawk had a chance to spin, flip, camel walk—the original version of the moonwalk—then tumble and land at Luke's feet. Toward the end of the solo, Ronnie would come back in singing like he was driving a mule train, and when he did the Hawks would settle into a slippery, swift locomotion behind his vocal.

Lefty Evans on bass was the only thing that kept the band grounded, or they might have become airborne and floated away. It was the most violent, dynamic, primitive rock 'n' roll I had ever witnessed, and it was addictive.

In the center of it all was a young beam of light on drums. Teeth gleaming, laughing, bleached hair glowing, whole body shaking, drumsticks twirling, pushing those red sparkle drums with a hawk painted on the bass drum like a white tornado. It was the first time I saw Levon Helm, and I'd never seen anything like it.

After the show I hung out while the Hawks packed up their guitars and drums, leaning in just to hear those southern accents, so rare up in Canada. I desperately wanted some of this mojo to rub off on me. They were playing at the club Le Coq d'Or in Toronto for a couple more weeks, and I hung around them as much as I could without getting in the way, trying to make myself useful. Their road manager, Colin "Boney" McQueen, let me help out, doing stuff he didn't want to do, but I didn't care: this was biblical and I was fast becoming an apostle of the church of rockabilly.

One afternoon at the Warwick Hotel, where musicians, strippers, and small-time con men stayed in downtown Toronto, I overheard Ronnie say, "Boys, I need some new songs. We're going in the studio next month."

A bell went off in my head. I had written some tunes for the little bands I'd been in, but this could be a breakthrough. I ran home, grabbed my guitar, went to my room, and stayed up all night trying to write something that Ronnie could wrap his voice around—hopefully something reminiscent of Gene Vincent's "Woman Love."

By morning I had finished two songs. That day, I taught them to Johnny Rhythm, who could sing them in a style similar to Ron's, and soon we were playing them for the Hawk himself. He listened to both songs with a little smirk on his face, but when we finished he stood up and said, "Play those again." Damned if they didn't sound better the second time around. Ron pointed a finger at me and declared, "I'm going to record both of them songs."

I tried not to get too excited in front of him, but inside I was overflowing. "Not bad for a fifteen-year-old, right?" I mumbled out of nervous joy. Ron just pointed his finger again and said, "I'll be keeping an eye on you, boy. You might have some talent." When it came to finding good material this incredibly funny showman became stone serious, and it was fascinating to see him turn on a dime.

When Ronnie returned to Toronto a few months later, he brought his new album, *Mr. Dynamo*, and presented me with a sealed copy. "Both your songs are on here, turned out pretty good." I tore open the LP and looked at the record label, thrilled to see their titles there—"Someone Like You" and "Hey Boba Lu." But when I looked for my name, I saw that the songwriting credit read "Robertson, Magil." Who was this "Magil" guy? What was this all about?

Ronnie laid it out for me: "Magil" was an alias used by a man named Morris Levy: the power behind Roulette Records, nightclub owner, business partner to the legendary rock 'n' roll disc jockey Alan Freed, and mobster known for having a recording artist hung by the ankles out the window of his office building. "See that Cadillac convertible parked down there?" he'd say. "I can let go and drop you down into that car . . . or you can walk down there with the keys and drive away. All you have to do is sign the papers." When you recorded for Roulette, Morris Levy usually got a piece of the songwriting. "Magil" was his credit.

I started to protest but Ron said, "Son, in this business there are certain things you don't even question. There are some ol' boys in New York City you don't want to mess with." I had heard such stories of the ruthless rock 'n' roll music business floating around, but I still couldn't help feeling like "The Fool" from the Sanford Clark song for not standing my ground.

A few days later, Ronnie came to me with an idea, one that would take me to New York City. If I could write songs for him, he said, maybe I also had an ear for other songs that would be good for him to record. Like many artists at that time, he didn't write much of his own music and was in constant search of new material. So with Levon doing most of the driving—daytime, nighttime, it didn't matter to Levon—we set off to New York. A friend of Ron's, Dallas Harms, who had written a couple of popular songs, came along. I felt as if I were part of an official song-search mission.

Crossing the bridge into Manhattan gave me chill bumps. I had never seen so many lights, so many movie theaters, so much neon, so many ladies of the night. I couldn't take it all in quick enough. We stayed at the Times Square Hotel on 42nd Street, and the next day Ronnie, with me in tow, hailed a cab. "Is Levon coming?" I asked.

"Nah, it's not his thing," Ronnie said. "He'll play it better than anybody, but he ain't a song person, or he wouldn't still be singing 'Short Fat Fanny' every night." Ron chuckled and slapped my knee as the taxi pulled away. "Son, that's what I brought you for. We gotta find me some good material."

We headed for the Brill Building. With its high entranceway and gold doors, 1619 Broadway was like a temple for tunesmiths. It was the Tin Pan Alley of its day, just north of Times Square, the eleven-story heart of the music industry, a warren of small and large production offices humming with songwriters, musicians, music publishers, and producers. Inside, a guy from the record company took us around to the different music rooms making introductions: Doc Pomus and Mort Shuman, Jerry Leiber and Mike Stoller, Otis Blackwell, and, oh yes, the outrageous singer-songwriter Titus Turner, who had just had his own hit on the King label with "Return of Stagolee." They were all tickled by Ron's stories and cutups. "Boys, I'll tell ya," he crowed, "there ain't no difference between me and Elvis Presley except maybe looks and talent!"

The Hawk headed off for a meeting elsewhere in the building, and now it was my job to listen to tunes by these brilliant songwriters to see if there might be something up his alley. I couldn't believe this was happening to me, but I tried to act as if it was all business as usual. First I went to Otis Blackwell's writing room, a small space with just a spinet piano against one wall. Otis, looking a bit worn, sat down on the piano bench, motioned me over, and proceeded to tell me how Colonel Tom Parker and Elvis completely screwed him on his song "Don't Be Cruel" while touchingly accompanying this story on the piano. *Okay*, I thought, *if it can happen to Otis Blackwell, it can happen to anyone. I'm not the only one getting shafted on songwriting, and Morris Levy isn't the only one doing it.* Otis sang a little tune he'd been working on called "Honeymoon Cottage." A sweet song, but I was hoping for something more rocking, like his classic "Great Balls of Fire."

Doc and Mort were incredibly obliging, and very much wanted to find just the right tune for Ronnie. Mort said, "Give us a little time. See what we can come up with." Give them time? These were the guys who wrote "Save the Last Dance for Me." "Yes!" I said. *Please take your sweet little time.*

Leiber and Stoller were the hottest songwriters around. They had written "Hound Dog" and "Kansas City" before they even hit their stride. I sat in their writing room as they tried to remember something that might suit Ronnie. First they refreshed their memory on a couple of his hits, "Mary Lou" and "Southern Love." They sang me one idea and I could barely breathe. It was amazing—not just the song, but the fact that Leiber and Stoller were sitting there playing it for me. "That was terrific, yeah," I gushed when they'd finished. "You got any more?" At this they paused. Jerry looked at Mike, looked at me, and said, "Who are you again?"

After I'd listened to tunes from all these songwriters, the Hawk said we were going up to the Roulette Records offices to meet with Morris Levy. *Good*, I thought, *I'll be able to get to the bottom of this whole "Robertson, Magil" songwriting matter.*

Levy's office looked like a scene out of a Damon Runyon story. Outside the door, tough guys in dark suits with broken noses looked us over. As we entered, a blond receptionist resembling Veronica Lake or Joi Lansing, her hair falling smoothly over one eye, barely glanced at us. Count Basie poured out of the speaker in the background. Morris welcomed Ronnie with his gravelly gangster voice (what happens to mobsters in their childhood that makes their voices go all gruff and raspy?). "Come on in, come on in, you wild man. I get such a kick outta this guy," he announced.

Ronnie started right in with his routine. "Hey, hoss, how you doing? I wanted to stop by and see if there was any papers you wanted me to sign so those boys outside don't have to hang me out the window."

Morris chuckled. "Don't believe those stories. I'm a sweetheart, you know that."

"Sure, I know that," Ronnie parried, "but does Frankie Lymon know that?" They both bent over laughing.

After a few more jibes, Ron did a little camel walk across Morris's Oriental rug and we all sat down. Ron gestured to me and said, "Morris, this is the kid I was telling you about. Think he might have a lot of PO-tential."

Levy looked over at me, nodded his head, and growled, "Yeah, he's a nice lookin' kid. If you had to do time, it'd be good to bring him along. I bet you don't know whether to hire him or fuck him." At that moment I decided to forgo bringing up any dispute over the "Robertson, Magil" songwriting issue.

AS MY TRAIN made its way through the Midwest, the conductor's song had a beautiful cadence to it, rhyming off the names of passing cities and towns. The farther south we got, the sweeter it sounded. When the conductor called out, "St. Louis, Missouri, gateway to the West," all I could hear playing in my head was "Saint Louis Blues" and "Meet Me in St. Louis, Louis."

A bus carried me from Missouri into Arkansas, and in Fayetteville, Ronnie Hawkins's home base, I asked the driver to let me off in front of the Starlite Motel. I saluted him, descended the steps with my old suitcase, and put my feet on solid ground. The air smelled like Ozark pines and fried food. I was here.

A voice called out from across the road as the bus pulled away, "Welcome to the South, boy!" I looked up and there was my old bandmate Scott "Magoo" Cushnie. I couldn't have been happier to see anyone. Scott had joined Ronnie's band a couple weeks earlier and helped persuade the Hawk that I was worth a tryout. He grabbed my arm and said, "Come on, Ronnie and some of his local-yokel friends are over in his room." As we approached I could hear howling laughter. "Check it out," said Scott. "These people are insane."

When we pushed open the door, everybody went quiet. They stared at me as if I were a full-blown alien. Ronnie took one look at my clothes and said, "Well hell, son, people down here never seen a Canadian hobo before. What in the world is that coat you're wearing?"

"It's reversible," I said, and everybody burst out laughing, Ronnie the loudest.

"Son, we're going to have to get you some damn clothes, immediately if not sooner. I can't be seen with anybody dressed like that 'round here. I'm much too good-looking and sophisticated myself."

The next few days I quietly but quickly adjusted to the surroundings. The local Fayetteville characters were classic, a rogues' gallery of wild southern types and small-time legends. Herman "Killer" Tuck, who had played drums for Jerry Lee Lewis, owned a furniture store in town. Chester, a mentally challenged fellow in a wheelchair, would yell bizarre phrases at girls walking by on the main drag—"Whoocha, baby, whoocha!"—prompting the store owners to threaten to push his wheelchair down the hill if he didn't stop scaring away the customers. And Don Tyson, the owner of Tyson's Chickens, loved four things: making money, rock 'n' roll music, having a few laughs, and pretty girls—though not necessarily in that order.

My favorite, though, was Dayton Stratton, whom Ronnie called Blinky. Together they were partners in the local Shamrock Club. Dayton was one of the sweetest, most gentlemanly people you ever met, but saints preserve you if you caused trouble in his club. He would first ask you, extremely polite and kindly, to leave the premises. If the trouble continued, he would start blinking and stammering. Then, like lightning, his feet would leave the floor and he would pound you several times about the head, so fast, so hard, you didn't know what had happened. Invariably, people who pushed too far with Dayton went *down*. Whether they were huge Razorback football players from the University of Arkansas or big, tough redneck farmboys, it didn't matter. You did *not* make trouble in Dayton's backyard.

Ronnie took me to his favorite Fayetteville clothing store and dressed me and groomed me. When it came to music, though, the expectation was that I'd quickly learn to measure up. The band rehearsed at the Shamrock in the afternoons and sometimes gigged there at night. I wasn't sure where I fit into the mix just yet, but they let me sit on the side, near the front of the stage, and take it all in. Technically I wasn't old enough to get into a club like this, but since I was with their coolest export at the time, Rompin' Ronnie Hawkins, the doorman never batted an eye.

I soaked up everything I could, fast as I could, especially when it came to the band's personnel. The guitarist I was trying out to replace, Fred Carter Jr., was ten years older than me. He hailed from Winnsboro, Louisiana, and had played with Ron's cousin, Dale Hawkins, of "Suzie Q" fame, and Roy Orbison. Fred was an experienced and accomplished musician, definitely the real thing. Levon Helm, who was probably twenty by then, already struck me as a veteran. He knew the ropes and had music in his bones. He was just born that way: the *real* real thing.

The presence of my old bandmate Scott gave me a boost of confidence and comfort in this strange new world. He seemed to roll smoothly with the routine. He wasn't as thunderous on the keys as Will "Pop" Jones, the piano man he had come down to replace, but he played his heart out. I liked the swing he gave the groove, not at all choppy or hardheaded.

Lefty Evans, a right-handed bass player, had a more traditional sound. It bugged Levon, who wanted something more driving, more eighth notes, more exciting, but Lefty's real calling was country music. Levon teased him about it. "How can you sing, play bass, and hold your nose at the same time to get that nasal twang in yer voice?"

Every day opened my eyes a bit wider to the Hawks' world. It became pretty obvious to me early on that in Arkansas they had their own rules when it came to sexual activity. It was understood that there was going to be some hanky-panky, but with whom seemed shockingly circumstantial: it was par for the course to see someone's sister or wife or neighbor slipping in or out of Ronnie's or Levon's motel room in the afternoons. Sometimes Ron would whisper under his breath, "Boys, I'll tell you, I had a little encounter this afternoon with what's-his-name's sister-in-law and she nearly devoured me. Got scratches all over my back to show for it." Later that night we would see the sister-in-law and her husband at the gig near the front of the stage, cheering Ron on. I was baffled—but also couldn't wait to get acquainted with the local customs.

SOON WE HEADED out for the Mississippi Delta, Levon's home turf. The six of us rolled in Ronnie's big Caddy, towing our instruments behind us in a trailer decorated on each side with a painting of a hawk holding drumsticks. Along Highway 540, Scott and I fell silent at the particular beauty of the Arkansas countryside, rolling hills of green on green as far as the eye could see. We turned onto Route 40, where we passed the town of Conway, namesake of Harold Jenkins, a singer with an incredible vocal range who found much greater success after changing his name to Conway Twitty.

We were headed to Charlie Halbert's Rainbow Court Inn Motel in West Helena. Ron described Charlie as a good old boy who loved music and liked to help out musicians. He also owned the *Delta Queen* ferryboat, which went from Helena over to Clarksdale, Mississippi, home and breeding ground of a lot of great bluesmen. Memphis was seventy miles upriver and was the center of music in the universe, as far as I was concerned. This whole area was a great mystery to me: How could Johnny Cash, B. B. King, Jimmy Reed, Elvis Presley, Muddy Waters, Bo Diddley, Sonny Boy Williamson, Robert Johnson, and on and on, all come from this particular place? What magic potion was in the water around here?

Shortly after we settled in at the Rainbow, Ronnie went to England to do a TV show and promote his new record. He took Levon with him, leaving Fred behind to familiarize Scott and me with Ron's repertoire. But I soon discovered Fred had little interest in showing me anything. He constantly avoided my efforts to learn from him, "Nobody ever showed me nothing," he would say, "so why should I show you?"

What was his deal? Was I a threat to him? Or was I nothing at all? Scott had already sat in with the Hawks and was familiar with some of the tunes, but I had barely a clue. To make it worse, Lefty Evans had decided to leave the Hawks too. He'd spoken quite seriously about becoming a preacher. "Preachers make some damn good money down here," he'd inform us with remarkable sincerity. His departure meant double trouble for me: now my challenge was to learn all the songs on bass *and* guitar. Which meant that I'd have to learn to play the bass—I had never really played it in my life. I wondered if Scott might have exaggerated my relationship with the Fender Precision Bass to Ron to help get me the tryout, but now wasn't the time to get confessional.

I tried to hustle Fred a little. "You can't blame me for wanting to learn from a master. Throw me a bone. I just don't want to let Ronnie down." Scott thought Fred was being a jerk and shrugged it off with a "who needs him" attitude, but I couldn't afford to think like that. I needed to absorb everything I could while Ronnie was gone. This was rockabilly boot camp.

In the meantime I tried to soak up as much local flavor as possible. Before he left for England, Ronnie had taken us to the Delta Supper Club in West Helena, a local dance joint where everybody went to hear music. Carl Perkins, Roy Orbison, Conway Twitty, and Ronnie all played here on occasion. The Delta Club was very basic and unglamorous—some tables, a dance floor, a funny-looking shell-shaped bandstand, a few neon signs, and a bar of legend that had been chainsawed down the middle by an angry patron. All kinds of folks came here; I noticed that down south older people and young people all went to the same clubs. Age didn't matter; it was all about the music, and who was playing it.

Scott and I ventured over there after dinner one night when we heard that Billy Lee Riley and the Little Green Men might be playing. He scored us some beer, though I hadn't yet developed a taste for alcohol. We got to talking with a couple of young girls who were dancing in front of us—they simply could not fathom that we were from far-away Canada. Scott and the two girls got a little tipsy and we all ended up back at the Rainbow Inn.

The Rainbow had a number of well-furnished bungalows—ours, which we shared with Fred, had a living room where we could set up our instruments, a kitchen area with a bar, and two comfortable bed-rooms. We were having a few laughs with the girls when Fred came back. He paused in the doorway for a moment, looked around, and liked what he saw. "Well, hello there. Where did you fine young things come from?" Suddenly he was all funny and charming, flashing his powerful dimples. He ended up embracing the girl I was with in a long, slow hug, speaking softly in her ear. Over her shoulder, he waved me good-bye. I'd been snookered. I stepped out for a bit, and when I came back both bedroom doors were locked. When I knocked, Fred called, "Go away, I'm busy." The night ended for me on a chair in the living room among empty beer cans and full ashtrays.

A couple of nights later Scott and I were waiting for a table at Nick's Café, the place everybody went for a late bite, when I noticed a striking girl grooving to the song playing on the jukebox. As I looked closer I could see that she might be an American Indian. I drew a breath, went over, and started gabbing about what a cool jukebox they had at Nick's. She said her name was Emma, and she turned out to be from the Kiowa Nation. I told her my mother was Mohawk, from Six Na-tions. "Mohawk! You're Mohawk? How come you don't have one of those scary haircuts?" We had an easy connection, and while the boys were sampling the chicken-fried steak, Emma and I sat by the river talking. She had the sweetest laugh. Miss Emma and me, we both felt the shimmer.

At the end of the week, Fred said he was driving over to Sun Rec-ords in Memphis to let Sam Phillips know he'd be available for session work in the near future. He asked if I wanted to come. Sun Records? The label that discovered Jerry Lee Lewis, Elvis Presley, Carl Perkins, and Johnny Cash? With the yellow label that was black in the begin-ning? *The center of the universe?* Yes, I wanted to go to Sun Records.

We hit the road and Fred pointed out pieces of music history along the way, like the Plantation Inn, Miss Annie's Place, and the Cotton Club in West Memphis, and then we drove over the Memphis-Arkansas Memorial Bridge into Tennessee. He dropped me off on Beale Street at the Home of the Blues record store while he went to make an appointment at Sun. Home of the Blues was just up the street from the Lansky Brothers, where only eight years earlier a seventeen-year-old Elvis working at the Loew's State Theatre had bought his first suit from Bernard Lansky, and where Carl Perkins and Johnny Cash got their sharp outfits. To me these were more than just shops: they were historic landmarks. I had heard of Home of the Blues only on fifty-thousand-watt southern radio stations that on cold, clear nights could beam all the way up to Canada.

The inside of the shop featured wall-to-wall record covers and rows and rows of records, ones you could never get up north and many I'd never heard of. I spent nearly my whole first week's paycheck on Warren Smith, Muddy Waters, B. B. King, Roy Orbison, Little Walter, Charlie Rich, Howlin' Wolf, Don Gibson, T-Bone Walker, Little Junior Parker, Ray Charles, Mahalia Jackson, and the Swan Silvertones. I was going to *my* music school, and to church. When Fred picked me up on Beale Street later and saw all my bags of records, his eyes went wide. "Boy, what did you do, buy out the store?"

"They've got everything you want and stuff you didn't know you wanted," I told him. I felt proud and equipped.

As we headed back to Sun Records for Fred's appointment, I was flushed with excitement. Inside I took a seat in a little lobby area while Fred was escorted to an office. The pictures of legendary Sun recording artists hanging up and down the hallway made me feel I was stepping into a rock 'n' roll cathedral. A man came out of the recording studio, and as the door swung open I thought I saw Jerry Lee Lewis sitting at the piano. *Must be imagining it*, I thought, but then the door to the control room opened and from the speakers I heard that voice and that piano—Jerry himself. So real I could barely stand it.

Back in West Helena, Scott pored over the jackets on my new LPs, commenting on the cool or corny artwork, and I cut my thumb on the plastic opening all the albums. I had found the holy grail. Those records played day and night on Ron's record player, which was worth its weight in silver. I always listened with a guitar and bass within reach and many times fell asleep playing along.

The next night I brought Emma, the beautiful Kiowa girl I had met at Nick's Café, back to the Rainbow Inn. We fell into each other's arms, went directly to Fred's bedroom, and locked the door. Scott was already asleep in the other bedroom.

Emma and I were deep in the throes of enchantment when Fred returned. He knocked sharply on the bedroom door with a sense of authority. I said, "Go away, busy right now."

He knocked again.

"Go away, thank you, I'm busy." Emma put her hand over my mouth to stifle my laughter.

When we surfaced in the morning, Fred was stretched out on the living-room couch with a cushion over his head to shield his eyes from the daylight.

Not sure why, but after that Fred started sharing some of his guitar knowledge with me. That afternoon he was changing his guitar strings and decided to show me how he used one banjo string for the high E and moved all the regular guitar strings down one place, meaning the A string was now the low E. It made all the strings much more bendable. He said it was a trick he had learned when he was playing the *Louisiana Hayride*, a radio show out of Shreveport, where country music and the blues met and got hitched. I was taken with the way he used a flat pick and two National finger picks on his middle and third fingers. I started trying that too. You could grab hold of the strings in a more deliberate way, steel on steel, and I even tried them playing bass—which might've been a first.

Fred finally started going over all the tunes with us, showing us where the live arrangements were different from the records. I was lapping it up, grateful for his generous turn. I'd been using a spare guitar and bass, but he suggested we go over to the guitar store in Memphis and check out some new equipment. Ronnie was always open to getting new gear for members of his band. He let you pay it off, a little out of your paycheck every week.

And then news came over the wire that on Friday night it was going down: Howlin' Wolf and his band were playing at the Cotton Club in West Memphis. I had just bought his record with the gray cover and a picture of a wolf howling, called *Moanin' in the Moonlight*, the one with "I Asked for Water (She Gave Me Gasoline)," "Smoke Stack Lightning," and of course "Evil," a real heart-warmer. Yes, Chester Burnett, known as Howlin' Wolf, was badass. I suggested we could piggyback a stop at the Cotton Club with our trip to the musical instrument store. But Fred wouldn't commit, mainly because I was too young to get into the club.

On Friday afternoon we "motorvated" over to Memphis and the O.K. Houck Piano Company, a place of true beauty. Guitars ran up and down the walls forever, as I had imagined in a dream. I tried out a red Gibson 335 semi-hollow-body, like Chuck Berry played. The body was a little bulky, but I liked it. The sound was smooth and wide, different from solid-body Fenders, Gibsons, and Gretsches, which had a tighter, brighter sound. James Burton, Roy Buchanan, and Fred all played Fender Telecasters, maybe because they had all come through the *Louisiana Hayride* school. These guitars were lighter in weight and didn't kill your shoulder when you had to play long hours in a club. I strapped on an unusual white Fender six-string bass with a tremolo bar, a halfway point between a bass and a guitar. This was new and different. I wanted it.

Back in the car Fred said the magic words. "Let's give it a shot. Let's go see Howlin' Wolf. If they stop you at the door, you can wait outside and just listen. I'll go in and tell you how great it was." I hoped he was kidding.

As we approached the entrance to the Cotton Club on Broadway Street, a huge African American bouncer looked at me and said, "How old're you?"

Fred answered for me. "He's with me, and we're musicians from over in Helena playing with Ronnie Hawkins. We're just here to listen to some good music."

The bouncer asked if we had any booze with us, and we both shook our heads no. "Well, make sure he don't drink any," he said, pointing at me.

We entered a music haven: a combination bar, restaurant, dance hall, and juke joint. The odor of stale cigarette smoke, perfume, liquor, and spicy food hung thick in the air. The crowd was almost entirely black, and I was too new to know whether it was cool for Fred and me to be here. Wolf and his band were already in the middle of their set, sweat glowing on their faces. Wolf's stage attire was a white shirt and dress pants, but on him it looked like straight-arrow blues. Above the stage a blue spotlight shining down on his face made him look like a haunted man, but this was no voodoo; this was hoodoo and the spirit of the "new blues," different from the traditional folk blues of Josh White or Big Bill Broonzy. This was down, dirty, and hard.

I was tripping over myself trying to get closer to that sound and fury. Wolf's vocal style came from another planet, sliding from his big growlin' tone into his pinched bullhorn stinger, then just as quickly lifting us with his hoot-owl falsetto. And those guitar parts from Hubert Sumlin, king of the blues riff—to hear them live was like hearing them for the first time. On Howlin' Wolf's records the music came bursting out of the speakers with a powerful authority, but when the band played live it had a surprisingly delicate blend. All the parts sounded beautifully balanced.

I was mouth breathing, my jaw hanging down. Fred looked at me and broke out laughing but I was locked in. This was Wolf in *his* element, in his backyard, with his devotees egging him on. When they hit the last blast of their set, the house lights came on and it was like snapping out of a spell. That night was the most frightening musical experience I'd ever had, and it felt way too good.

RONNIE CAME BACK from England with a deeper, more worldly look in his eyes. It sounded as if he and Levon had had a bloody good time. Ronnie kept preaching of England's glories. "Boys, if we could spend some real time over there, we could be big, we could stir it up big time. They love our music and I don't think they've got much music of their own, or maybe it's not very good."

Levon confessed he'd caught a case of albino crabs there. "Never seen anything like it," Ronnie said. "I swear, they were white. Hard to see those little albino suckers."

During the trip they'd run into Eddie Cochran and Gene Vincent, who were touring there. I'd played Gene's "Be-Bop-A-Lula" on the jukebox at the soda shop across from my high school nearly every day—just hearing about Ron and Levon seeing him was enough to give me a rush. "Gene was singin' good," Ron told us, "but he looked to me like he was missing his band, the Blue Caps." Not long after Ron and Levon got back, Eddie and Gene were in a car wreck while they were still on the road in England. Eddie was killed, and Gene was terribly hurt. The news devastated us. They were true rock 'n' roll heroes in our book.

I could tell Ronnie was trying to figure out if it was worth the trouble hiring an underage Canadian kid like me, who might bring down the law if I got caught by an inspector. It was virtually unheard of to consider hiring a sixteen-year-old to play in these nightclubs, where you had to be twenty-one. Levon was Ronnie's go-to guy, his musical ears. It was his job to figure out whether I could play worth a damn enough to take the risk of getting busted. But slowly I was convincing him. When we practiced, he could see we wanted to go musically to the same place. He could feel my hunger. When he saw the records I had bought while he was in England and heard how blown away I was by his meeting Eddie Cochran, he saw how much this southern music meant to me, how deep it was in my soul. All this made me feel like I was starting to get through to Levon, not just musically but on a personal level.

Then one day Levon said, "Hey, Robbie, come with me. Let's go visit my folks. I'm gonna show you Marvell, Arkansas, gateway to Indian Bay." We'd be driving up in Ron's big white '59 Cadillac Sedan DeVille. He smiled. "That'll turn some heads."

On the way he searched the radio dial, lit a Winston cigarette, told me about local legend Sonny Boy Williamson, and drove, all at the same time. Sonny Boy had a show on Helena radio station KFFA. "That's over on Cherry Street, 1250 on the AM dial," Levon told me. "At twelve fifteen King Biscuit Flour presents Sonny Boy Williamson and his King Biscuit Boys. Brought to you by Sonny Boy Cornmeal!" Levon mouthed the sound of a blues harp. "Wah-oo-whaaa! And that's just how the show gets started." He laughed. "They call it West Memphis Blues!"

It just sounded so good, all of it. To my ears, this was poetry coming to life. The names of the towns and rivers, the names of all these characters, everything had its own rhythm down here. Images and sounds started getting stuck in my head. I was sixteen years old and very impressionable.

Levon told me about all the folks I'd be meeting. "There'll be Jasper Diamond—that's Daddy—who you'll see is a one of a kind. And Mama, her name is Nell, but we all call her Shuck." I wondered why they called her Shuck but didn't want to interrupt. "Then there's Modena, my older sister. She might be there with her husband, Ralph. My younger sister Linda, that's who I played music with. She played washtub bass and I played guitar and sang. We were called the Jungle Bush Beaters. And my little brother Wheeler, he'll be there for sure." I felt privileged to have Levon introduce me to his family and show me his old stomping grounds.

When we arrived at his house, the first thing I noticed was how the house was raised well above the ground. "The water can get pretty high around here," Levon pointed out. "Sometimes you need a little boat to get to where you're going. They don't call it the Delta for nothing."

His sister Linda was the first one to burst out the front door, laughing and yelling, "Lavon, there you are! Hi, y'all. So nice to meet you!" Next came Levon's mom, with her arms stretched out toward her boy. "You better come here and hug my neck, right now." Then Jasper Diamond, smiling, coughing, and blowing cigarette smoke. "What kind of car is that you drivin'?" he hollered. "That's the biggest damn car I ever seen."

"Yeah, it's a beauty," Levon said, grabbing Wheeler's crew-cut head.

"Look at this big old boy." As we chatted, Modena came out of the kitchen, shaking a spoon with joy. "Somebody's got to keep this food from burning!" she called out. As they swarmed Levon, you could tell how much they loved their guy.

We sat down to an authentic, health-be-damned southern meal. *Real* corn bread, fried chicken, wilted greens, ham, biscuits and gravy, iced tea, pecan pie, the works. I looked around the table and felt a deep warmth and contentment—good people, good food. Levon had brought me into his world; it was all new to me, and wonderful.

We moved to the living room for an after-dinner smoke, everybody moaning about how full they were. As I sat down on the couch, Diamond passed wind like a foghorn. He looked back toward the kitchen and called out, "Hell, Robin, was that you? Sound like you stepped on a big ol' bullfrog."

"Diamond, you stop that," said Shuck. "You're embarrassing poor Robbie." But Diamond was grinning from ear to ear and knew he had me going. He jammed his cigarette out in the ashtray, coughed, and asked me, "Robin, tell me something. They got many niggers up there in Canada?"

I was stunned for a moment. "No," I told him, "we got mostly 'ofays' up there." Levon laughed out loud.

"Well, we got eight colored to one white round here," Diamond explained, lighting another cigarette, thumbnail on match. "I ain't saying anything bad about niggers. I know some hardworking, good folks, but we got some bad ones too. When I was sheriff here, I'd be throwing one too many of those drunk old boys in the pokey every Saturday night."

"Daddy, you better quit that," Linda chimed in. "You're 'bout to scare young Robbie all the way back to Canada." She reached for a mandolin and handed it to Diamond. "Here," she said, laughing, "stop talking and sing something."

Diamond looked around the room and smiled like he had pulled a rabbit out of his hat. He hit a couple chords on the mandolin and started singing an old-time story song. The timbre of his voice was gentle and deep-rooted. Levon passed me a guitar and motioned for me to play along. I did, and it made everybody sit back, just right. Levon had told me on the drive out, "My mama and daddy worked so hard all their lives, growing cotton. One of these days I'd like to give them some comfort and easy living. They deserve it." I saw what he meant.

BACK AT THE Rainbow Inn, Ronnie had worked out a rough timeline with Fred, who had agreed to stay in the band until things were up and running with the new inexperienced blood he was trying out. When Levon and I returned, we ran over some of the tunes from the repertoire, including many songs from Ron's first two albums, like "Mary Lou," "Forty Days," "Southern Love," and "Someone Like You," which was one of the tunes I had written for him. Ron was not known to be shy about making his band rehearse relentlessly. Levon showed me driving rhythm parts on the bass, twin-string and upper-octave stuff, playing it Chuck Berry style. I practiced on my own too and ran over the songs until my fingers were bleeding. I couldn't have been happier.

The Hawk was becoming half pleased with the possibilities of a lineup that featured Magoo, Fred, Levon, and me on six-string bass. This band was starting to have confidence and a "look," something that Ron was always very conscious of. He said, "If my band is good-looking, that'll bring the girls into the clubs . . . and sure enough the boys will follow." Fred was a handsome man with a weathered complexion and a more mature, southern manner, old-fashioned in many ways and proud of it. Levon was the opposite. He looked young, shiny, and magnetic with his blond hair, gleaming smile, and highly contagious laugh. Ronnie himself always had a unique, sharp style. He looked the part, mischievous and dangerous in a lovable way—a lethal combination. Magoo had thick glasses creeping down his nose and a blind man's smile. He looked a bit overly educated in Ronnie's eyes, but he sure could rattle those ivories.

Ron saw me as more of a work in progress, but he went out on a limb and offered me the job. "I can see how hard you're working, and you're hungry," he said. "I like that."

"Great, thanks!" I gushed. "What's the pay gonna be like?"

"Well, son," he said, "you won't make much money, but you'll get more pussy than Frank Sinatra."

TWO

A couple days later Ronnie announced that Harold "the Colonel" Kudlets, his booking agent, had called: we were booked for two weeks in London, Ontario, at the Brass Rail Tavern, then three weeks at Le Coq d'Or in Toronto. Ron liked playing up in Canada because the hours were easier and we made more money. This was exciting news: I'd be returning to my homeland a member of the Hawks. But nothing was certain: Magoo and I were still inexperienced Canadians trying to make it in a southern band, and Ron could boot us at any time. And while I was bangin' it out on the bass for now, I was sleeping with my guitar.

As we packed up at the motel for the drive, Charlie Halbert came over to say good-bye. I told him that his Rainbow Court Inn had to be one of the hippest places ever. He patted me on my back all fatherly and said, "Well, you're young and you ain't been anywhere, but I'm sure the Hawk is getting ready to show you places you never dreamt of."

Levon arranged our instruments in the trailer methodically so that nothing would get damaged. We had three Fender Bassman amps, the amp of choice around these parts, one each for Fred, Magoo, and me. Levon put his red sparkle Gretsch drums in their black cases inside the front of the trailer, the amps at the back, and the guitar and bass cases in the middle, and sat the suitcases on top. It made for a tight, secure fit. Our whole musical lifeline was back there in that trailer, hitched under the bumper with two safety chains to the back of Ronnie's white Caddy.

Levon always took the first driving shift. He knew how to back that trailer full of instruments into tough spots and maneuver it in rain, sleet, and snow. That impressed me, mainly because I didn't even know how to drive yet. And handling a huge '59 DeVille with a heavy trailer on the back could be dangerous. We would move to pass a truck on a two-lane highway, see an oncoming vehicle up around the curve, and have to abort the pass. Ron would grab the dash and scold Levon, "Boy, I want to get to Canada *alive*. I ain't into that James Dean shit." Levon would just crack up.

Watching Ron and Levon, I could understand their bond. They had a strong friendship and connection, like Cisco and Pancho. Ron had discovered Levon when he was still in high school in the Delta, and had to wait until he'd graduated to hire him full-time. It was apparent to everyone who met him that Levon was special, and Ron saw the light immediately. Levon could play like fire, but more, he had *personality*. The two of them had a wonderful dependence on each other: Ron was the older brother and teacher, but Levon had special musical instincts that Ron totally relied on—Levon elevated Ronnie's musicality. And they had developed their own rapport, based on a shared Arkansas sense of humor.

The idea of returning to Canada after a month down south seemed like a whole new program for me. I felt different on the inside and I looked different on the outside. Coming home was stirring up old memories.

MY MOTHER, Rosemarie Dolly Chrysler Myke Robertson, was born February 6, 1922, on the Six Nations Indian Reserve of the Grand River in southwestern Ontario, nestled between Lake Ontario to the east, Lake Erie toward the southwest, and the wide, beautiful flow of the Grand River on its northern border. Six Nations was then and still is the largest reserve of its kind in Canada, and the only one on which all six of the Haudenosaunee/Iroquois nations—Mohawk, Cayuga, Onondaga, Oneida, Seneca, and Tuscarora—live together.

My mother's family was of Mohawk and Cayuga descent—could be some Irish snuck in there too, which she would speak of proudly on occasion. At school on the reserve, it was made perfectly clear to her that this was a white man's country now, and being of native blood was no advantage. It was similar to the Carlisle Indian Industrial School in Pennsylvania, where they would take Indian kids from their homes, cut off their hair, and forbid them to speak their native tongue or practice any of their bloodline traditions. We heard the story of one kid at the Carlisle who was found in the bathroom trying to scrub the Indian off his skin with an iron bristle until he was raw. From a very early age I remember a phrase being quietly passed around among our relatives at Six Nations: "Be proud you are an Indian, but be careful who you tell."

My mother was raised by her mother and grandparents. Her father, Mr. Chrysler, lived at Six Nations but wasn't around much during her childhood. She remembered him as a good-looking man who sometimes came to visit, like a distant relative or drifter. But my mother adored her grandfather. He was kind, caring, and understanding and told her he believed she was something special. My mother didn't cherish much about her childhood on the reserve, except for playtimes with her cousins and school friends and those special moments with Grandpa Myke. He hunted and worked the land, and they lived by very simple means. They drank from a well, raised most of their own food, and had a strong basic connection with the earth.

When Rosemarie turned fifteen, her mother grew extremely ill and died soon after. This devastated her grandparents and broke up the family. Her younger brother Bun stayed on the reserve with their uncle Ferd and his family, but my mother was sent off to the city, to Toronto, where her mother's sister Beatrice lived. Aunt Beatrice welcomed her, but in Toronto my mother would find no more schooling, only work. The move completely changed my mother's world, but not for the worse. She took to city life naturally over the next few years. It helped that she was very pretty and could pass for a suntanned white woman.

She got a job working at Coro Jewelry, a gold- and silver-plating factory, and there she met James Patrick Robertson. She already knew his brother Albert, so they became easy friends and soon started going out. But war in Europe was brewing and soon it disrupted their lives— Jim Robertson joined the Canadian Army and shipped off to Newfoundland, ready to be deployed to Europe in the war effort. Dolly, as my mother was called for her strikingly pretty face and figure, began getting a lot of attention from gentleman admirers. But when Jim visited Toronto on leave, he and Dolly grew closer, and during those brief respites from his service, they would ponder the idea of someday getting married. He was twenty-three, she was twenty . . . and uncertain.

Jim finally returned from his tour of duty in Newfoundland—to his family's relief he wouldn't be sent to the front lines. They took pictures of him in uniform, six feet tall, thin but solid, with broad shoulders and a widow's-peak hairline. Jim was a truly handsome man with a kind smile, and he and Dolly made a fine-looking couple. In 1942 they got married without too much fanfare and went down to Niagara Falls for their honeymoon.

Starting out with little money, they moved in with Jim's parents on the north side of Bloor Street in downtown Toronto, about a block west of Bathurst Street. The Robertson clan lived an extremely modest lifestyle, basic working class, but they got by. The neighborhood felt very homey and worldly at the same time to the young couple, with family and extended family all around. Jim went back to work at Coro Jewelry with Dolly, and they began to build a future.

On July 5, 1943, at 10:25 p.m., Dolly gave birth to a healthy baby boy, nine pounds, eleven ounces, at Toronto General Hospital. She named me Jaime Royal Robertson, partially after her cousin Royal, Aunt Beatrice's son. She chose to spell my name with the *i* before the *m*, because the reverse looked to her like it should be pronounced "jam-me." Jim Robertson thought his son should be named after him and spelled the name "James" on the birth certificate. My mother called me Jaime and my dad called me Jame or Jim.

I grew up surrounded by busy, vibrant neighborhoods alive with immigrant sounds and smells. Some of my very earliest recollections are of rows of storefronts, each one memorable from all the various indelible scents of the neighborhood. The corner drugstore with its medicines, chemicals, and soda fountain mixture. Sweet aromas of pipe smoke from the smoke shop downstairs, proudly displaying Cuban cigars behind glass in the back. A Jewish deli poured out the scent of hot corned beef and dill. The bakery around the corner was my favorite—when you passed by you could almost taste the fresh-baked bread and cinnamon pastries. The candy shop, a close runner-up, made its own maple squares, marzipan, and Turkish delight. The shoe repair shop had a leathery, musky, shoe polish odor that impressed my young nostrils. The fish market had its ups and downs, of course, but in its freshest moments the smell of the ocean, lakes, and rivers carried in with the fish was wonderful. Alley cats would sit out front, waiting for a donation. Another gem was the Nuthouse, where they roasted and cooked so many kinds of nuts it was almost impossible to choose which to buy. The fruit and vegetable stand and butcher shop were next door to each other, so poultry and citrus intertwined. At the end of the block the smell of buttery fresh popcorn from the movie theater filled the air. At Honest Ed's giant bargain store over by Bathurst Street they had one section where they kept the denim, and the jeans had this *new* scent to them. What was that particular smell? You never forgot it.

Police on horseback patrolled the back alleys, parks, such as nearby Christie Pits, and main streets too. Rag-and-bone men with horse-pulled wagons roamed the back streets singing out, "Rags, bones, old iron," and the scent of manure played its own part in the mixture of downtown city life. And this was all in one block.

"WELL, BOYS, we're here," Ron announced a couple hours later as we cruised up to the front of the Embassy Hotel in London, Ontario. London had been a music town since the nineteenth century and in the fifties home to many jazz venues. The Embassy didn't look like much of a hotel, or even like a hotel at all. It wasn't what you'd call sleazy, maybe two notches above. But at this stage any hotel looked like a palace to me, and I had a full-on grown-up feeling when we checked into the Embassy and I got my own room. Ron and Levon took a two-bedroom poor man's suite with a little sitting room to one side. This gave them the opportunity to entertain lady friends with the option of close, convenient privacy. Their setup looked pretty suave and "road cool" to me.

We set up our equipment Sunday afternoon at the Brass Rail Tavern so we could run through a few tunes and get used to the sound before the first show the next day. It was the nicest place in town to hear rock 'n' roll music, with a long brass railing in front of the bar, a stage about a foot and a half high, and a ceiling only ten inches above my skinny six-foot frame. Every time we ran over the songs I gained a touch more confidence. Ron stood off the stage facing us while singing, to check out the playing and the look. We tried a song called "Odessa," about a prostitute in Helena (of whom Levon and Ron spoke very highly: one time when they had visited her, Levon had gone into the bedroom with her first, and when they emerged, Odessa said, "Mr. Ron, I'd like to give you *some*, but I believe young Mr. Levon done took it all!"). Ron paced back and forth in front of the stage with a frown on his face as we rehearsed. He stopped, looked up at me, and said, "Boy, you look so damn young, I hope that liquor inspector don't come in here and shut me down. I don't know if I can even pay the son of a bitch off for this. Have you tried shaving?"

"Hell, Ron, it'll be okay," yelled Levon from behind the kit. "We'll just draw a mustache on him with an eyebrow pencil."

I went out that same afternoon and bought an electric razor, a Remington, and started shaving three times a day, based on the theory that the more you shave the faster your beard grows. I didn't have much to shave, so all it did was irritate my chin and neck. Raw from razor burn, I didn't look older; I just looked like an abused teenager.

On our opening night, my debut, my head was reeling but I was determined to remember all my parts and lock in with Levon's beat. I didn't have a chance to worry about it once we walked up on that stage. Ronnie had arranged that I stand under a blue light by the back wall for the lowest profile possible. I played looking at Levon's hands the whole time. After a raging version of "Dizzy Miss Lizzy," Magoo spun around from his piano and gave me an encouraging nod.

When I called my mother the next day, she was thrilled—and relieved to hear my voice. I had never been gone this long, though I had checked in once while we were in Arkansas and sent some postcards and a little money. I told her we would be in Toronto in a couple of weeks. Mainly she was glad to hear I was okay and that I had not fallen into a world of debauchery and destruction. I couldn't confess the jury was still out on that one.

Almost every night girls came back to the hotel after the gig. Scott and I watched Ronnie and Levon closely: we were trying to learn the tricks of the trade from the masters. These southerners could get away with mischievous behavior that Scott and I wouldn't dream of trying: lines like "C'mere you pretty thing and give me some sugar" weren't something you could pull off without a southern accent. Most of the women thought I was just a kid and that I should probably go and get an ice cream cone and stay out of the way.

THE FIRST TIME the power of music really struck me was on the Six Nations Indian Reserve. I was about eight years old, sitting in a kitchen at the house on Second Line road while a couple of relatives played guitar. It rang my bell—the sound, the rhythm, the fingers on the strings, the voices blending together in unison and then slipping into harmonies. My uncles and cousins were so lost in the music that it mesmerized me.

Sometimes there would be a mandolin or a violin joining in with Iroquois hand drums and water drums. On the rez there was no other entertainment—everything was homegrown. Nobody there had any "money honey" and it didn't matter. Things balanced out in other ways, through the wilderness, the Grand River, the changing seasons, and always the dancing and singing. From my earliest impressions, I knew there was a deep beauty in this place. The water we drank straight from the well was cold and clear and I never knew water could taste so good. We picked wild berries from the fields and grew sweet corn so tall you could get lost in it. Every day was a celebration of nature with the three sisters, beans, squash, and corn, like nothing I experienced back in the city. My cousins didn't climb trees; rather, they would run up them. I studied their hands, their feet, trying to find the secret of this supernatural skill. Over and over I tried to keep up with them, most of the time falling on my butt and once, when I was seven, breaking a wrist, the white bone itself jutting right out of my small hand. In the summertime we would head over toward the railroad tracks like a ritual. Stop at the water pump, splash a little water on your face, have a drink out of a tin cup. There was a path that led through a field of wild strawberries, and we would grab a couple of handfuls on the way. Once my cousin Doug spotted a dried plant of some kind that was probably a type of wild tobacco, the Ontario tobacco belt being not far from Six Nations. Doug picked a few leaves, rolled them in his hands, retrieved a stray piece of newspaper, rolled the plant into a small square of it, lit and smoked it. He might have been eleven or twelve at the time.

With the heat bug singing in the late afternoon, we stopped by a longhouse to hear an elder share a story. That turned out to be a particular highlight for me. When everyone had gathered round, an old man appeared out of the trees like a vision. With his walking stick he pushed himself past everybody and into the longhouse, where he settled into a chair made of birch branches covered with deerskins. We gathered in front of him as he banged his walking stick twice on the wooden floor and began speaking, first in native tongue, like a short prayer of gratitude. Then, switching to English, he told the story of Hiawatha and the Peacemaker who brought the nations of Onondaga, Oneida, Cayuga, Seneca, and Mohawk together after years of war and introduced the Great Law of Peace. When he told that story, it sent a charge right through me—the cadence of his voice, the power, the violence, the righteousness. I only hoped someday I could tell stories like that.

———

ONE NIGHT about a week into our gig at the Brass Rail, we were in the middle of a song when Ronnie motioned me to step forward on the stage. "Come out into the light. Let's see what you got." He motioned for me to take a bass solo. This was confusing primarily because so far as I knew there were no bass solos in the middle of songs. "Go ahead," he nodded, "go on." Fred stopped playing and looked at me wide-eyed, like I'd just stepped on a land mine.

Well, I was on the spot, so I walked that dog. I locked in with Levon's kick drum, leaned back, and wailed. The crowd started clapping along. Ronnie started hollering, "Go on, son, walk that baby!" Soon the crowd started yelling and whistling. It went over so well that the Hawk made my bass solo a staple in our set. Ron said I looked older when I played a solo because it made me appear more experienced. I hoped the young ladies coming to the clubs would think that too. At least being featured helped me overcome my nervousness about getting busted by the liquor inspector.

Levon was a locomotion every night, machine-gun eighth-note bass drum if need be. He kept a Kotex pad under the top skin of his snare to keep it tight, popping like a whip, an idea he got from Jerry Lee's drummer Jimmy Van Eaton. I found myself playing directly toward Levon to get that rhythm-section connection. It made the vocal phrasing feel better and gave the music a solid foundation. I kept an ear out for when "the pocket"—the groove—was alive and breathing. We came to the conclusion that the thick, four-stringed Fender Precision bass had more low authority to it than the six-string. Levon said, "Let's go for the low down."

Those first weeks flew by for me: the pure excitement of being in *this* band, making a living playing music and learning the code of the road. But London was just the warm-up; the real live-wire shows in Toronto would be the true barometer for whether the Hawks' personnel changes would stick. After our last night at the Brass Rail we headed out on the highway for Toronto, the center of the Canadian rockabilly circuit. This had been a band of southern Arkansas cats, but it now had two Canadians; and our lineup was edging toward a questionable reading on the rockabilly authenticity meter.

Toronto had become a major music town, with hot jazz clubs like the Colonial and the Town Tavern and new after-hours spots blooming as well. There weren't many places up north where a rockabilly band like ours could play for three weeks at a time, but Toronto had Le Coq d'Or, which also featured Conway Twitty and Narvel Felts. Then there was the Edison Hotel next door, where Bo Diddley, Jerry Lee Lewis, Carl Perkins, and Big Jay McNeely and his band would play. There was the Brown Derby, a Vegas-type joint where Louis Prima and Keely Smith with Sam Butera and the Witnesses could play. Just up the street was the Zanzibar, half strip joint, half local talent. A couple blocks down you'd find the venerable, legendary Massey Hall, where you could hear Sinatra, Segovia, or Ray Charles. All these venues were on one side of Yonge Street, forming a remarkable row of music temples.

Cruising along the highway, I could see the glow of the Toronto skyline in the distance. It felt good coming home with a little experience under my belt. Heading into the center of the city, we passed the Alhambra movie theater on Bloor Street, where my mother took me when I was little. The Alhambra showed coming attractions, a cartoon, a newsreel, a serial, and a feature film, sometimes a double feature. It tilted my imagination like nothing else; some of those first movies made an impression that I would only come to realize years later—films like *It Came from Outer Space* in black-and-white 3-D, or *Streets of Laredo*, where a guy throws a knife at William Holden and it sticks into his guitar with a vibrating thud.

We checked into the Warwick Hotel, with its air of muted prestige, a haven for streetwalkers, hustlers, and tin men (slang for aluminum-siding salesmen). Most musicians staying in Toronto checked into either the Warwick or the Westover; they stood right across from each other at Dundas and Jarvis, the city's vibrant crossroads of vice. I had told my mother I couldn't stay at her house because of our rehearsal schedule, but I really wanted to be with the band, to be part of the *ritual*.

As we set up our gear at Le Coq d'Or Tavern, I noticed that Carl Perkins and his band were playing next door at the dark and dingy Edison Hotel. He and Ronnie were friends and had both worked this circuit before. Carl was one of the fathers of rock 'n' roll. He wrote his own songs, played lead electric guitar on his baby blue Gibson Les Paul, and moved and sang perfectly in the Sun Records rockabilly style. He had been a tremendous inspiration for a lot of young musicians, including me, and his song "Blue Suede Shoes" had become a rock 'n' roll anthem, even more so after Elvis cut it.

The club manager at Le Coq d'Or took a look at me and asked Ron, "How old is that new guy?"

If they busted me for being underage at Le Coq d'Or, they'd be busting Ron too, and since he didn't have a backup bass player that meant all our eggs were in one basket. But he didn't hesitate.

"He just looks young, hoss," said Ron. "He's got so much talent it don't matter. Get me some of that Canadian Crown Royal rye whiskey in those purple satchels for gifts. If the authorities show up that always goes over pretty smooth with those ol' boys. Had to do it a couple times with Levon. Hell, he looked fifteen forever with his bleached-blond hair and schoolboy smile—part of the reason they came to see our act."

Unfortunately, the way the stage was situated, there was no place for me to stay "out of the way." For our whole run I never smiled, never looked directly at anyone. My mother came with a friend the first night and I didn't look at them once.

As vulnerable as I felt, I had no control over my future. All I could do was play like a demon. But I was that much closer to where I wanted to be. I had crossed the border. I had gone to the Mississippi Delta. I'd gotten hired by an official southern rockabilly band, one of the hottest around. Now I was onstage at a big-time club in my hometown, and I stepped forward into the spotlight to take my solo.

THREE

I was at my mother's house at 193 First Avenue, in a part of Toronto called Cabbagetown, enjoying a wondrous home-cooked meal. It was the best food I'd had since going down south. There was fine food in Arkansas, but I tell you my mother had the magic touch.

"Ma," I said, "you wouldn't believe the South. You wouldn't believe all that I've seen down there."

"Try me," she said, smiling.

"It's magical," I said. "There's music everywhere. Age doesn't matter. Background doesn't matter. Big or small, rich or poor, *everyone* shows up for the music."

My mother nodded, enjoying my excitement.

"I mean," I continued, my voice rising with enthusiasm, "I always kind of sensed there would be magic down there when I listened to my records. But actually going and smelling the air, seeing the way people walk and talk, all in the rhythm of the South . . . it's so beautiful."

My mother said, lowering her voice slightly, as if confessing a secret to me, "I just *knew* that's what you would feel. I don't know how, but I just felt all along that you'd discover something special down there."

We grinned at each other.

"You had a feeling, huh?"

My mother wiped her hands on her apron and nodded modestly.

She did believe in her own powers of precognition. I made my way
back to the hotel with a full belly and a warm heart.

Every night at Le Coq d'Or, I was growing by leaps and bounds
musically and coming out of my shell in other ways too. Magoo and
I, both still pretty green when it came to playing with an act of this
caliber, were slowly gaining acceptance from the crowds, though we
drew some smirks when the audiences caught on that we were Canadians. None of the famous rock 'n' roll or rhythm-and-blues bands
had Canucks; it was unheard of. Some people even began accusing
Ron, Levon, and Fred of not actually being from the South, either,
saying that the whole act was a put on, right down to phony accents.

"Canadians in disguise!" they yelled.

"What the hell is this about?" Levon asked Ron.

"Hey," said the Hawk, calm as ever, "as long as they're talking, it's
okay. It's when they *stop* talking that you have to worry."

Friends and family came to Le Coq d'Or to witness our first Toronto shows with the Hawks. Ronnie had become a master at "working the room," and he made a big fuss over my friends and relatives,
especially my mother. The Hawk was born to entertain—he made everybody feel a part of the evening, singing along, joking, having a rare
time.

And he and Levon charming the ladies was a sight to behold—
the humor, the timing, an art form unto itself. They started pointing out particular girls they had gone out with and thought I should
meet, giving me a little backstory and setting my imagination afire.
Night after night, an array of teachers, nurses, waitresses, students,
hairdressers, salesgirls, elevator operators, and telephone operators
passed before my eyes. The recommendations came with careful consideration as to who could teach me the most the quickest. I tried to
follow their advice and thought I saw in the mirror a boy turning into
a man before his time.

For the next few years I lied about my age to everyone but my
mother. It was part of the routine, but real life to me was playing
music, traveling, meeting girls, listening to and collecting lots of records, practicing day and night.

OCCASIONALLY, BETWEEN SETS at Le Coq d'Or, the Hawk would head next door to the Edison Hotel to catch Carl Perkins and his band. I'd run after him.

"Hey, Ron! Hold up. I'm coming too."

He would give me that sideways grin. He knew I was tagging along with him so that the doorman at the Edison wouldn't ask to see my ID, but I loved being there with him and Carl together. Watching Ron and Levon interacting with Carl and his boys was like observing a tribal community gathering. Magoo and I stood to the side and let the good old boys have at it, Carl and Ron trading humble remarks.

"Well, hell, I must've tripped over a rabbit's foot and landed here," Ron declared. "It sure ain't for talent and looks, that's for damn sure."

"Tell you what, I'm just trying to get a bit better than I was yesterday," Carl rejoined. "And God did bless me with a little luck."

At Le Coq d'Or, Ron began featuring me as his young show dog more and more. It was the role Levon had once filled, but Levon didn't have a problem passing the torch. He felt the same way about using me as Ron did: "Let that boy roll on," he'd say. Whenever Ron's fears of our getting busted for my age temporarily subsided, I was allowed out of the club's back room, and he would call me over to certain people's tables, introducing me as his new "find," like a circus act. While I shuffled my feet, he'd brag about my talent, that one day I would be this and that. "And on top of everything," he'd say, building to his punch line, "he's hung like a mule!" Then he'd bust out laughing, slapping me on the back.

"Please don't listen to him," I'd beg.

"Too late, son. The word's out!" the Hawk would cry.

He always wanted his boys looking sharp. That meant a trip up Yonge Street to visit tailor extraordinaire Lou Myles in his famous shop. The Hawks' style was evolving—no more black vests and short-sleeved red Orlon shirts. Now we rocked black mohair suits, white shirts, black ties, fake white hankies, black shiny pointed shoes, and black socks. Nothing missing. The satin lining of the suit jackets was usually red, though I got mine in purple. Jackie Wilson or Roy Orbison couldn't have done it any better. Lou Myles designed the suits to emphasize the positive; his was definitely a sensual cut. He had the flair of an international Italian designer, but it was his street savvy that made him Toronto's hottest tailor. My first "Lou suit" made me stand a little taller, but there was a price: the uniform of an official Hawk had to be paid off, fifteen dollars a week. I could handle it, though. My starting pay was $125 a week, which covered wardrobe, food, hotel, and occasionally a new instrument. I felt rich and complete.

WHEN I WAS around eight years of age my parents moved to Scarborough Bluffs, in the east end of Toronto, a considerable distance from downtown. It was a whole new scene for me. The Bluffs overlooked Lake Ontario with an edge of danger, a hundred-foot drop-off to the shoreline. Our house, white clapboard with a basement and an unfinished second story, had a real backyard with a hill, fruit trees, and rose bushes. No retail stores downstairs anymore; in fact, no stores for blocks. I'd landed square in the heart of suburbia.

Jim and Dolly started making new friends—the neighborhood teemed with characters, and that too felt like a departure from living at Jim's parents' apartment downtown. Family made sure we weren't too lonely. All the Robertson relatives enjoyed coming out to visit. Uncle John, Aunt Mary, and the kids were always a welcome sight. My uncle John worked for Seagram's, selling whiskey—he seemed to me trustworthy and impressive, and I thought he must be very good at his job. Uncle Bill and Aunt Vi were more the quiet type. Bill had continued to serve in the air force, and you couldn't imagine a more gentle military man. I can still see him standing there in his blue uniform with ribbons on his chest, Aunt Vi beside him, her head turned to hide the scar that ran right across one side of her face. I never asked what had happened; I didn't want to know.

My favorite of my father's brothers, Uncle Al, an ex-boxer and magician, would cruise out to Scarborough in his yellow and white Chevy convertible. Sometimes he'd bring a blond honey; other times one of his cheering-squad buddies would tag along, funny characters with names like Sleepy or Knuckles. It was as if the circus had come to town when Al walked into the house, pulling money from behind my ears or long colorful scarves out of his mouth and making them disappear. Cool and funny, Al knew card tricks galore, and I wanted to be just like him when I grew up, pleading with him after one of his dazzling displays to teach me some magic tricks. He sometimes used the name "Robbie" when he performed, which was interesting because that's what kids at school had started calling me, after my last name.

"A real magician never reveals his secret," he'd growl. But every once in a while he would give in and show me a couple of sleight-of-hand techniques. He sent me books on magic in the mail and I ordered some on my own out of my allowance. Sitting in my bedroom, shuffling a deck of cards like the Great Robingo, I questioned my true calling: magician or musician? I was approaching an age where this kind of decision was considered on the scale of "how to impress the girls."

On my mom's side of the family tree, her uncle Waddy and cousins Herb and Fred Myke came by sometimes to play music. All three drove dump trucks, delivering stones, gravel, and asphalt to Toronto from Caledonia and the Six Nations area, and they would stop by on their trips. They carried their guitars with them, or sometimes borrowed the acoustic guitar my parents had given me for Christmas, a sturdy model with a cowboy painted on it, straight out of the Eaton's department store catalog. After a couple of beers at the kitchen table, everybody was ready to sing. Because the Mykes lived in the country, a good portion of their repertoire turned out to be country music, and it was funny to see Indians singing cowboy songs, like Marvin Rainwater. Everybody had a little chuckle when they did "Kaw-Liga," Hank Williams's tune about a wooden Indian who fell in love with an Indian maiden. Then they might slip into the Kitty Wells classic "It Wasn't God Who Made Honky Tonk Angels." Every time one of the Mykes visited, I tried to learn another little thing on the guitar from them.

My mother and I usually made trips to Six Nations four or five times a year. We mostly stayed with her uncle Waddy and aunt Alice Myke on Second Line between the towns of Hagersville and Ohsweken. Alice and Waddy had twelve kids ranging in age from mine to my mother's. I still don't know how we all fit into their little house, but it worked. Nobody ever thought to mention its being crowded.

In Scarborough my dad was spending the weekends remodeling the upstairs of our house into two bedrooms and a sitting area that we could rent out to make a little extra money, always needed. He came off as an easygoing, gentle guy, but he had a rough side, and whether this came from his time in the army I couldn't say. He had a strict workout program with weights and a high bar he built in the back-yard, and between the kitchen and the hallway he installed a chin-up bar. He would lift me up to hang from it while offering cheers of en-couragement. "Pull yourself up, that's it," he'd say. "Do it again, come on, one more. Don't worry, I won't let you fall." Pretty soon my hands would get tired and slip. He would let me fall until my feet were just about to touch the ground and then catch me at the last moment. He would laugh, saying he was teaching his boy to be a "man's man." But trying to be like my father or be what he expected didn't come natu-rally to me.

Still, over time we made some connections. During visits to Six Nations some of my relatives showed me tricks in knife throwing and bow-and-arrow skills, and my dad, who was a pretty good carpenter, built a large wooden target area in our basement and got me a new set of balanced knives. The sound of those knives plunging into the wood gave me a thrill—my dad too. He made me a powerful new bow and a whole batch of arrows. I could spend hours down in that basement fighting off imaginary enemies and bad guys. And one Christmas my parents got me a Daisy Red Ryder BB gun—with one simple warning, "No shooting birds with that thing." I have to confess I did shoot one bird and felt terrible afterward, as I buried it.

Walking home from school one afternoon, I came upon a house that was just a basement with a tar-paper roof—the rest of it hadn't been built yet—and the man who lived there was chasing a couple of young boys away from his yard, swinging a rake and yelling about their having done something to his property. They were already out of reach, but when I strolled by, he whacked me on the back. More angry than hurt, I quickly moved out of range and made my way home. When I walked in the door my dad asked me why I looked so sour. As I told him what happened, I could see his jaw clench and his eyes narrow.

"Show me where he lives," he snapped as he took me by the arm.

I could hardly keep up with the pace of his walking; somehow I was following him even as I was leading. The rake guy was working in his backyard as we approached his fence.

"Hey there, YOU!" my dad called out. "Did you hit this kid with a rake?"

"There were some kids throwing garbage in my yard and I chased them away," he answered. "He might've been one of them."

Jim stared at me. "Did you throw garbage in his yard?"

"No! I did nothing. I don't even know those kids."

My father gritted his teeth and pointed his finger. "You ever come near my boy again, I'll climb over this fence and wrap that rake around your neck. Do you understand me, you son of a bitch?"

"Yes, yes, I understand," the guy said hurriedly. "I'm sorry. I understand."

My father put his hand on the back of my neck as we walked away. I'd heard kids say, "My dad could beat up your dad," but only as a bluff. This was real, and I couldn't help but feel a jolt of pride.

That Christmas we got our first television, black-and-white, of course, with a rabbit-ears antenna on top. My dad and I would watch the telecast of Gillette's Friday-night boxing matches together religiously. Sometimes his brother Al, who had been a boxer, came over and watched with us, giving insight and commentary on what we were seeing on the fuzzy TV screen. I remember tuning in to see Sugar Ray Robinson defeat Bobo Olson to win the middleweight championship, in a helluva fight. My dad and I probably made our tightest bond watching those fights together.

———

ABOUT A YEAR or so after we moved to Scarborough, my parents and their friends began having weekend get-togethers. Though I was just ten years old, my parents frequently left me on my own: no babysitter, no brothers, sisters, or relatives. They went off to meet friends at the Scarborough House, a Canadian beer parlor divided into two rooms with separate entrances—one door with a sign above it instructed, "Ladies and Escorts"; the other, "Men Only." Gradually my parents started to drink deeper into the night, and no matter what time they said they would be back, they never were.

One evening somebody came beating on our side door, yelling and threatening to kick the door in. When my parents got home and found me crouched in my bedroom, I told them what had happened, but they shrugged it off. "Oh, that's just Frank from up the street. He probably had a few too many." This did little to calm my growing paranoia. But in that moment what really stunned me was just how unaware they were of their unawareness.

Drunk people made me uncomfortable, including my parents, but I seemed to be spending more and more time around this kind of behavior. My parents' get-togethers with drinking buddies and trips out to beer parlors grew more frequent. My father had an issue with his nerves, and his hands shook noticeably the morning after. Soon it began to register with me that my mother took on a different personality after she had a beer or two. She spoke with a strange Indian country accent, threw her head back in a different manner. She even walked with an unusual rhythm. Eventually I discovered this was an "Indian thing." Native people and alcohol: a rough combination.

My dad, on the other hand, just got sloppy drunk, one eye half shut, ready to fight. Every once in a while somebody would do something or say something that would piss him off. In the middle of the night I'd be awakened by feet slamming against the floor and things breaking.

In my bedroom I would escape into a world that I knew must be out there somewhere. I had no problem spending hours playing guitar or practicing magic. My privacy and isolation felt good to me.

Soon my parents informed me that I was going to have a new baby brother. We were all excited about having an addition to the family, and they were particularly warm and comforting to each other; relatives came from around Toronto and the reserve to visit and celebrate the anticipated new arrival. I enjoyed my solitude, but there was no denying that at times it did feel a bit lonely. My mother was convinced she would be having a boy—she wanted to name him Michael. Some months into the pregnancy, when the baby was moving around inside her, she would smile and say, "Ah, there goes Michael, knocking on the door." Then one night I was awakened by the sound of panic in the house and my mother crying. Jim was taking her to the hospital. The next day she explained she'd had a miscarriage, saying that she had a "blue baby." I didn't know what that meant and found the phrase disturbing, hard to imagine. I didn't realize at the time what a toll such a thing can take on a family.

WE WERE HAVING a tough winter and, remembering the flyer I'd been given in the ice storm, I asked my mother if we could check out those guitar lessons. She seemed pleased to indulge my interest and took me on the bus and streetcar with my little cowboy guitar to check it out.

The instructor was a tropical-looking fellow in a Hawaiian shirt named Billy Blue. I took out my guitar and played a few chords for him, picking out a "Three Blind Mice"–type melody. Billy watched my hands the whole time. Then he went into another room and returned with a new Stella black-and-red sunburst guitar that looked much sharper than mine. I started to get excited, but then he laid it flat on my lap.

"Your hands aren't big enough yet to fit around the neck of your Spanish-style guitar," he said. "So I'm going to start you out on Hawaiian guitar."

What? Gene Autry, Hank Williams, and Roy Rogers didn't play Hawaiian guitar, but Mr. Blue sold his reasoning quite well, and for me just playing music was the key; looking sharp would have to come later. Before long I could play "Honolulu Sunset."

Next I began working on a tough one called the "Hawaiian War Chant." Waiting for my lesson one day, I could hear another student in the next room playing the same song on an electric lap steel guitar, with Billy Blue accompanying him on an acoustic. It sounded so good coming through the wall. When they finished, Mr. Blue introduced me to his student, Joey, who, as it turned out, lived one street over from us.

"My friends call me Scooter," said Joey. "You could come over to my house and practice if you want."

We played together a couple of times, and I found I learned faster the more we did. Scooter must've been about four years older than me and a couple of years ahead in lessons. He took his playing pretty seriously; he almost seemed pushy, in fact, with his steady requests for me to come over and practice up in his room.

One night after dinner, we were working on a pretty tricky tune.

"Let's take a break and play a game," he suggested, which came as a relief since we were struggling with the song.

"We both start with our fly open," Scooter continued. "Or no, even better, we pull our pants down." With that, I suddenly developed a toothache and had to go home.

My Hawaiian aspirations in general were winding down. I picked up my cowboy guitar, reached my left hand around the neck, and said, "I'm ready." I quit my lessons the same day, and that was the end of my only formal music training.

DURING THE THREE WEEKS at Le Coq d'Or, Levon kept offering me advice on music, life on the road, and bass playing. We listened to a lot of Jimmy Reed, who didn't even have a bass on some of his records, but what a feel!

Levon continued to introduce me to funny downtown characters and women he thought would take me under their wing. Along the way I managed to steal a guitar lick here and there from Fred, who by now had stopped treating me like an underage foreigner. Meanwhile Ron started pushing me to "put on a show" while I played. He acted like I was a stray pet he'd rescued by the side of the road. Perhaps he wasn't that far off. "You know, kid," he loved to say, "if I hadn't hired you, you'd be in reform school or jail."

Ronnie seemed bent on never letting me forget the time a year or so back, before I'd joined the Hawks, when the Bear, Thumper, Magoo, and I had hooked up with a singer from England by the name of Billy Kent. He'd had some success back in his native country, where he was known as the Singing Milkman (I didn't ask why). We played a couple of sock-hop dances together, and all of us were convinced we could make a go of it as a group.

"Come back to England with me," Billy encouraged us. He thought having a band from North America would put him on top. As his pitch was our best and only offer, it grabbed our attention right away. I'd just turned sixteen, and I couldn't see anything standing in our way. So Billy, Pete, Magoo, and I immediately checked into the Westover Hotel to make plans and work on music.

Every day we awaited the arrival of money from Billy's management, which would give us something to live on and let us fly to England. But between our room rate and Billy's business calls across the Atlantic, our hotel bill started adding up. The front desk at the hotel started getting antsy. "Patience," Billy advised, promising the cash would be arriving any day now. As our discomfort grew, we took to slinking past the front desk, hoping to go unnoticed.

Nothing takes the sting out of an awkward situation like a couple of pretty girls. One night Billy invited me to come meet two English girls he knew who were sharing an apartment. They were both very attractive and fun. We had a bite to eat, shared a few laughs, and began necking for hours. In 1959 I'd call this a near-perfect night.

But when we got back to the hotel, the hammer came down. The hotel manager wanted payment for the room "NOW!" Cornered without a backup plan, I said the only thing I could think of to buy us time: I told him we were guests of Ronnie Hawkins.

"He'll be here in a few days," I stammered. "He'll be taking care of the bill."

Ronnie and the Hawks were good customers at the Westover, so this took the heat off a little, but now we were ready to strangle Billy Kent. A couple more days of long-distance calls and finally our doom was confirmed: even though Billy had every intention to make this work, he realized he would have to go back to England in order to get everything straightened out in person.

We were screwed, and since Ron wouldn't arrive for a few more days, we couldn't leave. At this point Ron had already offered Scott the piano job, but Scott was holding out, hoping Ronnie would also hire Pete and me. So we had no idea if Ronnie would be feeling charitable toward us when he finally turned up. All I knew was that he would probably have a nervous breakdown when he heard I'd said he would cover the bill.

Sure enough, when the Hawk arrived at the Westover and the hotel manager told him the story, he flew off the handle. "If it wasn't for me," he yelled, "you'd be doing time somewhere, without a pot to piss in!"

I had no choice but to agree, as he proceeded to take care of the hotel bill.

"This Billy Kent guy's a phony," he added. "You were suckers to be fooled by him in the first place." I liked Billy and didn't want to think the worst of him—though it might have been the English girl he introduced me to that had made me a believer.

Now, at the beginning of our fourth week playing at Le Coq d'Or, that same pretty English girl showed up. *Now that I'm playing in the Hawks*, I thought, *I'll be able to impress her properly.* Hoping to expand upon our necking session, without hesitation I asked if she'd like to come back to the hotel afterward and meet everybody.

"Yes, that would be nice," she agreed.

When we got to my room, I couldn't help but start kissing her and making my move, but she pulled away. "No . . . I can't. I'm not ready for that."

Maybe I'm being a little impatient, I told myself. *But I'm a professional rock 'n' roll musician now. This should be working.*

Discouraged, I told her I'd be back in a few minutes and went over to Levon's room to see what he was up to. A couple friends were visiting, and we sat and chatted for a bit. When I went back to my room, she was emerging from the bathroom, straightening herself.

"I'm very sorry," she said, "but I need to get going. I've got work early in the morning."

At a loss, I hugged her good-bye and she disappeared into the night.

The next day Ron kept looking at me with a grin on his face like a cat that had just eaten a mouse. Finally he pulled me aside.

"Son, I got a little confession to make. When you went over to Levon's room last night, I happened to stop by your room."

"Oh yeah?"

"Well, that girl of yours opened the door. I slipped in, locked the door, laid her down on the bed, and bogged her."

The news hit me like a gut punch. I didn't know who to be mad at.

"She told me she wasn't ready for that," I stammered.

"Well, she might not have been ready for *you*," Ron explained, the grin never leaving his face, "but she was ready for me. Sweet young thing just wanted somebody a little more grown up, that's all."

I could hear Fred and Levon snickering in the background. I began to understand a bit more about the rules of the game in the Hawks. There were none.

FOUR

Two years earlier, in 1958, Morris Levy's Roulette Records had contacted Ronnie in a frenzy to record a song about Caryl Chessman, the "Red Light Bandit," who was on death row and scheduled to be executed. It was a controversial idea, possibly a highly commercial one, but there was a catch: Roulette envisioned a folk ballad as opposed to a rock 'n' roll tune. Not every rockabilly star would've been up for it, but Ronnie had expressed a deep but somewhat obscure appreciation for folk music that came from a part of his Arkansas background. Unfortunately, Ron's "Ballad of Caryl Chessman," with its plea to "Let him live, let him live, let him live," wasn't that memorable, nor was its plea very effective—Chessman was eventually put to death. Now Ronnie decided he wanted to make an entire album of his favorite folk songs. The Hawk was ahead of the curve on this one: the peak of the folk-music movement, when finger-picking protest singers would swarm coffeehouses across North America, hadn't yet arrived. Still, it was in the wind, and Ronnie had picked up the scent. Of course, none of the rest of us had any idea what to do on a folk album, so we just tried to be respectfully supportive. After all, if something was good for Ron, it was probably good for us.

The folk album didn't garner much attention, so we headed back south to play some honky-tonks and keep sharpening our blades. Moving around all the time, doing one-nighters, the Hawks were like a blur going by. The more time we spent in Fayetteville, the better chance we all had to get a little settled. Fayetteville was Ron's Ozark stomping grounds, and he felt comfortable and appreciated there, though my being from Canada was like being from just this side of Mars. Ron's friends were welcoming and hospitable but mostly older. I just tried to blend in with them.

By this time, Fred Carter was finally making plans to leave the Hawks, though Ronnie and Levon and I were encouraging him to stick around as long as he could. "We're going to put you on rhythm, behind Fred," Ron decided, pointing at me.

"Rhythm guitar?" I had just mastered that damn bass. But my passion truly was playing guitar, lead guitar, and this was a stepping-stone.

Ron nodded. "I'll go looking for a new bass player. Time to find out what's really going to work here."

Soon he found what worked: a smooth young operator originally from Alabama named Rebel Payne who had played Fender Precision bass in a band up in Buffalo, New York. Rebel's bronze Indian skin glowed against his near-perfect white smile. He played in a gliding, steady style that went down easy, just like his personality. Rebel melted effortlessly into the Hawks.

Unfortunately things weren't going smoothly, personally or musically, between Ronnie and Magoo. When you're spending hours at a time together rehearsing, or packed into a car hustling from town to town, bad vibes amplify quickly. Magoo and Ron always seemed to be working each other's nerves. They had almost completely opposite senses of humor: Magoo couldn't roll with playing the joker on piano like Will "Pop" Jones had, and most of his humor Ron didn't really get or want to get. The atmosphere they created when they were together became increasingly uncomfortable.

I could see it happening, but there was nothing I could do. It was sad to watch. Magoo and I had chased this dream together. Hell, he had initially turned Ronnie down because there was no place in the band then for me. But the reality of being in the Hawks just didn't feel right for him. "This isn't my scene," he confided. Eventually he tendered his resignation and headed back to Toronto. It was strange and depressing to see him go. But he acted lighthearted and in some ways seemed relieved to be moving on, which helped take the sting out of it for me. We'd shared a goal and it was hard right then to think we wouldn't be on the same team.

IT WAS ONLY four years earlier, at the end of the summer of 1956, that—*wham!*—the world had changed overnight. Rock 'n' roll had fully arrived. On Tuesday we were listening to Patti Page's "How Much Is That Doggie in the Window?," Perry Como, Teresa Brewer, maybe a little "Sh-Boom." Come Wednesday, we had the Big Bang of rock 'n' roll with Chuck Berry, Elvis, and Little Richard. It struck me as a miracle. Where were all these rock 'n' rollers last week? Were they just waiting in the wings for their moment to arrive? Of course, I would go on to learn that this new music had been seeping under the door for years with artists like Fats Domino, but to me it felt like it happened in the blink of an eye.

Wherever it came from, I was thirteen and ecstatic. I'd just reached puberty; suddenly, girls were a revelation. I already had a guitar in my hand. So there I was, standing at the crossroads as rock 'n' roll exploded. Everything changed: my clothes, my hair, my focus. Music became my calling.

Now I just needed the proper equipment. I loved my acoustic guitar, but becoming the rock 'n' roll hero of my dreams would require something more. Sure, Elvis played acoustic to accompany his singing, but I wanted to play lead and tear off explosive guitar solos. So I saved my money and begged my parents for a copper-colored Harmony electric guitar I'd seen in the Simpsons department store catalog. I had to have it. Each day I willed Christmas to come so I could finally wrap my hands around that guitar.

Then, finally, on Christmas Eve 1956, we opened presents just after midnight; there would be no waiting until morning. I ripped open the big box with my bare hands, pulling out that beautiful guitar. To my eyes it glowed in the dark. I tuned it, turning the knobs and marveling at its size, at how lightweight it seemed. Then, as I strummed away, I suddenly realized a major flaw in my plans—I had no amplifier. Wailing a solo was out of the question. I had been so caught up with just getting the guitar that I'd never stopped to consider how to make it scream. So one afternoon I took the guts out of my parents' combination record player/radio console in the living room and managed to turn it into a makeshift guitar amp without electrocuting myself. When my mom got home, she saw the speaker and tube chassis in the middle of the living room floor with a wire running up into my guitar. I was beaming.

"Jaime . . ."

Before she had a chance to get upset, I hit the strings, and a hot rush of noise came blasting out of the speaker. Mom laughed, somewhere between amused and impressed, but thankfully not mad. "Okay," she said, "we'll see if we can afford to get you a little amp. But first you've got to put that thing back together."

Around the same time, the rebel rock 'n' roll spirit that had taken over music was bleeding into movies too, in pictures like *Crime in the Streets* and *Rebel Without a Cause*. Soon our teenage lives began to imitate art. Gangs formed in different neighborhoods. Hot rods and souped-up cars became the thing. Kids wore brotherhood denim jackets with the name of their club or gang sewn onto the back. Gang rumbles broke out up by the railroad tracks over territorial disputes. I joined a Scarborough outfit called the Black Orchids—one half Bowery Boys, one half Devil's Disciples—and wore the name proudly. Boots were a big deal. You could tell the most serious members of the Black Orchids by the size, cut, and toughness of their boots. "I'm going to feed him the boots!" was a promise we often heard. Although some groups had weapons, the Black Orchids mostly stuck to well-timed kicks in the crotch. A boot that found its target would send the crowd into hysterics and also had the added benefit of ending a fight immediately.

I soon discovered I wasn't much for the physical end of things. When rumbles first became popular I felt brash, ready for anything.

Then I got smacked around a couple of times, kicked in the gut, and I thought, *I have to find another way to rebel.*

WHEN SCOTT LEFT, Ron invited Will "Pop" Jones to come back on piano. Willard already knew most of the songs and Rebel was an experienced bassist, so it came down to my finding just the right place in the mix for a rhythm guitar. Levon came to my aid, showing me some twin-string parts that supported Fred's lead in a funky, feel-good way. I played the red Gibson ES-330 semi-hollow-body guitar, which matched Levon's red sparkle drums. Its fullness balanced out tonally with Fred's Fender Telecaster, which had a thinner and more piercing sound. I went back to "school" with my record collection from the Home of the Blues and more, and ravaged the style of Eddie Cochran and James Burton. I thought back to how Jimmy Ray "Luke" Paulman used to play for Ronnie in the driving, explosive fashion of the white Mississippi Delta rhythm guitar—that bone-dry, percussive sound, the way he muffled the strings with the palm of his right hand and slid into all the chords with his left.

While playing a date in Conway, Arkansas, we ran into Conway Twitty and his band, the Twitty Birds. Made me relieved to be in a group called the Hawks. Still, the name didn't let on how wicked his band was: Big Joe Louis on guitar, Tommy "Porkchop" Markham on drums, and Blackie Preston on bass. They were a crackerjack outfit, tight as a drum, and I noticed that Ronnie felt a bit competitive with them—on a friendly level, of course. Right then Conway and his boys were all in an uproar. They told us that Big Joe and Blackie had been out driving with a couple of girls, Big Joe behind the wheel and Blackie in the backseat making out with one of them. He'd undone her top and was "tasting her milkshake" when Big Joe went flying over a hill at a railroad crossing. The car came crashing down, and Blackie accidentally bit the girl's nipple off. It was horrible. They took her straight to the hospital but weren't sure whether Blackie would end up in any legal trouble.

"Blackie's kind of crazy anyway," Ron observed later. "Something eventually was bound to happen."

"Well, hell, you can't blame him," Will responded. "It was Big Joe that went over the bump." It sounded like a joke, but he was stone serious. Getting used to Willard's deep country ways was still a work in progress for me. Sometimes he made Ronnie and Levon seem like Harvard graduates.

The young southern belles from the University of Arkansas made me feel much more at home. Every time we played clubs or a school dance around town, I would try to meet someone a little closer to my age. Levon and I would double-date sometimes with girls from the university. We often took them to drive-in movies, mainly for the purpose of making out.

"I hope it's not a good movie," I said to Levon as we got ready one night.

"Don't worry," he assured me, "I think this one's even in black and white."

He wasn't wrong. But the movie was John Ford's *The Grapes of Wrath*, so powerful, so beautiful, that it tore your heart out. Making out in the backseat couldn't compete with Henry Fonda's acting and John Steinbeck's epic story.

The next night, Levon and I pulled into the local Tastee-Freez for a corn dog and thick shake. We had just picked up our order when some guy started pointing his finger at me, claiming that I had been hanging around with his girl. I had no idea who the guy was or what he was talking about.

"Don't pretend you don't know *exactly* who I'm talking about, you son of a bitch!" he yelled, jabbing his finger in my face.

Levon put his corn dog down and got right in between us. "Don't you be *pointing* your goddamn finger over this way," he growled, "or I'll gnaw your fucking ear off. Get out of here, you sorry-ass bastard."

The guy threw his cup of soda on the ground and walked away.

"I'll kick his ass all over this town," Levon declared, picking up our box of food. I followed him into the car, catching my breath.

"Who do you think he was talking about?" I said, bewildered.

"Come around here pointing his goddamn finger . . ." Levon mumbled as he sucked on the straw of his thick milkshake.

It was the first time I'd experienced the protection of an older brother. And it felt pretty good.

RONNIE'S AGENT, Harold "the Colonel" Kudlets, had us booked into Hamilton, Ontario, then back to London and Toronto. We packed up the trailer once again, and naturally Levon took the first driving shift. With six of us in the DeVille, I was stuck riding the hump in the front seat. Soon Levon and I were the only ones still awake. The radio station WLAC out of Nashville was pumping out the gospel sound of the Harmonizing Four's "We're Crossing Over." I turned it up as Levon kicked the Caddy into passing gear and we cruised by a big rig.

"Listen to that bass singer," I said. "Man, is he good."

Levon blinked his lights at a truck, and the truck driver blinked back. "You know, I became friendly with Herb, the bass singer in the Platters."

"Really?" I replied. "I wasn't sure I even liked that kind of music, but their lead singer, Tony Williams, has to have one of the finest voices in all of rock 'n' roll. Hey, did you ever listen to the Hound?"

"Who?"

"George 'Hound Dog' Lorenz. He was an R&B disc jockey with a real smooth rap. Sometimes he broadcast out of the Zanzibar club in Buffalo." Lavern "Jim Dandy" Baker or Bill "Honky Tonk" Doggett could be onstage while the Hound was doing his show in the back of the club. "Every night while I was doing my homework I would listen to him. He had this theme song to open his show, 'The Big Heavy.' The horn line would come in, and he'd say in this cool, deep voice, 'Dig, man, the Hound's around.'"

Levon laughed. "That's beautiful."

"He was amazing," I said. "In the next open space between horn lines, he'd say, 'Movin' and groovin'. Layin' the sound down.' Then he'd play 'Blue Monday,' yelling out, 'Comin' at you from New Orleans, none other than the great Antoine *Fats* Domino.'"

I loved the Hound's jargon. His rap had the authority of a preacher laying down an R&B gospel. I was such a fan, in fact, that once I convinced my friend Don to drive me to Buffalo so we could actually see the Hound in person at his radio station, WKBW 1520. We walked into the station, acting like we knew where we were going, and there, through the glass, we spied the Hound, live on the radio, spinning "Lawdy Miss Clawdy," by Lloyd Price. Finally we could put a body to the voice. The Hound was actually a white guy, a bit chunky, with a salt-and-pepper goatee. You could tell by the joy on his face that he lived for this music. During a commercial break for "What's the word? Thunderbird" wine, he came out of his studio and called over to a young boy I assumed was his son. The kid was bouncing a rubber ball.

"Hey, look out," warned the Hound. "You're gonna fall. I told you before—no *ball* in the *hall.*"

With that, he walked back into the studio and sat down behind the mic just as the commercial ended, hit the ON THE AIR switch, and purred, "Hey, baby, can you dig? 'Young Blood' by the Coasters." As far as I was concerned, Moses couldn't have said it better.

Levon laughed and lit a Winston. "So, I took you out to Marvell to see my humble beginnings," he said. "Now tell me your story. When did you start getting serious about playing guitar?"

"Well," I said, grinning, "after I finally managed to score a little amp to go with my Harmony electric, there was no stopping me."

AT OUR HOUSE in Scarborough Bluffs I received a welcome surprise. Our new boarder, Doug Willis, happened to be a guitar player. He had a pretty black F-hole acoustic with a DeArmond pickup on it, so he could plug it into my amp or play it acoustically. We often practiced and sang songs together. I had turned thirteen and was playing with a band, the Rhythm Chords, which had come together when we all answered a newspaper ad placed by a drummer named Johnny Diamond and included Pete Traynor, his brother Steve, and a sax player named Bob, who were all in their late teens or early twenties. We played school dances, parties, anywhere we could get booked. Little Richard's "Rip It Up" and "Miss Anne," Jimmy Reed's "You Got Me Dizzy," and Elvis's "Heartbreak Hotel" were mainstays in our repertoire. Chuck Berry's "Maybellene" too. I love that first line: "As I was motorvatin' over the hill, I saw Maybellene in a coupe de Ville."

On the weekends, Doug Willis would play guitar and sing for my parents' friends. A couple named Len and Betty, who were a few years younger than my parents, would often come by with their friends Willie and Helen. Doug would do a couple of standards, like "Ain't She Sweet." But then, when I'd pick up my guitar and play a few rock 'n' roll tunes, like Big Joe Turner's "Flip, Flop and Fly" or Little Richard's "Send Me Some Lovin'," the mood in the room would change. The neighbors would get all fired up and cheer me on. I could see in their eyes the effect my playing had on them, the power of rock 'n' roll.

One night Doug pulled me aside. He told me he'd been hooking up recently with Betty, Len's wife, and this time Helen, Willie's wife, was coming too. She said she wanted Doug to bring me along. "Helen's really pretty," Doug said encouragingly. I wasn't sure, but Doug kept pushing. "Come on, no big deal. We'll go get a Coke or something."

We didn't get a Coke. Doug piled the four of us in his car, Helen and me in the backseat, and set a course for a remote country road. As we drove, Helen moved closer to me. "Your music gave me chills, and I thought you were so cute singing." Her attention was intoxicating. When we were sufficiently far from anywhere, Doug pulled over and hustled Helen and me out of the car, tossing us a blanket. "Here, go have fun. I'll be back in an hour." We went into the field, laid the blanket on the ground, and went at it with a teenage sweetness. She was sensitive to my youth and inexperience.

The next weekend, when my parents' friends came over again and the guitars came out, I reached a little higher, stealing glances over at Helen to see if I was getting through. Doug arranged to take us out again, same country road, same blanket, and this time Helen and

I rock 'n' rolled—my first real grown-up romantic encounter. The power of this music was changing my life.

Our rendezvous went on until one evening Betty and Helen said they needed to cool it; their husbands were starting to ask questions. I tried to look disappointed, but inside I breathed a sigh of relief. As surreal and wonderful as this experience had been, I wanted out of this craziness before things got out of hand.

I often felt like a kid moving through an adults' world. I had worked at a ragtag carnival the year before in Scarborough, so that summer I got a job on the midway sideshow at the Canadian National Exhibition, beside the lakeshore in Toronto. This show featured contortionists, barkers, dwarfs, an armless man, a hermaphrodite, Siamese-twin brothers, and an alligator man, all gathered for display in the name of family entertainment. My duties seemed incredibly simple. Make sure everybody had what they needed, make sure they showed up on time. How hard could it be? But I hadn't understood just who I'd be dealing with. These were true sideshow freaks, hardened by long lives on the circuit and God knows what else. Some had done time, and some had done too much time. They looked at me like a lamb ready for slaughter.

Looking for something less dangerous, I got a job at the Midland Bargain Center, run by Max and June Applebaum. I worked after school and on weekends for one dollar an hour, decent money for a kid my age. The Applebaums were kind people, happy to teach me what they knew about sales and retail. They had an employee named John who seemed like the coolest guy around and I really looked up to him. But every once in a while when we worked together, I noticed him pulling out a big wad of cash.

"Did you get all that money from working here at the store?" I asked him.

"No, I get it from rolling queers downtown on the weekend. It's easy. You pretend you're going to let them blow you, then you ask for some money, ten bucks, whatever. When you see how much money they pull out, you just take it, push them over, and run off. Usually they just start crying. When you're a little older, I'll take you with me."

I acted unfazed but inside I felt nauseated. It seemed like I was walking from one nightmare alley to another.

IN THAT FALL of 1957, I heard that Alan Freed, the legendary radio DJ, was bringing his Rock and Roll Show to Toronto's Maple Leaf Gardens arena, featuring an amazing lineup: Fats Domino, LaVern Baker, the Everly Brothers, Chuck Berry, Frankie Lymon, and Buddy Holly and the Crickets would all be performing. For the next few weeks I saved every penny I could to buy a ticket. This was the holy grail of rock shows, and there was no way I was missing it.

By the night of the show, I was so out of my mind with excitement that I arrived hours early to watch the road crew prepare the stage, the lights still dimmed. As the Gardens filled up, the smell of strong cologne, body odor, and cigarettes wafted through the air. Then, at the appointed hour, a crowd of men slipped through the darkness and took the stage. The lights went up and Alan Freed charged the microphone at center stage as the Paul Williams Orchestra kicked into gear.

"Ladies and gentlemen, teen queens, rockers and boppers, I'm Alan Freed and welcome to the Cavalcade of Stars. Without further ado, let's get started with Mr. Rock and Roll himself. . . . Let's hear it for *Chuck Berry!*"

The sound of Chuck's Gibson 350 sent lightning bolts through my body. His voice echoed through the arena like that of a prophet spreading the gospel of a "Brown Eyed Handsome Man." It was a whole show of headliners; one after another they came on, looking fantastic and sounding amazing. They all rocked the house, and by the end I could hardly breathe. But fasten your seatbelt, there was one more: Buddy Holly and the Crickets appeared, romping into "Peggy Sue" and "That'll Be the Day," with Buddy down on his knees pounding out a guitar solo that ran up my spine.

After the show, as the musicians packed up their equipment, I slipped up to the security railing by the stage and caught a glimpse of Buddy Holly putting away his guitar.

"Excuse me, sir," I called out. "I gotta know, how do you get that huge sound out of your amp?"

He looked over at me and smiled, then closed the latches on his guitar case and walked toward the railing. His black horn-rimmed glasses looked much bigger offstage and he dressed more like a university student than a rock 'n' roll star.

"You a guitar player?" Buddy asked.

"Yes sir, I'm trying."

"What's your name?"

"Robbie," I quickly replied. "Robbie Robertson."

"Robbie Robertson, all right!" Buddy laughed. "Here's the thing. I got this Fender amp with two twelve-inch speakers. I blew one of the speakers, and thought it sounded better, so I left it. Some guys I know even cut holes in the speakers or put paper in them to get this tone."

I couldn't believe it: not only was Buddy Holly a genuinely nice guy, he was willing to reveal the kind of inside information I was hungry for. As he walked back to pick up his guitar case, Holly raised his arm over his head, calling back, "Good luck to ya!"

When I left the arena I didn't know what to do with my nervous energy—if I got any higher I worried I'd just combust into smoke. I'd just been through something transformative, a wondrous experience that had given me a glimpse into a different life, and it was both thrilling and terrifying. I couldn't go home, so I went to a restaurant and didn't make it back until two thirty in the morning. My parents were pissed, and I had no way of communicating to them that this had been the most important night of my life.

All of my focus now went into sharpening my chops, and soon various local bands started inviting me to join them for gigs at dances. Pete "Thumper" Traynor joined me on occasion. Our band, the Rhythm Chords, had by then evolved into Thumper and the Trambones, or sometimes Robbie and the Robots.

Nothing could compare to a lesson in rock stardom like Alan Freed's Rock and Roll Show, but we learned a lot from local bands too. Toronto had an incredible scene in the late fifties, and we got to see plenty of great acts, night in, night out. Pete and I both liked a hot group called the Gems, featuring Bobby Blackburn on vocals, one of the only young black R&B singers in Toronto. The Gems had a full horn section, so they were definitely official. And of course there was Little Caesar and the Consuls, whom I played with and from whom I learned a wicked version of Huey "Piano" Smith and the Clowns' "Rockin' Pneumonia and the Boogie Woogie Flu." I soaked up everything I could from all these bands. I wasn't sure if I could ever play better than these guys, but I thought I could dream bigger than any of them.

At home, I felt a distance growing between my dad and me. When I talked about my musical ambitions, he said, "Look at your relatives on the reserve. Look at the people in our neighborhood. That doesn't happen to folks like us. So don't set yourself up for disappointments." When he pushed back against my dreams, my resentment grew. And I saw something too that was getting worse with him. It had started to become apparent one night a couple of years earlier. We had a black and white mutt named Buster, a beautiful dog, half collie, half something else. He went on all kinds of adventures with me, trailing behind as I tromped through the willows or ran errands. Buster went anywhere I could take him, and when I'd get back from school, he would be waiting for me faithfully. One summer night my father came home late from drinking with friends. When he came in, Buster barked and growled, protecting the house. My father kicked and beat the dog down into the basement in a drunken rage. I never forgave him for that.

Another time I came downstairs after practicing my guitar and accidentally left a fan running. When my dad got home and found the fan still on, he stormed down into the kitchen and smacked me across the head, knocking me into the stone chimney. It might have cost a half a penny's worth of electricity to leave it on, but that was his reasoning. Shaken and angry, I ran out of the house and down to Kingston Road, where my mother had taken a job in a restaurant to help make ends meet. When I walked in the door, she could see the welt on my face and the sadness in my eyes. She knew instantly what had happened, and with a red fury in her frown tried to settle me down while she prepared to read Jim the riot act.

Over time my mother and father fought and argued more and more. And there were episodes, drunken and not, when he hit my mother, whenever he thought it was warranted. He always tried to make up afterward, but one time he beat us both and blackened one of my eyes. That would be the beginning of the end for my mother; as for me, I just disconnected. And when my father's violence started to become a regular thing, my mother said she was leaving. She gathered many of the photos of the two of them and cut them in half or destroyed them. He didn't know how to undo the damage and fix the situation, so he agreed to a divorce. They both came to me separately to ask who I wanted to live with, my dad in an awkward, sincere way, my mother as if she knew I had no choice but to go with her.

Then one morning my mom asked me to join her at the kitchen table. "I've got something to tell you. Sit down." She looked across the table and spoke of Jim with ice in her voice. "I have to tell you this now. And maybe I should've told you before. . . . He's not your real father."

"What? He's not?" I gasped. "I don't understand. He's not my *real* father? Then who is? And who is he?"

"I'll tell you later," she whispered like it was a secret, and would say no more.

Trying to go to sleep that night, I couldn't quiet my mind. I wanted to feel like nothing could rattle me, even such powerful news, but a voice in my head kept saying, *I don't know who I am anymore— orphan, bastard, stepchild?* I was desperate for more information, but my mother never had been much for sharing stories about our background.

Over the course of the next few days, though, she gave me bits and pieces of the true story regarding my birth father. His name was Alexander David Klegerman. She met him when they were both working at Coro Jewelry, after Jim had deployed to Newfoundland. Alex, as they called him, had taken the job at Coro to learn about the different degrees of gold plating, but his main talent was gambling. He was a card shark who'd become convinced by his mother that he possessed an extraordinary gift of memory. She herself had an incredible memory, honed through years working as a bootlegger after the Great

Depression, never committing anything to writing—no addresses, no phone numbers, nothing. She made the money in the family, cooked, cleaned, and raised her four kids while her husband prayed and met with other respected Jewish intellectuals in the community.

Alex became a card counter. The game, he saw, was not luck but mathematics. In time he became quite successful at the local poker games. The stakes grew, and he began winning not only bigger pots of money but also cars, jewelry, sometimes even mortgages. A handsome, well-dressed, street-smart hustler with money in his pocket and a silver tongue, Alex had never seen anything quite like Rosemarie "Dolly" Chrysler before, with her high cheekbones, red skin, big eyes, and glowing smile. To him she seemed possessed of a pure spirit not found too often in the big city. Inspired, he brought her gifts and made her feel special. Their contrasting backgrounds felt intriguing and fresh.

If Jim Robertson was a down-to-earth, regular guy, Alex Klegerman was the polar opposite. There's no doubt Dolly was taken by the excitement of Alex's scoundrel ways. Jim wanted to get married, and a twenty-year-old Dolly appreciated his commitment, but she wasn't sure of her feelings and didn't know what to do. Jim was stationed over a thousand miles away. As the months passed, Alex and Dolly grew closer and closer.

Then, tragically, Alex was killed in a hit-and-run on the QEW highway while changing a flat. A passing truck slipped onto the shoulder, hit him, and kept going. A friend who was with him wasn't hurt but witnessed the whole horrible thing. They had been on their way to New York City for some kind of "sting" that the friend wasn't at liberty to discuss. Rumor spread that Alex's death wasn't an accident. There were all kinds of nefarious theories, but nothing was ever proven.

Scared and devastated, Dolly went into seclusion at her aunt's. Not long after, she received a letter from Jim saying he would be returning to Toronto soon and wanted to marry her. Under the circumstances, she agreed.

Though she didn't yet know it, Dolly was pregnant.

I TOOK ALL this in with surprising ease, though there was a numbness in my heart. I wasn't sure if it was because I held a deep anger toward Jim or because it now made sense that I had never felt a strong connection to him. In any case, my mother's anger was enough to go around.

My last days in Scarborough were full of Jim explaining that Doll had driven him to this bad behavior and that he wasn't really a hurtful person. "It was her fault," he kept saying. "And this stuff about me not being your real father—that's ridiculous. Of course you're my son. I don't know why she would even say that. It's just out of anger." I felt a little sorry for him trying to convince me of *his* truth, which he truly believed, but I still couldn't accept what he'd done to my mother and me. It could never be undone.

My mother decided to call Alex's brother, Morrie Klegerman, whom she'd known even before she met Alex, to tell him the truth about my birth, and she arranged for Morrie and his younger brother Natie to come out to Scarborough. A few days later they met us at a restaurant down on Kingston Road. Morrie seemed very happy to see my mother after all these years, but Natie asked questions with an undertone that suggested he was wary of her intentions. My mother wasn't asking for anything; she just wanted to make them aware of Alex's child.

I could tell Natie was sharp and had a keen eye by the way he spoke and looked me over. He had blond hair and a very likable face, and he stared with piercing eyes over the bridge of his crooked nose as he smoked and drank coffee. Morrie, on the other hand, had dark hair and a warm, round smile. Only when they laughed could you see the resemblance.

"Well, I'll tell you something," Natie said finally, leaning back, "there's no doubt in my mind that's Tutor's son."

"Are you kidding? Of course, he looks just like him." Morrie laughed.

"What are you talking about?" Natie said. "He looks like his

mother, thank God, but I could tell a mile away. His voice, his gestures, his forehead. I can tell for sure."

I felt like I was passing a test that I didn't even know if I wanted
to take.

"Well, Jaime, how about that?" Natie continued. "I bet you didn't
know you were Jewish."

Morrie, with a wide smile, added, "Doll, you ever tell him he was
Jewish? Look at that, he *looks* Jewish sitting there."

"Doll, you did a great job," said Natie. "Good kid. Right, Morrie?
Great-looking kid."

THE CADDY WAS doing close to eighty miles an hour as we cruised along
through the night toward Hamilton. "Oh, man"—Levon grinned at
me as I wound up my story—"you're Jewish? How about that!"

At that moment Ronnie rustled awake. "What, who's a Jew? Let me
check and make sure I still got my damn wallet." He shook his head
and rubbed his eyes. "You saying young Robin here's a Jew? You better
pull the car over and shake him down."

"Aye, aye, Ron," said Levon. "Next chance I get, I'll turn his pockets
inside out."

"Well, I'll be damned. Bad enough he was a redskin, now he's a Jew
on top of that."

"I'm afraid so." I laughed. "Yeah, you could say I'm an expert when
it comes to persecution."

They kidded me the whole drive to Canada, but it became obvious
that Levon looked at me differently after I'd shared some of my past.
After all those stories, I became somebody he wanted to know. This
was the beginning of a brotherhood.

FIVE

My new uncles, Natie and Morrie Klegerman, were, I would soon discover, products of Toronto's Jewish underworld; both were streetwise, reared by their tough bootlegger mother. The brothers were close but extremely different in mind and in body. Natie had a wholesale business selling fur coats and diamonds, while Morrie owned and drove a taxicab. Natie was intellectually gifted, with a remarkable ability to connect with people and delight them with his dangerous imagination, while Morrie, more solidly built, fit naturally into the role of protector.

They quickly pulled me into their world and went out of their way to make me feel like family. By then I was going to R. H. King High School, even farther east in Scarborough, but I made regular trips downtown to the heart of Toronto's Jewish neighborhood at College Street and Spadina Avenue. Natie introduced me to his lovely wife, Fran, and their two kids—my cousins—David and Vicki. And even though this world couldn't have been newer or more different from the suburbs or the reserve, I felt quite at home. Maybe it was the mysterious bloodline connection—or maybe they were very sweet and caring people.

My uncles were keen to know what made me tick and showed concern for my future. Natie took me to his business headquarters and showed me someone cutting and sewing fur skins. He poured out diamonds from a piece of crepe paper and explained they would later be mounted in jewelry. He told me about money lending, another part of his broad business model, which seemed to cover a range of very traditional Jewish trades. I could tell he was trying to see if any of this touched a nerve in me.

When I told Natie that playing rock 'n' roll music was my passion, a stunned look came over his face. "What kind of a cockamamie thing is that?" Then he realized, "Oh, show business. I get it. But rock 'n' roll? Isn't that a bunch of goofy, crazy people?" The concept was as foreign to the Klegermans as being a shylock was to me.

I grew ever more fascinated the deeper they drew me in to my new-found heritage. One powerful moment came when Natie took me to meet his father, Shmuel Chaim, a devout-looking Jewish gentleman dressed in a black suit. They spoke in Yiddish, and Natie explained the whole situation to him, that I was Alex's son. The old man trembled with emotion. He put his hand on his chest and lowered his head as if in prayer. Then slowly he raised his eyes to look at me, a combination of joy and sorrow on his face. I felt frozen in the moment as he studied me, searching, I'm sure, for traces of his departed son. He gave a nod of recognition and a tear rolled down his cheek. Then he spoke in English. "Alex was my favorite. Your father was my favorite." I managed a slight smile in acknowledgment before glancing at Natie with sympathy, concerned he'd be upset by his father's stark favoritism, but he waved it off—as if it didn't bother him in the least. He signaled for me to join them. I walked over and took both their outreached hands, profoundly moved by the whole experience. But though I knew Natie meant for it to bring me closer, in this strange new world I still couldn't help feeling like an outsider.

So while my uncle Natie tried his best to pull me into his business and family, music took me away. That summer of '58 he got me a job selling dresses in the wholesale district, but I also opened for the Hawks with my band, wrote the two songs Ronnie recorded, and got rock 'n' roll permanently under my skin.

Just as I would go my own way, Uncle Natie went his. After that summer, as I fell deeper into the world of professional music, he began to organize a new and mysterious business enterprise that no one but him completely understood. It still involved diamonds, but this was more like an investment venture. From his vague explanation, I gathered it was an extension of the six-for-five money-lending business but with a much better "vig," or interest. And there was an international element, connecting Natie in Toronto to others in New York and Antwerp. Some investors were putting up hundreds of thousands of dollars, and Natie had diamonds from a New York 47th Street connection that he was using as collateral. He recommended that my mother and I invest whatever money we might have while we had the opportunity. "It will be worth twice as much in about a month," he promised.

The whole thing was over my head, but I completely trusted my uncle and admired his ambitions. He was by far the smartest, most charming person I had ever known—one of those people who, whatever the subject, knew much more about it than anyone else.

"How do you retain all these facts, and keep all these numbers in your head, without writing anything down?" I asked.

"Our bloodline is blessed with a very special gift of memory," Natie explained. "My mother never wrote down a name, a number, an address. And maybe it was for the best, too, when it came to dealing with the authorities. Your father also had this, especially when it came to poker. You're very lucky. Have you ever noticed you can remember things that other people couldn't imagine?"

I had a flash of realization. "You know," I said, "in school, I could remember everyone's name, where they lived, stories they had told. After a while I had to pretend not to remember, just so the kids and teachers wouldn't think there was something peculiar about me."

"There you go." He smiled, gratified. "You got it, that's the Klegerman memory."

THE HAWK LOVED hearing about my colorful family. "Well, I hope they come to the club," he said. "I'd like to meet this uncle of yours." We pulled up to the Warwick Hotel, unloaded, and checked in like the regulars we were. Ron liked to stay at the Warwick rather than the

Westover because the hotel had a roof that was good for sunbathing. Duane Eddy and the Rebels were playing next door at the Edison, and rolling in the following week was none other than the man himself: Bo Diddley. At this point, I thought, life *might* be perfect.

Then one night Ron's wish to meet my family came true: Uncle Morrie, Uncle Natie, and Aunt Fran came down to Le Coq d'Or to check us out. I introduced them to Ron, not quite knowing what to expect. I couldn't imagine two more different worlds coming together. Ronnie could be funny and likable, but he was half wild man, half savvy entertainer; I knew my aunt and uncles had never met anybody like him. But Natie asked Ron questions about life on the road and the record business, and Ron answered seriously and respectfully. All seemed to get along perfectly well. Later Ron pulled me aside. "That uncle of yours is one smart son of a gun," he declared. "You could just feel it. I liked him. I liked them all. And your aunt is so damn pretty." Morrie didn't say much. He was just measuring Ronnie on his bullshit detector with my best interests in mind. So was Natie, of course, but you would never know it.

A few nights after that, my dad, Jim Robertson, came to the club by himself for a beer and a little visit. I hadn't seen him too much after the divorce, partially because we were always on the road and partially because my mother still held hard feelings toward him. I introduced him to Ron and the boys, which completely confused everybody; I had family showing up left and right. Afterward Jim told me he was proud, and had known all along that I would turn out to be something; it touched me that he'd come by and said so. Despite the violence and the difficult days, I had a warm place inside for Jim. He was still the only father I had ever known.

But of all my family, it was my mother who would come to hold a hallowed place in the affections of the Hawks. Ron and Levon had met her briefly a few times before I ever got tangled up with them, back when she'd come to Le Coq d'Or with friends. Sometimes, Ron told me, she would mention "her talented son." But after my Jewish relatives came to the club and I told Levon and Ron a little more about my background, they looked at my mother in a whole different way.

With so many threads of my ancestry to keep track of, they mistakenly thought she was Jewish and started calling her "Mama Kosh," as in "kosher." She didn't mind, and I got tired of trying to explain the whole story again, so the nickname stuck.

Come Monday night, Bo Diddley started his engagement at the Edison. Ron liked Bo's music, so it didn't take much to convince him to go check out his set and to bring me along. The spell was woven as soon as we walked through the Edison's doors. There onstage stood Mr. Diddley, armed with a square-body guitar and an amp strung with chicken wire, and Jerome, his maraca player, shaking the joint down. I concentrated on Bo's hands, his fingers—it was like watching some kind of voodoo magic, where you can only believe half of what you see. How could someone make that rhythm, make that beat, sing with such mourning and move that way? It was a great musical Mississippi mystery I deeply needed to solve. Every chance I got that week, I slipped next door and took in a bit more of Bo's jungle medicine. His stripped-down combo made a raw, hypnotic noise that could stop a train on the tracks. And when we hit the stage back at Le Coq d'Or for our own sets, I incorporated bits of his rhythm into our songs.

Then, one night after the show, the Hawk and Levon decided to have some company over to the Warwick, and Ron suggested that I go next door to the Edison and ask Bo if he'd like to join us. I jumped at the chance, and as I approached him I took in his shiny, silky-straight hair and those thick black glasses. Somebody had asked him for an autograph and he took something out of his jacket and stamped his name on a piece of paper.

When I told Bo I was with the Hawks and invited him to come by, he looked amused. "I like Ronnie Hawkins. He's a funny cat," said Bo. "Yeah, I'll come by, what room you in?"

Earlier I'd met a young lady named Patricia who was at the club with her aunt and invited her to our postshow get-together. As she and I strolled over to the Warwick after the show, I stuffed my hands in my pockets and tried to make a little conversation.

"Are you really twenty-one?" I asked.

"No," she admitted. "A friend loaned me her ID. It's the first time

I've ever used it." She was a little uncomfortable going to a hotel room with someone she barely knew, but I assured her she had nothing to worry about. Up in the room Patricia waited while I changed out of my show clothes in the bathroom, and just as I emerged there was a knock on the door. I opened it, and there stood my hero: Mr. Ellas McDaniel, known to the world as Bo Diddley.

"Come in," I said, trying to act as cool as I could. Bo was carrying a guitar case that he laid at his feet as he sat down. "Ron will be by soon. This is Patricia." I couldn't believe that Bo Diddley was sitting right there in my hotel room. After a few minutes of small talk he reached down, unlatched his guitar case, and pulled out that incredible looking square-body ax. The Gretsch guitar company had built this custom for Bo. Mostly country-and-western musicians played Gretsch guitars, so this was quite unusual—and nobody had a square-bodied one. His foot started patting out a tempo, and then he kicked into his pulsing "I'm a Man" rhythm—*boom bap boom* bah boom. Was this really happening? The sound, the feel of just his thumb strumming and his foot on the carpeted floor sent chills up my spine. When he began to sing, it took me a second to realize that he was making up words on the spot about what he was going to do to this young girl called Pa-*tri*-cia, once he got rid of me.

> When this young man's gone
> And Bo Diddley moves in
> Patricia gonna know
> Real loving ain't no sin

My mouth hung open. Patricia started squirming and looking at her watch. Just then Ronnie knocked on the door and let himself in. "Son, you got Bo singing in your hotel room," he cried as he surveyed the scene. "How much did you have to pay him for that? We know he don't play for free."

Bo slapped me on the back. "You can pay me later." He put his guitar back in the case.

"Well, don't put that thing away now," Ron whooped. "We're going down to my room and have a little party!" He put his arm around Patricia's waist. "Darlin', you and I might have to run off together before this night is through." She blushed.

"Yeah, I was trying to tell her the same thing," said Bo. "But I sang it, for free."

Bo and Ronnie headed down the hall whispering to each other. "Really, I have to get going," Patricia said softly. "I have to get up early for work."

"Work?"

"Well, actually, school."

I could tell she was unsettled by all the attention and tried to explain that she was in no danger: I promised I'd keep these Casanovas away from her, but Patricia just patted my cheek, smiled, and said, "Call me a cab."

THE HAWKS HAD a wilder, slightly out-of-control force to us now, with Willard back on piano. His style wasn't as musical or refined as Magoo's, but it made for an exciting ride. My rhythm guitar, matched with Will's left hand and Rebel's solid bass style, held down the foundation well enough to give Fred free rein to wail. And wail he did—his solos were the best I'd ever heard from him, and that pushed me to raise my game.

Despite the difference in our age and experience, Fred still regarded me as a junior-sized version of himself, which probably explained his enduring competitiveness. Ron liked to feature Fred singing a down-and-dirty version of Muddy Waters's "She's Nineteen Years Old." He played guitar solos that stung like a bee—the piercing sound of the back pickup on his Fender Tele could jab you right between the eyes. It was hard to imagine anything could top it, but gradually Ron started pointing to me to take solos on the same song. I played most of my leads in a go-for-broke fashion, and Ron got a kick out of this youthful, pedal-to-the-metal approach. "Burn that baby up, son!" he kept yelling, and my confidence bloomed nightly. Levon too would be laughing and nodding at me to keep on pushing. Fred, on the other hand, did not like anyone trespassing on his turf.

The Hawk had a strict rehearsal regimen, and many afternoons were spent learning new songs and pushing our skills. Ron was dead serious about having the best band around, and proclaimed, "If you're not working at it, you ain't getting better." I took these words to heart. One afternoon at rehearsal, Fred made a snide remark about my practicing all the time.

"Well, you need to be practicing yourself," I shot back.

"Oh, really? Why's that?" he said.

I looked up at him. "Because someday I'm gonna cut you."

Fred granted me the courtesy of a small laugh but then muttered, "Okay, that's it. The guitar lesson is over." After that he never played another solo facing me so I could see what his fingers were doing.

Yep, this was high noon and the Wild West.

WITH FRED ABOUT to depart, the pressure to hold up my end on lead guitar was mounting. My youth and limited experience made Ron nervous about my taking over this responsibility. So he decided to try out someone else: a top-flight Arkansas guitar slinger named Roy Buchanan who, like Fred, had played with Ron's cousin Dale Hawkins. I had no choice but to roll with the punches, though when Roy showed up in Toronto with just a Fender Esquire guitar and a small duffel bag, I thought the Lone Ranger had never looked this solitary. He plugged into a small amp we had at the hotel and proceeded to blow our minds. Roy had more tricks up his sleeve than Houdini: his fast runs and extreme string bending, his rhythm and soloing at the same time, like it was two guitars. The thrilling part was that he didn't mind showing me things in slow motion, quite the opposite of Fred. Roy would play something amazing, break it down for me piece by piece, and then hand me his guitar. I began hoping we could both fit into the next incarnation of the Hawks. I wasn't overly naive: I knew this could mean I'd be out of a job—Ron might not want two guitar players. But right then it didn't concern me. Just being around somebody that good lifted me up.

Soon after Roy arrived, though, Ron observed there was something a bit demonic in his eyes, and in his nature. The suspicion was confirmed when one day, out of the blue, Roy confessed to us, "I'm half human and half wolf." We all stared at him. "And sometimes it's a problem, especially late at night when there's a full moon."

"Why? What happens?" I asked. Sure, Roy did look more bohemian than us, with his goatee and pasted-down hair, but a wolf?

"Well," said Roy gravely, "sometimes I wake up in the night howling from a nightmare. One time there was blood on my beard, and in the bed."

"That sounds like a werewolf to me," Ron teased.

"Right. Same thing." Roy then declared that he'd made a vow to marry a nun; only then would his wild ways be settled. I heard later he actually did marry a former nun. But Ronnie wasn't willing to wait for that day. I recognized the expression on his face when something got too far out for his liking. "That shit's too damn weird for me," he finally declared. And like that, Roy was gone, and I was once again the lone entry in the guitar lineup. Ron gave me a long look. "You better start playing real good real fast, that's all I can tell you."

I now had three weeks before Fred left for good. I didn't talk to anybody, didn't hang out; I just listened to records and practiced nonstop in my hotel room. The Hawk liked my monastic dedication, assuring me he could hear an improvement in my playing night by night. But we were pressed by more changes. Willard wanted to leave—you could tell he needed to get back to Arkansas for some kind of family reasons, or maybe he was just homesick—so the Hawk checked out another piano player from Buffalo, a former bandmate of Rebel Payne's named Stan Szelest, a handsome, James Dean–looking nineteen-year-old who could keep up with the high standard set by Willard and Magoo. Stan had a stern, serious side that made Levon and Ronnie want to push him to lighten up and at least act like he was having a good time, but I liked his natural intensity. It made me think he really meant what he played.

Right around this time Ron and the boys started coming to dinner at my mother's house in Cabbagetown for a feast of her cooking. She'd make her chicken imperial, baked ribs with corn-bread dressing, a melt-in-your-mouth Chinese pot roast, mashed potatoes with sweet corn, her rouladen, Swiss steak, coleslaw, three-bean chili, potato salad with cheddar, meat loaf with dressing in the middle, cheese bread, tamale pie, shepherd's pie, turkey pot pie, crispy pork chops, scalloped potatoes, Christmas goose, sausage rolls, four-hour pot roast, hot apple crisp with ice cream, lemon meringue pie unequaled anywhere, her extra-light pastry for strawberry-rhubarb pie, blueberry, peach, cherry, apple with a whole wheat crust to die for, pineapple upside-down cake, butter tarts, date squares, on and on to the point of paralysis. This was food for the soul, feasts of near-spiritual experiences, everybody moaning nonstop "oohs" and "ahhs" of satisfaction and delight. Ma blew their minds with every dish she made, and they weren't shy about telling her so. "I don't care where in the hell in the whole wide world you go," Ronnie declared, "you ain't gonna get better food than this. Damn, boys, I gotta go lay down before I faint." Because of my mom's deprived childhood, devoid of much appreciation, a few compliments went a long way.

Before long, the Hawks started kicking around the idea of staying at my mom's house when we were in town, to get fed like this on a more regular basis.

WHEN WE HEADED south again, we were a new band. Stan was in, Fred and Will were out. With Fred gone for good, the Hawks felt a bit like a boat without a rudder. Fred had more miles on him than the rest of us, and we had looked to him for musical direction, especially me. In his own way, he'd become an important teacher and a major inspiration.

When I graduated to lead guitar, it felt like a natural transition to start playing a cream-colored solid-body Fender Telecaster, the guitar du jour for the likes of James Burton, Roy Buchanan, and of course Fred Carter Jr. So I traded in my red Gibson 335 and became a man. Glued to that Fender, during the next few weeks I went on a rampage of screaming overdrive and deployed all sorts of high-flying guitar tactics that I hoped would convince everybody that I was a force to be reckoned with. At least I had the right attitude, if not quite the skills. I didn't possess the refined fingering and accuracy that Fred or Roy had, but neither did Bo Diddley or John Lee Hooker, two of my faves. I tried to make up for my rawness with aggression and excitement.

We were booked into the prestigious Cimarron Ballroom in Tulsa, Oklahoma, and the Hawk wanted to put on a good show to give the people their money's worth. As we played, I noticed right down at the front of the stage a young Indian guy with very long black hair, watching me and my fingerwork without blinking. He would nod his head slowly whenever I played some flashy lick. I could feel a musical communication between us.

After the show, as I was carrying my Fender Bassman amp down off the stage, he came up and said, "Let me get that for you."

"That's Indian Ed," Ronnie shouted to me. "He's a young guitar player from around here."

I thanked Ed for helping with my amp. "My name's Ed Davis," he said shyly. "I love your playing. That's just the way I want to play someday. Nobody around here plays like that—nobody. Where are you from?" I told him about my background on the Six Nations Indian Reserve, and boy, he couldn't have been more thrilled to hear that. Not only could I wail, but I was also a damn half-breed from the Mohawk nation.

All that practicing and my willingness to take risks onstage had transformed my guitar playing. Along with my own blind ambition, I was becoming the youngest, whitest—well, not really *that* white— blues boy around. This was 1961 and, if nothing else, I was for sure *early*. Levon's trust in me pushed me further. Almost daily he gave me reasons to believe. "Son," he said in his down-home, brotherly way, "*nobody's* doing what you're doing. You want to know why? Because nobody can *do* what you're doing."

I wanted to believe him. In Ronnie Hawkins's music I'd found a sweet kind of violence: it was hard and tough and rugged and fast— but tight. I was trying to do something with my playing that was like screaming at the sky. Levon understood on a deep level what I was going for, and in those moments when I doubted my progress, he showed the generosity and willingness to hold up a mirror and wink approvingly. If Mark Lavon Helm from Marvell, Arkansas, digs what I'm doing, I figured, it must be okay.

WHILE WE WERE in Arkansas, Ron had helped Levon buy a beautiful mint-condition 1956 Cadillac Coupe DeVille with a dark green roof and light green body. With his own ride, Levon (and by extension, me) could claim a little more independence. Having two cars for the band also gave everyone more elbow room when we traveled.

We played a round of colleges and graduation parties in Oklahoma, Texas, and Arkansas, and on that tour it struck me: as eye-opening as life with the Hawks was, I was missing something. Mixing with all these young people at their schools, I was witnessing a part of growing up—an educational experience—that musical roadrats like us would pass right by. It left me feeling empty. I grew deeply interested in reading and developed a thirst for words that would help fill the void left by dedicating my future to music. Southern writers felt most appropriate for the scenery passing me by on the road, and I loaded up on William Faulkner, Eudora Welty, and Flannery O'Connor. I read *As I Lay Dying* again, captivated by the fate of Addie Bundren and Faulkner's fluid stream-of-consciousness technique. Ronnie thought my reading binge was making me too distant and heady. "Son, what the hell are you reading now? You're gonna get your head all tangled up in those damn books."

As summer set in, the Hawk informed us that we were headed back to Canada, but not to the usual Yonge Street or London haunts—we had been booked for July and August at a summer resort in Grand Bend, Ontario, on Lake Huron at the Imperial Hotel. "They're building us our own quarters," he announced, "an annex for us to stay while we're there." It had six bedrooms and our own bath facilities on top of the hotel, where we wouldn't disturb anybody. We had never heard such an offer before, and the prospect of staying put in one location was appealing, especially at such a beautiful summer spot. Grand Bend had everything we needed, so let the party begin, and *that* we did. Just up the street lay the sandy shores of Lake Huron, with its clean and (for the Great Lakes) reasonably warm water. The area had several good food stands and restaurants, and there was always the sundeck on the roof of the Imperial Hotel, where you could lie out. It was an easygoing atmosphere all around, scores of girls around every corner. It was so relaxed that Ron didn't even show up at the club until it got crowded.

During that summer all seemed at peace, and yet the revolving door of the Hawks personnel never quite came to rest. Our first month at Grand Bend, there were rumblings that Rebel Payne might be moving on. His girl wanted to settle down and have a more normal life. We liked Rebel and wished he would stay, but deep down we already knew what he would choose when push came to shove. He wasn't really a music addict like the rest of us.

At the same time, a strange tension began growing between Stan and Levon. Levon didn't feel that Stan was a good bandmate. He thought he was too moody and distant. Stan didn't give a shit what Levon thought and went his own way. One night the tension boiled over, and they really got in each other's faces, which turned to pushing and shoving.

"If you guys really need to get this out of your system," I suggested, "why don't you take it outside?" They both tore off their shirts and said, "Let's go."

"I want to see this," Ron cried. "If there's gonna be some ass kicking, I want a front-row seat. Shit, we should be charging admission."

Everybody marched outside, and Stan and Levon went at it, punching and wrestling, smacking and shoving, though to me they looked more like two blond modern jazz dancers. They threw some good shots and scratched each other up a bit, but you could see they were both more lovers than fighters. Finally they got winded.

"Have you had enough?" Levon groaned.

"Have you?" Stan responded.

They ended up shaking hands and calling it a draw, but it was pretty clear Stan had gotten the best of it. I tried to comfort Levon, telling him he came out on top, but he probably knew better.

On Sunday nights we would play in Port Dover on Lake Erie, at Pop Ivy's Summer Gardens. My cousins from Six Nations, which wasn't very far away, would come, which made me feel good. Ron would announce over the mic, "Some of Robbie's kin are in the house, so if anybody gets scalped, you'll know who did it."

One night a little band from Simcoe, Ontario, opened for us. We had seen them before, and I remembered especially their leader, the youngest guy in the group, a good-looking eighteen-year-old kid who played rhythm guitar and sang in a voice reminiscent of Sam Cooke. You can just spot a musician who's got the goods. You can sense it in an almost tribal way. Rick Danko had it. Levon and I nudged each other as he sang—this guy was a contender. And when we met him, there was a connection between his personality and his performance, a nervousness and excitement that came out as a kind of jittery electricity. We pointed him out to Ron, but the Hawk was already on it. With one of Rebel's feet already out of the band, Ron wasted no time in offering the kid a job if he would learn to play bass.

Young Rick was overwhelmed by the proposition. It was an incredible opportunity but it would mean undoing his entire life. Despite his obvious musical talent, the band he led was little more than a hobby. He had a full plate back in Simcoe, with a serious girlfriend he planned to marry and a job as a butcher's apprentice that promised a steady career cutting meat. Picking up with the likes of us meant taking a huge risk, but Rick could see something serious with Levon and me that held great appeal. And in the end he did the right thing: he blew off his past and gambled on the future. Over that summer in Grand Bend, Rick went from butcher's apprentice to bass player apprentice, with Rebel, Levon, and me as his would-be teachers. Levon was spreading the word at the time about a new album called *The Best of Muddy Waters* on Chess Records. This collection of music would go on to indelibly influence the course of music in North America and England. Rick was half confused and half enchanted by it—his tastes ran more to R&B. I was already deep in the Muddy Waters club, and I wanted to share what I loved about this music with Rick, who appeared pretty open-minded about anything you threw his way. Levon, though, was a little impatient. He yearned for a rhythm-section partner who had that down-in-the-mud feel like Duck Dunn from Booker T. & the M.G.'s. Rick had a different way of playing bass, like he was skipping over ice. It made Levon strict with Rick's learning curve when it came to our music. "Either you feel it or you don't," he declared. "Let's not waste one another's time." Rick was also constantly restless and fidgeting, which drove Levon nuts. He'd have to get fully on board with the program for it to work, not just with the music.

Rick had entered a whole new world, one that was light-years away from small-town Simcoe. He was finding out quickly that this adjustment involved changing everything: his tastes, his abilities, his backward personality and unhip ways, and even his approach with girls. But boy, was he a quick study. He watched, he learned, he practiced. He was on a mission to turn himself inside out.

THE NEXT THING I heard, Ron had invited Roy Buchanan to come back for another tryout. At one point this development might have troubled me, but by now I had thicker skin and I believed in my own path. Ron enjoyed seeing a good knock-down-drag-out, whether it was a match in the boxing ring, a fight in a club, or musicians trying to play each other under the table. So he would set Roy and me against each other in a guitar duel to see how the sparks flew.

The house was packed at the Imperial Hotel club the night Roy was invited to sit in with us. Levon winked over at me during the set. "Go ahead, baby, do your thing, and do it well!" Near the end of the night, Ron called out for a down-and-dirty blues jam so he could see Roy and me really go at it. Roy kicked it off and began crawling around on the low strings like a swamp dog, deep and mysterious. I picked it up and started sawing out lower notes in a language usually saved for arctic wolverines. Roy grinned, enjoying this little tit-for-tat game. When he began changing the tuning of his guitar in the middle of a solo, I suddenly felt like Doc Holliday trying to sober up before a shoot-out with Wyatt Earp. Everybody played along with Roy's amazing tricks, but then I came out swinging. I made my guitar cry like a baby, and suddenly this duel got serious. Roy kicked his guitar's back pickup into ear-splitting overdrive until the audience was on its feet.

"Take it, son! Make that sucker scream!" Ron yelled at me over the crowd.

I stepped to the front of the stage and started playing notes that weren't even on the fret board. The veins in my neck bulged, and sweat flew from my brow. Levon got on the bottom of the beat and kicked the rhythm section into high gear while prompting me on: "That's it, baby! Here we go!" I hit a stuttered run-up to the top fret of that Tele, and the crowd jumped to their feet and screamed and whistled. I didn't know how to get back down from that high note, so I stayed there, trilling on it until I got dizzy. My arms were flying, the guitar was airborne, my hands were a blur. The audience couldn't stop clapping. Roy couldn't stop grinning out of the side of his mouth.

He might have played better than me; certainly his solos were more technically advanced. But I stole the show. And nobody thought otherwise, not my bandmates, and especially not Ronnie. Levon raised a drumstick at me while the audience kept clapping for what felt like minutes. Of course, Ron loved the battle. I could tell he was terribly proud of me. Only Roy and I really understood what had just happened. We'd reached a musical wavelength and both of us had pulled the trigger.

The next day Roy packed up his things to make his departure. I walked downstairs with him and thanked him for his inspiration and generous sharing. Ron met us outside and mentioned to Roy that we were going down to New York soon to do some recording. Would he like to come and join us?

"I'll be there," said Roy. He made a saluting gesture.

I watched Roy walk toward the bus, duffel bag in one hand, guitar case in the other. *There goes an amazing talent that needs to find a home*, I thought.

BETWEEN SETS AT the Imperial one night, Rebel and I wandered across the main drag in Grand Bend to a little burger stand for a snack. As we ate, a guy walked up and introduced himself, mentioning that he played piano and sang in a band that had opened for us a while back called the Rockin Revols. I remembered him—he'd sung a terrific version of Bobby "Blue" Bland's song "Little Boy Blue." Rebel made some crack about this guy's "schnoz," his long, pointed nose, but rather than take offense, the guy laughed. "Yeah, that's why they call me Beak," he replied. "My name is Richard Manuel."

I shook his hand, but Rebel stood behind him making mocking gestures like he knew something I didn't. Then I got it: Richard "Beak" Manuel was drunk—a laughing, fun-loving sort of drunk, but drunk nonetheless. Richard's condition had puzzled me at first since nobody in the Hawks drank. We could hear Ronnie taking the stage, so we had to head back over.

"I'm not old enough to get in the club," Richard called to us.

"You're not old enough to be loaded either," replied Rebel.

Looking back at Richard as we walked toward the club, I thought, *I hope this guy doesn't have a problem. Maybe it's just one of those nights. . . .*

SIX

Coming after the 1950s and the big bang of rock 'n' roll, the early sixties didn't have quite the same fire. But there's always magic out there, and Roy Orbison, Ernie K-Doe, the Shirelles, Timi Yuro, Ray Charles, Ricky Nelson, Ben E. King, and Patsy Cline kept the flame burning. Who would have thought Hank Ballard and the Midnighters' song "The Twist" would come back and haunt the dance floors of the world? You couldn't avoid it, and this craze would come back to haunt us as well.

The early 1960s were not a high point in the popular musical landscape. A bit of a drought, you might say, which meant that to find the good stuff, we had to dig deeper, trolling the further reaches of the AM dial, the stations I called "the secret airwaves." One refuge was an old standby, WLAC out of Nashville, Tennessee, where DJs like John R., Herman Grizzard, Bill "Hoss" Allen, and Gene Nobles always got their hands on some wicked R&B and killer blues. The gospel-hour shows delivered too, with new and old gems that made us crank the volume just to feel the thunder.

In the South, AM radio stations that played mostly electric southern blues via Chicago were on the rise. What had felt a couple of years earlier like scattered sounds from a dark underground had begun to rise over the land like a misty revelation. We even heard rumors that this blues music was beginning to spread like a holy virus across the Atlantic to young musicians in England.

RONNIE AND THE HAWKS were back at Le Coq d'Or Tavern for a three-week engagement, now with Rick Danko on bass. The lineup wheel kept right on turning. Stan had grown less certain about his future with the Hawks, and soon he confessed that he needed to be moving on. Ronnie accepted his resignation and immediately turned his attention to finding a new piano player. He was constantly thinking about how to have a better, stronger band.

We were now holed up at a different, slightly more upscale hotel on Jarvis Street in downtown Toronto called the Frontenac Arms. Some of us would stay at my mother's house from time to time too. Her cooking and the reasonable amount she charged could be very appealing given our modest paychecks, and the easy rapport she shared with the guys only added to the charm of the arrangement.

There were a few minor complications, however, in involving my mother so deeply in our lifestyle. Although she kept an open mind and knew when to look the other way, we all felt a bit uneasy about having girls coming and going at her house. Often she would see young women leaving in the morning, and as a matter of etiquette she would see them to the door. Sometimes in the late morning or at lunchtime, female visitors would swing by, and Mama Kosh would greet them, forever the kind hostess.

"Come on in, dear. You too, come right in."

She would then point them in the direction of one of our rooms with a genteel smile. My mother took it all in stride. She looked young and was used to people asking if she might be my sister. She dug that image, and it helped her feel like one of the gang.

Ron had come up with the brainstorm of opening an after-hours club called the Hawks' Nest in the banquet room downstairs at the Frontenac Arms. When the clubs that we played closed at 1 a.m., the Hawks' Nest became the spot to continue the party. You could even have called it a late-night rendezvous joint and "booze can." We stayed upstairs in good-sized two-bedroom suites, which was convenient, to say the least. This may have been the most successful sexual atmosphere Ronnie ever created. We were booked solid, days and nights, with a steady flow of "lovelies" coming and going. "Sharing is caring" was our motto.

Ron asked my mom if she would be a hostess at the Hawks' Nest, and she was happy to oblige. But as free-minded as she was, I couldn't get completely comfortable having my mother around to witness some of our shenanigans. First of all, I couldn't even remotely imagine any of the other guys' mothers being around us like this. Though this was part of what made Mama Kosh unique, I nonetheless felt I needed to put on a bit of a front in her presence. None of the guys ever wanted to come off as sleazy or inappropriate in front of her, and that went double for me.

Around this time I got some disturbing news: my uncle Natie had gotten caught up in a police investigation over passing illegal diamonds. I called Uncle Morrie as soon as I heard to find out what was going on, but he was hesitant to say much on the phone. "It's probably a big mistake," he advised, "a business deal gone bad. Don't worry too much." One afternoon I got a call from Natie. "Meet me at the Capri Restaurant on Yonge Street." The Capri, he told me, was a place where we could get a little privacy so he could fill me in properly on this whole diamond business.

Midafternoon, the lunch crowd had thinned out. In the dark-cornered Italian restaurant with its scent of secret underpinnings, Natie sat alone, smoking Black Cat cigarettes at a table amid the darkened decor. He waved me over to sit beside him.

Natie's presence could make you feel that something special was happening. He carried a light inside him, and you could feel its glow. You couldn't help but be drawn to his unusual features, the smart eyes that saw right inside you. When he laughed, his whole face lit up with joy. He was a knowledge gatherer and stored everything he learned within the vast troves of an indelible memory. When he explained something to you, his narrative had the detail and precision of a diamond cutter.

"Kid, I don't want you to get false information from what's in the paper or what you hear," he said in a hushed tone. "I'm doing a business operation, and some unexpected complications turned up, so it looks a little different from what it really is."

I had no idea what he was talking about, but the confidential way he spoke made me feel I was in on something very curious and daring. He continued in the same nebulous vein for a while and finished with these words: "Your father was my hero. I truly looked up to him, and what I'm doing here is no different than what he would have done. Tutor, your father, would have been my partner. This is a very big business deal. I want this for you too, Jaime. Do you understand? You're my nephew and I've got to protect you. If I tell you too much, you could be vulnerable and in danger." *Welcome to the underworld*, I thought.

"If anybody asks you questions about this situation," he advised, "just say, 'I don't know anything about my uncle's business.'"

After that, he and I would check in on the phone regularly. Natie always spoke under his breath, as if somebody might be eavesdropping. He called me from phone booths only and told me that when I was out on the road touring I should always call him collect and say it was Mr. Hutchins calling. It made me feel like a confidant, and I dug it.

RONNIE HAWKINS'S southern Ontario tour circuit kept us crisscrossing paths with other bands, which gave us the chance to see all sorts of talented young musicians. One of our most striking new discoveries was the young man Rebel Payne and I had run into on the street in Grand Bend: Richard "Beak" Manuel.

We were playing an auditorium near Stratford, Ontario, Richard's hometown, and his band, the Rockin Revols, was opening. Everybody in the group was talented, but Richard's voice particularly stood out—it had such richness and power, such maturity for an eighteen-year-old kid. You heard it most on those Bobby "Blue" Bland covers—when Richard sang, you melted away. His piano playing wasn't as rollicking as we were used to in the Hawks; he wanted to be more like Ray Charles than Jerry Lee. But he had all of the standard R&B piano licks down, and he was just the right age for Ronnie to believe he could be broken in and shaped. Richard's volatile relationship with beer, which Rebel and I had witnessed firsthand, appeared to have mellowed, which helped his chances with Ronnie. Now he seemed more like a "good-time Charlie"—a guy who liked to sometimes have a brew. Best of all, he was hungry to play with us and eager to prove he could cut it as a Hawk.

Richard's voice was there from the start, but when I got to know him, I found he was also one of the nicest, sweetest people you'd meet. He was funny, but when someone else was funny, no one appreciated it more than Richard. His great big teeth stood out when he smiled, and he could laugh as good as Levon, which made him even more lovable. Richard's joining the Hawks would be an easy fit.

There was an unwritten law about hiring musicians away from other bands, so after Levon and I gave Richard our full recommendation, Ron hired the Rockin Revols to serve as the house band at his club in Fayetteville, Arkansas. There would be a transition period— Stan would stay until he figured out his next move, and Richard could be initiated into the group while the Revols looked for his replacement.

In the meantime, Rick was getting more comfortable in his skin as a Hawk. He had a keen ear for music and for his new surroundings. Levon felt Rick needed a total makeover and Rick stepped right up. And though Richard didn't have the jackhammer rockabilly piano style of his predecessors, when he sang, all was forgiven. It didn't take Beak long to look the part too. Since Levon and I always hung together, Rick and Richard quickly bonded and became running mates. When they sang Sam Cooke's "Bring It on Home to Me," the sun came out.

A solid core was forming. Bill Avis, a friend of ours from Lake Simcoe, Ontario, had joined our posse as road manager. "Business Bill," as we called him, was always right there when you needed him, memorable for his poise and courtesy. You couldn't help feel good having him around—he took care of business and then some. "Whatever you need," he'd say. "You need equipment? You need cigarettes? You need me to go collect the money? I'll be right back."

Before we hit the road for the South again, Levon and I headed over to my mother's place for a last meal. As usual, we stuffed ourselves to the point of total satisfaction and utter discomfort. Ma had gone out of her way to make dishes that Levon especially loved, items with a southern flair to them. On this evening we feasted on all of these, plus a quintessentially southern salad that Levon had told Ma about some months before: wilted greens.

"You cook some well-done bacon and crumble the bacon into small bits," he had explained. "Then you mix it into a beautiful salad with plenty of greens. Then you pour a little of the very hot bacon fat over the salad until it sizzles." In those days nobody flinched when you talked about pouring hot bacon grease or hot butter over a salad. My mother followed his directions, and according to Levon, Toronto's own Mama Kosh made the best wilted salad on earth, bar none.

We motored on to Oklahoma, ready to tackle the next few gigs. On the way, Ron reminded me of a horn player who had started showing up at some of our London, Ontario, gigs, sitting in on occasion. Jerry Penfound played tenor sax, flute, and baritone sax and seemed like an easygoing guy. "I like that old boy," Ron said. "I'm strongly considering giving him a job." It was a bold feeling, the power a couple horns could bring. But finding the right people would be key. One of the guys we had tried out played mostly jazz in after-hours clubs. His goal, he told me, was to make enough dough to buy a plane ticket to London, where he could become a steady heroin addict. "Doing dope and playing jazz, that's all I want," he said with remarkable earnestness. Somehow, Jerry Penfound seemed a better bet.

When Ron brought up Jerry's name, I felt inspired to mention a piano player we'd heard in London, Ontario, who'd come to Grand Bend. "You remember Garth Hudson?" I asked. "Well, I talked with him, and besides being a really skillful musician, he's a fascinating and unusual guy. He mentioned this new gizmo that hooks up to a piano and sounds like an organ. It would make us sound twice as big."

"That right?" Ronnie looked up.

"Yes," I said. "He plays different saxophones, and he's a monster of a piano player. He can play any kind of music."

I could see Ron turning it over in his head. "Yeah, to have an organ and horns, that would be a big sound," he admitted.

Soon we arrived at a desolate concrete building outside of Pawhuska, Oklahoma. The manager of the club let us in and showed us where to set up. After the trailer was unloaded, I stood at one of the club's windows and looked out at the dazzling Oklahoma landscape, mesmerized. The whole horizon was a burnt orange, and nothing seemed to be moving. An eerie quiet surrounded the whole area. I called Levon over to look at this beautiful and unusual stillness.

He took one look out the window and turned pale.

"Boys," he shouted, "we got one coming!"

Everybody rushed to the window and stared out in awe. Then I saw it, a gray funnel in the distance, zipping back and forth and heading our way. As it edged closer, we saw trees torn from the ground, cars flipping in the air, and buildings ripped apart like they were made of matchsticks.

Levon seized the club manager by his shoulders. "You got a basement or a storm shelter?"

"Follow me," the manager said. He rushed over to open a trap door to the basement. I grabbed my guitar and scampered down the stairs, everyone else hustling down ahead of or behind me. Huddled together below, we heard what I imagined sounded like a cyclone and an earthquake happening simultaneously. It was the most frightening thing I'd ever heard.

I was holding my breath and clenching my teeth as Levon, alert but calm, spun Tornado Alley stories from his Arkansas youth—tales of broom bristles plunged into the sides of trees and a whole building blown away while a pile of soda-pop crates sitting right next to the building were left perfectly undisturbed. "In fact," he recalled with satisfaction, "we had a tornado come through town once that lifted my parents right in their very home, carried them away, and then saw fit to set 'em down. They survived, but they were never the same. So you can understand my particular fear of these damn things."

The tornado passed without hitting the club or our cars and equipment. *Holy miracle*, I thought.

A few nights later we played a club in Tulsa called the Canadian

Club, thanks to its location by the Canadian River. The gig was nothing all that memorable but for one crucial wrinkle: we never got paid. Now, haggling with proprietors over payment wasn't exactly new to us. Dayton Stratton, Ron's club partner and southern booking agent, would sometimes accompany us to gigs, and Dayton had a knack for getting checks out of club owners, sometimes even cash from the door receipts. But after we played this show in Tulsa, Ronnie and Dayton ended up with a promise rather than money.

This wasn't the first time somebody had asked to pay later, but you could tell there was concern we might get screwed on this one. Ron and Dayton went back and forth with the club owner, to no avail. Their discussions grew increasingly heated and soon escalated to shouts, slurs, and improper insinuations. Ron, furious, threatened everything this side of boiling him in oil.

"I'll go kick his ass," Dayton promised, but that wasn't enough for the Hawk. Ron and Dayton started making a plan. Soon it became clear they would need the services of Ron's pro-football-player buddy, Donnie Stone, and a fearless and crazy local legend named Kenny Brooks, from whom Ronnie had lifted a lot of his sayings and humor.

As I heard the story, Dayton, Donnie, Kenny, and Ron went back to the Canadian Club in the dead of night and forced their way inside. The piano player Leon Russell had played the night before us, and his band still had their equipment stored there, so, with the utmost care and caution, Ron and the boys removed every piece of Leon's equipment from the club, placing it safely outside. Then they torched the place, and burned it to the ground.

The police got involved and confronted Ronnie about the incident. "I have no idea whatsoever who would have set that fire," he told them. But you couldn't help noticing as he said this that his eyebrows were completely singed off. It was no great mystery who did the deed, but the police knew this club owner was a scumbag. So the authorities gave Ronnie an ultimatum: if he promised not to come back to this part of the country, they would chalk it up to dust-bowl justice and leave it at that.

I TOLD LEVON about my uncle Natie's predicament with the diamonds and he was intrigued. "Is this some kind of a diamond heist, a money-laundering thing? It sure smells fascinating to me." Levon and I had become thick as thieves. We went everywhere together. Ron thought we were a good duo, even if I was stealing his old running buddy. As the months wore on, Levon and I separated from the rest of the pack, going our own way and discussing future plans. In London, Ontario, Richard "Beak" Manuel finally took over on piano and vocals. Rick had become pretty solid on bass, and his singing was getting featured more. Ron always liked the idea of having Rick, Richard, or Levon take a lead vocal here or there, making the show more like a Ronnie Hawkins Revue. By now too my guitar playing was becoming a crowd pleaser unto itself. And Jerry Penfound finally came on board officially, bringing a fresh new sound to the Hawks with his flute and saxes.

And then there was Garth Hudson. With his dark hair, long forehead, and pale skin, Garth looked jazz-musician cool, or like someone who hadn't been out in broad daylight for ages. He played brilliantly, in a more complex way than anybody we had ever jammed with. Most of us had just picked up our instruments as kids and plowed ahead, but Garth was classically trained and could find musical avenues on the keyboard we didn't know existed. It impressed us deeply. Levon and I pushed Ron to try to get him to join us.

Garth was quiet and clearly a bit offbeat. While Ronnie understood that he was an amazing musician, he was a bit concerned about his being so different from the rest of us. We'd been through ups and downs with personality mismatches like Magoo and Stan, and Ron preferred having guys who fit easily into the fold. But I embraced Garth's difference, and it helped that Levon did too. I was studying Garth, sensing there was something special to be learned from him. It really caught my attention when he spoke about playing the organ in church and at his uncle's funeral parlor. He talked with real passion about emotionally controlling the crowd with his music, making people break down or rejoice through the hymns he chose. "I found some true enjoyment in helping people get to the bottom of their feelings," he explained in a manner that sounded anything but condescending. "I felt I was doing a service, in a way. It did seem like they appreciated that." He added humbly, "It was more than just a job to me."

When Ronnie had first floated to Garth the idea of joining the Hawks, he had put up a good deal of resistance. Now Ronnie made him a real offer, and once again he hesitated. I could see that Garth had serious reservations that we didn't quite understand. Levon and I tried to entice him with tales of our promiscuous lifestyle and the promise of upcoming opportunities, but he just smiled and said he didn't think that would be possible. Ronnie finally corralled him. "All right," he said. "Let's get down to it. What's it gonna take?"

Garth explained that if he went off to join a rock 'n' roll band full-time on the road, his parents would be devastated. He was twenty-four, older than all of us except Ronnie, and his parents were old-fashioned and conservative; given all the support they had invested in his classical music training, they would see this as a waste. It would break their hearts. At the same time, he was interested, and recognized the power of Ron's charm and persuasive ways. "Maybe," he proposed to the Hawk, "if you were to speak to them personally, they might see this as a good career opportunity for me."

That evening Ron, Levon, and I gathered together to hash everything out. I felt strongly about how much we could learn from Garth and his astonishing multi-instrumental talent. If he were to join the Hawks, I reasoned, it would help all of us become better musicians.

So Ron met with Fred and Olive Hudson and turned on his magic full throttle. With sophisticated, soulful conviction, he sold them beautifully on what a big *break* this was for their son. He would perform for large and appreciative audiences, Ron told them, receiving more than adequate compensation. The bottom line, though, was that Garth would assume the role of *teacher* to the rest of the members of the band. This was an extremely prestigious position.

No one was a match for Ronnie Hawkins. Garth's parents gave their blessing, and he became a Hawk. Ronnie paid Garth his customary salary, but the clincher was that the rest of us had to pay Garth ten dollars a week for music lessons. We were thrilled that Garth was finally in the group, but in quiet moments we wondered: *Did we just get scammed?*

Most everybody who was ever in the Hawks played by ear; none of us knew how to read or write music. Undaunted, Garth showed us some shortcuts to more sophisticated chord progressions and introduced us to some funky jazz blues that gave us a better template for incorporating the two new horns into our repertoire—songs like Bobby Timmons's "Moanin'," as well as some choice cuts by jazz giants like Art Blakey and Horace Silver. Between Garth and Jerry Penfound, who also knew how to read music, our cool factor was on the rise.

Jerry also had a knack for electronics and proved helpful in hooking up Garth's Organo, the device that produced the sounds of an organ and could be played with a piano keyboard. It was a temporary, cost-efficient solution; as much as Ronnie loved outfitting his band with new gear, the cost of the Lowrey organ that Garth wanted exceeded the Hawk's pocketbook at the time.

With Rick, Richard, Garth, Jerry, Levon, and me, Ron had himself a strong lineup, and he knew it. He felt we could go up against anybody. Ronnie was deeply competitive but he was very aware of his talents and his limitations. He knew he didn't have the vocal abilities of many of his peers, although he would sometimes joke, "Hell, Caruso's got nothing on me." To him, having a hot musical band with some good-looking guys helped balance out the big picture.

Colonel Kudlets had booked us into a new Toronto club called the Concord Tavern, closer to the west side of town on Bloor Street. The Concord had a bigger stage than we usually played and featured a dance floor right up front, with tables and chairs lining its sides. The club doors were manned by a legendary bouncer named Big Lou, whom everybody was fond of unless he had punched you in the face and thrown you down the stairs. Then you weren't so fond of him. Big Lou had lots of nervous twitches, but you got used to them pretty quickly. He would seat all the "nice" upstanding-looking people on the right side of the room and all the rounders, thieves, and tin men on the left. Of course, he would sit most of the hip chicks and the pretty women on the left side too.

Most of the Hawks were staying at my mother's house. Rick and Richard had rooms on the third floor, while Levon, Garth, and I lived on the second. The Hawks' Nest at the Frontenac Arms was on-again, off-again, but Ron wanted to keep the after-hours club going in hopes of pulling down some extra money—and he appreciated the "social" benefits as well.

One afternoon my uncle Natie came by and picked me up at my mom's place. "The situation has changed considerably since you've been away," he said as we drove. "We've moved into an apartment up Bathurst Street. It's safer for the family."

"Safer?" I asked. "Safer from what?"

The business operation Natie had developed had by then taken in a few million dollars—an enormous amount of money back then— and some of the investors were demanding their return. Natie told me it was taking longer than he had planned for all of the deals to go through; people were getting angry and impatient, and some had threatened violence.

"Jaime, I don't want you to be worried," he said. "It's all going to be worked out, it's just taking longer with my people in New York to get everything organized. It's all aboveboard, and everybody's going to do extremely well."

I believed him because I believed *in* him, but then he dropped a bombshell. He explained that for business reasons he had to involve some heavyweight people to keep things from getting out of hand. Natie had brought in the Volpe family as partners.

Even I had heard about the Volpes. They were four brothers who, with various associates, were said to head Toronto's Cosa Nostra affiliation. Nobody wanted trouble with the Volpes.

Natie said he was dealing directly with Paul Volpe, the head of the family. When Paul had gotten wind of Natie's situation, he'd come to him with an offer: "There are quite a few people very upset with you, and some really want to do you harm," he'd told my uncle. "We've been told that at this point you've taken in a lot from these investors, and they want their money or else." Volpe proposed a deal: "If you give us a cut, I'll make sure nobody hurts you. No one will bother you because they'll have to go through me." Paul Volpe was very direct about what he wanted and what it meant to have his organization behind you.

A couple of weeks earlier, one of Natie's creditors had become so irate that he'd hit him, opening a cut over his eyebrow. Volpe's protection at this point made sense. Natie agreed but insisted that everything stay very low-key: no threats, no rough stuff—unless there was absolutely no other choice.

I thought, *This is so surreal.* It felt like something from a movie; at the same time, it felt intriguing to be part of this underworld scenario. After all, I was just the long-lost nephew who played guitar in a rock 'n' roll band. Nobody was after me.

Over at the Concord, though, we got to know all kinds of hoods and gangsters. Normally, neither the Volpes nor Natie would come to a place like the Concord, but one day, to my surprise, Natie informed me that he and Paul were going to stop by the club to pay me a little visit and hear some music. When I pulled Levon aside to fill him in and told him about the Volpes, his jaw dropped. "Damn, this is some heavy shit, but I like it."

"Let's keep this on the Q.T.," I urged. "I don't want Ronnie making any jokes about them from the stage. They do *not* appreciate that kind of attention."

On a Thursday night Natie and Fran, along with Paul Volpe and his lady friend, showed up at the Concord around 9:30 p.m., while we were in the middle of our set. Big Lou seated them where he put most people he wasn't familiar with—over with the nice folks on the right side of the dance floor. As they ordered drinks, I nodded subtly to Natie from the stage. A couple songs later I noticed a bit of a buzz coming from the other side of the club, where the rounders and tin men were seated. Somebody had recognized Paul Volpe, and word was getting around that "the big man" was in the house. Mouths whispered, fingers pointed. For these wise guys, Paul Volpe showing up at the Concord was an event.

We finished our set and I slipped through the crowd to join Natie. He introduced me to Paul and his lady friend and pulled up a chair for me. I realized I had seen Paul Volpe before at the Capri Restaurant, where I'd met Natie a few times, but hadn't known who he was. Tallish and slightly bulky, he had a kindly-looking face that also had a hard edge to it.

"So, Jaime, you like this rock 'n' roll music," Paul said matter-of-factly. "You guys sound good. I'm having a good time. Right, Natie? They sound real good."

Natie responded with a slight laugh. "What am I going to say? He's my nephew. I'd tell him he's the best no matter what."

Paul seemed outgoing and pleasant enough, not your storybook Mafia boss. Ronnie came over to the table and shook Natie's hand. "I knew you couldn't stay away," he said, smiling. Natie didn't introduce Paul, so I didn't say anything. As Ron wandered on from our table to joke and slap the backs of familiar regulars, I waved Levon over and introduced him to Paul. He greeted everybody with an outstretched hand and his broad smile. Natie commented that he thought the music and especially the drums sounded better at this place.

"We like it too," I said. "You can hear everybody better, and it has a proper sound system."

"Leon," Paul said, "you think this music's a little loud in here? You like it that loud?"

"Well, it's sounding pretty good from where I'm sitting," Levon said without missing a beat. "You know, if it isn't a little loud, you just can't get into it."

"I'll keep that in mind," Paul said, patting Levon on the arm as if to say, *Thanks for stopping by. You can go now.* As Levon left the table, Paul looked at Natie incredulously. "What are these guys, cowboys? They sound like they're from the hills or something."

"You know, I like that kid," said Natie.

Ronnie's voice called out from the stage, "It's *racket* time," which was his humble way of saying, "It's *showtime!*" I strapped on my guitar and we kicked into one of our requested songs, "Ruby Baby." Toward the end of our set I saw Natie and company stand and head for the exit. As they went, Natie caught my attention and signaled that he'd call me. Levon threw me a grin—"Oh, man." Ron looked over at me—I could see he was putting the pieces together.

On my way to the restroom after that set, some second-story guys and a tough, fearsome chap named Tony stopped me. I knew this guy in passing from his ruthless reputation—during a fight here one night he'd stabbed someone in the eye with a fork.

"Robbie, come sit down for a moment. Let me buy you a drink."

"I don't drink, but thanks. What's happening?"

"Pull up a chair, come on," Tony said. "Somebody told me the guy with Paul Volpe is your uncle."

"Yeah, he is. Why?" I answered.

Tony puffed hard on a Rothmans cigarette. "I've heard things about your uncle, some big things. And do you know Mr. Volpe, who he is? You know anything about his background? It's not a pretty story, let me put it that way."

I shrugged. "I don't know, he's just a friend of my uncle and aunt. Seems like a nice fellow, though. Excuse me, I gotta go water the flowers."

"Go ahead, Robbie," Tony said as we both got up. "You're okay, kid. I'll catch you later."

SEVEN

Many southern rockabilly bands had a fondness for uppers—bennies, dexies, black beauties, take your pick. "Diet pills" they called them, because they suppressed your appetite. They made you talk a lot, set your heart pounding, and could make sex iffy for men. If you were a smoker on these "pep pills," you hated to put one out. They were also known as truck driver pills, for overnight long hauls. As a road band, constantly on the move, we found them handy for getting to the next job.

The sixties had rolled in and with them the counterculture quest for expanded consciousness. Like most musicians, we were ready, our curiosity in tow. Some of the rounders who frequented the clubs had pot connections, and of course the jazz cats always knew where to find a hookup. Levon couldn't wait to try marijuana and went on the hunt. You had to be careful whom you confided in, though; back then the authorities considered pot no different from hard drugs. The consequences of getting busted could be disastrous, especially for bands like ours that had to repeatedly cross the border.

Levon and I got close to a new friend we'd made at the Concord Tavern, Connie B. The *B* was for the last name of her boyfriend, who was doing time. Connie was blond, with powerful cheekbones and a smile that lit up the room. Everybody accepted her into the club: she was sharp and cool, gifted with an intelligent-sounding voice that matched her strikingly rich vocabulary. Connie was in her midtwenties, a few years older than us, and she knew most of the rounders and thieves and where to score some grass. In time she became a dear pal of Levon's and mine, almost a sister. Having discovered that we could talk freely to her about girls we liked and get pretty accurate feedback, we began to come to her for counsel on a regular basis. We ran together and smoked pot together. After gigs the three of us made a habit of hiding ourselves away to smoke, snack, listen to music, and laugh the night away. Ron, who would sometimes refer to our little gang as "the Three Musketeers," was concerned about our behavior. He didn't drink or smoke cigarettes, just the odd dexy once in a while. The mystery of drugs still lingered in the air, like steam from the shower.

On one occasion when Ron caught Levon and me smoking a joint, Levon impressed upon Ron that he was really missing out. "You gotta try this shit."

"If I try that stuff I might start speaking in tongues," Ronnie said.

But we got him to take a few puffs, and pretty soon he said, "Boys, I'm gonna have to go lay down before I float away," and excused himself. The next morning Ron raved about what a crazy night he'd had after he left us. "I'll tell you what, I started dreaming in Technicolor and I couldn't stop. I spent the whole goddamn night seeing things I ain't never seen before."

Late one night, Levon and I decided to turn Rick and Richard on, up in their rooms on the third floor of Mama Kosh's. After we passed around a joint and Levon ate the cocktail, the usual giggling and cackling ensued. Pretty soon my mother called up the stairs from the second floor, "Stop all that noise up there, or I'm gonna come up there with a broom!"

That just made it worse. We were falling apart, crying with laughter, burying our faces into pillows and blankets to muffle the sound. Richard laughed so hard he nearly peed himself. Finally we all managed to bring it back to a whisper. "Okay, Ma," I called back. "We were telling a joke. We're gonna step out for a snack anyway. Sorry for the racket."

"It's *not* racket time," Levon whispered, and we all buried our faces in the pillows again. The four of us slipped as quietly as we could down the stairs and out the front door, headed for the closest all-night doughnut shop. Rick and Richard were the perfect stoner brothers. They laughed harder and more often than anybody around. "Business Bill," our road manager, would go up to that doughnut shop counter too and say, "I would like to order six creamy maple," then fall to his knees laughing and have to turn his back until he pulled it together. Garth and Jerry were older, and their jazz backgrounds had given them a measure of cool we still lacked; they just blurted out random, strange, poetic lines that no one understood.

Garth was in many ways an enigma. He had narcolepsy and could fall asleep at any time, and maybe because of that he lived a unique lifestyle. Some of his habits were unusual, to say the least. He claimed he didn't sweat, no matter how hot it got. He would buy orange juice but wait for two days to drink it until all the pulp had sunk to the bottom. He would eat around the seeds of a tomato. Ronnie found it all downright strange, but he could tolerate it because Garth was such an incredible musician. He could've been playing with the Toronto Symphony Orchestra or with Miles Davis, but he was with us, and we were lucky to have him. Levon had tremendous respect for Garth as a musician, so when it came to any weirdness, he just looked the other way.

WE WERE CAUGHT UP in our music and our lives, paying little attention to the world around us. The U.S. military offensive in Vietnam was only beginning to escalate in 1961, but the military draft had been reinstated. Levon got word from back home that he was being called up. Bad timing: we were on track with the band and wanted to do something to make our mark in music. Plus Levon really, *really* didn't want to go. Connie and Levon decided that if it came down to it, the three of us would drive to Buffalo or Niagara Falls and they would get married so he could avoid it. I'd serve as best man.

Meanwhile, we were excited that Roulette Records had a new producer for us, Henry Glover, who had worked at King Records for Syd Nathan. Henry's credits shone: he had produced James Brown and Little Willie John and had written "Drown in My Own Tears," one of my favorite Ray Charles tracks. Now he had us booked to record some new tracks at Bell Sound in New York City. He brought a tremendous amount of experience to the table—I probably asked him too many questions about recording "Fever" with Little Willie John and how James Brown worked out his musical arrangements.

The Hawk lived up to his promise and called Roy Buchanan to meet us for the sessions. I looked forward to seeing Roy again, and if having him on board made the sessions stronger, I was all for it. Roy and I set up our amps in the studio and sat across from each other. Ronnie said, "Let's run over 'Bo Diddley.'" Levon started playing that jungle beat, and we all kicked in. I hit that "Bo" rhythm hard and Ron started rapping out the words. After Roy played a stinging "ride" in the middle, I closed it out with more fire. Henry came on the talk-back mic from the control room. "We're just getting a sound on everybody. Robbie, I love what you're playing. Keep doing that."

Suddenly Roy stopped and said, "I think I should play bass. That's what I'm feeling." So Rick handed over his Fender bass and we launched with abandon into "Who Do You Love?" A few seconds in, Henry called out, "Hold on, hold on, I want to record this. Okay, tape rolling." We ripped into "Bo Diddley" again and with no break straight into "Who Do You Love?" with Ronnie growling and screaming and my guitar on eleven. One take and that was that. When they released the record, they put "Bo Diddley" on one side and had to fade into "Who Do You Love?" on the B side.

Later we recorded a couple of blues tunes with Levon singing. He and Henry had bonded quickly over their shared Arkansas background, laughing about little towns they knew in common. I mentioned to Henry that Ray Charles's live version of "Drown in My Own Tears" in Atlanta in 1959 was one of the most extraordinary recordings I had ever heard, and he was delighted I knew that performance. He said he'd like to do a whole session with the Hawks sometime. "Robbie writes songs," Levon piped up, adding that we would love to take him up on that offer in the future. I asked Henry if he would be interested in writing a tune for us to record, and he said he'd see what he could come up with.

I was on an all-consuming guitar-slinger mission, and I hadn't been giving as much thought to writing songs. I couldn't help being a song person, but at that moment Garth had me checking out the horn tonalities of Coleman Hawkins and Ben Webster. I especially enjoyed the sound of saxophonist Johnny Hodges, who played with Duke Ellington: his tone was somewhere between a violin and a toy sax, so beautiful. And of course there was always Monk, Mingus, and Miles; Coltrane, Cannonball, and (Ornette) Coleman. I was captivated by Bill Evans's touch on the piano: remarkable. For good measure Garth would throw in a dash of Bach, preferably played by the charismatic young Toronto composer and pianist Glenn Gould. Garth was a reservoir of brilliant music, and I wanted to dive in deeply to learn and understand enough of it to appreciate its rewards.

NATIE CALLED from Toronto. "I'm in a phone booth." His voice was low with intrigue. "Even the pay phone outside the Capri Restaurant is bugged now. Kid, I need you to do something while you're in New York. There's a very important older gentleman you should go visit. You would never know it by looking at him, but he's one of the biggest diamond merchants around. He turns over hundreds of thousands of dollars in stones every week. Anyway, you'll go to his office. He already knows you're my nephew, and he'll give you a package. Then you'll go to the Taft Hotel and meet somebody in the bar. There'll probably be a couple of guys. Neither one of these parties can be seen together or know each other, you understand?"

"Sure," I answered, understanding little except that it sounded like risky business.

"First of all," Natie continued, as if he sensed my doubts, "there's nothing illegal going on here. Nobody's going to bother you, and I'll make sure you get well taken care of for your trouble." The word "trouble" stuck in my head. But I had to trust my uncle, right? And I could use the extra money.

"How much longer will you be in New York?" Natie asked.

"A couple more weeks," I told him.

"That's good," he said. "I'll give you a ring in a day or two with more information."

When I related the story to Levon, he said, "Man, this is some big-city shit going on. We don't have nothing like this in Arkansas, I guarantee you."

"It sounds like this is a legitimate diamond dealer who doesn't want to get his hands dirty doing business with mobsters," I said.

"Maybe you should just take the stones and disappear," he joked. "Retire to an island somewhere. Or maybe you don't want either one of these parties chasing your ass."

Levon and Connie had started calling me "the Duke" for a sharp new suit I'd just had made at Lou Myles's tailor shop, and I was sporting it one night when Levon and I got back to the Forrest Hotel, a legendary spot for musicians to stay in New York. The songwriter Doc Pomus had staked out his usual position across from the lobby check-in desk. Doc was a heavyset Jewish guy who'd survived polio as a kid and now got around on crutches. It was always great to run into him. Doc called: "Robbie, that's some fine-looking threads, baby."

"That's why we call him the Duke," said Levon as we walked over to greet him. "By the way, Doc, do you know where we might be able to score a little reefer?"

Doc motioned us closer. "There's a girl named Doris who stays here. She sells pot, pills, junk, whatever you need. I'll call her room and tell her you guys are okay. If she's here, you can go right up and see her." He picked up the house phone and dialed. As he spoke into the receiver, he started nodding "yes" to us. He gestured toward the elevator with one of his crutches. "Go on up. Room 709. She's waiting for you." As we headed across the lobby, Doc called out under his breath, "By the way, she's a girlfriend of Ray Charles."

At room 709 the door opened to reveal a woman in her late twenties or early thirties, attractive, with dark hair and vanilla skin. "Well, look at you," said Doris, eyeing us. "Come on in, but I have to leave in a few minutes." She had a "been around the block" attitude, and her hotel room had the scent of something hard-knocked, a mix of rubbing alcohol and tar. I wondered if she was a heroin addict. "Tell me a little about yourselves," she said.

"Well," said Levon, "we're here in New York doing some recording and playing at the Roundtable, a brand-new supper club, kind of upscale. And we're in a pretty damn good rock 'n' roll band."

"Oh, I like your accent," she said. "You from down south?"

"Yes, ma'am, from southeast Arkansas, born and bred. The Duke here is from north of the border, up in Canada."

"Really, and you play in a band together? The man I'm with right now plays music, Ray Charles. Going to see him shortly. He's recording some new stuff."

That was exciting news. "I can't wait to hear new music from Ray. Do you mean you just go to the studio and listen to what brilliant thing he's gonna do next?"

She smiled, almost sadly. "Something like that. You're so sweet—what's your name—Duke? You want some grass?"

Levon gave her a double sawbuck and she handed him two ten-dollar bags wrapped in little manila payday envelopes, same as they did in Toronto. "Maybe I'll see you around," she said. "Gotta run now." She rode down with us in the elevator, and when Levon and I reached our floor, I said to Doris, "This is us. I'm in 505, and Levon's in 507."

"Levon," she said, letting the sound of his name hang in the air. "Don't think I've ever heard that name before. All right, catch y'all later."

JOHN COLTRANE was playing for the next week at Birdland, and Levon and I couldn't wait to check him out. We showed up on his opening night, and though we'd been to Birdland before, this time there was such a different vibe in the air. The club felt darker and heavier. Even the black greeter at the door, a little person, was more subdued.

When Coltrane and his band took the stand, they kicked into some of the most angry, powerful, strident jazz I'd ever heard. The stage lighting made Elvin Jones, the drummer, look like a demonic octopus, and he wailed with Trane like they were speaking a secret language. Coltrane didn't address the audience. Half the time he played facing his band. You could feel his rage all over the wall. I had never witnessed a more antishowbiz stage performance. It felt like they had an ultracool, long-distance connection, and I swam in it.

The next afternoon, as I was laying low in my room reading Steinbeck's *Cannery Row*, the phone rang. It was Doris. "Duke," she said, "I saw how thrilled you looked when I told you about Ray and me. I'm heading over to the studio now. You want to come check it out?" I closed the book and grabbed my coat. "I'm ready."

Doris hailed a cab outside the hotel. In the daylight I noticed the glassiness in her eyes. I didn't know what she was into, but a drug dealer most likely enjoyed the fruits of the trade. "You can just sit quietly in the control room," she explained, "and I'll introduce you if I feel it's cool, you dig?"

We entered the studio control room, and there behind the glass sat Ray Charles at the piano. He wore a light brown shirt and black pants, and his feet shuffled a bit nervously. He pushed his dark glasses up on his nose and scratched at his face. Doris showed me where to sit on a couch over to the side.

The man behind the soundboard said on the talk-back, "Ray, let me know when you want to run this one down. Everybody's in place." No response. The producer repeated, "Ray, whenever you're ready."

I could see Ray rolling his head around, almost squirming now on the piano bench. "Let me talk to him," said Doris to the producer. "He's just not feeling well."

An African American fellow pacing in the control room piped up. "Yeah, go see if Ray's feeling right. I'm here if you need me." I guessed he was Ray's manager.

The producer looked frustrated. "We've got a studio full of musicians waiting," he said impatiently. "Boys, take a ten-minute break."

I watched Doris walk into the big studio and over to Ray. The mics were live and we could hear her softly spoken words through the speakers in the control room. "Hey, baby, it's me, I'm here. You need to talk to me." Ray rose up from the piano and took Doris's arm. She led him out to the hallway.

"Yeah, he just needs to use the john, we're cool," Ray's manager murmured.

About fifteen minutes later, Doris emerged from the restroom alone and came back into the control room. "Joe, Ray's looking for you," she said to the manager. He sprang up and went to help Ray back into the studio. The orchestra musicians and singers all took their places while Joe led Ray back to his position at the piano.

"Okay, let's go," the producer announced. Ray sat on the piano bench and lowered his head, almost as if he were in prayer. I thought, *Look at this, Brother Ray, the genius, doing his thing.*

"Ray, we're rolling," said the producer. But again there was no response. "Ray! Okay, we got to do it. This is costing money and time." Ray sat there barely moving.

The producer kicked back his chair with exasperation and charged into the studio, raising his voice at Ray as he approached. Doris tensed up. "He's okay, man," she murmured, "just give him a minute."

But the producer was already on him, scolding about wasting everyone's time. Then, suddenly coming to life, Ray stood up and smacked him across the side of his head. "I'm ready, motherfucker. Get off my ass!" he declared. "Who the fuck are you, talking at me!" Ray sat down and called out, "All right, one, two . . ." The engineer hit "record," and they slid right into the tune. Ray's vocal sounded like he'd just woken up, and that wasn't even the best thing about it. His phrasing of the words, his take on the melody—it was like the best caramel sundae you ever had.

When Levon and I met up back at the hotel, I enthusiastically told him the story of my afternoon. "Holy shit," he said, "I guess that Doris really knows her way around."

The next thing we knew, Doris had checked out of the hotel and was gone. Doc Pomus guessed she might be going on the road with Ray. "That will be interesting," he said, "because Ray's wife is traveling with him these days, and I heard he's having a thing with one of the Raelettes too."

I put my arm around Doc's shoulder and said with all the worldly wisdom of an eighteen-year-old, "Ah, show business."

I'D ONLY JUST settled back in my room for a nap when the phone jarred me awake. I fumbled for the receiver. It was Natie, speaking quietly. "Jaime, write down this address and name I'm going to give you." He gave me the address of an office on 47th Street, and a very biblical-sounding man's name. His instructions were short and clear, and his tone left no room for interpretation: this was serious.

The next afternoon I walked over to the address, entered a nondescript doorway, climbed the stairs to the third floor, and knocked on an office door. A man in his thirties wearing a yarmulke answered the door and waved me into a sparsely furnished room, just a card table and some chairs. In one of them sat an older bearded man in a black suit and hat. He was having a phone conversation in Hebrew or Yiddish, I wasn't sure which.

The older man was the one I was here to see. Even though I had no idea what he was saying on the phone, I couldn't miss his tone of authority and impatience. The younger man shook his head with disappointment at the phone conversation, looking at me as if to say, *Can you believe this? Oy.* I managed a weak smile. The old man hung up the phone and introduced himself to me in a heavy Jewish accent; the young man, he said, was his son. He told me how much he liked my uncle Natie. "Very, very much I appreciate your uncle. A terrific man to do business with, right?" he asked, looking approvingly to his son. Then the older man reached into his inside pocket and pulled out a square envelope. "This," he said, looking at the envelope and then at me, "is what I'm no longer giving you to take to our business associates. Natie just informed me he doesn't trust these people to have this package, which I understand. So I'm not going to ask you to take this, because I have just found out it's not in our best interest."

"Of course," I said. He grunted a small laugh. "Well, young man, I hope your uncle comes here himself sometime." He passed me the envelope. "Feel that? Heavy, huh? Maybe at a later date. We'll see."

I stood and shook hands, and as I closed the door behind me, I wondered if it had been divine intervention. Who knows what or who was on the other side of that envelope at the Taft Hotel: mobsters? smugglers? creditors? I was relieved to be out of it—this wasn't my bag—but I couldn't help but be curious.

When I got back to Toronto, Natie and I met to talk about the Taft Hotel. "In terms of the handoff to the people at the Taft, I've found another way to keep them satisfied without having to give them the stones," he said, "although, to tell you the truth, they're getting a little anxious again anyway."

I mentioned to Natie that it was way past the date when he'd said I would be making money from what my mother and I had invested. Everybody was getting anxious, including me, and I wanted to feel like I was an exception and not getting screwed. He ducked the question for a while but finally said, "Okay, I'll make a call and get it straightened out."

We went to a place where they had a bank of public phones, and Natie pulled a dime out of his pocket and put it in the pay phone. He spoke into the receiver, saying that he needed to get some interest money back from my investment. He listened carefully, then said, "All right, I want to get this taken care of immediately. Yes, I'll call you back on Wednesday. Okay, bye." He hung up and looked at me. "It's being taken care of. I'll call on Wednesday and get it straightened out."

We got in Natie's car and drove off. Several moments later, with real hurt in my voice, I said, "I heard the dime come down into the coin return. There was no one on the other end. How can you try to fool me like this?"

Natie pulled the car over to the side of the street. My eyes had welled up a bit. I had come into this family just a few years earlier, and in a whirlwind they'd taken me in and made me part of their lives. Natie especially had seemed keen on bringing me into the fold—all those calls on the road, the meet-ups, taking me around like the heir apparent. He'd made a tremendous impression on me in a short time. This was a punch in the gut.

He apologized profusely and said he should have known better than to try to fool Tutor's kid. "I have to play the part of a ruthless con artist. You see what I mean? I can't show vulnerability. If I show any weakness toward anyone in my family, I'll be putting us all in danger." Natie put the car in gear and we drove on. I didn't say anything. I understood the impression he believed he needed to give his creditors, but I also realized he was so deep in his own con game that he didn't know how to be real with me. This street lesson had an effect on me; I knew at that moment that Natie's world wasn't what I was looking for. I'd take music.

EIGHT

There was a different tone in the air. The war in Vietnam was looming larger in our lives as American involvement deepened. As we had planned, our friend Connie B. married Levon to keep him from being drafted.

At the same time, I met a girl named Carolina, a classic beauty, maybe five or six years older than me, who had previously been the girlfriend of a major operator in Toronto. She was well known and respected in the rounder world and often had pot. She had an edge to her, and I learned quickly that she had no tolerance for bullshit. With her cat eyes and pouting lips, Carolina had a look that shot straight through you. I was just eighteen, and flattered that she found me interesting enough to spend time with. I felt a little more mature in her presence. Everyone seemed to have an opinion on my relationship with her. Connie wasn't thrilled about it, and Ron thought I might be getting in too deep. But Levon, my partner in crime and closest friend, said it was good experience for me to date a woman on her level—a gangster moll chick who was a knockout, and powerful in her way.

Our gigs at the Concord Tavern ended at 1:00 a.m., but Ron would keep us rehearsing deep into the night, always driving us to get better. Sometimes he would join us, rehearsing songs he wanted to try, but more often than not he left us to toil alone. In many ways this was a good thing, as his choices weren't always our cup of tea. Left to our own devices, we took to venturing into new territories. Mainly

Levon and I selected rare gems, though sometimes Garth and Jerry would suggest some instrumental bluesy jazz numbers. Rick and Richard kept an ear out for cool Motown delights. The next evening at the show, we would audition our new stuff in front of the audience, songs like "Turn on Your Love Light" and "Stormy Monday" by Bobby "Blue" Bland and "Please Please Please" by James Brown. Often we'd be auditioning for Ron too, who had never heard us play this material. Some of it was a little beyond his comfort zone, but for the most part the Hawk embraced the songs and challenges we were embarking on. He stood proud of how his band was advancing.

At our Saturday matinee shows at the Concord, local talent would regularly sit in with us, like Jon and Lee, two white teenagers who sang like Sam and Dave on steroids, and David Clayton-Thomas, whose powerful R&B voice raised the roof—he would go on to become the lead singer of Blood, Sweat & Tears. One Saturday we were joined by John Hammond, a good-looking folk-blues artist from Greenwich Village with a likable stammer. Hammond was an authentic student of early bluesmen like Robert Johnson and Mississippi John Hurt, as well as other brilliant acoustic-blues artists who followed in the tradition of Huddie "Lead Belly" Ledbetter. John's father was John Hammond Sr., the Columbia Records A&R master who had signed Billie Holiday, Pete Seeger, Aretha Franklin, and Bob Dylan. We didn't know many white cats on a dedicated blues journey like John Hammond Jr., and we certainly appreciated his respect for the music. He had a unique, before-its-time, raw musical persona. Normally he played acoustic guitar, sang, and blew harmonica, but on this afternoon he played with the Hawks and something magical happened. Afterward John was ecstatic, and said he wanted this electric experience to be his next record. He invited us to record with him in New York. This was the beginning of something: we all felt it.

By this time folk music had developed an enormous swell of popularity in Toronto: Gordon Lightfoot was causing a stir around town, and Ian and Sylvia Tyson were on their way to wide recognition. And just as Yonge Street had hosted the rock 'n' roll explosion, a street in town called Yorkville became a focal point for the folk scene, drawing talent from all across the land. For the Hawks, folk came from the other side of the tracks. It was a kinder, gentler music, sung in coffeehouses where university students sipped cappuccinos. There was nobody drinking cappuccinos where we played, and we had only ever played electric, loud and hard. Ronnie had a special admiration for folk music, but the rest of us Hawks were definitely cut from a different cloth. "If I had a hammer, I'd hammer in the morning" had a certain toughness to it, but it still was no "Smoke Stack Lightning." We wanted a sound that cut through you, music with a sense of danger and sex that reflected our world.

You could see it in the characters we hung around with. During our tenure at the Concord, our crew included a fellow named Teddy "the Hungarian," a strong, grizzly chap who would accompany us to the hotel after the gig and park himself in a corner, reading comic books and giggling to himself. If we asked nicely, sometimes Teddy would rip phonebooks in half for our entertainment.

"What exactly do you do for a living, Teddy?" I asked him one day.

"I'm a strong arm for certain businessmen," he explained modestly.

"What do you do when you go up against a mob guy?" I asked. "Or another money collector who thinks he's more of a badass than you?"

Teddy looked around the suite and grinned at me through his stubby little teeth. "A while back I was hired by a major bookie organization in Windsor. There was a territory dispute, and I ran up against a very dangerous guy who was working for some heavies out of Detroit. They sent him to threaten me and chase my people away. He told me he was going to break my legs with a baseball bat unless I took a walk."

I lit a smoke and sat back in my chair as Teddy looked right through me with his beady eyes. "I grabbed this big monster so fast and so hard around the throat, his head nearly exploded. Robbie, you've seen my teeth, right? They're very thick and sharp. I told him if I ever saw him again I would bite his lips off. Ever seen somebody with no lips? It's not a pretty sight."

I couldn't even look Teddy in the face at this point. Downtown Dougie, a professional "booster" thief, was in the room and overheard us. He just shook his head, let out a little laugh. "That's a real fucking pipper."

Sometimes Levon invited a small, mentally challenged dancing dynamo who talked in riddles over to the hotel after the show. Freddy McNulty delighted Levon. He brought him to our Sunday-night gigs and let him get up and sing and dance with us; he gave him money, fed him, protected him from bullies, bought him clothes, and made everybody around appreciate Freddy's unusual ways.

Freddy knew that one of Levon's secret ambitions was to get him laid. One evening a band came to town that had a dwarf in their group, and Levon invited him to join our party. A couple of girls were hanging out, and Levon began working on them, convincing one to take care of Freddy and the other to take care of our small new buddy. "You might never have the opportunity to bring this much joy to someone's life ever again," Levon told them. They finally agreed and led their boys toward a pair of private bedrooms. Some minutes later the dwarf and Freddy reemerged, flushed. The girls appeared next, like sexual Mother Teresas who had done a pious deed. "Well, how was that?" Levon called out. "How did you boys do?" Freddy and the dwarf looked at each other, mumbling awkwardly. Finally one of the girls popped her bubblegum and said, "That was pretty fucking weird." Levon fell apart laughing.

Experimenting with different drugs in those days seemed like it came with the job. One friend of ours, George—or "Dr. M.," as we called him—had every kind of pill one could imagine. But drugs could be like a roll of the dice, and every so often we rolled snake eyes. One night Ronnie invited a pretty young lady who looked to be about twenty-one back to the hotel, where we were hanging around with our dates and friends. Before long one of the road managers brought out a selection of pills, and we passed them around like they were jelly beans, everyone choosing their favorite color. The girl with Ron picked out a Tuinal. He laughed and warned her that she could get very stoned on those babies, but she took it anyway and ended up completely wasted. We were all young, thought we knew everything, courted danger without thinking about the consequences.

A few nights later this young lady's brother showed up outside the Concord at closing time with a crew of street thugs, yelling and threatening that they were going to kill the guys who had abused the sister. They had guns and knives. This felt serious. We ducked back into the club, where the owner, Jack Fisher, a savvy guy who rarely lost his cool, reached in a drawer behind the bar and pulled out a .38 pistol. He told someone to call the cops. Then he walked outside. "The police are on their way," he called out to the mob. "So if it's a gun battle you want, then that's what you'll get."

The angry gang turned on their heels, scowling and swearing they'd be back. Revenge became the name of the game. In the days that followed they called the hotel over and over again with threats: *We're watching you. We're going to meet again.* They showed up in parking lots or stood across from the hotel and put everybody on edge wondering when the next showdown would be. They were serious and we were on guard. Luckily, life on the road meant never staying in one place for too long. Much to our relief, Ronnie got a call to do some recording in Nashville for a Hank Williams tribute album, and we were able to leave the death threats behind. We were packed up and on the road before you could blink an eye.

THE DANGER WAS behind us but still in everyone's thoughts. After we'd officially passed into the South, we pulled off the highway to visit a gun shop. The plain-fronted stone building seemed nondescript enough, but inside we found a candy store for weapons, endless racks of guns and knives, and cases filled with ammo of every shape and size. We bought small derringer pistols, switchblades, an assortment of blackjacks, brass knuckles, even tear-gas pens—whatever could be easily concealed and quickly accessed. By the time we pulled back onto the highway, we'd spent nearly our last dime, and the Caddies were like two mobile arsenals.

We were headed to Fort Worth, Texas, for a job at a club called the Skyline Lounge, where we had never played before. When we arrived, our jaws dropped open. The club was burned out, blown up. It was hard to imagine it was habitable, never mind the kind of place that would actually attract paying customers.

"Looks like we finally hit the big time, son," Ronnie said to Levon. "Man, I hope you boys saved up your paychecks, because if we can't draw nobody here, we're up shit creek without a paddle."

But inside we learned why the place was called the Skyline Lounge: there was no roof. A fire had burned it up, and the owner either had decided to go with it or couldn't afford to fix it. You could still smell the singed wood. Dubiously we set up our gear and checked out the PA system. Our voices sounded like barkers at an amusement park. Ronnie turned to us on the bandstand and said, "Well, boys, you live and you learn. If we can get through this alive, we can do anything."

We checked into a motel and returned to the club that night, ready to go on at 9:00 p.m. sharp. All told, the audience numbered less than ten. The place was so empty you could make out individual conversations in the crowd.

About halfway through our first song, a girl started dancing her way toward the stage from the back of the joint. As she came closer, I gradually realized that the club employed a one-armed go-go dancer to entice people to get up and dance. She spun over to one table, sprightly swinging her lone arm in the direction of the people seated there. We were spellbound, watching the patrons trying to avoid her gaze, but the wind from her swinging arm eventually brought on nods of approval from the people brave enough to witness her gyrations. She cruised to the front of the stage doing the Twist and gave us a few twirls and spins, like we were all part of the same attraction. Then bam! She hit the floor and did the splits. I nearly peed myself. Then she broke into the Stroll, another popular dance of the time, and strolled her way over to the other table of people, who toasted her with whoops and hollers. At last, a few songs later, a lone couple got up and joined her on the dance floor. Things were picking up. The owner of the place looked on approvingly. Still, I wondered, *How is the guy going to pay us?* A song or two later a couple from the other side of the dance floor joined in. Gyrating back and forth to our music, these four people all looked so lost in this huge venue, meandering about a dance floor that could have easily accommodated eighty couples. We played, and they danced and drank, while the stars shone down on us.

Suddenly, a tussle broke out in the middle of the dance floor. It seemed to me that there weren't nearly enough people here to cause a ruckus, but the next thing I knew, one of the guys had pulled out some kind of weapon. With no warning he shot tear gas at the other guy from very close range. The man clutched his face and crumpled immediately. Everyone shrieked and ran from the dance floor. As the cloud of gas drifted on the wind in our direction, we were left teary-eyed on the stage, playing for no one.

When we wrapped up—which wasn't much later, as no one could breathe for the gas—the club owner approached us with more great news. "Boys, this building ain't exactly secure enough for you to leave your musical equipment unattended."

"You've got people stealing drum sets and guitars?" Ronnie asked.

The owner nodded. "We sure are sorry about that."

"Well, what are we supposed to do?"

He folded his arms. "If I were you, I'd stay here and guard 'em."

Our booking ran for a week, so we decided to take overnight shifts in pairs, guarding our instruments with our new handguns. Rick and I agreed to take the first shift. We played cards and tried to push off our tiredness and boredom in any way we could. Rick devised a scheme to jimmy open the cigarette machine, so we had no shortage of smokes. There was a soda-pop machine too, the bottles hung between metal slats. We discovered if you had a bottle opener and a straw, you could drink all you wanted, right out of the machine.

Rick helped make our guard duty less grim. He was upbeat and funny, telling me about his former band with his schoolteacher and his older brother Junior, and the crazy gigs they'd played. He booked the gigs, sang and played lead guitar, taught them the songs, and was the youngest pipsqueak in the group. They had played some jobs around his local area opening for Frankie Yankovic, King of the Polkas. "That was my whole reality," he told me. "Thank the stars above that you guys came along, or I might have ended up leading the second-best polka band in the country."

Around 4:00 a.m., Rick and I were deep into a game of crazy eights, when suddenly we heard a terrifying sound that seemed to be coming right toward us—a loud clawing on the floor and fast, hard breathing. Rick grabbed the gun from the table, and we both inched back from the doorway, pressing our bodies up against the wall. Rick leveled his pistol and pointed it into the blackness.

Around the corner came two German shepherds, growling threateningly, bound on tight leashes. Two policemen stood behind them. "Damn, boys, what the hell are you doing here this late at night?"

We sank back against the wall. I told them we were the house band for the week, and we were here to guard our musical equipment from burglars.

One of the cops grinned. "Man! If I'd let these dogs go, they woulda eat y'all up and spit you out."

"It's more likely you would have had two dead dogs," Rick muttered, still gripping the pistol in his hand. There was a pause, and then both cops cracked up, like that was the funniest thing they'd heard all day.

"We usually stop by here during the night to see if everything's all right. It's kind of a strange place, you know."

"Well, thanks for coming by," I said, relieved.

"Sure thing," said the cop. "Try not to shoot anybody with that gun, y'hear?" They snickered as they left, the dogs scratching and pulling them forward on the wood floor.

The next night it was Richard and Levon's turn to play watchmen. Garth had narcolepsy and could be asleep at any given moment, so he was off the hook. I never knew if he was more exhausted or more rested than any of us. Ron, on the other hand, pulled rank, claiming that he had to figure out how to get us our money, so it was important for him to be rested and sharp. So Richard and Levon took their positions, and we bade them good night.

In the morning Ron met Rick and me with a big grin. "Turns out Richard and Levon had a similar experience to you fellas, only when the police came in, Richard panicked and sprayed the dogs with mace!"

Levon and Richard trudged into the room, looking dead tired.

"You guys maced the dogs?" I asked.

"The cops should have announced themselves first," grumbled Levon.

The Skyline was tethered to reality by the flimsiest of strings. Throughout the week the owner, whose name was Jack, would pop in on us in the middle of the night. Maybe he realized we were ready to maim any man, monster, or beast, because he always called out, "It's me!"

"Does that guy ever sleep?" Rick groaned, shifting his pistol to his other hand.

You could tell by Jack's grinding jaw that he was into uppers. He had another club over in Dallas that seemed to be doing well, and he was trying to get the Skyline off the ground too with some help from groups like us.

The crowds were picking up night by night, but Jack didn't want to pay us until the weekend. We were hungry. Desperation set in. Being from Canada, we had brought big overcoats with us, so we threw them on and headed to the nearest Piggly Wiggly grocery mart. One of us picked up a loaf of bread and some mustard, while the other filled his overcoat with bologna, cheese, cold cuts, and a few cupcakes for good measure. The guy with the bread and mustard headed to the checkout counter to pay and I called out, "Oh, good, you got some bread and mustard. Go ahead and pay and we'll meet you in the car, thanks." We stuffed our bellies like long-lost refugees and headed back to the Skyline for another trip to the Twilight Zone.

By the time we finished up our gig, the tear-gas fumes had cleared up, and we no longer played with watery eyes. We got paid—not as much as we'd hoped—and hit the highway, thinking that the strangeness was over.

Only it wasn't. A few months later, on Friday, November 22, 1963, President Kennedy was shot in Dallas, Texas, and two days later his assassin, Lee Harvey Oswald, was in turn shot by a mysterious nightclub operator with ties to the mob. As the assailant's face was splashed repeatedly across television and newspapers for days on end, a bizarre

realization settled in for all of us Hawks: Jack, the owner of the Skyline Lounge who always seemed to be tweaked on pep pills, was none
other than Jack Rubenstein—otherwise known as Jack Ruby. The man
who had hired us only a few months before to play his weird, burned-
out Skyline Lounge in Fort Worth, Texas, had shot and killed the assassin of President Kennedy.

NINE

When we got back to Arkansas from Texas, Levon pulled me aside. "We got to make a connection down here," he said. "We got to find us some Mary Jane." He and Ron knew a guy named Jim Bob who could get his hands on a variety of pills. Levon and I tracked him down and picked him up in our new white '63 Cadillac, which Ron had helped us buy. As we pulled up to a stoplight where three young kids were playing, Jim Bob rolled down the window and said, "Hey, kids, you want to see something funny?" He stuck his right hand out the window. The kids stared, then let out a horrified scream as they realized he was missing some fingers. Jim Bob laughed as we pulled away. "Kids these days have no sense of humor."

"Hey, do you know anybody who sells grass around here?" I asked him.

"Well, of course I do," he said. "There's a couple of old guys out here a ways that got sacks of it in their barn. They grow it themselves. You want to go see 'em?"

Levon and I looked at each other, wide-eyed. We cruised out into the sticks, following Jim Bob's directions. Soon we pulled up to a funky farmhouse with a weather-beaten barn. A grizzly-looking geezer came out of the house yelling, "Who's that? Who the hell are you boys?"

Jim Bob jumped out of the car. "Hey, Clo, it's me, Jim Bob. I would have called, but I don't think you even got a goddamned phone yet."

Just then, another old fellow came out of the barn, carrying a rifle under his arm. Levon spoke up. "I'm from down Helena way, and this here is the Duke. Jim Bob said we might be able to purchase a little reefer from you gentlemen."

"This here's Bertram," said Jim Bob, gesturing to the guy with the rifle, "and that's Clo." He smiled at them. "I told Levon and the Duke, you boys grow some pot that will set them on their *ass!*"

Bertram looked at me, looked at Levon, then looked at the Caddy. Finally he said, "Well, you sure as hell ain't the *po-lice*, with a ride like that."

"Go on, sit in it," offered Levon. "It still has that new-car smell."

"No, if I sit in it, I'm gonna want to keep it," said Bertram. "And then I'd have to kill you."

Bertram invited us into the house while Clo went to get the pot. "Clo and I don't smoke that stuff no more. We prefer something a little harder."

A minute later, Clo came into the house carrying a small black doctor's case and a paper bag full of pot. "Here, smell this," he ordered, pushing the paper bag in front of Levon and me. Then he reached into the doctor's case and pulled out a syringe and a spoon. He cooked up some heroin, looked into a small mirror, and shot it into a vein in his neck.

I cringed and reached into my pocket to pull out a C-note. "Here you go."

Bertram reached over and touched Levon's hand. "You boys want to come and stay over sometime, just say the word. We got lots of dope and you can have all you want."

"We should get back to town," Levon said, slowly withdrawing his hand. "We got a show to do."

"We can get close, if you know what I mean," said Bertram.

Jim Bob slapped his hand on the table. "I'd bet the rest of my fingers these cats don't go that route," he laughed.

"We sure appreciate the smoke," I said. Things had taken an awkward turn, and we knew it was time to move.

A NEW SEASON of changes was upon us. Our song repertoire was evolving at a faster pace. Over the last year you could feel the Hawk going in one direction and the Hawks going in another, and it went beyond the music. A while back Ronnie had gotten married to a wonderful girl, Wanda Nagurski, sister of the famous football player Bronko Nagurski. Wanda was like one of the guys, with a remarkable sense of humor and an extraordinarily high tolerance for Ron's shenanigans. Ron became understandably involved in his new family life. Some nights he didn't even show up at our club dates, and people coming out to see Ronnie Hawkins and the Hawks only got half the marquee.

He had also decided he wanted to hire Bruce Bruno, a young Italian American singer we had met through Morris Levy in New York during our run at the Roundtable nightclub. Adding Bruce was part of Ron's idea for building his Ronnie Hawkins Revue stage show. Bruce looked good, danced good, and sang his butt off.

When Bruce came into the fold, it was immediately clear that he came from a different planet from the rest of us. Here we had five true-blue Canadians, plus a favorite son from the Mississippi Delta; now we were adding a New York Italian. And while we were grounded in rock 'n' roll and R&B, Bruce specialized in power ballads like "The Twelfth of Never" and songs that showed off his considerable talent for Jackie Wilson–like vocal acrobatics and dance moves. When he wasn't singing, he played tambourine and tried to blend in as naturally as he could, but onstage with the Hawks he sometimes looked as out of place as a kangaroo in a dinner jacket.

Performing that big vocal material meant his throat had to be in top form, which it frequently wasn't. Almost half of the time, Ron would introduce him and Bruce would point to his throat and shake his head. Soon Ron grew impatient with Bruce's excuses. He would turn his back to the audience and chew Bruce out in front of the rest of us. "I didn't hire you to play fucking tambourine, I hired you to sing, and you better start singing quick or I'm gonna stop paying."

"Sorry, man," Bruce would respond. "I got a sore throat and I can't hit the notes."

"You're gonna have more than a sore throat to worry about," Ron would snap back.

When Bruce smoked weed, he became incredibly funny, doing voices and accents and improvising scenes with characters from his old neighborhood in New Rochelle, New York. He would come into the room doing a funky walk, with one arm hanging low, one leg stiff as a board, and the other arm swinging front to back, mimicking one of his favorite buddies. He'd make a face, then croak, "I'm Stone the Bone. And I want to be left alone." He'd give us some skin, then turn and do the walk right out of the room. We'd all fall down laughing. You could tell he was just nailing it; the voice and swagger felt totally authentic. It made us totally dig Bruce and enjoy having him on board.

I NOTICED SOMETHING changing about Levon during this time, a certain maturity setting in. His southern drawl softened, and he began to dress in a more sophisticated way. He became more inquisitive about worldly things, more citified. He grew a goatee, and an unusual one at that—it curled forward at the bottom and became quite full. Levon's wild beard didn't sit well with the Hawk. Every once in a while he would say, "Son, you look like an old billy goat with that damn thing on your face. Hell, girls don't want to be kissing a dirty old billy goat."

Levon got tired of seeing a bunch of different girls all the time and started dating a girl named Sandy from a more upper-class family in the west end of Toronto. Sandy had one brown eye and one gray eye, dark hair, and an electric smile. She and her girlfriend Rosalind first came to the Concord Tavern with their boyfriends. Then the girls started coming on their own. Soon they had both dumped their boyfriends, whom Levon referred to as "Greasy and Bumps." Levon starting going with Sandy, and I started seeing Roz, who also came from an upscale family but looked the opposite of Sandy: tall, with white-blond hair and delicate, pale skin, very pretty.

Sandy and Roz traveled with us to many of our gigs throughout Ontario. Levon and Sandy were crazy about each other, while Roz and I were along for the ride; we had a lovely time but we weren't in the same league.

On one of our nights off, Levon and I, along with Connie and Mama Kosh, drove a couple of hours to the Buffalo Auditorium to catch Otis Redding; Jerry Butler, with Curtis Mayfield and the Impressions; and Junior Walker and the All Stars.

Otis was astounding; that voice slayed me. He could be such an exciting performer, but it was the ballads that completely took me away, songs like "These Arms of Mine." Junior Walker and the All Stars were a very different Motown act—raw, sax-blowing energy in a league all its own. A four-piece unit, they sounded like eight. When the guitar player fell to his knees on "Shotgun," Junior Walker tore the roof off the joint. And during Curtis Mayfield and the Impressions' set, the hall became an R&B prayer meeting. The crowd stood and swayed to the music in a trance. Curtis had a mellow, fluid guitar style, and used a certain tuning that I had never seen before.

After the show we were speechless and left in a daze. Wanting a bite, we found a nice-looking club and stopped to digest the incredible music we had experienced. Just as we got some drinks and started to recover our senses, some musicians took the stage, and a woman came out and sat at the piano. The lights came up and, lo and behold, it was Aretha Franklin. We couldn't believe it. She took us to church and beyond, and this became one of the most memorable musical nights of our lives.

THAT FALL, I ran into a couple whom I had met once through Natie. They were involved in his business scheme. The husband seemed overly happy to see me. "Listen," he asked very gently, "would it be possible for my wife and I to talk to you for a few minutes? It's quite important."

I didn't feel comfortable with this, but I tried to be congenial. We went to their house for coffee and what I hoped would just be a little chat, but it turned out to be an interrogation. "Jaime, there has been crazy talk that your uncle has been collecting bags of cash from investors, taking it home, going down to the basement, and burning it in the furnace." The guy wrung his hands. "This is very disturbing, Jaime. We've invested most of our life savings in this venture and need to know what is going on. Can this insanity be true?"

I told them I had never personally seen Natie burning money but I had seen him take some shopping bags down to the basement of his old house in Willowdale.

"Oh God, no!" his wife shouted. "Should he be institutionalized? Please, is he burning our money?"

Increasingly agitated and bewildered, they kept asking each other what to do. Suddenly their radio playing in the background stopped for breaking news: The president of the United States, John Kennedy, had been shot.

"Oh my God, did you hear that?" I asked. "This is horrible. I'm sorry, I have to be going." Shaken, I showed myself out and headed back to the hotel.

Like so many of us, I would always remember exactly where I was at that terrible moment on November 22, 1963. By then I'd been gigging in the United States for a couple of years, and it felt like my roots straddled both sides of the border. Kennedy's assassination was devastating. It seemed to me that everyone loved him. How could this happen? The news hit me hard, like a blow to the chest.

I WENT TO VISIT Natie a few nights later after we had finished playing our evening's set at the Concord. In those wee hours everyone in the house was asleep except for Natie, who thought sleeping was a waste of valuable time. I related the couple's story about his burning money. He laughed. "That's a good one! I wish everybody thought I burnt it. They'd stop giving me so much aggravation."

The next weekend I went up to Natie and Fran's again for a little family visit. As I entered the lobby of their apartment building, I saw someone I recognized from the Concord—Tony, the fellow with the notorious reputation who had cornered me to ask about Natie and Paul Volpe. Tony looked sharp in a sleek gray tailored suit. When he spotted me, he smiled and waved me over.

"Hey, Robbie! Just the person I wanted to see."

I kept walking, but he caught up with me in front of the elevator just as the doors opened. He pushed me inside and stuck an ice pick under my chin. "We're going up to visit your uncle."

I was terrified. Tony was known to be fucking crazy and this wasn't for show. I tried to calm him down. "Tony, come on, what are you doing? I thought we were friends."

"We are," he responded. "But I've got a job to do, and there's a big payday in it for me. It's business. We're going up to the apartment, and you're going to knock on the door. Just say it's you. I'll take it from there."

My mind raced through my options as I stared at his clenched jaw. The ice pick pressed deeper and I lifted my head to ease the pressure. I felt numb with fear and knew I had to think fast.

"Natie's not there," I said finally. "He's upstairs at Saul's penthouse."

"Then we'll go up there," growled Tony. He banged the button for the top floor. Saul was a creditor and friend of Natie's who had hung in with him for the long run, hoping to get paid by wearing Natie down with patience and loyalty.

When we reached Saul's apartment, Tony slipped the ice pick in his pocket and knocked politely on the door. Saul answered the door with his wife a few feet behind him, and before I could say anything Tony pushed past me and grabbed Saul by the face. He started making demands. I signaled to Saul's wife to call Natie to alert him.

"Natie's not here," stammered Saul.

"Then where the fuck is he?"

Saul shook his head. "I don't know, Tony."

Tony slapped him across the face. "We're going to their door, and you're going to knock." He dragged Saul out of the apartment and pushed him toward the elevator. "Robbie, you and Saul are going to knock and say it's you."

"Tony, I can't do it," Saul said. "I can't."

Tony grabbed Saul's face again. "You'll do it, Saul, or I'll rip your fucking head off."

"Leave him alone," I said. "I'll knock on the door and see if he's even there." Knowing Saul's wife had called them, I knocked. "It's Jaime. Hello?" I knocked again. No answer.

Tony charged the door with his shoulder, then tried kicking at it. He landed a couple of powerful blows, but the door was too thick. It didn't budge. After a few more minutes of kicking and cursing, Tony gave up and walked away, shouting threats.

I watched him make his way down the hall. Before he'd gone more than a few paces, he turned around to face me. "I'm not done here," he promised. He pointed the ice pick at me. "I'll be back, and I get results."

A few minutes later, when Saul and I told Natie and Fran what had happened, Natie looked at me with sadness and terror in his eyes. He said, "Jaime, you shouldn't come up here anymore until I take care of this." Then he picked up the phone and called Paul Volpe.

The next day I heard that Natie had been committed to a mental hospital. When I spoke to Fran, she claimed he'd had a breakdown. He wasn't looking after himself, she said, and he needed proper care to make sure he was going to be all right. I knew she was protecting him—I didn't believe for a minute that this was anything but part of a plan for him to "disappear." Then Natie called me from the "funny farm," as he called it.

It had been necessary, he explained, to remove himself from the scene until things settled down and Paul Volpe had gotten things worked out. He also had a court appearance coming up in the dia-monds investigation. "The authorities are suspicious that the stones were stolen, but they can't figure out who they were stolen *from*."

"So where does that leave you?"

"I'm in good shape. There's no way they can prove I had any knowl-edge of the stones being illegal in any way."

It wasn't long before Natie had himself sprung from the mental in-stitution. Assuring me it was now safe, he invited me over to the apartment for one of our usual meals and a visit with the family. Everybody looked refreshed, calm, and collected, and as usual, it was lovely to see my cousins David and Vicki. Fran took me to the kitchen, where an older man wearing an apron over an expensive-looking shirt and tie was standing at the stove, humming an Italian ditty as he stirred a pot of sauce.

"I'd like you to meet my nephew, Jaime," Fran said to the man. He smiled, bowed his head to me politely, and continued stirring.

"Jaime," Natie called to me. "Come here, sit down. I haven't seen you for a while." I joined him in the living room. After about fifteen minutes, the older man came in, still wearing his apron. He spoke quietly with no preamble.

"This is the way it works," he said. In his right hand he held the ladle, pointing it like a baton as he explained. "If anyone rings that buzzer or knocks on that door, *I* will be in charge of dealing with that. I'll step outside and sort out whatever the problem is. *You do not open the door* unless I say so, to let me back in. We all understand?"

Everybody nodded, and he returned to the kitchen and went back to cooking. I turned to Natie.

"What was that all about?"

"Paul Volpe and his brothers, they're looking after things. This gentleman has come up from New York to make sure everything works out without any crazy nonsense," Natie said. I nodded, but I wondered what this old gentleman was going to do about a vicious guy like Tony.

A couple of hours later we were watching the new president, Lyndon Johnson, on television when we heard a commotion and a hard knocking at the apartment door. I startled to my feet, but the man from New York held up his hand, motioning us to be still. Nobody moved.

Carefully, he took off his apron and donned his suit jacket. He tightened his tie, opened the door, and stepped out into the hallway.

"Fran, you take the kids, go into the back bedrooms and close the door until this gets settled," Natie said. As I sat with him he seemed remarkably composed, puffing on his Sweet Caporal cigarette. "He'll get things worked out," Natie assured me.

A few minutes later there was a knock. Natie got up and peered through the peephole. "It's me," the man said calmly. "You can open the door."

Natie opened it and the man strolled in. Natie lifted his chin questioningly. The man looked at me, wondering if he could speak freely. My uncle nodded.

He explained that he'd informed the four people at the door that they were in a different league now. This was no longer local hoodlum stuff. "You mustn't come around here bothering these people ever again," he'd told them. "Or I will come and take care of you personally. If you ever bother this man again, I will find you and kill you, and I will kill everybody in your family. *This is what I do.* Now I want you to leave." He looked at Natie and me, shrugged, and said, "They understood."

And with that, he took off his suit jacket, put the apron back on, and returned to the kitchen, singing the same Italian song.

"He's responsible for Mafia kingpin Albert Anastasia's assassination in the barbershop in New York," Natie told me under his breath. "He is a very, very dangerous man. I don't like all this threatening of violence and gangland tactics, but sometimes you have to settle things down."

An hour later the family gathered around the table for a quiet dinner. The man served us pasta with the sauce he had cooked, and it was delicious. I asked where he got the recipe, and to my surprise his eyes grew watery. It took a moment before he was able to speak. "From my grandmother in Sicily," he said finally, "before she passed on."

IN EARLY 1964, Uncle Natie was put on trial for possessing stolen diamonds. The Volpe family and its associates could protect him from his irate creditors, but not from the Canadian authorities—Natie's connection with Volpe and the Mafia left him with a reputation for being a Canadian Meyer Lansky, the major Jewish crime figure in the U.S. known as "the Mob's Accountant."

Natie didn't want his trial to become a big public spectacle, so he hired an inconspicuous, low-key attorney. I attended the hearings to lend support to Natie and the family, but also because I wanted to experience a real trial firsthand.

Natie spoke cautiously at the trial, always calm, never admitting anything. If he was going to be convicted, they would need to have him dead to rights. Aunt Fran displayed little emotion as she watched everything play out. I was fascinated but frequently found myself distracted by Natie's lawyer, who had a habit of scratching the back of his balding head and picking at the scabs. I had my concerns about Natie's defense, and as soon as I could I told him straight out that I didn't feel his lawyer was doing a good job. "He doesn't make me confident," I said. "He keeps picking at the scabs on his head."

Natie just laughed. "He has some kind of nervous tic. He's serving a certain purpose, Jaime. I think it's going to work out for the best." Natie spoke often of his plan to secure enough money to start some new insurance or finance company, a business that his son David and I could one day take over, similar, he said, to the Bronfmans' Seagram's business in Montreal—they had started out as bootleggers.

The hearings consumed me during the days. I went as often as I could, and though I found the procedure fascinating, it also made me feel sick. When the verdict finally came down, Natie was sentenced to six years in prison. All his dreams for the Klegermans' future evaporated into thin air. He acted as if this wasn't necessarily a terrible outcome. But I felt awful for Aunt Fran, David, Vicki, and Uncle Morrie, and I was devastated to see someone I loved and appreciated being hauled away in handcuffs. Natie had lovingly made himself my mentor and had become a father figure. It was a terrible feeling of helplessness to have him taken down. It broke me in two, a loss that pushed me deeper into my refuge, music.

Back at Le Coq d'Or down on Yonge Street, things were rocky too. One night Ronnie told Rick he was banning Rick's girlfriend from our shows at the club. He said that if Rick only sat with his girlfriend between sets, he wasn't doing part of his job, which was to mingle with the crowd. Rick objected to being told whether he could see his girl at the club or not. Levon didn't like it either and asked Ron what he would actually do if Rick's girlfriend came to the club.

"Well, I guess I'll have just to fire his ass," the Hawk shot back.

Levon frowned and half laughed. "Ah, man, you can't do that. Hell, you can't tell someone who they can have come to the club and who they can't. That ain't right."

"Just watch me," Ron answered sharply. "I'll do whatever the hell I want as long as I'm paying the wages." You could feel a chill in the air.

I was twenty and my life felt in turmoil. What was right, what was wrong, who was my family, who my friends? Tension and distance were growing between Levon and Ronnie too. The battle over Rick's girlfriend had stuck in Levon's craw, and the bigger issues that had been dividing us, in terms of both Ronnie's absences and our diverging musical directions, were starting to boil over. One of the main sticking points was that Levon felt we should be paid more if Ron wasn't going to show up to perform. A reasonable point, but Levon took it to a place of deep and growing anger. He kept preaching to the guys that Ronnie was cheating us and treating us like shit.

I saw a side of Levon I'd never seen before. He stewed with bitterness toward his old friend and mentor. He showed a profound paranoia about being treated like a country fool. The rest of us felt that Levon was the senior and original member of the Hawks, so we supported him, but I felt sorry to see two friends who had been so tight turning to such hostility.

Ron took a hard line: he was the boss and that was that. Finally, one night things came to a head: Rick's girlfriend had been making sure she stayed away from the club on nights when Ron showed up, but one time she came with a couple of friends just before the Hawk arrived. Ron spied her in the middle of a song and his face turned dark red. He nodded harshly at Rick. Levon shook his head at me as if in warning: *Okay, boys, here we go.* I knew it was about to get bad and ripped off a raging guitar solo, trying to let off some steam.

When we wrapped for the night, Ronnie announced in a kindly but stern voice, "Well, it looks like I'm going to have to replace young Ricky here. We had a deal, and he broke it, so I'm gonna keep my side of the deal." And with that, he turned and walked out of the club.

The Hawk didn't show up the next couple of nights. We held down the fort at the club, contemplating our next move. We were all of the same mind—that he was being a complete jerk in threatening to fire Rick. Levon said he was going to call Ron and demand more money for the nights he didn't show up, and not just going forward but also retroactively. I knew Ron would never agree to these conditions and thought we should put our demands in a more clear-cut framework: we wanted a significant raise, or we were going to leave; we also wanted a bonus when we played without him; and if he fired Rick, he'd have to fire us all.

"But the son of a bitch is fucking us," Levon yelled. "And I want to rub it in his face."

"He's not screwing us, he's just offering us a deal we don't accept," I said. "And we're making changes. That's it. No animosity, no revenge, just plain business. Let's not get caught up in personal crap."

The others agreed. They didn't hate Ron; they just wanted to be treated fairly. But when Levon called Ron, he had venom in his voice.

It was by now sadly obvious how this would turn out. I had already started imagining the musical challenges that lay ahead. We had to find our individual sound and identity, and head in a more ambitious creative direction.

As expected, Levon fired up, Ron fired back, and the Hawks left Ronnie Hawkins. I knew it was time to go, but I couldn't help but recognize that Ronnie had discovered me at the ripe old age of fifteen and hired me at sixteen. Ronnie could be rough, but he had never personally treated me badly, even if I didn't agree with all of his decisions.

It was tough, it was rough, but how you gonna stop this train?

TEN

Our first order of business was to see if Colonel Kudlets was willing to book us on our own. As it turned out, Ronnie had just notified the Colonel that he wouldn't be using him as a booking agent in the future—which left an empty slot on his roster for us. Now we had to start thinking about getting our own record deal. We expanded our repertoire until it slowly represented solely our taste and not the best of Rompin' Ronnie.

The Colonel told us he could book us for six weeks of shows in Quebec and Ontario—the first way up north in Timmins, Ontario, not far from what's called the "tree line," where it gets so cold that even trees can't grow. Levon sold the '63 Caddy and leased two navy blue Monarch station wagons for the five of us and Business Bill Avis, who stayed on as our road manager. Our haul was expanding: not only did we have guitars, amps, and drums, but we carried Garth's big Lowrey organ and Leslie speaker, which he'd gotten soon after he joined the Hawks. The weight of all the gear and trailers beat the hell out of those Monarchs. They reminded me of a couple packhorses from a western movie; we could have called them Poor Ole Blue and his brother Whiplash.

We rolled through Timmins, Sudbury, Rouyn-Noranda, Montreal, and as far as Quebec City. The venues we played boasted a very different clientele than we were used to. Some were in blue-collar mining towns or lumberjack areas full of true roughnecks, hardworking people who drank just as hard. When a fight broke out in the bars, beer bottles being smashed and used as weapons was par for the course. Guys hit one another with chairs, sometimes tables. We soon developed one simple rule: if a fight breaks out, keep playing; don't stop the music no matter what happens. If we were between songs, we'd kick right into the next one. Maybe a slower tempo might help ease the tension. Richard singing "Stormy Monday" was always a good choice, as it was rhythmically difficult to brawl to.

After that trial by fire, the Colonel had us booked back in Toronto at Le Coq d'Or for the first time without Ronnie. Our set list of songs and our whole stage presentation were shaping up, and our confidence grew a little bit each night. Levon and I started imagining that all of our hard work and "dues paying" was coming to fruition.

One night between sets Levon and I slipped down the street to a new Jack Fisher–owned club called the Friar's Tavern. The famous Cannonball Adderley Sextet was playing and we couldn't wait to check it out. Cannonball and his brother Nat were on horns, and they had a new guy on tenor sax and flute. We watched the new guy in awe—he was one of the coolest-looking cats you'd ever seen, tall with longish hair, in a tailored suit, tinted French wire-rim glasses, and a goatee. Cannonball stepped to the mic and said, "We'd like to feature a new member of our group, Mr. Charles Lloyd."

Mr. Lloyd not only looked sharp—he was a great musician. I immediately loved his sound, his phrasing: southern, modern, fresh. We rushed back the next night and he played even better. After that set I spoke to him and told him I was in a band playing up the street. He replied that he was from Memphis and had played with B. B. King and some R&B bands. I mentioned that a friend had some hash and we were gonna have a smoke, if he wanted to join. "Of course," he said. Later he confessed that playing with Cannonball was a temporary thing—he was interested in starting his own band in the near future. I was surprised to hear it since I thought the band looked so solid onstage. But I could tell he was seriously on his own wavelength.

The next booking the Colonel had for us was a full left turn into the Twilight Zone. The dance craze called the Twist had become hugely popular, and we were on our way to the very center of its existence: the Peppermint Lounge on 45th Street in New York City. Before we left Toronto, Levon and I told Garth, Rick, and Richard that we weren't going to be able to afford to keep Jerry "Ish Kabibble" Penfound in the group. We all really liked Jerry, but we were barely making ends meet. It was heartbreaking to see him go. As we headed for New York City, chasing a record deal, I looked back at the skyline of Toronto with a blue feeling at leaving behind my uncle Natie and Rompin' Ronnie Hawkins.

On this trip to New York I felt a stronger connection to the big city, which seemed more familiar and less cold. People in Canada and in the South were known for their friendliness and hospitality, but a first impression of New York City was that someone would just as soon walk on you as look at you. And the more time I spent here, the more I dug that in-your-face attitude.

The Peppermint Lounge was an auspicious New York debut for Levon and the Hawks, but we soon found that the club owners only wanted us to play like the kings of the Twist, Joey Dee and the Starliters and Chubby Checker. We needed the gig, so we agreed, though this wasn't our thing at all and we soon fell back on playing our kind of music. People danced to it the best they could, but night by night you could feel the tension growing with the management. The last straw came when our friend John Hammond showed up and sat in with us. We played Billy Boy Arnold's "I Wish You Would" and Howlin' Wolf's "Spoonful," which were both shuffles you could dance to—but they weren't Twists. One of the owners flipped out and pulled Levon aside. "What is this shit you're playing?"

"We're playing good music, sir. That's what we do," Levon answered.

"If you don't do more Twist music, we're going to fire you."

"I can't wait to get out of this piss-ass joint," Levon fumed.

Before heading back to Canada, we learned that our number would be shrinking again: Bruce Bruno, who had long pined to get back to his old neighborhood and his girlfriend, BJ, decided to leave the fold and stay in New York. We understood, but I was really going to miss "Stone the Bone."

We hadn't been offered a record deal in New York yet, but now we heard that Duff Roman, a local Toronto DJ, had put together some backing for us to go into the studio and cut some tracks for his label, Roman Records. That was welcome news from a welcome source: many moons ago Duff had put together the Dixie Arena show where my band had opened for Ronnie and the Hawks.

I always enjoyed getting back in the studio to learn a little more about the recording process. We took a loose approach, deciding to try some different ideas and see what stuck. We dug into the songs we'd rehearsed back at the Concord before we left Ronnie. To warm up we cut a cover of James Brown's "Please, Please, Please." And even though I hadn't had much time to focus on songwriting, I tried to throw some things together for the occasion. We recorded a track I wrote with Garth called "Bacon Fat," inspired by the wilted salad my mother made for Levon, her other favorite son. With a few minutes left in our session, we laid down "Biscuits and Taters" and then a one-take version of "Robbie's Blues," a jam we played at gigs to show off a little. No matter what we cut, it was always good to hear ourselves in playback to understand what sounded good on tape, as opposed to just live in the room.

As he'd promised, John Hammond asked Levon, Garth, and me to play on his new record when we were next in New York. He said some real good blues musicians were coming in from Chicago to join us: Charlie Musselwhite on harmonica and another guitar player named Mike Bloomfield, along with bassist Jimmy Lewis, who had played with the Drifters and Sam Cooke. In the studio we jumped right in with "Baby, Please Don't Go," and John prompted me to wail hard. Mike Bloomfield didn't yet have as much experience under his belt as I did and decided to play some piano, but he was tremendously obliging and enthusiastic. Musselwhite was a pure pleasure on harp. He knew when to burn and when to cool. Every time we went into the control room to hear a playback, John's producer from Vanguard

Records would make some suggestions and John would get red-faced and disagree. I thought, *Maybe this is how it works, the artist and the recording company representative always at odds with one another.*

We recorded a pretty mean version of Otis Rush's "So Many Roads," and John later decided to make that the album title too. The recording went by in a flash. I didn't know if we had done great work, but there was no question we'd had a real good time. Afterward Bloomfield invited Levon and me to come to Chicago sometime, to take in the blues clubs on the South Side. He said he even had a place where we could stay. I left the studio and walked along the New York City streets alone. Funny, I thought, how you can be in such a bustling, crowded major city and still feel isolated at the same time. I strolled through the diamond district on 47th Street, missing my uncle Natie and thinking of all the madness he had put us through. *How can he be doing in prison, swallowing all those dreams?*

John Hammond was so appreciative of the work we had done on his record that he surprised us with an ounce of Panama Red, which to us was the marijuana of kings. I opened the bag to have a whiff, and sure enough, it was the real deal: orangey red in color, rare as pink diamonds. It smoked with a utopian flavor.

We had to decide whether it was okay to bring this very special weed across the border with us. Typically we would never take chances carrying drugs through customs because the Canadian authorities looked at pot through the same lens as heroin or any other hard drugs. But we'd been back and forth many, many times and had never had our clothes searched, so we figured the risks were minimal. Consensus was we couldn't leave the Panama Red behind.

I put the bag in the inside pocket of my beige overcoat and threw it in the back of the station wagon with everyone else's coats. At the border crossing above Buffalo we held our breath as the immigration and customs officers gave us the once-over. They just looked at our papers and waved us on through. We let out yelps of relief as we drove toward Toronto. Bill Avis pulled out some rolling papers from his briefcase, took the bag from my coat, and proceeded to roll a nice fat one in celebration of our smuggling act. The six of us smoked that joint with deep, lingering pleasure.

Bill had left our other wagon in the parking garage at the Toronto airport, and we needed to stop and pick it up. Levon pulled up next to the other car and we all got out to stretch our legs.

"I'll drive the other one," Rick said, and Levon passed him the keys. As Garth, Richard, and Rick got ready to load into the other vehicle, we heard a shuffling sound. Suddenly, four men appeared from behind cement pillars, moving quickly. One of them pulled Levon out of the car and shouted, "Police!" Then a sedan roared up behind us and screeched to a halt, blocking us in. "Don't anybody move! RCMP!"

There were local detectives, airport police, Toronto narcotics squad, and Mounties. All together, seven plainclothes police officers surrounded us. We were so shocked that we were frozen in place. They searched the station wagon we'd left at the airport and came up with a small film canister with some pot in it. Then they searched the car we were driving and found the bag of Panama Red. The undercover Mountie held them both up in front of him as he walked toward us. "This is bad. You're under arrest." Then he turned to Garth. "Hello, Garth. I'm sorry to see you involved in this."

Garth lifted his head. His eyes opened wide in recognition. "Hello, Don." The Mountie was an old schoolmate of Garth's named Don Docker. We had met him before when he'd come to a club in Toronto to see one of our shows. He had a reputation for being a tough little SOB.

The cops piled us in cars and drove to the Mississauga police station near the airport. They booked us and threw us in jail. We were confused, terrified, and speechless, not sure who to call, what to do next. A few hours ago we'd been smoking a celebratory spliff, and now our freedom was in jeopardy. None of us could make sense of what had happened. How did the police know we were going to the airport, and that we had some pot? My mind was racing. This could mean anything—that we were done, that our music career had just come to a dead end. And we might be going to prison.

A little while later the booking officer brought us out of our cells. "You can make a couple calls. You're going to have to see if you can make bail, and you're going to need a lawyer. These are serious charges against you that can carry a ten-year sentence for importing drugs into the country for the purpose of sale, and—"

"Officer, we're not drug dealers, you know that," I interrupted.

"No, I don't know that!" he said, slamming his hand on the desk. "Make your calls. I need you back in that cell."

We called Colonel Kudlets, who gave a Jewish cry of dismay. "Oy, don't tell me. How could this happen?" He suggested trying Jack Fisher, the owner of the Concord and the Friar's. So we did, and a couple of hours later he and the Colonel came to the jail and bailed us out—we were very grateful. Jack said he knew a retired judge in the Mississauga precinct who still practiced law and sometimes took on a case. "I'll try to convince him to represent you," he said.

The next day our bust was all over the newspapers. We were staying at my mother's and had to explain to her that this was all a misunderstanding and that there was nothing to get upset about. She went along, but we could tell she didn't really buy our story. Rick put his arm around her and said, "Have I ever let you down, Mama Kosh? Well, I'm not about to start now," which brought a smile to her face.

Two days later we began our stint at the Friar's under duress. The place was packed with patrons who wanted to see the druggies live and in person. People called out requests for songs like "Smoke Gets in Your Eyes." To make matters worse, Ronnie and his new band were playing up the street at Le Coq d'Or, and we heard he was making jokes about our pot bust from the stage, no doubt enjoying our predicament.

Between sets Jack Fisher told us that the ex-judge in Mississauga had agreed to represent us. Bill Avis drove us out there so we could meet him and tell our side of the story. He looked to be ninety years old and his hands shook as he made notes. He didn't seem to be a stickler for detail, and I couldn't tell if it was age or disinterest. Needless to say, we were worried sick about the choice of attorney, and that night we expressed our deep concerns to Jack Fisher. He nodded but told us the old fellow was our best bet in Mississauga. "He was the main judge there for many years, and the new judges all respect him."

"Sir," Levon said, "we're so thankful for your help and advice. But our ass is on the line. Are you sure about this?"

"No," Jack replied. "But he's going to get the trial postponed for a few months, and it will give us time to look at it closer. In the meantime you guys better be careful. They're going to be watching you."

Our next booking was at the Grange, a new club in Hamilton, Ontario, run by a Chinese family. We drew good crowds, ate lots of Mandarin food, and started feeling like we were getting back on our feet. Between sets I hung out downstairs in a little dressing room and worked on an idea for a song called "Leave Me Alone." While writing a few lines and pacing back and forth, I noticed a square door in one of the walls, about waist high. The door blended into the woodwork and was almost invisible but for a latch with a padlock that hung loose. The door had an *Alice in Wonderland* vibe to it, and I decided to take a peek inside. I removed the padlock, opened the door, and after a second's look slammed it shut immediately. I went and got the other guys.

"You wanna see something?"

They all followed me to the dressing room and gathered around as I opened the little door. Inside in the darkness, about fifty glowing eyes stared back at us. Cats, lots and lots of cats.

"Maybe they have a problem with mice, maybe rats?" Richard offered. "Or . . ."

We all had the same horrible thought, and never ate Chinese food there ever again.

ELEVEN

One of the stipulations of our bail was that we had to stay in Canada, but our southern agent, Dayton Stratton, had already booked some April gigs in Texas, Oklahoma, and Arkansas. Thankfully, in a few weeks our lawyer was able to secure permission for us to go back and forth to the U.S. for work purposes. The pay for these gigs wasn't really enough to sustain our expenses going south again, but Levon was convinced more opportunities would arise once we got there.

We were relieved to be free to go back to the States, and Levon and I arranged to take one of the Monarchs and visit Mike Bloomfield in Chicago on our way down to Texas. So we headed to the mecca of big-city blues. I offered to drive, but naturally Levon jumped behind the wheel. "Son, you drive like an old lady. We gotta cross the border before next winter sets in."

"Hell, I ain't that bad," I said as we blew past the Toronto city limits, picking up speed. "Let's not get arrested all over again."

He pulled a Marlboro out of his pocket with a cocktail roach stuck in the end and handed it to me. "I wouldn't think of it."

We crossed the border at Windsor-Detroit and met up with a couple of friends, who took us to a club where a hot blues band was playing. It was an all-black joint, packed to the rafters. Levon pointed out a couple of cute girls at the front of the stage. He exchanged smiles with them. Our friends said that Bobo's Blues Band was up for us sitting in, if we wanted.

The crowd cheered when Bobo and his men took the stage. Bobo looked like a Bobo, big, dark, and jolly, with a mile-wide smile. He strapped on his guitar, and from the enthusiasm of the crowd you could tell he had a strong following in the Motor City. After the band had rocked three or four tunes, he looked over to see if we wanted to jam with them, but Levon suddenly got cold feet. He didn't think the drummer looked keen on someone taking over his kit.

They had an extra guitar amp on the stage, so all I had to do was plug in. The musicians didn't quite seem to know what to make of this white guy sitting in with them, but they kicked into "Kansas City" with the grooviest shuffle of the night. Bobo took the first solo, cranking out a rhythmic riff that I completely got behind. My turn was next, and I signaled the band to break, then threw in some low-string growls. As they came back in I ripped into high gear, screaming to the stratosphere. It wasn't a competition, but I had a natural instinct to pull out the stops. Bobo looked over at me like *Who is this guy, and what's this shit?*

The crowd didn't like seeing Bobo get shot down, especially by some white out-of-towner. Even the cute girls standing in front were waving me off, as if to say *Don't be messin' with our Bobo!* Catching on, I immediately backed off and played a support rhythm, letting Bobo take all the solos for the rest of the song. When the tune ended, I bowed to him and applauded his effort. He flashed that big Bobo smile. I threw my guitar in the case, and Levon and I slipped out the stage door and into the night. "Man, it got raw in there for a minute," said Levon, laughing as we drove through the dark city.

We "motorvated" into the Midwest the next morning, through Battle Creek and Kalamazoo—places of legend, places where you sent cereal box tops for mail-order goodies. Passing a sign that said CHICAGO, 47 MILES, Levon flicked the dial over to a local "race" radio station that played mostly R&B with a touch of blues. The whole atmosphere changed. Chicago was a big, badass American city, and you could feel it in the air. Approaching downtown, we pulled into a gas station to call Mike Bloomfield.

Right off the bat, you got the idea Bloomfield had this town wired.

He took us to a funky little place to grab a bite, and as we ate told us about the circuit he was playing with Paul Butterfield, who shared his devotion to the blues. We had heard wild stories about Paul and his friend Nick "the Greek" Gravenites, another white Chicago blues singer. The circles they ran in and the places they frequented, well— you'd have to be some tough, crazy sons of bitches to seek out danger like that.

When we hit the street, Mike had a plan. "Let's go by Butterfield's place. He's got some rare blues records, killer stuff—you'll love it, and we'll smoke some weed."

We arrived at Butterfield's apartment, and Paul came out from a back room and greeted Mike in a quiet, casual way. He had a pale, street-hardened face with remnants of freckles, and his hair was pushed back like a bohemian Bela Lugosi. Mike introduced us with little backstory or fanfare. Paul looked as if it would have been difficult for him to care any less who we were, but I liked him anyway. He had a dry sense of humor and seemed like the kind of guy who got straight to the point. When I looked over at Levon, though, I could see he had reservations. He was eyeing the sweat stains on Butterfield's shirt. One thing that turned him off about some of our newfound acquaintances like Bloomfield was the fact that they weren't overly concerned with personal hygiene. The funky beatnik body odor didn't sit well with Levon. He was a true believer that cleanliness was damn close to godliness, and both he and the Hawk were sticklers about being showered and fresh no matter how hard we might sweat while playing. They inspired all the Hawks to embrace the full routine— "shower, shit, shave, and shampoo"—often before and after a gig.

I figured I'd get us talking music. "You got any blues gems we ain't heard yet?" Paul's face lit up at the challenge. Right away he reached for a 45, looked at one side, and flipped it over with a smile. It was a B-side by his true-life blues-harp hero, the great Little Walter. Paul was a dedicated disciple of Walter's and had studied his sound and licks closer than probably any other human being. He dropped the needle and turned up the volume on "Boom, Boom, Out Goes the Lights." The record slayed us.

As we came out of its spell, Bloomfield took the situation in hand. "Hey, Butter, you got any smoke? We'd love to enjoy a little reefer." Paul looked at us warily, trying to decide if he wanted us smoking up his weed. "Come on, man, let's have a smoke," Mike urged. Paul went in the back—we could see him opening a drawer—and returned a moment later with some papers and a couple of plastic bags. He gave us a pack of rolling papers and a bag of grass, and he kept the other bag and rolled a joint from it for himself.

"Thanks, Paul, we really appreciate it," I said. "Is there a difference between the two bags?"

Paul kept on rolling, didn't look up. "This grass here is really good, and that bag there is dog shit."

I laughed incredulously. "So you're going to smoke the good stuff while we get the shit. Is that what you're saying?"

He looked up and said, "That's right, I'm not giving you the good stuff. Smoke that or don't, I don't really give a fuck."

We huffed and puffed on that lemonade trying to get a buzz while Paul, red-eyed and shuffling through his records again, picked out a Little Junior Parker cut and said, "Oh, I got a Big Walter track you probably never heard too."

When we left, I asked Bloomfield, "Is that behavior normal around here? Seems kind of cold and selfish, like a 'screw you.'"

"Yeah, what a piss-poor attitude," Levon grumbled.

"That's just the way he is. Like he said, he don't give a fuck. Don't worry about it. We're going to a club on the South Side called Pepper's. Muddy's playing . . ."

"WELCOME TO BLUES HEAVEN," I said to Levon as we sat ourselves at a table close enough to hear Muddy Waters's fingers moving on the strings.

He smiled. "Don't get no better."

Muddy was belting it out, hard and unforced at the same time. "Forty days and forty nights, since my baby left this town." There was something so true, so honest about his performance. He didn't move around much or give any sense of trying to put on a show. He just stood there and sang with his incredible voice. It knocked the wind out of you. One fist would go in the air, and you would feel a touch of gospel, just for a moment. It was hard for me to watch him and breathe at the same time.

Like Howlin' Wolf back in West Memphis, Muddy's band didn't play loud; they played so they could hear one another, balanced. The power of the sound on the record didn't prepare you for what you heard in person. Bloomfield waved to Muddy as the drummer counted off "I Just Want to Make Love to You," a gem written by my songwriting hero, Willie Dixon. Muddy's voice glided through the music like a crawling king snake. Pure magic. You don't learn to sing like that: you're either born with it or you ain't.

And Muddy was just the first half of a great night of blues that Mike had planned for us. When Muddy's band finished up, Mike steered us over to Curly's to catch the late set from Otis Rush. We got there just in time, and boy, was Otis on fire. He and Buddy Guy and a few others had pioneered what was being called the "West Side sound," a style of blues considered more modern, a little grittier and more forceful, than the sound of legendary South Side bluesmen like Muddy and Little Walter. A certain drive and aggression sliced through the air at Otis's show. He played a couple of guitar solos that made Bloomfield's and my hair stand on end.

We made plans to meet up with Mike for dinner the next day, then catch the Butterfield Blues Band, who were playing a club called Big John's over near the University of Illinois. Levon and I took the day to catch our breath and cruise around Chicago a bit. We wanted to see as much of the city as possible, to feel it in our bones, but time was tight—we had to head for Texas that night after the show to meet up with the rest of the Hawks.

As the afternoon rolled on, we wanted to smoke a joint. So we went back to Butterfield's apartment with a sob story, hoping he'd give us a taste, even of the bad stuff. We knocked and knocked at his door. No answer. After we'd knocked for a while, Paul's landlady appeared to see what was going on. She seemed pleasant enough, so I told her that our friend Paul wasn't home and we had left a wallet at his place, but now we had to head out for Texas. Could she help?

"Don't worry," she said. "I have a key, it's no trouble at all."

When we stepped inside the apartment, I kept the landlady talking while Levon slipped into the bedroom, found the stash, and took the good stuff. He pulled his wallet out from his pocket and came to the front door.

"Found it, all set, thank you."

"Well, you boys have a safe drive to Texas."

"Thank you, ma'am, much appreciated." We drove two blocks, pulled over, rolled a sweet one, and got ripped.

That night we went with Mike to the venue where the Butterfield Blues Band was performing. According to Mike, Big John's served the best burgers in town, and he was right once again. Then the house lights went down, and the stage lights came up. With Paul on harmonica and vocals and Mike on guitar, the whole band was tight and tough-sounding. They played with such youthful vigor and excitement: louder, faster, right in your face. This was yet another evolution of the blues.

Toward the end of the show, Paul pulled me up to sit in, and we blasted through a couple of songs, pushing higher and harder. When they finished for the night, Mike looked kind of pale and said he was sorry but had to get going. We said good-bye and thanked him for a wondrous time. Then he disappeared quickly. We told Butterfield we were about to hit the road, and he followed us into our car. He seemed distracted and bothered about something. Suddenly, he smacked the back of the seat with his hand.

"Goddamnit!" he erupted. "Somebody stole my grass, my good grass! And I think it was Bloomfield. That motherfucker, I'm gonna break his fuckin' neck."

"Whoa. You guys just played, and it seemed like everything was cool."

"I'm just now putting the pieces together. And he's the only one who knows where my stash was. Bastard. I can't believe it."

"Naw," Levon said. "Mike is such a good guy, he wouldn't do that."

"Then why did he run off so quickly tonight?" Paul snarled. "Something don't smell right to me."

"Paul, I'm sorry but we've gotta ask you a special favor," I said, with all the sincerity I could muster. "Levon and I have to drive to Texas tonight. Could you spare us a little grass? We'll repay you next time for sure. I'd really appreciate it."

Paul looked almost hurt by the request. "Hey, man, I just got robbed. I don't have that much left. What are you asking me for?"

"Just a couple of joints for the trip, or one, whatever you can spare," Levon said. Butter rolled his head back. "You guys, shit. Lemme check my bag and see. Where's the papers? I'll roll you guys one for the road. . . . I can't believe I'm doing this."

"We'll pay you back twice as much next time," I said.

Once we'd said good-bye and Levon and I were speeding out of Chicago, I pulled Butter's joint from my pocket.

"Maybe he'll learn a lesson about stinginess and treat people right in the future," said Levon.

"I believe he's already started learning."

Levon laughed. "Now light that sucker."

I felt kind of bad for ripping off Butter. We were musicians, not thieves, but we were picking up bad behavior from the lifestyles of the crooked and the bent. Street hustlers and road dogs surrounded us in the clubs and on the road, and don't let anybody tell you "it don't rub off." The game had become normal to us, but it wasn't who we were. Bad habits, we were collecting them like coins, and we knew how that worked: the more you get, the more you want. I wrestled with these thoughts late at night when my mind was too tired to fight them off.

AS WE DROVE past Memphis, talking about all the great music we loved, I put a question to Levon about our own studio ambitions and the kind of songs we hoped to record. Were we shunning popular music to our detriment because of our particular taste in music? We liked finding obscure records by unknown artists—southern R&B, Chicago blues, rare mountain music. When we were asked by audience members in clubs to cover some radio hits, we almost resented it and tried to fulfill their needs with something they'd never heard of. But it made me wonder if we were building a wall between the audience and ourselves. Were we shooting ourselves in the foot by always looking for the unobvious?

"I don't know what other people like," Levon said quietly. "I know what I like, and maybe that will go a long way, and maybe it won't."

I realized in this moment that my partner, for all his extraordinary musical skills, didn't have a strong relationship with what was trendy or popular, and for that matter none of the other guys did either. Whatever direction we were going with our music, we would have to make it on our own terms.

WE PLAYED a stretch of dates in Texas around the Dallas–Fort Worth area, typically hard-edged kind of places. I called up my old girl Virgie, and she said she'd never been to the South and wanted to come visit. We were still terribly low on cash and had some fairly uninspiring venues coming up.

"This might not be the most ideal time to come down here," I told her. "We have some real unglamorous joints scheduled."

"If you were on the moon, it wouldn't matter," she insisted.

So Virgie came down, and of course I was thrilled to see her. With her modern, metropolitan wardrobe and style, she looked stunning and wildly out of place. Her mere presence made these honky-tonks easier on the eyes. One night after a show we all went across town to a blues club where Little Junior Parker and his band were playing. I loved the slinky smoothness of Junior Parker's blues style and harp playing. He had a full band behind him with a horn section and everything, which signified a level of prestige and class. The staff knew we were in a band playing across town and set us up at a table right down in front of the stage. We ordered drinks and felt right at home, even if we were the only nonblacks in the packed audience.

Junior Parker's band took the stage and kicked into a wicked groove. His guitar player must have weighed 350 pounds, and he put his full weight into his thick, funky sound. Then Little Junior came on and glided right into "Driving Wheel," a raw blues shuffle. I stood and applauded, it felt so damn good. Junior looked over at our table and bowed his head lightly. He was dressed to the nines, with a sharp cream-colored suit, orange and brown tie, two-tone shoes, and big diamond rings on both hands. Every song they played hit the mark. Junior owned the night.

Toward the end of the set, Junior was singing one of my favorites, "That's Alright": *"I know you're loving another man, but that's alright."* He came across the stage right in front of our table, looked straight down at Virgie sitting beside me, and held out his hand, flashing his giant diamond ring. He started singing, *"Take my hand, take my hand."*

"Go ahead," I whispered to Virgie, nudging her.

"No, I don't even know him. I'm not gonna hold his hand," she said in her gangster-chick tone.

"It's nothing," I whispered. "It's just a gesture."

"No, screw him," she said stubbornly. "I don't want to take his hand."

Now Junior had come closer to the edge of the stage, still singing, *"Darling please, take my hand,"* his head bowed down low, his arm stretching out in supplication.

People in the crowd began yelling out racial remarks and fuming at her tactlessness. Levon shot me a look, which I took to mean, *She's going to get us killed.*

"Take Little Junior Parker's fucking hand," I whispered in her ear, "or you're going to get our fucking throats slashed. Do it!"

She pulled back, startled. She had never heard me use that tone before, but we'd never been in a predicament like this before either. After a moment she stood, stepped elegantly to the front of the stage, and took his hand. And without missing a beat, Junior sang, *"Well, that's alright."*

There was a mild smattering of applause.

"I'm going to get the car," Levon muttered to me under his breath, "and I'll meet you right out front. Let's not all walk out together."

We slipped out quietly, jumped in the car, and peeled out of there with our lives intact. Virgie lit a smoke, cracked her window a bit. "I hate it when men act like you owe them something," she said. "But I sure do love that music."

TWELVE

Breaking out on our own as Levon and the Hawks was a struggle, and we were feeling it. Survival was hand-to-mouth and week to week. Over the next month, as things got tighter, Levon and I were constantly trying to figure out ways to get by. Some of our friends in Fayetteville knew we were feeling the crunch, and one day a friend— I'll call him Jay—approached Levon with a proposition.

Every Thursday night, he told us, big-money guys gathered at a high-stakes poker game just outside of town. They got drunk, bet wildly, and didn't care that much about winning or losing so long as they had a grand old time. Jay proposed that Levon and I get some guns, wear sock masks over our heads, and go in and rob the game. We could score about thirty grand. They'd be scared to death and glad to hand over the money with no trouble; he'd wait outside in a getaway car.

Levon and I had spent enough time around gangsters and thieves that the idea didn't seem preposterous. And since we were in a tough bind for money, it was worth considering. The game itself wasn't legal, so they couldn't go running to the cops. Jay kept insisting that there wasn't much danger and that we'd be in and out of there in minutes.

Levon took to the idea wholeheartedly. "Duke, we need the scratch. Let's get it over and done with. Jay's got it all worked out."

Levon was my closest friend, my partner, and the leader of the Hawks. I didn't want to let him down. But I had a serious, very specific concern: who was going to do the talking during the stickup? Some of the card players knew us, Levon had an extremely recognizable voice, and I sounded like I was from Canada. It wouldn't take much chatter to figure out who was behind the masks.

Every day, though, Levon kept pressing me to go through with it, and every day Jay would show up to urge us on. Levon tried out different growly voices on me: "Put the money in the bag and no one will get hurt. No . . . Put all the money in this sack or I'll blow your fucking head off!"

"That's it, that's it," Jay yelled. "They won't do nothing but hand over the dough. We just don't want Robbie saying 'about' or 'out' or 'house' in Canadiana."

I told Levon that this was truly insane. "There's so much that can go wrong, and I really don't like the idea of robbing anyone to begin with. What are we thinking?"

Levon smiled. "Well, you're the one that's got the big gangster background with your uncle and everybody. I need you to stick by me on this one."

The next day, the Wednesday before Thursday's card game, Jay came by our motel with sock masks, plumbers' clothes, two guns, and a bag for the money. We were in the middle of checking everything out when Richard came in. He looked at the masks, the clothes, and the guns and said, "Uh, what's going on here?"

Levon looked up with a sense of authority. "We gotta go get you some money, son. Tired of this scrounging by."

I still felt uneasy about the whole thing. But I wasn't going to chicken out on Lee.

The next day, Jay drove over in the car we'd use for the heist. The plan was that he would head over to the spot first to check it out. Then he'd meet us down the road from the building to give us the okay.

Levon and I changed into the clothes we were going to wear, tried on our sock masks, and loaded the guns. I looked at Levon with his mask on. "How do you feel?"

"I feel a little shaky," he said. "Let's get this over with."

We got in the car and drove to the location of the game. Not much was said. No radio, no music, just the sound of our deep breathing. I opened the side-vent window and bent it toward me, hoping to blow off some of the raw feeling in my gut. Levon reached over and slapped me on the knee.

"It will be over before we know it, son. Don't worry, we got it, baby."

When we got close to the spot where we'd meet Jay, Levon pulled over to the side of the road. He put his mask on, took one of the guns out of the glove box, and stuck it in his pocket. I did the same. I felt the adrenaline kick in. As we rolled forward, we could see the building up ahead where the game was being held. But no Jay.

"Damn, where the hell is he?" Levon murmured through his sock mask as we crawled along slowly. Suddenly, Jay came busting out of the darkness, waving his hands, and ran up to the side of the car.

"I just came from around back. I looked in the windows and nobody was there. They must have called off the goddamn game this week or something. Shit, we'll have to do it next week."

Levon and I sat there staring at Jay, sweating and puffing through our masks. We looked like idiots with our stupid disguises and plumber's clothes. Jay got in the car and we drove back to the motel. Rick, Richard, and Garth were outside, waiting for us anxiously.

I got out of the car and gave them the news. "They called off the game. We couldn't do it."

As I sprinted to my room to change, I felt a tremendous sense of relief. I fell down on the bed, and the gun popped out of my pocket. Staring at the ceiling, I thought to myself, *Yeah, sometimes the Lord works in strange ways.* There would be no going back next week for me now that we'd gotten out of it by the skin of our teeth. Loyalty can be a scary proposition at times. This episode rarely came up in conversation ever again.

LEVON WAS ALWAYS courteous and warm to his folks when we played near his hometown—he was proud to be there, and I found it an interesting contrast to watch him with his friends and family with their traditional southern ways. But you could tell it didn't play quite the same anymore: he was torn about shedding some of his past in favor of the new, modern-day outlook he was in the process of discovering.

After we played our gigs in Arkansas we had a day off, and I asked Levon if he thought Sonny Boy Williamson still lived in the town of Helena. "Probably so," he said, "and there's one way to find out. Let's drive down to the holler and ask around."

"What's 'the holler'?" Rick asked.

"It's the strictly black part of town, where you'll hear the best music and find the best whorehouses."

Richard jumped in. "Well, let's go!" Then he paused. "Wait, is it okay to be hanging there, or will we get our asses kicked?"

"Nah, mostly nice people just trying to make a buck," Levon answered.

Garth piped in, in his very slow monotone voice, "Well now, I don't know. Sometimes it's just better to stay out of the way." We laughed at his subtle wisdom and headed for one of the station wagons.

Levon jumped behind the wheel and we cruised. He was very familiar with the landscape, calling out sights along the way. Pretty soon we were the only white faces on the street. We stood out like clowns in a VW bug.

Levon spotted a fellow who looked like he knew his way around and pulled over to the curb. "Excuse me, sir, would you know where I might find the legendary bluesman, Sonny Boy Williamson?"

Levon had such charm in his voice. Without hesitation the man answered, "I just saw him two blocks down the street here"—pointing his finger—"and you might be able to catch him right over yonder."

We motored straight in that direction, wondering if it could be this easy. We came around a corner and there he was, Sonny Boy himself, like a vision, walking with his back to us. As we approached, I studied his lanky form shuffling down the street. He wore a black bowler hat and a two-tone suit: the jacket was black on the left side and gray on the right, and the trousers were the opposite. He carried a black briefcase. As we pulled up beside him, I could see his gray hair and Fu Manchu goatee.

Once again Levon spoke for us. "Mr. Williamson, my name is

Levon Helm, and I'm from up Marvell ways and have been listening to you on KFFA most of my life. We're a music group who love what you do and just wanted to come down here and pay our respects."

Sonny Boy seemed comfortable getting attention from us young white musicians.

Levon continued, "We just wanted to spend a little time, or play some music, anything you want, sir."

Sonny Boy looked us over one by one. Then, to our surprise, he said, "Okay, come on, I'm going right up here." We parked and followed him inside a building to an upstairs apartment. A woman welcomed him; her young son was sitting over to the side, and a couple of hustlers in their midtwenties were hanging out too. Sonny Boy sat in a chair in the middle of the room, and we all found seats surrounding him. He looked over at the woman and she brought out some little cups, pouring a clear liquid into two or three of them. Sonny Boy took a sip and let out a cough of appreciation. I tried a sip and it nearly set my mouth on fire. I'd just had my first taste of pure "white lightning" corn liquor—or "corn," as they called it.

I didn't know much about Sonny Boy's backstory, but I had heard his real name was Rice Miller and that he'd changed it to Sonny Boy Williamson even though there already was a blues singer with that name—*How can you do that?* I thought. Some people referred to him as Sonny Boy Williamson II. It was all a bit baffling, but I sure wasn't going to ask why.

He took another sip from his cup, reached down into his briefcase, and pulled out a harmonica, checking to see what key it was in. Then he played a couple of amazing warm-up licks and started stomping his foot. He tipped his bowler hat back and kicked into singing about "fattening frogs for snakes." Without blinking an eye, the young boy picked up a pair of homemade drumsticks and started beating out a perfect rhythm on a cardboard box. Sonny Boy played that harmonica like it was a part of his body, and he sang his heart out. We were breathless and cheered him on. He played another one called "In My Younger Days" and spit into a can sitting at his feet. I thought he was

With my mom and dad in Toronto

Portrait of my mother, Dolly,
hand-painted by my dad, Jim

Me with my first ax

My first guitar, with a
picture of a cowboy on it

My first group, the Rhythm Chords

Alexander David Klegerman

With my uncles Morrie and
Natie Klegerman

Early days with Ronnie and Levon in a nightclub

Burning it up for Ronnie

Ronnie and the Hawks with new members Rick, Richard, and Garth

Ronnie Hawkins and
Mama Kosh

Stan Szelest, Rebel Payne,
Ronnie, me, and Levon, with
Freddy McNulty in front

Richard's birthday at
my mother's house

Levon and the
Hawks with Jerry
Penfound and
Bruce Bruno

With John Hammond (*at left*) at Bob Dylan's *Like a Rolling Stone* recording session

With Michael McClure, Bob, and Allen Ginsberg at City Lights Bookstore, San Francisco

My first gig with Bob Dylan, during sound check at Forest Hills Stadium

Dominique Louise Bourgeois in
Montreal, Quebec

With Dominique on our wedding
day, Woodstock, New York

chewing tobacco or dipping snuff, but when I looked down at the can, I realized he was spitting blood. It made me shudder.

We suggested he come with us back to the Rainbow Inn, where we had our equipment set up, so we could show him we were no slouches either. "Let's go on out there, then," he said, and spat a little more blood into the can.

As we drove, Sonny Boy explained that he had picked up the bowler hat and the two-tone suit during his recent trip to England. He also laid a couple of tall tales on us. Little Walter and Little Junior Parker were his illegitimate children, he said proudly, and they weren't the only ones. "I got many, from Chicago to Houston and back. When Walter and Junior were young, I would put one on my left knee and one on my right knee, and teach them how to play mouth harp. They wouldn't have even known how to play the blues if it wasn't for me, but that's what you do with your children, you teach 'em, right?"

"Isn't that something," I said. "Walter and Junior on your knee. You should tell the world about that."

"Nah, I'd rather keep it to myself. Their mamas get all upset and wanting me to be sending them money."

When we entered our practice room, Sonny Boy drawled, "Well, look-a-here, you boys got it good." We plugged his vocal and harp mic into a guitar amp, and I started a little groove on guitar; the boys joined in. Sonny Boy looked at my fingers to see what key we were in, reached for his harmonica in the attaché case he carried, and started playing along. Pretty soon, sparks flew. He looked around the room at each of us, showing off his wide, crooked smile with a couple of missing teeth. Garth and I traded solos, and Sonny Boy wailed back at us like a coyote in heat.

We ran through some more tunes with different people singing and Sonny Boy weaving in and out with his harp. He fit into the groove so naturally. I looked around at Levon and the other guys and could see in their eyes that they were as jazzed as I was. Sonny Boy threw his hand in the air for a break and we stopped on a dime. He stood up and rocked back and forth, taking the whole harmonica into his mouth, never missing a lick. I ripped off some high harmonics of a blues riff and Sonny Boy fell back down in his chair, grinning and slapping his knee.

We were really feeling buzzed, and between songs we talked about how to keep this connection going. Sonny Boy said that while he was in England he'd jammed and recorded with different musicians. "Boys, I'll tell you what, those young English cats over there really wanna play the blues bad, but unfortunately that's just how they play it . . . bad." He broke up laughing. Then he said, "You fellas as good as anybody I ever played with." That was a huge compliment coming from a master.

Levon got up from his drums. "You guys hungry? Damn, I'm starving. Sonny Boy, can we take you for some of the best soul food in these parts?" He nodded and headed to the bathroom. We could hear him in there coughing violently. I exchanged a worried glance with Levon. When Sonny Boy came out I put my hand on his shoulder and asked if he was okay. "Oh yeah, I'm fine, just a bit of a cough."

We drove straight downtown to a restaurant Levon had raved about. Sonny Boy knew it too and gave it the high sign. On the way, we committed to telling our respective booking agents that we wanted to do some gigs together. Sonny Boy said, "Man, I'd like to get into the studio and cut some things with you guys. I'll tell Leonard Chess we onto something here."

"Chess Records in Chicago?" I said. "That would be so fine."

Richard said, "I would just like to see the inside of that studio. Love the sound of those records."

We walked into the restaurant and sat at the counter so we could watch them cook the food close up—collard greens with smoked ham, corn bread, black-eyed peas, fried chicken, biscuits with gravy. Hog heaven is what you call it, and we were smack dab in the middle.

Just then, two police cars pulled up in front of the restaurant, their high beams burning our eyes. Two cops got out of one of the cars, swung through the door, and marched up to us. "What in the hell is going on here?" one of them asked. They looked behind the counter at the black cooks and server, who shook their heads like they didn't know nothing. The cops looked at us with blood in their eyes. "What do you think you're doing?"

Levon stood up and introduced himself. He explained that he was from up in Phillips County, where his uncle was the sheriff. "We were just having a bite with the legendary bluesman Sonny Boy Williamson. We're all musicians, sir."

The other cop, who was holding a club, said, "So do you think your uncle, the sheriff up in Phillips County, would be proud of y'all's behavior?"

Sonny Boy just sat there, his back to the cops. He knew better than to get involved. "Yeah, your uncle'd be real proud of you, eatin' with niggers," said the other cop. "What in the goddamn hell are you thinkin'?"

Levon wouldn't be cowed. "Well, sir, I'll tell you what I'm thinkin'. I'm thinkin' we can eat wherever we want, with whoever we want. Especially with somebody of the caliber of this gentleman right here. It's our honor."

The cops looked at each other. One stepped in closer to us. "That car out front with the Yankee plates, that yours?"

Levon answered, "Those are Canadian plates, sir."

The cop stuck out his jaw. "I don't give a fuck where they're from. What I want you boys to do is get in that car and drive as fast as you can outta here, back to wherever those fuckin' plates are from. I'm tellin' you right now, you're looking for big trouble around here, and we don't stand for that. We're all gonna follow you outta town. You understand me?"

I could see Levon getting hotter, and as much as I appreciated his trying to take a stand in his old stomping grounds, the last thing we needed was to get thrown in jail and beat up. Before he could say anything I intervened. "We just have to stop at the motel and pick up our things, and we'll be on our way." Levon looked tight as a knot, but he calmly shook hands with Sonny Boy and said we'd be in touch. "We got work to do."

Sonny Boy smiled. He gave everybody a wave as we went on our way.

The cops rode our tail back to the Rainbow Court. After we'd packed up our gear in record time and turned back onto the road, those high beams chased us for miles until we crossed the county line.

OUR MONARCH CONVOY cruised north toward Yankee country, where we were set to cut some tracks with Henry Glover for his new label, Ware Records. We looked forward to having a real producer/arranger/song-writer helping us make a record. In the past we'd mostly just played the songs and the producer had pressed "record." Henry offered to write us a song too—which had us dreaming big. I couldn't wait to hear what he had in store.

As I pulled my Telecaster out of its case, Henry sat down at the piano and started playing some chords and singing the basic idea of a tune. It was okay, but it didn't fully connect for us. I played him "Leave Me Alone" and "Uh, Uh, Uh," the songs I'd been working on at the Grange in Hamilton.

"They're better," said Henry. "Let's cut those."

Henry wrangled us pretty well, but I also realized that for him this was the opposite of working with studio musicians, who were able to go directly to a hook that felt good and familiar. We were trying to look for the unobvious and didn't know how to do it any other way. For a record producer like Henry, that could seem like taking the long way around. Yeah, wrangling the Hawks was probably a lot like trying to herd cats. When the record came out, Ware had changed our name from Levon and the Hawks to the Canadian Squires. *Oh dear.* I went along with it to be a good sport, and since it was okay with Levon, but that "square" name spoke something significant about the conceptual difference between us and Henry. We loved him for all the brilliant work he'd done, and he wanted to help us, but this was a new era.

IN THE SUMMER of 1965 we had booked a gig at Tony Mart's big dance club in Somers Point, New Jersey. Tony's was a hot spot, a popular club that sometimes had three bands playing on separate stages over the course of the evening. A big round bar sat in the middle of the club, handy for a refill no matter where you were standing. Tony Mart himself was an unusual club owner, a real character. A bit stocky, no-nonsense, and Sicilian born, Anthony Marrota spoke broken English and hardly ever smiled. He ran his "circus" with a strong hand, wandering through the crowds while yelling orders at bartenders and bouncers. Every once in a while he'd walk by the center stage we were playing on and call out, "Hey, turna downa tha jukebox!" We took this to mean we were playing too loud for an early-evening crowd.

On the first weekend we were there, you could tell the audience was into our type of music. Conway Twitty and some of his original band were in residence too, which was a nice surprise. When we went on, the place came alive. By Saturday night the club was so packed you couldn't move. Tony Mart pushed his way through the crowd and called up to us, "Hey, turna upa tha jukebox!" and gave a little grin.

After the first two weeks, Tony asked us to come back for two more weeks later in June. It was very unusual for us to play two stands so close together in one spot like that, but we were glad to plant our feet for a while. And lo and behold, our old road manager, Bill Avis, showed up in Somers Point too, managing a band of lesbians calling themselves the Female Beatles.

In between dates in Somers Point, we would head up to New York City to meet with production companies that had seen us play and were interested in signing us. We listened to songs they thought we could record, but none of them really connected. Part of their deal would be to sign us to a song-publishing agreement, at which point they would try to push their catalog on us. The acoustic folk setting was thriving in New York. You could feel it growing in Toronto's Yorkville district, but Greenwich Village was the epicenter of this world. John Hammond asked me to come hear him play at the Gaslight Club. He talked up Dave Van Ronk, Fred Neil, and a couple other guys he thought were very soulful folk singers. The Gaslight had a sign out front announcing the next act that would be performing there,

Mississippi John Hurt. I told John about our jam with Sonny Boy Williamson, and he said, "Sonny Boy one or two?"

I had to laugh. "Two."

He said, "Love his harp playing!"

ONE AFTERNOON, John came by the Forest Hotel to collect me for a trip downtown to a hip record store. I threw him the keys to one of the Monarchs and he floored it, ripping down Seventh Avenue like we were in a movie car chase. Then he hit the brakes and said, "Oh, man, I forgot something. A friend of mine is recording around the corner and I promised I would stop by. Can we go in for a minute and say hello?"

Before long we were on the elevator in the Columbia Records building heading for Studio A. In the control room people were listening to the playback of a song they had just cut. John said hello to a man in round wire-rimmed glasses with shoulder-length grayish hair.

"Robbie, this is the great music manager Albert Grossman." Sitting in the corner silently was Dion of Dion and the Belmonts. Then John went over and gave a big greeting to his friend who was recording. He turned to introduce me.

"Hey, Bob, this is my guitar-player friend Robbie, from Canada. This is Bob Dylan." You could barely see his eyes through the dark glasses he wore, but there was high voltage in the room coming from his persona.

Bob said hello, and then to John, "You wanna hear something?"

"Yeah, I'd love to."

Bob teased, "You sure you want to hear this? You never heard anything like this before."

Albert Grossman and the record producer nodded in serious agreement.

"It's called 'Like a Rolling Stone,'" Bob said with a little smirk. "All right, go ahead, play it back."

Bob was right—I'd never heard anything like this before. The studio lit up with the sound of toughness, humor, and originality. It was hard to take it all in on one listen.

After the playback John shook Bob's hand and showered him with compliments, and just then I noticed through the glass the studio musicians that played on the track. There was Mike Bloomfield. He waved and I stepped into the studio to say hello, but for some reason he looked a bit out of sorts. He whispered, "I'll be off to Chicago in a couple days. This is pretty weird, but it's all cool. There's something I need to talk to you about." I didn't know what he meant, but this wasn't the time to get into it.

When John and I were back in the car, barreling downtown, I expected him to comment on the song or the experience we'd just had. But he didn't say anything about it, and I got the feeling that for John it was still all about the blues.

THE HAWKS WERE finally getting closer to signing a deal with a record company in New York. The talent scout from Aaron Schroeder's production company, Eddie Heller, had shown tremendous interest in us. Eddie had seen us during our miserable stretch at the Peppermint Lounge, and we appreciated his determination. The advantage of a production deal was that they would find material for us to cut, though at the same time we weren't sure if we shouldn't be signing directly with a record company. Schroeder gave us the whole music-biz sales pitch, which sounded impressive to our naive ears. They had the lawyers draw up a contract.

"It's a very good deal for you gentlemen," Schroeder told us when they gave us the paperwork. "You can sign it now or, if you want to, you can have a music attorney go over it. That's your choice. What do you think, Eddie? Should they have a lawyer take a look at it?"

Eddie scratched his receding hairline. "Well, yeah, you can have an attorney look at it, but it's gotta be a music guy so he understands the business. But that's gonna cost money. And those guys don't come cheap, if they're half decent."

It felt a little like we were buying a rug or a used car. Levon had the idea to ask Henry Glover if he would take a look at the contract and let us know if it looked fair. Henry read it and said he wouldn't sign it. It locked us up for a long time on everything from recording to publishing, with a very low royalty. We took notes on what Henry said and asked some questions about what we should push for.

Levon was pissed that they were trying to screw us, but I said it was only worth being angry if we had already signed the deal. "Let's see if we can do better," I said. When we presented our counteroffer to Schroeder and Co., they acted like we were asking to put up our own tollbooth on the Brooklyn Bridge. Levon started yelling back, but I told them, "That's what it's gonna take. Either you want us or you don't." In the end they compromised on a few things, and we made a somewhat reasonable deal. Now they would go to work finding material for us to record.

By then we'd begun our second stand at Tony Mart's club in New Jersey, and on our nights off we would slip over to the Wonder Garden club in Atlantic City, where we caught some of the best jazz-organ combos going. Jimmy Smith played there, and we also saw Brother Jack McDuff, whom Garth appreciated for his unusual style. Shirley Scott, "Queen of the Organ," was a favorite of mine, with her husband, Stanley Turrentine, on sax. Most of these jazz organists played a Hammond B3 with bass pedals, which meant they could play without a bass player. It was fascinating to watch them play a lead part with their right hand on the upper keyboard and chords or counterparts (and sometimes lead) with the left hand on the lower keyboard. At the same time they'd be changing sounds and controlling the speed of the Leslie speaker, pulling and pushing buttons and stops with both hands while playing the bass part with their feet. The whole thing was a remarkable balancing act. And of course the groove and texture of the B3 was sexy cool. It made you want to order a Cutty Sark and soda. Garth played a whole other kind of organ, the incomparable Lowrey. Different sound, different touch altogether from the Hammond B3, and you could bend the notes like a horn or guitar, which completely baffled a lot of listeners. So great when Garth would kick into a free-for-all jam by himself, with those bass pedals in full effect. Gave you the shivers.

One night after we finished playing at Tony Mart's, Garth began telling me about some ideas and effects he was experimenting with. He was always devising new modes of "hot-rodding" the Lowrey organ and its Leslie speaker to create brilliant new sonic wonders. As he described his research-and-discovery approach, most of it went over my head, but the results were undeniable. The sounds that came out of Garth's keyboards or wind instruments had originality stamped all over them. Garth experimented endlessly, like a Harry Partch or Les Paul. He never stopped wanting to expand on his technical abilities inside or outside the instrument. None of the rest of us Hawks was so inclined. Some people want to know how a watch works, and other people just want to know what time it is.

Quite regularly on our off days I would head up to New York City, sometimes crashing with our Canadian pal Mary Martin, who had taken a job working for Albert Grossman's management company. She was always so supportive and would try to turn us on to new music that was happening, like John Sebastian's new group, the Lovin' Spoonful. Sometimes one or two of the other Hawks would join me on these excursions into the city, but it soon became evident that I was the one most drawn to the metropolis.

Catching up with my new friend Charles Lloyd was a must on these trips. All sorts of interesting people moved through his world. One time, when I stopped by his pad in the Village, Ornette Coleman was there. He seemed pretty reserved and mellow for a guy who played such wild, aggressive, challenging music. Charles had formed his own band and recruited pianist Keith Jarrett, drummer Jack De-Johnette, bassist Cecil McBee, and a fantastic guitarist named Gabor Szabo, who played with an otherworldly, gypsy jazz tone. Upstairs in Charles's building lived a character we called Third-Floor Richard, who kept the Lebanese hashish flowing. But I would have come back to Charles Lloyd's apartment regularly anyway, just to listen to music on his amazing hi-fi system.

Of all the groups that played Somers Point in the summer of 1965,

Tony Mart's personal favorite was Levon and the Hawks, though it was sometimes hard to tell whether he liked the swampy sound of our music or the ringing of the cash registers. Toward the end of our stint, our relationship with Tony had grown warm, almost familial. He hired us to finish out the season, which proved ideal for future recording sessions and continued access to the city. Everyone in the band seemed to be in a good place during those days.

The only dark cloud that passed over us that summer (other than the enduring stress of the drug bust) was when we got word that our dear Sonny Boy Williamson II had passed away from tuberculosis, and that the beautiful dream we had of recording together had died with him.

SOON AFTER, I got a message from Albert Grossman's office, asking me to come up to the city on our next day off to meet with Bob Dylan. I'd met him only briefly with John Hammond when they were record-ing "Like a Rolling Stone." I asked the guys if they knew any of Bob's music. I wasn't that familiar with it myself, though I remembered a song he'd done a few years back called "Oxford Town." It rang true, and the tone of his voice really stood out for me. Richard offered that Bob's record "Subterranean Homesick Blues" reminded him of Chuck Berry's "Too Much Monkey Business." "Yeah," I said, "that staccato rhythmic phrasing is reminiscent."

Albert Grossman's office set it up for me to meet with Bob the fol-lowing Monday. I couldn't help but wonder what this was all about.

THIRTEEN

Come Monday morning, I drove solitaire from the Jersey Shore to Albert Grossman's office on 55th Street, just west of Park Avenue. I pushed the elevator button for Gross Court Management, on the fourth and fifth floors, and a few moments later an assistant escorted me to a room stockpiled with new Fender guitars and equipment—a Precision bass, a Stratocaster with a rosewood neck, a Jaguar guitar, and some amps with separate heads and speakers. It was comforting to see our old friend from Toronto, Mary Martin, who'd been raising the Hawks' flag around the office for a while now.

As I made a list in my head of the stuff in this room that I considered the "crème," a lightning bolt entered the room: Bob Dylan, puffing on a cigarette harder than Bette Davis, one knee bobbing in time to a shotgun monologue. He was dressed in a dark red polka-dot shirt and blue striped pants. Electricity seemed to be shooting up through his hair. His dark prescription sunglasses accented his nocturnally pale skin and wiry build. This wasn't the folk traditionalist Dylan; this was the emergence of a new species.

Bob filled me in on his recent experiment playing electric with the Butterfield Blues Band at the Newport Folk Festival, which had elicited a controversial response. He said some people didn't like it but that those people for the most part never understood what he was doing anyway.

Bob claimed to have considerable experience with rock 'n' roll, mentioning by way of example that he'd played with Bobby Vee for a while. I wondered to myself if playing with the teen idol who made the rather square 1961 hit song "Take Good Care of My Baby" necessarily amounted to a real injection of rock 'n' roll in the veins. But at least it shed light on Bob's openness to collaborate and experiment. I confessed to my own limited experience in the acoustic, folk world.

I still had no idea why I was here, but I tried to dole out a few insights regarding the electric guitars that surrounded us. I told him I was a maple-neck guy, that I found the rosewood a little scratchy for playing lead. "Have you ever tried a Telecaster?" I asked him. "It's lighter on the shoulder and stays in tune easier than the Strat, or any of the Fender guitars that come with a tremolo bar."

Bob lit a cigarette off the one he was smoking and laughed. "Yeah, that Stratocaster I've been using doesn't stay in tune for long." He called to somebody in the next office. "Hey, can you get that Fender guy to bring over a Telecaster?" An assistant named Johanna came into the room and wrote down the request.

"Will they know what color or any details I should ask for?"

"They usually come in a cream color," I answered, "but maybe you should ask for a black one with a white pick guard. That could look good."

Bob left the room and came back a minute later carrying an acoustic guitar case. "Hey, man, you wanna go somewhere?" he asked. "There's something I wanna play for you. Why don't you grab that Fender acoustic guitar, and we'll go downtown."

Our destination was Albert Grossman's place in Gramercy Park, where Bob was staying while he found a place of his own. The Grossman house was stately, with high ceilings and tall windows, beautiful woodwork, and brass hardware. I had never seen this kind of New York elegance before. We took our instruments into Albert's living room, and Bob pulled an acetate disk out of a paper slipcover and put it on a turntable. He played two or three songs from the record, giving me some background on the sessions as we went along. I couldn't quite take it all in, with the music playing loudly and Bob talking over it, but it did feature his vocal way up front, pouring out some of the most amazing lyrical gymnastics that had ever been pressed to vinyl. His incredible feats of imagination and original vocal phrasing floored me. Where had this even come from? Rock 'n' roll wasn't born of a sophisticated attitude toward wordplay, but you wouldn't know it from these songs.

It didn't take me long, though, after hearing several cuts from his new album that would be released as *Highway 61, Revisited*, to realize that Bob at times was steaming down the tracks too swiftly for the musicians to keep up with his epic poetic energy.

I took the Fender acoustic out of its case while Bob tuned up his beautiful Nick Lucas Special. The headstock of his guitar said "The Gibson"—not just "Gibson"—which meant it had some years on it. We kicked into a rhythm, which Bob soon steered into one of the songs we had just heard. The texture of his voice and his guitar playing were as good as if not better than on the record. I watched his fingers to follow the chord progressions until I had a handle on the tune. I couldn't help but start floating between the vocal lines, swirling and stinging with fills when necessary. Bob lit up immediately, and after running through a couple songs, it almost felt like we had done this before. We laid down our guitars and lit up some smokes. Then he offered me a job.

Finally it became clear why I was here. He told me he had two concerts booked in a few weeks, with possibly a whole tour to follow. Some of the musicians who played on his record had agreed to be part of his live band, but he needed a lead guitarist.

I didn't know how to say that I wasn't here auditioning for a job. I asked why Mike Bloomfield wasn't joining him for these dates, and he said Mike had a full-time gig with the Butterfield Blues Band. "I do too," I responded, explaining that the Hawks had a solid bond, and that we were together through hell or high water. Bob said he was playing Forest Hills Stadium in New York and then the Hollywood Bowl in Los Angeles. He asked if I could at least see my way to join him on those two jobs.

The offer presented me with a dilemma. I could immediately see the appeal of playing with Bob. I really enjoyed our musical connection. But I couldn't conceive of doing anything that would jeopardize the Hawks.

I told Bob I might be able to do it if Levon played drums with us for the two gigs.

"Is he as good as Bobby Gregg?" Bob asked, smiling.

I smiled back. "Oh yeah, and better."

I only knew of Bobby Gregg from a cool instrumental record he had put out a couple of years earlier called "The Jam," featuring Roy Buchanan on guitar. Bobby was a known New York City session drummer and surely had great chops. But this wasn't about who played better; it was about my not wanting Levon to think I would abandon ship. Bob said he thought they already had Bobby Gregg booked.

"Well, let me know if we can do it with Levon," I said, "and I think we might be able to work something out."

Back at Somers Point I described Bob's offer to my bandmates. I could see different levels of concern on their faces. The idea of somebody making one of us an outside offer to play live had never entered the picture before. I made it clear that we were a unit, and nothing was going to change that.

When I explained that I wouldn't do the shows with Bob unless Levon could be a part of it, Lee still didn't embrace the idea. "We got our own thing," he said, "and we don't need no distractions." My personal curiosity and sense of adventure were the only things that made him give the experiment even the slightest consideration. As for the rest of the guys, Richard was the only one who showed any interest in exploring what might be stirring on the Bob Dylan front. Not even excitement and encouragement from Mary Martin made much of an impression on the Hawks.

To some extent, I could completely understand. We had left Ronnie to get out of this kind of situation, and now someone was coming along to suggest another backing opportunity, and even then, possibly just for two of us. And with a record contract under our belts and a great summer at Tony Mart's behind us, it felt like we were getting somewhere. But to me, what Bob was doing was strong and fascinating, and I thought there could be something in the discovery process that would be valuable to all of us.

After we talked as a group, Levon and I spoke about it one on one. "We have to see what's behind this door," I told him. "It's too interesting. Plus, these two jobs are bigger than anything we've ever been a part of. We've gotta feel it out."

Soon word came down from Bob's camp that they'd be happy to have Levon play drums for the gigs. I couldn't wait for Bob to meet Levon, and vice versa. They asked if I could come to the city for another get-together to iron out more details in preparation for the shows.

We drove up to the city to meet Bob at Albert Grossman's office. This time Albert came in to say hello and expressed his enthusiasm that Levon and I had agreed to do the shows. While we chatted, I tried out a couple of newly arrived guitars and plugged into one of the Fender amps in the room. It was a bit loud for the office, but Albert smiled wide when I ripped off a couple runs. I handed a new Telecaster to Bob when he came in the room. He just strapped it right on and raked out a few chords approvingly. We jammed back and forth for a few minutes, sending ripples down the hallways of Gross Court Management. Workers peeked out of their offices to check us out like a parade had come to town. You could tell there hadn't been much electric music bouncing off these walls before.

For the two upcoming gigs, Bob had enlisted Harvey Brooks to play bass and Al Kooper on keyboards. He stressed how well they played on his new record, and how easy they were to work with. "They'll fit in so smoothly that after a while you won't even know they're there." I assumed that was a good thing, and asked when we'd start to run over the songs together. In a cryptic way, Bob answered that it would all be worked out soon. He laid his guitar on the amp, which immediately started to feed back and roar through the office walls. We had a laugh as I scrambled to hit the standby switch and realized that Bob might find that this electric thing took some getting used to.

I wanted to make Levon more comfortable with this venture if I could, and commented that besides Bob being a unique talent, I thought he seemed like a great guy.

"I wanna get in the studio and do some recording," Levon said. "That's all I care about."

Eddie Heller, Aaron Schroeder's persistent talent scout, had brought some demos of songs for us to consider recording. He had set up some time for us to get into the studio. We listened and listened but couldn't get behind any of the material. *Here we go again*, I thought, *all dressed up and no songs to record.* So I grabbed whatever time I could and tried to come up with some tunes we could cut. That night I locked myself away with an acoustic guitar between Tony Mart's 2:00 a.m. closing time and dawn, and wrote a gospel-flavored tune called "The Stones I Throw." It reminded me of Pops Staples and the Staple Singers, who at that time sang mostly gospel music. For a B-side I found a riff that I turned into a song called "He Don't Love You."

Our first recording experiences all seemed to follow the same pattern. On a Wednesday someone would sign us to a deal, and Wednesday night I'd have to try to come up with something to record on Thursday. I could have called my music-publishing company "Eleventh Hour." Sure, I enjoyed throwing together a couple of songs for the occasion, but I had tremendous respect for songwriters and wanted to do better than what these circumstances would allow.

AS SOON AS Levon got behind the drums for our first Dylan rehearsal, Bob could tell he was the real deal. We met Al Kooper and Harvey Brooks, and everybody wanted to find our groove, looking to make some honest and good music. We tried and tumbled through the tunes with the best of intentions, but for Levon and me the music felt somewhat disorganized. We rolled with the punches as best we could. Al and Harvey were terrific guys and recognized that we were on a free-floating raft. The saving grace was that Bob didn't seem to be bothered by any of this. It could be that he played so much as a one-man band—just his voice, acoustic guitar, and harmonica—and slayed audiences everywhere, so why would he look at it differently with a few musicians?

On August 28, at Forest Hills Stadium in New York, we took the stage for our afternoon sound check. It was a huge tennis stadium that had been reconfigured for live events. It held maybe twelve or fifteen thousand people, a far cry from the clubs we'd grown so accustomed to on our circuit. Our sound echoed loudly through the empty stadium, and I asked Bob if he could hear himself well enough. "Nah, but that's okay. Just remember, tonight, don't stop playing, no matter what." He said it like we were going into battle.

As the hours passed, you could feel the scale of the event building. Albert Grossman seemed to be everywhere at once, checking last-minute details. The other Hawks showed up to see what Levon and I had gotten ourselves into; they too seemed awed by the size of the stadium. But I was worried less about the big crowd than about how we'd play, and how they'd react. We had heard what had happened at the Newport Festival with Bob and the Butterfield Blues Band: Bobby Neuwirth, Dylan's road manager, said Pete Seeger had wanted to pull the plug on them—but that was at a folk-music show. Not knowing what would happen tonight made for a tense backstage vibe that felt exciting and unnerving at the same time.

Bob went out and played the first half of the show doing his acoustic set, and it sounded real good. It gave us some confidence that the show was going well; all we had to do in the second half was follow through.

As soon as we hit the stage and plugged in, the audience unleashed its fury. From the first notes of the first song, "Tombstone Blues," people started booing viciously. I looked at Bob, but he just shrugged. People charged toward us, like they were staging a massive coup in an imaginary war. We followed Bob's advice and didn't stop playing "no matter what." Some people busted through the barricades and got on the stage, knocking Al Kooper over. Albert was directing security to help hold the crowds back. Bobby Neuwirth was waving frantically, like we might have to make a run for it. I looked over at Levon, who just shook his head. Harvey saw this and started laughing, and

I couldn't help but laugh too. Soon even Bob joined in, because this whole thing was too far gone to comprehend. I thought, *What's the big deal? Let the man play his music how he wants.* This was such a strange situation, and Levon and I had nothing to compare it to; these folk traditionalists were rabid. We felt like we were on a desolate island where cannibalism hadn't been outlawed yet.

Afterward, Bob assured us our next gig at the Hollywood Bowl in a few days should be a lot better: people out there in Los Angeles, he said, would be more open-minded. The Los Angeles band the Byrds had released a cover of Bob's song "Mr. Tambourine Man" a couple months earlier, paving the way for what some were calling the "folk-rock movement." Perhaps this was a sign we were just a little too soon with our "electric" current.

When we landed in Los Angeles, it did feel more welcoming. I'd never been there before, and I happily found the Sunset Strip alive with hundreds of people gathering in the name of a new day and dancing in a potion of love, peace, music, drugs, and sex. What truly blew my mind was the sheer *number* of kids: the Strip was overflowing with them, some smoking weed, some heading to the Whisky a Go Go, some with no money to be doing anything except hanging out. Los Angeles was open and spacious. A youthful, hopeful, almost dreamlike feeling was in the air.

Musicians, actors, hipsters, and more came by to see Bob, with his friend Victor Maymudes sometimes leading the charge. The photographer Barry Feinstein, who was married to Mary Travers of Peter, Paul and Mary, brought the best reefer I'd ever had. The Hollywood Bowl was big, beautiful, and of course legendary. It felt like an honor just to be performing in this world-famous venue.

We arrived that night knowing that Bob would sing and play his heart out in the acoustic first half of the show and the audience would love it. Then he would sing and play his heart out in the electric second half, and the audience might hate it.

"This is so strange," I said to Levon before we went on.

"Never felt anything like this, man," he responded. I had never seen my friend look more unsure of the ground he was standing on.

As we walked out onstage for the second half, the audience seemed to be waiting for a cue. A murmur ran through the crowd, cresting in a couple of shouts: "Go home!" "No rock 'n' roll!" After we played the first song, I looked out at the crowd and noticed something odd. People would look around and try to boo louder than one another, laughing and screaming with anger like this was a game or part of the show. Individually they didn't seem offended by the music; it was more of a mob mentality—"When Dylan goes electric, you boo." Jeering was just a thing to do. I saw it, and I got it. From that moment the cheers and jeers no longer affected me. I pushed it all aside and got lost in the music.

After the show, Al Kooper and Harvey Brooks seemed to think it had gone better than in New York. Bob and his team and various friends felt reasonably good about it. All the talk rolled off me. What did bother me was I knew we could play this music better, and I could tell Levon felt the same, though it probably wouldn't have made that big of a difference to an audience distracted by its own agenda. Bob had done his best, pounding those amazing songs out with all the firepower he could, but as a band we didn't have it yet.

I didn't say much at the time because we had only signed on for these two gigs. But when Levon and I returned to New York, I got a message. I told Levon, "Bob called and said they're booking an additional fifteen dates, and they want us to do the tour."

Levon laughed. "I would have thought he'd learned his lesson by now."

"Yeah, I told Bob we couldn't do it. We have our own band, and that's what we're all about. But he says he wants to meet me tonight at a bar in the Village. I'll see what's up."

I had walked by the Kettle of Fish on Macdougal Street before but had never been inside. It was known as a gathering place for members of the beat generation as well as musicians. By the time I got there, the place was hoppin'. Dylan was with his road manager, Bobby Neuwirth, and they had a table staked out near the back. Bob was in good spirits and very funny, pointing out characters in the bar and making up elaborate backstories about them. Neuwirth jumped right in. They made cutting, sharp jabs, and the whole thing seemed like a routine between them.

Neuwirth ordered some wine and Bob asked me straight out if I could do his upcoming tour. I told him again that the Hawks were a close unit and we were on our own mission; I would never do anything to get in the way of that. Neuwirth interjected that I could come back to "the Hawks thing" later; playing with Bob was a big deal, and the Hawks' future was a big "maybe" at best.

"That's not the way I look at it," I said. "We've been through so much together, and we're gonna see it through. I'm sure you'll find some guys that will play well with Al and Harvey." Bob said that he didn't think he'd use those fellows on the tour, that they seemed more suited for the studio. (I heard a couple of days later that Al Kooper didn't want to do the tour. He thought playing music under these circumstances could be dangerous and took a pass.)

Without having really discussed it with the guys, I took the liberty of saying the only way I could consider doing the tour would be if the Hawks were the backing band. "It's kind of an all-or-nothing situation," I told Bob.

"Whoa, how do we know that these guys could even cut it?" Neuwirth said.

"You don't. Bob would have to come hear us play."

"Where?" Bob asked.

"In Toronto next week. We're playing a club there."

"Really? Yeah, maybe I could do that."

"Well, we're going into the studio tomorrow to record some new songs. I'll talk to the boys and see what they think," I responded.

"Did you write the songs?" Bob asked.

"Yeah, I do most of the writing, although I've been a little strapped for time with all that's going on. Richard, Rick, and Levon do the vocals. They're all really good singers. Garth and I take the solos."

"I'd like to check this out." Bob nodded. "Yeah, I'm going to try to come up to Toronto."

Neuwirth paid the check, and on the way out we ran into Phil Ochs, a popular folk singer at the time. Neuwirth and Bob verbally tore into him on the spot, laughing the whole time. You could tell there was some history between them, but I didn't know a thing about it. Neuwirth and Bob seemed pretty harsh with Phil Ochs, but I guessed Bob had his reasons. I was just glad that it wasn't me stranded on that firing line.

The following day, as we headed to our recording session, I told the boys about my conversation with Bob. Nobody seemed to have any real objection to our checking out the possibility of a tour. It was an intriguing opportunity and it was only for fifteen dates.

Aaron Schroeder and Eddie Heller had booked us in a studio called Mira Sound, conveniently located downstairs from our hotel in the city. A girl group called the Crystals was working on a session at Mira too. We decided to collaborate—though not so much on the music.

Eddie liked an up-tempo version we did of the traditional song "Little Liza Jane," so we decided to cut that along with the new tunes to satisfy the production company. Our recording engineer, Brooks Arthur, knew what he was doing, which gave us a chance to rehearse the new material while he worked on the sound. We had a vibe going on "He Don't Love You," and I thought we were off and running. We cut "Go Go Liza Jane" in two takes, and though it felt like a novelty rendition to me, Eddie liked it. Garth played a nice melody on "The Stones I Throw," with his own hint of gospel. I felt somewhat satisfied with the session but knew we hadn't gotten to the real magic I imagined we could produce. I longed for a situation where I could have a little break, some space, so I could concentrate on songwriting.

Aaron Schroeder informed us that Atlantic Records was going to release our tracks on their Atco label. The Drifters, Aretha Franklin, Bobby Darin, Ray Charles, and so many other greats were on Atlantic, so this came as superb news.

ARRIVING BACK in Toronto in mid-September for a stand at the Friar's, we were forced to deal with the reality we'd been pushing away for

months: our marijuana bust and the upcoming trial. A strategy meeting with our elderly attorney and Jack Fisher made plain our situation:
we could do serious prison time if convicted. Ten years, maybe seven
for good behavior—these were the numbers thrown around the room.
Ontario, Canada, was a conservative place in 1965 with extreme views
on drugs. Not quite as extreme as Texas, where a stripper called Candy
Barr (coincidentally a friend of Jack Ruby's) had been sentenced to
fifteen years for a couple of joints. The idea sounded horrific. I was
twenty-two. I tried to hold it together on the surface, but inside I was
freaked out.

But we weren't beaten yet. When we'd played the Friar's Tavern
in the spring, some of the arresting policemen had begun stopping
by the club after work to hear us play. Sometimes a couple of the officers would come by together; other times Don Docker, the Mountie,
Garth's old schoolmate, would drop by on his own. On occasion they
would bring their wives for a night out, and soon their presence became a regular occurrence. We were working overtime to give the
strong impression that we weren't in any way bad people or common
criminals.

One evening, while I was sitting with two of the officers and their
wives between sets, one of the wives looked directly at her husband
and said, "You better not do anything harmful to Robbie and the
boys. These are some good kids and we don't want to see anything bad
happen to them."

The other wife joined in. "Absolutely. They play wonderful music
and look so handsome doing it. I believe they are going to be very
successful in the near future. We don't want to see anything get in the
way of their careers, do we?" she asked, looking at her husband. "Or
things could get very lonely at home, if you know what I mean." They
all broke into laughter as I took the stage for our next set.

A few nights into our run, the lead arresting narcotics detective
came to the club. We did our "palsy-walsy" routine with him, even inviting him to back to the hotel for a little party after the show. There I
pulled him aside, poured him a Crown Royal, and lowered my voice to
ask him a question. "Just outta pure curiosity, how did you guys know

we were going to pick up our other car at the airport parking lot, and that we had some pot?"

He took a sip of the whiskey, looked around the room, and leaned in toward me. "We got a call from Rick Danko's girlfriend—or ex-girlfriend. She told us when you were coming back and that you had marijuana."

I gasped. "Rick has been trying to get her off his back for months. He broke it off but she keeps hanging on." Ironically, this was the girl who had prompted Ronnie Hawkins to fire Rick.

Now the pieces started to fit together. Just then, Levon came over and put his hand on the detective's shoulder. "I've got someone I want you to meet," he said, and introduced him to Katy, a pretty, shapely sometime girlfriend of Levon's and a pal of ours. She shook hands with the detective and didn't let go. Katy looked very beautiful and sexy in her white skirt and sheer top. After a few minutes Levon said to Katy and the detective, "Why don't you guys go into the next room so you can talk privately?"

Levon had explained to Katy that we needed to beat the charges against us, or we could end up going to prison for years, and she had offered—if it would help us—to let the detective "get his rocks off."

After Katy and the detective got it on, she said, "Oh, God, I forgot to tell you something. . . . I'm sixteen years old." The detective's eyes bulged out of his head. "I don't want to have to tell anybody about what we've done," she continued, "but I need to know that the boys aren't going to have any problems with these awful charges against them."

The next day the Hawks and Business Bill Avis gathered to size up the situation. "How about our dear Katy," Levon said. "Did she come through or what? I had no idea she was gonna play that underage stuff. She's seventeen but she told him she was sixteen." I told everyone what the detective had said about how Rick's ex had set us up. Rick looked upset but didn't seem that shocked by the news. He rattled it around in his head a few seconds and said, "I'm gonna take responsibility for this. I'm going to say the Panama Red was in my overcoat pocket. It was mine, and it was me who brought it across the border. I don't want anybody else going down."

Rick was being a stand-up guy. It was a big, bold move for him to offer to take the rap, whatever it might be, for the charges.

ON SEPTEMBER 15, Bob Dylan came up to Toronto with his girlfriend, Sara Lownds, to hear the Hawks play live. I set them up in a discreet corner of the Friar's to check us out. We played pretty good that night, and when we finished our last set at 1:00 a.m., Bob put Sara in a taxi to go back to the hotel. As she was leaving, she told me that she really liked our music and hoped that everything would work out. Sara was kind of a quiet type, with a mystical side. She had dark hair, fair skin, and sad eyes. I thought it was very sweet what she said, and I knew she didn't have to do that.

After the club had emptied out, we got a mic for Bob and plugged in his guitar. Some of the songs on his records had particular arrangements we tried to follow, though that wasn't necessarily our strong suit. Never playing something exactly the same way twice was more up our alley. We played a few tunes through—"I Don't Believe You," "Just Like Tom Thumb's Blues," then "It Ain't Me Babe"—which he had played acoustic in the past.

As we ran through the material, it sounded a bit messy; we didn't know the songs that well. I tried to help lead the arrangements by giving signals, waving my guitar neck and playing a little louder on the chord progressions. We played the songs with no concrete beginnings or endings. Bob would usually start strumming away to set the tempo, and we would stagger in when we got a feel for the rhythm. I suggested that when we neared the end of the song, Bob could give me a nod and I would signal the boys that we were coming in for a landing. We ran through about ten tunes before Bob put his guitar down and called it a night.

He returned to the Friar's the next day for another session, and as we kept running through the songs, I could tell we were drawing somewhat closer as a unit. I was enjoying Bob's singing and the level of intensity this collaboration brought to the songs. He wasn't too fixated on details or fussy about how tight we were. Finally Bob appeared to have heard enough.

"Yeah, that sounds pretty good. So why don't we do this first tour and see how it goes. What do you think?"

Truth be known, we didn't know exactly what to think. But we all agreed to give it a shot.

When I sat down with the guys to talk about how this music felt to them and their take on working with Bob, Richard offered, "He seems like an okay guy to me, but that run-through wasn't very good on our end. We have to start by really learning these songs."

Bob had asked Garth to play some of the organ parts from his record, but these didn't necessarily fit Garth's style or aesthetic.

Levon shrugged. "So far it's sounding rough as a cob to me."

Rick chimed in with the voice of reality. "We gotta give it some time and see how it goes. Besides, we've still got our trial to face—we may have to phone in our parts from Kingston Penitentiary." The possibility of doing time for our drug charges still loomed large.

The next day we got together for lunch with Bob and Sara and a special guest, Bob's mom. She had come to visit him from Minnesota, which surprised me a bit. When Bob mentioned his background to us in conversation, he made it sound almost as if he'd had an orphanlike upbringing. But his mother was warm and outgoing—a regular, proud, loving mother. She liked Rick, chatting him up and asking where we got our suits made, and that's when I insisted Bob come to check out our tailor, Lou Myles. Bob didn't seem like much of a suit guy, but Lou was on top of his game. He pushed to make Bob a brown and black houndstooth wool suit, and a salt-and-pepper tweed with black leather piping around the jacket. As Bob concluded his visit in Toronto there was a very positive feeling about us doing this tour together, but the outcome of our trial still remained very much up in the air.

NOW WE HAD to turn our attention exclusively to our legal problems. The prosecution would be calling us individually to the stand. "The less said the better. Don't let them trick you into saying things," our law-yer advised. We shared with him some of the stories about different officers coming to the clubs to see us over the last few months. Other stories, of course, we held back, especially the one about the detective and Katy.

On the morning of the trial, the six of us dressed respectfully and drove in our two Monarch station wagons to the Mississauga court-house, nervous as hell. The Colonel and Jack Fisher came out in full support—and to get their bail money refunded. I had a sick feeling in my throat, but this was our high noon, and we had to see it through.

"The court will now come to order." The judge entered the court-room, poker-faced. I put my hand on Rick's knee and gave him a reas-suring pat. He nodded, looking straight ahead, and patted me back.

The judge asked our attorney and the prosecution a question about procedure, but our attorney didn't respond. Dead silence. Confused, I looked over and saw that if our lawyer wasn't asleep, he was having a moment of deep thought.

Oh no. I cringed.

The judge addressed him again, and as he wobbled to his feet with a document in his hand, he passed gas. Everybody acted like it didn't happen. I wondered if it could be a clever sympathy maneuver on his part—I sure hoped so.

Our attorney called the arresting officers to the stand one by one to sketch out the details of the arrest. First came one of the policemen who had come to the club with his wife. He answered the questions very professionally, describing how the arrest went down and what they found on us. His testimony wasn't particularly harsh, but it didn't do us any favors either. A cold chill ran through me.

Don Docker, Garth's old schoolmate, looked right at us as he tes-tified. No patsy here. He described the arrest and the importing of marijuana, and said that although he didn't think we were a threat to society, we had committed a crime. I looked at Garth, who had a weariness in his eyes.

Next they called the narcotics detective, whom we'd introduced to Katy, to testify. He claimed there were questionable circumstances leading up to the arrest and that it was possible the marijuana was part of a setup to get us in trouble. When the prosecution started to drill him, he declared that, in his professional opinion, we were not drug dealers in any way, we had never been in trouble before, we were on the cusp of becoming successful, and there was nothing whatsoever to be gained from treating us as a threat or as criminals. Levon gave me a little nod. You could hear a slight gasp in the court: he was doing a better job of defending us than our lawyer.

Then it was our turn to take the stand. The court called Bill Avis and asked about the rolling papers found on him. He said he used them on his face when he cut himself shaving.

"You use cigarette rolling papers that are commonly used to roll marijuana joints? You use them for shaving?" the prosecutor asked.

"Yes, sir, in case I nick myself," Bill answered.

They called a couple more of us to see if someone would make a false or incriminating statement, but we held our ground. The only one to cause a stir was me. All along our lawyer had told us that he wanted to plant in the judge's mind the idea that there was something fishy about this whole setup. I took a chance when he asked where the pot in the little film canister under the car seat had come from. Did I put it there?

"No, sir," I answered truthfully, not knowing where it came from.

"Did one of your bandmates put it there?"

"No, sir."

"Did perhaps the police put it there?"

"I don't know . . . possibly," I answered. Another gasp in the courtroom. A few of the cops' eyes widened at the suggestion.

Finally they called Rick to take the stand. He confessed that the grass we had brought from New York was his. It was found in his overcoat and a friend in New York had given it to him. He assumed full responsibility for bringing it across the border into Canada but said he'd had no intention of selling it. "I made a terrible mistake, and I apologize to my family and my bandmates for being so foolish, and I will never do anything like this again." I thought, *Man alive, Rick couldn't have played it better.*

Our moment of truth had arrived. The judge picked up his notes and said, "Here's my ruling: for Garth Hudson, Levon Helm, Richard Manuel, Jaime Robertson, and William Avis . . . no charges. You are free to go. For Rick Danko, I'm giving you a one-year suspended sentence, probation, and, I hope, a lesson well learned."

The Hawks exhaled collectively. We shook hands and thanked our elderly lawyer over and over. Rick looked more relieved than anybody. No jail time! He was bouncing around, hugging and laughing with everybody he could find. He'd have to get a work visa and a waiver to travel, which were already in the works with the lawyer. We notified Albert Grossman that we were free to do the tour with Bob.

We drove back to Mama Kosh's house to tell her the great news, and she made us a fantastic meal to celebrate. Now all that was left was to wait for our first trip on a private plane—they were sending a twin-engine thirteen-seat Lodestar to pick us up and fly us to our first gig of the Bob Dylan tour in Austin, Texas.

FOURTEEN

Going out on tour with Bob Dylan was like heading into the great unknown, and I couldn't think of a better place to kick things off than in the heart of Texas. One thing you knew down there was they loved their barbecue and they loved their music. The morning after we flew in on the Lodestar, Bob, the Hawks, Albert Grossman, and Bobby Neuwirth all gathered at the hotel before we headed over to the Austin Municipal Auditorium. This was a true state-of-the-art concert hall that had over four thousand seats. This was the first time all five of the Hawks would be playing together in such a big space.

For this first show of the tour, we didn't know what to expect. Everybody's nerves were on edge, waiting to see if the Hawks were going to be a good fit. Of course we felt like we could have been more rehearsed, but Bob only had so much patience for any of that.

Still, it felt good to have our little army together on the front lines. Bob ran through a couple of acoustic songs at the sound check, and I went out in the house to listen. Then we played part of "Just Like Tom Thumb's Blues," getting a balance onstage while the soundman checked settings for the whole band. Bob stopped about three quarters of the way into the song and said over the PA, "How's it sound?"

"More, please," the soundman asked. We ran through two more songs, but the soundman still wasn't satisfied. "Almost there."

We moved Bob's amp so they could get more isolation among the instruments. It was hard to hear ourselves and get a balance onstage while they worked on the sound in the house. What they usually say at this point is, "You can't tell how it's going to sound until the place fills up with people."

"You want me to tune that guitar up for you?" I asked Bob. "They put light-gauge strings on it, like mine, but for rhythm you should probably have a heavier gauge. They'll stay in tune better."

"I like these strings," Bob answered.

"That's because they're easier on the fingers for bending, but the trade-off is they go out of tune quicker. Let me stretch them out real well, see if that helps."

That night, when we made our way back into the auditorium, the Hawks felt a bit like outsiders in this tried and true world of folk music. How odd to be invited to the party but not sure if your name is on the list. We couldn't even know for certain if some of Bob's gang wanted this to work.

Could have been beginner's luck, but we got through the set reasonably well that first night. We might have played some tunes a little too fast or too slow, but nothing fell apart, and the audience put up with our noise pretty good. There were some hoots and hollers, but we didn't get the feeling they hated it. The auditorium acoustics were more forgiving than at Forest Hills or the Bowl, and though it's possible I was reading too much into it, Texas just felt like a musical place; this crowd seemed more open to the whole experience.

We got some feedback from the crew after the show, and it was such a bizarre scale on which we were measuring our performance. "Well, they didn't charge the stage." "Didn't hear too many boos."

I mentioned to Bob that maybe I was taking too many solos. "Nah, the more the better," he responded.

Truth be told, we were all learning how to make this music come together in front of an audience. Bob had limited experience playing with a band, so coming from our background as a tight unit, this felt pretty loose. "We keep breakin' meter," Levon complained. "I don't know where we are half the time. Can't tell when Bob's gonna come in singing, so I don't know when to lead in or lay out."

"We can't count on specific arrangements yet," I said. "Wherever Bob goes with the tempo or timing, we just gotta be on top of it and go with the flow."

"We'll get it," Rick insisted. "It's just a bit of a free-for-all right now."

THE NEXT NIGHT, September 25, we played Dallas, which rattled our nerves even more than Austin, being such a major American crossroads. You couldn't help but recall that only two years earlier President Kennedy had been assassinated here.

The Moody Coliseum was a big hall, probably seating around seven thousand people, and the roar of the crowd was overwhelming. Bob sounded very strong in the first half. I watched most of it from the back of the hall, wondering, *How in the world does this man remember all the words to his songs?* Lots of singers can memorize many song lyrics, but with Bob this was a feat above and beyond, not only because of the complexity of his lyrics but because some of his songs seemed to contain more verses than the Bible.

After a short intermission the Hawks and Dylan hit the stage, ready or not. As in Austin, either the Dallas audience was more accepting of our electric bombardment or the news had yet to reach Texas that booing the second half of Dylan concerts was *de rigueur.* We chose to believe the first option.

After the show a couple of interesting characters Levon had met joined us back at the hotel with an assortment of pills and weed. One of the guys was real good at knife throwing and boasted serious expertise in fighting with a straight razor. He gave me a lesson, showing me how to whip the razor out of my back pocket, flip it over my fist, attack with it, and make the razor disappear, all within a split second— very flashy and dangerous. Both guys were cool and seemed friendly enough, but you definitely wouldn't want to cross them.

There was a knock on the door.

"Hey, it's Neuwirth. Open up." I let him in. He took one look at our guests and started joking. "Who are these guys, local pimps or drug dealers? Come on, I nailed that one, right?"

The vibe in the room instantly went sideways. My straight-razor friend stood up and looked at Neuwirth with a deadly smile. I pulled him back down to the couch.

"You better go," Levon told Neuwirth. "You know what your problem is? You don't know what's fuckin' funny and what's not. Go on, before someone whips your ass." As he walked out the door, Neuwirth shrugged. "Sorry, man, I was just kidding around."

When he left, I added, "Don't worry about him, that's just Neuwirth being Neuwirth. He's a good guy, he's just got that New York attitude."

Levon snarled. "That crazy son of a bitch is gonna get his ass whooped talking that big-city shit down here."

WE HAD a few days off until our next job back in New York, a performance at world-renowned Carnegie Hall. The venues we had played so far with Bob were much bigger than any the Hawks had played before, but Carnegie Hall was on another level: this was one of the most prestigious concert halls anywhere. I was excited and concerned at the same time. Of course we wanted to do our very best under these circumstances; given that, more rehearsing seemed the obvious move. But the one thing this organization wasn't was *obvious*.

Running over a few tunes at the Carnegie sound check, I could tell the acoustics were more delicate than in the other places we'd played. Rick and Levon said we needed to turn Bob's amp down. We figured that if all Bob could really hear was his guitar, we'd have no way of finding a balance or the pocket.

"Hell, that's what's wrong," Levon said. "There ain't no pocket. We're all just clamoring along until we get to the end of a song."

"We should play quieter here," I told the guys, "try for a more subtle blend."

Sometimes, however, the excitement of playing live and rocking out can send subtleties right out the window, and that's precisely what happened at Carnegie Hall. Finding the pocket got sacrificed in the

name of reaching for the sky. Bob turned up, I turned up, and, conse-
quently, so did everybody. Loud ruled.

The Carnegie Hall audience didn't take it lying down. The crowd
may have been lying in wait to see if anything rubbed them the wrong
way, and apparently we provided them with plenty to hiss about. I
wondered how many people had ever been booed at Carnegie Hall.
Levon and I had been through this at Forest Hills Stadium and the
Hollywood Bowl, but Rick, Richard, and Garth had an otherworldly
look on their faces. Bob appeared unbothered by it. It seemed to me
that he realized that in a folk-music center like New York, we were
bound to get a strong backlash for playing electric. But toward the end
of the show, the crowd enthusiastically rushed the stage. To experience two such extreme reactions at one concert was really odd. The
evening was like a roller-coaster ride.

After the show, back in our dressing room, I could hear a conversation coming through the wall. Some friends and music-business
people were telling Bob and Albert quite bluntly, "You've got to get rid
of this band. They're ruining the music. The audience loves you, loves
your songs, but when those guys come out, they hate it. You heard
how the crowd reacts. It's plain to see they gotta go, and the sooner
the better."

I couldn't hear how Bob or Albert reacted, but when I looked
around the room at the other guys, I could see hurt and confusion on
their faces. The comments knocked the wind out of me too, but they
also left me feeling intent on vengeance. Somehow we had to win this
battle.

A FEW DAYS after the Carnegie show, Albert, who also managed Richie
Havens, hooked it up for us to catch his show at the Café Au Go Go
in the Village. The set was really good; Richie's voice stoned me, and
afterward Levon and I went to a bar across the street just to come
back down. We hadn't been there long when a voice behind me said,
"Hey, guitar man, what's happening?" I turned and was so glad to see

the smiling face of Mike Bloomfield. He was in town for some shows with the Butterfield band, and I thanked him again for arranging our fantastic time in Chicago.

When I told Mike that we were doing a tour with Bob Dylan, he looked puzzled. "Really?"

"We're feeling it out," Levon responded. "We'll see."

"Why didn't you hang in there longer with Bob?" I asked Mike. "You played good on his record. But when I saw you in the studio cutting 'Like a Rolling Stone,' you mentioned something about it being kind of weird."

"Well, first of all, the song 'Rolling Stone' is by Muddy Waters," said Mike, sticking his hand out for me to give him some skin. "That's where that English group got their name. And Bob's song is 'Like a Rolling Stone,' right?"

"Hail, Muddy Waters, right?"

Levon answered, "Hail, hail, Muddy Waters."

Mike was a hardcore blues guy, beyond a devotee. He talked about the blues like a religion, and I could see how playing with Bob, who loved the blues but incorporated so many other influences into his music, might not totally jibe with a purist like Mike.

"Bob's a cool guy, but he doesn't know that much about playing with other musicians," Mike added.

"Well, that's gonna come with time," I said. "And he's done so incredibly well on his own, the majority of people think he should carry on that way. The Hawks are like the uninvited guests who won't stop ruining his music."

Mike laughed. "Exactly—that's why I didn't want to stick around." He paused for a second. "Look, I gotta tell you something. It's what I couldn't talk about at the recording session with Dylan. I gotta make a confession." His face turned red. He closed his eyes for a moment. "You know that grass you took from Butterfield's apartment? Well, I had to tell him it was you guys that stole it."

"What? You told on us? You finked on us?"

"I had to," he pleaded. "He thought I took it, and he was literally gonna kill me. He went crazy. And we play in a band together. . . . I'm sorry, man. But the thing is, he's on his way here now to meet Albert, and if he sees you . . ."

"Well, let's get the hell outta here and we'll figure it out later," Levon said. Across the bar I caught a glimpse of a musician I knew who also sold pot. I went over and said, "Hey, you got any weed? I need to score some."

He reached into his pocket and quietly pulled out a whole ounce. "It's expensive. It's the best. It's Acapulco Gold."

"Let me see," I said. It did look special, with hardly any sticks or seeds. "How much?"

"Sixty dollars."

"Holy shit."

I went to Levon and said, "We need sixty bucks. We'll pay Butterfield back ten times over." We had eighty between us, and I bought the grass.

We stepped outside to wait for Paul, and sure enough, we soon spotted him coming across the street.

"You *motherfuckers*!" cried Butterfield the moment he saw us. He started reaching into his pocket and racing toward us.

I didn't wait to find out what he was reaching for. "Paul," I yelled back, "I told you we were gonna pay you back, and baby, we are paying you better than anybody's ever paid you back. Check this shit out— Acapulco Gold, man." I held up the big bag of weed.

Butter put on the brakes when he caught sight of the bag. Levon smiled. "That's the best damn weed known to man. Look at that shit."

Paul grabbed the bag, opened it, looked inside, and smelled it.

"I think we can call this deal *even*," Levon said. "Okay?"

Paul stuffed the bag in his pocket, scowling. "All right, man, all right."

As he and Mike walked into the restaurant to meet Albert, I let out an enormous sigh of relief. I heard Bloomfield saying to him, "See, I told you they were good guys. I told you they'd come through, right?"

WE HAD a couple of days off, and I think Bob did some writing, because a few days into October we were asked to go into the studio to record some new tunes. Bob and I might have run through one of them in a hotel room, but for the most part we did these songs cold.

After we had run through the first, "Can You Please Crawl Out Your Window?," I asked Bob if we could take a few minutes and let the engineer get a sound on everything, so that the boys and I could put together a more solid arrangement. But Bob just wanted to move forward. "I think we got it, let's record it. I got another song I'd like to get to." So we laid it down, playing too much and pushing too hard. Bob sounded good, and Levon and I had a pretty good little break section, but Richard and Garth were wailing when they should have been sailing. Still, we had a good time doing it. Next we launched into "I Don't Want to Be Your Partner" with a funky little vibe. (Later this would evolve into "I Wanna Be Your Lover.") The song was over before we could get a handle on it, but it had some cool words. Another tune that had terrific possibilities was one called "Freeze Out." I completely zoned out and played too many blues sevenths, which did not belong in the song. Bob recorded it later as "Visions of Johanna," and it turned out brilliant. There was one song idea, or at least a chord progression Bob had started with no vocals yet. I think Bob called it "#1." Garth played some beautiful little melodies and background on that, but we never came back to it.

Compared to session musicians, our studio inexperience showed that day in spades. Don't remember who the producer was for the session, and maybe there's a reason for that. Bob and his people mostly seemed to like "Can You Please Crawl Out Your Window?" and wanted to release it as the next single. Bobby Neuwirth didn't dig the song or our recording. When he said so, Bob lashed back at him, and things got heated. Some people were afraid to go against Bob's instincts, but if honesty was the bottom line, Neuwirth could play that card. I respected him for speaking his mind, even if I hoped he was wrong about the single. We were all too close to it to have a real perspective on the record, but deep down I sure didn't think it was the best the Hawks could do.

WE TOURED with Bob for the next two months, getting better all the time. Some of the shows were recorded, and back at the hotel we listened and learned. I heard things we could improve on, but we were definitely starting to find some amazing dynamics. Still, the audiences didn't seem to notice or care how much better we were getting. They came to these shows with their minds already made up. They booed, chanted, and hissed; sometimes they even charged the stage or threw things at us. I joked at the time that I learned how to play guitar without looking at my fingers because I was so busy dodging flying objects. It was harsh. We were in the midst of a rock 'n' roll revolution; either the audience was right, or we were right.

In the middle of November, we were booked for two nights at the beautiful Massey Hall in Toronto, built in 1894. What a way to return home—playing the classiest concert hall in town. All the guys were jazzed about seeing old friends and showing off a little. I took Bob over to my mother's house for one of her specialty meals but ended up eating both my portion and Bob's. He wasn't doing too much eating in those days. Could it be that those little truck-driver pills had found their way into Bobby's medicine chest? Or perhaps he was keeping a watchful eye on his figure. Bob said Mama Kosh was exactly how we'd described her: like a young Ma Barker, loving, loyal, and street savvy, taking no guff from anybody.

For our first night at Massey Hall, friends and family came out in droves to witness their native sons play the big time. We had gangsters and thieves, hustlers, tailors, cooks and contortionists, carnies and gamblers, you name it. Levon invited Freddy McNulty, our mentally challenged little friend, backstage before the show. We introduced him to blues giant John Lee Hooker, who was playing a club in town; Bob had invited him to stop by and say hello.

I said, "Freddy, you know John Lee's song, 'Boom boom boom boom, I'm gonna shoot you right down, right offa your feet, boom boom boom boom.'"

Freddy twirled around, did a few little dance steps, and murmured, "I'll knock you right down, I'll show the chicks some boom boom boom."

Levon and Bob cracked up. "John Lee, what do you think about taking Freddy here on the road?" I asked.

"I don't know what this cat's on," said John Lee, "but I knows he's far out."

The lights went down, and we took the stage in darkness and slammed into "Tombstone Blues." The most extreme booing and yelling erupted. Our friends and families were astonished at this reception and looked like they wanted to punch somebody. We had thought that in Toronto, our old hood, things would be different. We had bragged to Bob and Albert about Toronto, sure that it would be spectacular when we made our triumphant return. So we couldn't believe it when the crowd proved us wrong. It was hard to hide our disappointment.

The second night's show was just as bad, if not worse. We had our small rock-and-R&B contingent on our side, but the bulk of the crowd came from the dedicated folk scene in Toronto. A local music critic wrote a review scolding Bob for playing with a "third-rate Yonge Street band." Not second-rate: third-rate! You could hardly come up with a lower blow than that. At least we got to stop by Lou Myles's store while we were in town, and Bob picked up his two suits, which he wore for the rest of the tour. I had never seen Lou design anything like these before, and I have to say that both suits turned out fantastic and unique.

A dark wave passed over the Hawks on the trip to Toronto. Typically thick-skinned, we all felt hard hit from this particular rejection. Rick looked let down, as if an old friend had betrayed him. Richard wanted to put it all behind him and move on. Levon was completely pissed off. Only Garth seemed to understand why this was happening and chalked it up as a sign of the times.

But Toronto was my hometown, and I took it personally. The city felt small and insecure, like it would never be important enough. When we left town after those shows, I really didn't know if I would be coming back.

Anyway, New York City was the headquarters for what we were doing these days, and it felt like the center of the world. After staying at a few different Gotham hotels—the Albert, the Gramercy Park, the Chelsea—I secured a suite on the top floor of the Irving Hotel overlooking Gramercy Park, a small, lovely square of trees and flowers that required a key to enter.

For a while, whenever Bob was going to hear someone play, or even just hanging out, he called me to join him. His world revolved around art, poetry, and music, and the scene swirled with an almost atomic energy. Whether uptown or downtown, the streets were alive with music. I felt like I had a front-row seat for the cultural explosion that was changing the world.

My job in life at age twenty-two was to learn, to absorb the magic, and to have a real good time along the way. Bob brought me into his world with a generosity that made Albert Grossman and Bobby Neuwirth accept me—both of them were tough nuts but amazing people. We would go out to clubs, bars, meet up with people. We'd be at the Kettle of Fish regularly, and when we weren't downtown, we'd go to a place called Ondine, or the Scene, uptown. Bob was becoming a phenomenon, but he didn't live large. It was interior, all coming from within. And his girlfriend, Sara, had a daughter—she wasn't some silly rock 'n' roll girl. There was something completely outrageous about Bob and at the same time something quite grounded as well. We traded stories about our pasts, and though it had been a fairly short time that we'd really known each other, we already shared a unique experience on a musical battlefield; in the process we'd become like war buddies.

Every day it seemed that Bob's fame was growing exponentially. A lot more people were trying to get a piece of him. I'd never seen this kind of idolization—no one had, unless you'd been around someone like Elvis Presley in the fifties, or the Beatles. Even still, this was on a scale that felt unprecedented, and for some reason Bob insisted I have a front-row seat for it.

Levon didn't want to join me in these new experiences with Bob, which put me in a hard place. I knew he felt somewhat alienated. He was becoming uncomfortable with the "show biz" aspects of rock 'n' roll; he didn't even like people taking his photograph. The music, the people, the lifestyle, even the private Lodestar plane we traveled in bothered him. "I ain't that interested in touring in a Buddy Holly special," he'd tell me. "Sometime, if the weather's bad, that sucker could get blown right outta the sky."

Levon was like an older brother to me. He'd taught me a great deal about music and about life in our years together. But in New York that was a role he couldn't quite play anymore, and he withdrew. Bob was pushing forward and Levon was pulling back. I couldn't help being drawn to the positive energy.

Richard, Garth, and Rick were also caught up in this magical storm. They thought we had a job to do and were rolling with the punches. It was an extraordinary experience, overwhelming to the point of numbness. We had a plan: to ride this storm, see if it would take us to a higher place, do a smooth landing, and take it from there. Well, maybe that's not a plan. Maybe that's blindman's bluff.

ONE MORNING in November, Bob called me with a quiet tone in his voice.

"Hey, are you by yourself? Anybody with you?"

"No, why?"

"Can you do me a favor?"

"Sure, what's happening?" I said.

"Sara and I are going to get married," he said, "and we need a witness. You know, a witness when you sign the papers for when you get married."

"You mean a best man at your wedding?"

Bob laughed. "Well, I don't know about 'best man.' That's quite a commitment. Maybe 'good man' or 'very good man.' How would that be?"

I laughed. "Well, when's the big day?"

"Today, like in two hours. We're going to the courthouse. Can you make it?"

"Well, I'll have to take my best suit out of mothballs and get it pressed, but I'll meet you outside in two hours."

"Okay, but you don't need to tell anybody," he said. "Let's keep it quiet, you know what I mean?"

We drove over to Long Island, nobody saying much, like we were a little embarrassed. Sara looked beautiful, and Bob and I looked like immigrants trying to dress up for Labor Day. They said their vows, and it was kind of touching. There was a small reception afterward in a banquet room at the Algonquin Hotel, hosted by Albert and Sally Grossman. This day was important for Sara, who was with child and understandably wanted a grounded setting for raising a family. Neuwirth and the journalist Al Aronowitz came, and several friends drifted through as well. The whole thing was low-key but lovely and it felt right.

Before you could blink, we were back out on the road, finishing up this leg of the tour. Night after night, town after town, the same hostility rained down on us from the crowd. At Chicago's Arie Crown Theater, the crazy nature of the whole routine sank in for me: We come to a city, set up our equipment, and play a show. People throw stuff at us, hooting and trying to boo us off the stage, but we just play on. After it's over, we pack up our equipment, go on to the next town, set up, play the show, and get booed all over again. I thought to myself, *What a strange way to make a buck.*

"It's like a freak show," Richard said, "but that's what I like about it." Garth seemed more sanguine: "You get up in the morning and mow the lawn, or you get up on the stage and get booed. What's the difference?" Rick insisted he was digging it for what it was worth: an incredible life experience, unequaled in many ways. My feeling was if Bob could take it, then I could take it too. Now we had to show the world it was *truly* about the music.

After a show at the Coliseum in Washington, D.C., we had a few days off in New York to catch our breath. I liked being back at my pad at the Irving Hotel. Girls and friends floated by. I met a girl named Pam through John Hammond, and she understood this crazy life-style; she came and went like the wind, never once saying, "What about tomorrow?" I dug her, and we would lie in bed and watch great old movies and leave the world behind.

One night, must have been around ten o'clock, there was a knock on my door. It was Levon. He looked drawn and distant. We sat and both lit cigarettes. He undid his jacket, leaned in, and said, "I'm leav-ing tonight. I can't do this no more. I don't like it and I gotta go."

I knew he wasn't thrilled with our situation with Bob. I knew he wanted above all for the Hawks to do our own thing. But still I was stunned that he would up and quit.

"How can you leave? You can't leave your own band. This is an ex-traordinary opportunity. Why would you wanna pass it up?"

"Well, I'll tell you," Levon said, stubbing out his cigarette. "I don't like this damn music. I don't trust Albert Grossman and these people. And I don't wanna be around Bob Dylan and all these New York . . ." He stopped himself. "All this booing is some kind of bullshit game that I don't wanna be any part of."

"Come on, it's not about all that. It's about the music," I pressed. "And we're getting so good. Sometimes it feels like these songs reach such a height that they're going to explode in midair."

"I don't feel it," Levon responded, "and I don't wanna play drums for him or nobody."

"Bob sings the hell outta these songs, and he's been so stand-up for us," I said. "When people around are saying, 'Get rid of these guys, they're ruining your music,' he doesn't budge, he stands his ground. Let's finish up the tour and then we'll see what we want to do."

"Not with me." Levon shook his head. "I just can't do it."

At this point I realized how tough it must have been for him to come to this decision. And how committed he was. I backed off. "Where are you going to go? What are you going to do?"

"First I'm going to Arkansas, see everybody for a few days, then I think I'll go to New Orleans and see about getting a job working on an oil rig off the coast in the Gulf."

I didn't want to disrespect Levon's plans, but this sounded completely horrible to me. I could not imagine working on a damn oil rig in the Gulf—that sounded like a nightmare.

Bewildered and shaken, I said, "Whatever you gotta do, I'll back you up, you know that."

"You wanna walk me to the corner?" he asked. "I gotta catch a cab to the bus terminal."

"Of course." I threw on a coat. It was almost December and growing cold. "You have a reservation for a late-night sleeper or something?"

"No," Levon said, "I'm just gonna go to the bus depot and wait for the next one going my way."

While we walked to Third Avenue, I put my arm over his shoulder. He felt smaller and a bit fragile. I could hardly contain my sadness. This was killing me.

"You already told the boys you were heading out?"

"No, you tell them for me," Levon said. "And you can say I wish them all the best in the world." We reached the corner. He raised his hand and hailed a taxi. We hugged like it was hard to let go. I had a lump in my throat when Levon said, "Okay, Duke, I'll catch up with you a little further on down the road. You take care now."

I couldn't believe this was happening. We shook hands good-bye, and the taxi drove off. I walked back to the hotel with a tear in my eye and a pain in my heart. I felt broke down the middle. Maybe I should have seen it coming, but I probably didn't want to look. A soft rain started to fall, and for some unknown reason I started singing quietly to myself, "This train don't stop here no more, this train. This train is bound for glory, this train."

FIFTEEN

The next morning, I woke up feeling emotionally drained. I dragged myself out of bed, knowing I had to break the news to the guys. Garth and Richard were staying at the Irving, but Rick had been seeing a very sweet girl named Robin, who had a little apartment not far from Gramercy Park; he would often stay there when we were in New York. Levon had been going out with Robin's friend Bonnie. It had been a bit surprising, from my perspective, to see the two most "country" boys in the Hawks taking up with a couple of nice Jewish girls in New York City. I wondered if Levon had told Bonnie he was leaving.

When the guys arrived, they came up to my room. "Boys, I've got some really harsh news. Brother Levon has split. He said he couldn't continue like this—it didn't feel right, and he had to go. I tried to change his mind, but he wouldn't be swayed, he wouldn't hear it. He's gone. He asked me to pass it on, and said that he wishes us all the best."

A silence hung in the air. We all knew Levon wasn't overjoyed with the experience, but none of us had ever imagined him just taking off.

Then Rick spoke boldly with a chill in his voice. "Seems pretty weird to me, him just slipping off in the night, not saying good-bye, see ya later, go screw yourself, nothing."

"Hey, not everybody's cut out for a big, strange, unusual challenge," Richard said. "He hated it, I know. He just don't dig this music like we do, and I'm liking it more every day."

Garth stood up and paced a bit. "Isn't that something—he just up and left?" He added that it did seem like the audience's disapproval of our treatment of Bob's songs had really gotten to Levon. "I don't pay attention to that anymore, though. Just makes me want to play harder."

I was surprised that they didn't seem more distressed by the news. For me it was really tough. I couldn't fathom my best friend bailing on us like that. I felt forsaken and hurt inside in a way I didn't recognize.

Taking care of business seemed the best way to keep the whole thing from backing up on me. "We gotta find a drummer," I said. "I have to tell Bob, and we need to think of someone that can possibly take Levon's place." But even as I said it, I thought: no one can ever possibly take Levon's place in the Hawks. His unique voice and rhythmic feel were deeply embedded in our sound.

When I told Bob about it later that afternoon, I wasn't sure how he'd react—if he'd be pissed off, if he thought it would throw a monkey wrench into our touring schedule, or if he'd hold me responsible. When I first shared the news with him, he did look a bit confused, like he didn't exactly know how to take it. But then he started to laugh. "He's really going to Arkansas? What's Levon going to do there?"

We had only a couple days until our next concert, so Bob decided to call Bobby Gregg to fill in until we found someone to take over on drums for the rest of the tour. We didn't have much rehearsal time with him before heading to Seattle to kick off a West Coast run. Bobby caught on pretty fast and fit in the best he could, but for me it was like starting over.

FROM SEATTLE WE wound our way south to the Bay Area. A vibe was stirring in Berkeley and San Francisco—the Black Panthers, Oakland's Hells Angels, the Beat poets, and a burgeoning music scene that dovetailed a bit more with our musical direction. The audience even appeared a little more open and receptive to the electric thing.

One day Bob said he was going over to City Lights, Lawrence Ferlinghetti's bookstore in North Beach, and asked if I wanted to come along. I wasn't sure if I'd fit in. But I was getting used to going on

intriguing adventures with Bob, so I grabbed my coat. Allen Ginsberg had put this gathering together, and I had come to appreciate the
strong link between Bob and the Beat poets. Before Bob, nobody had
written songs overflowing with the kind of imagery he conjured; he
shared with these writers a kind of fearlessness when it came to pushing limits.

We arrived at City Lights and were met by the brilliant poets
Michael McClure and Allen Ginsberg. This get-together was a "moment," but I would come to learn that such moments are rarely recognized when they're happening. Seeing Allen and Michael and Bob
referring casually to different writers and poets made me think back
to my high-school days or the years with Ronnie, when even talking
about poetry was reason enough to get your ass kicked. That was all
changing now—even the heavyweight boxing champ, Muhammad
Ali, recited poetry, and rock 'n' roll was embracing it too. The shift
seemed overdue.

While we were standing outside the bookshop, a couple of photographers showed up and took some pictures of Bob and the poets.
I stepped to the side to get out of the frame, but they said, "No, get in
the shot." McClure and Ginsberg were such vivid characters, full of
life and proclaiming that huge changes were on the horizon. Bob's
presence seemed to lift their spirits even more, and as they all talked
their voices rose to a preacher's peak. "Politicians will crumble, and
the legalization of marijuana will rise across the land!" Ginsberg
added that in India, "for God's sake," parts of the culture looked at
smoking pot as a sacred experience.

When we played that night at San Francisco's Masonic Hall, the
poets brought several Hells Angels with them, making for a pretty
unusual coalition. After the show we were all invited to a big party at
someone's house. "Let's go," Bob said. "The rest of the guys will meet
us there."

We arrived at a packed gathering, and before long Ginsberg took us
aside. "A few of us are going upstairs for a little privacy to smoke some
Hells Angels weed." The rest of the band hadn't arrived yet, so we adjourned to a room upstairs and joined a circle of people seated on the

floor. Ginsberg played host and introduced Sonny Barger, head of the Hells Angels, Oakland chapter, along with Terry the Tramp. Barger was already a notorious biker of legend; he seemed like a sharp, cool, been-around-the-block outlaw. He didn't need to prove nothin'. Terry the Tramp looked like the perfect picture of a biker—big, raw, rugged, and ready for any shit that might go down.

About ten of us sat in the circle and Ginsberg brought out some weed and hallucinogens. Soon the room got so smoky from ciga-rettes and pot you could hardly see the person beside you, and things started getting gritty. Intoxicated sexual bravado turned to shouting. Laughing and madness settled on a room full of would-be pirates. As the smoke got thicker and the drinks got stronger, Ginsberg and his partner, Peter Orlovsky, suggested we all take our clothes off—saying something to the effect that "nakedness is pure freedom." One of the Angels started hollering and tearing off his jacket and shirt. I flashed a nervous look at Bob, but then I had an even more terrifying thought: *Oh, man, what if he* likes *this idea?*

Bob didn't blink. He started talking about something so elliptical and beside the point that everybody was trying to keep up with his train of thought; it killed any talk of "pure freedom."

Driving back to our hotel after the party, I said to Bob, "That got a little creepy back there," but he gestured like it was no big deal. I had thought I was pretty street savvy, but right then it felt like I was getting a lesson from an older brother in the "code of the road."

FOR THE NEXT few concerts in Southern California, we worked out of the classic Chateau Marmont Hotel in West Hollywood. Bob stayed in one of the newer, more spacious bungalows in the back. The producer Phil Spector sent over a spinet piano for him to use while he was in town, and I learned that Phil was interested in producing some songs with him. Word was, he thought Bob was a great songwriter but didn't care for the production on his records. I had a hard time imagining the two of them working together. Phil was very much into "the sound" and big production, and it seemed to me that Bob was more interested in capturing a song in a very direct and honest way. It was as if Phil—like the later Beatles and Beach Boys—was making "movies" with his music production, and Bob was more interested in the documentary, in purely nailing the live performance.

After we checked into the hotel, Bob invited some people over and asked me to bring some of my records to his bungalow. I headed over, and within minutes the doorbell rang. It was David Crosby of the Byrds, whom I hadn't met before, though I'd seen his band on a TV show. David was actually wearing the same outfit he wore on the show, a flat dark hat and short cape with a fancy shirt and boots—his own rock 'n' roll uniform. He bounced his skinny frame all over the bungalow with joy at seeing Bob.

David reached inside his pocket and pulled out a couple of the biggest joints I had ever seen, then lit one with a flamethrower lighter. David had brought an acetate of a new Byrds track, "Set You Free This Time," but didn't seem that thrilled with it. Instead he talked at length about the Beatles' "Nowhere Man" and "Norwegian Wood"—the album *Rubber Soul* had just come out, and David had clearly spent some time with it. Bob asked me to put on one of the records I'd brought, so I played "I've Been Trying" by the Impressions and "Tracks of My Tears" by Smokey Robinson. Crosby's huge joint had kicked in, and Bob and I got chills from these songs. David didn't react to them, though—his head was still filled with the Beatles.

After David left, Bob's friend Victor Maymudes dropped by. Victor was a warm, funny guy, very Los Angeles, and he came bearing an envelope that had been left at the front desk. Bob opened it and found a couple of photographs of us from outside the City Lights bookstore. He looked at the shots carefully.

"Why don't you let your hair grow?" he said to me. He looked back at the photo, then looked at me again. "Yeah, you should definitely grow your hair out."

"You mean like the Beatles or the Byrds?" I said. "With those cute little bangs and the whole bit?"

"No, not like the Beatles," Bob said, grinning. "Just let it grow."

Victor chimed in. "You know, it's healthier too. Tests have shown that long hair is better for your scalp, which means it's better for your whole body. I don't cut my hair anymore and I just feel better, inside and out."

"I don't know," I said. "A lot of the joints the Hawks played down south, if you had long hair, they'd kick your ass or shoot you. We were more into haircuts from the forties, like Tyrone Power or Gary Cooper. We hung out with a lot of gangsters and they thought if you had long hair, you were a fruit."

"Yeah, but it's a different time, man, look around," Victor said. "Bugsy Siegel ain't around no more. Let it grow, you'll feel better."

WE WERE BOOKED all over the Los Angeles area and down in San Diego. The concerts were going fairly smoothly with our fill-in drummer. Each night, whether the audience erupted in squalls of rejection or gave a slight sign of acceptance, we were doing our job. We showed up for every show ready for whatever the crowd's reaction might be. Here in California, it felt like we might be getting somewhere with our fight for musical independence. It wasn't just playing Bob Dylan's music with electricity that caused a revolt; it was how we played it: tough, aggressive, with raging dynamics that cleared the sweetness out of everything in sight.

While we were in LA, I met a girl through mutual friends who I thought was terrific. Her name was Ann Marshall. She was the daughter of the actor Herbert Marshall, and I think James Cagney was her uncle. We had a sweet connection, we were comfortable with each other, and she was special to me. When you're on the road, most of the girls you meet are brief encounters. Rock 'n' roll can callus the heart into believing shallow is less complicated and therefore better. The "code of the road" lifestyle is so nomadic that you can actually start to believe that *we're all better off letting a rolling stone roll.* But Ann was like a friend, and I never thought of her that way.

In LA people spoke of healthy food and fresh juice with an almost religious zeal. Just to counteract that, photographer Barry Feinstein took Albert Grossman and me to a killer hot dog stand. We smoked a joint on the way over, and Albert found these particular dogs heavenly. Just one completely satisfied me, but he doubled down and got one more to go.

We took a walk to check out a couple of stores along Sunset Boulevard that sold hippie clothes and paraphernalia—floppy hats, fringe vests, American Indian jewelry, and colored lava lamps that made one want to partake in some Timothy Leary–type exploration. We laughed our way from store to store. Albert had a wicked sense of humor and was open to whatever madness might roll his way. He looked somewhere between a jolly Benjamin Franklin and an intimidating bear. On our way back to the hotel, we crossed the street, Albert walking ahead of Barry and me through a red light, in typical New York City jaywalk style. From out of nowhere a motorcycle cop pulled up fast, deliberately cutting him off. Now, you have to picture Albert: six feet tall, shoulder-length salt-and-pepper hair, wire-rimmed glasses, intimidating jowls, chest stuck out with arrogance. The policeman scowled at him.

"Let me see your ID," he ordered. "You just crossed against a red light."

Albert handed over his driver's license. "I'm here from New York, where we don't have these kind of rules."

The cop looked at the license and looked at Albert. "Okay, what year were you born? When's your birth date?"

"That was a long time ago," Albert said. "I don't remember."

The cop looked agitated. "Really now, what color are your eyes?"

Albert shook his head. "I have no idea."

The cop moved a step closer. "You don't know what color your eyes are?"

"I don't stand in front of the mirror studying the color of my eyes like some people," Albert shot back. "If you need to give me a ticket for crossing the street or whatever law I've broken, please do. I'm a very busy person."

I had to turn away, laughing to myself.

"I'll get to that," the cop said. "What do you do? What is your work?"

Albert proudly answered, "I prefer not to work, but I have my own bodybuilding business."

The cop looked at Albert's protruding gut and realized he was being put on. He looked at Barry and me, then looked back at Albert, as if he couldn't quite figure out what was up.

"You broke the law," he said, "and I'm going to write you a ticket. In this part of the country, you walk on a green light and stop on a red. Do you understand that?"

"Yes, and thank you for explaining that so profoundly." Albert smirked.

The cop looked at him with venom in his eyes as he wrote the ticket. Albert took it from him, and I felt a sense of relief when he simply put it in his pocket and didn't tear it up. It was a hilarious exchange, but it reflected something that was shifting in the relationship between the counterculture and law enforcement.

WE FINISHED THIS leg of the tour a few days before Christmas and got back on the Lodestar, headed for New York. About an hour into the flight, Rick pulled out a perfectly rolled joint and lit up. We'd always smoked cigarettes on the plane, so no one thought anything of it. He passed me the joint, grinned, and said it was a gift from the Byrds. I took a hit and passed it around. Suddenly Tony, our chief pilot, came storming out of the cockpit waving his arms. "Put that out right now! Are you nuts? The air circulates in airplanes and goes right up front where it could affect the copilot and me. Don't ever do that again!"

Richard stubbed it out and apologized. Bill Avis assured Tony this would never happen again, even though Bill's eyes were more blood-shot than any of ours.

BOB'S 1966 TOURING schedule gave us a few weeks over the holidays to find a new drummer, visit our families, and digest what we had learned from the Dylan experience. Our journey to the outer limits had so far been unpredictable and challenging.

When we got back to New York, Bob was now staying at the Chelsea Hotel on 23rd Street part-time while sorting out his next residence. I hung out with him there sometimes, watching him pound away on his typewriter into the night. Bob wasn't someone who went off into a corner to seclude himself during his creative process. He did it right where he stood, just picked up a guitar or sat down at the typewriter right in front of you. Lyrics came flying out of that machine; it was a feat to witness. Whatever else might be going on around him didn't matter. The radio could be playing, television on, someone on the phone—Bob never looked up, just kept typing away.

During our break I would drag Richard or Rick to movies that sparked my curiosity. The past year, 1965, had been a boon for a movie lover like me, with the release of Jean-Luc Godard's *Alphaville*. I still hadn't gotten over his film *Contempt*, where I fell madly in love with Brigitte Bardot. But now it was all about Catherine Deneuve in Roman Polanski's *Repulsion*, and the fascinating Julie Christie in John Schlesinger's *Darling*. I loved these movies. They were art films, okay, so bring on the art, but oh my soul, were these women beautiful.

In early January, Sara gave birth to her first child with Bob, a baby boy they named Jesse. He was a cute little devil, and together with Sara's daughter Maria they made for a real pretty family picture. Even in the context of our crazy rock 'n' roll lifestyle, Bob seemed like a natural father. He played it quite cool but I could tell he was a proud papa.

Meanwhile the Hawks held a meeting to discuss new drummer possibilities. We debated the merits of all kinds of candidates, from guys in bands we knew down south to people we had played with from Canada. There was a drummer we liked from Buffalo, and then when we asked ourselves who Levon would choose, we realized it was the same guy: Sandy Konikoff. So we got in touch and asked him to come try out for the job. He was astonished that Levon had left and was thrilled to be considered.

Bob had booked Columbia Studios in New York to do some recording in January. We thought it would be a good chance to try out some drummers at the same time. When Sandy Konikoff showed up, the Hawks were a bit confused by his appearance. He looked *very* different from the last time we'd laid eyes on him. Sandy said he'd been "studying drums seriously" for the last year, but "studying drums seriously" meant one thing: jazz. And all that jazz had evidently rubbed off on the way Sandy carried himself, spoke, and dressed. He now wore a beret, black pants, black turtleneck, and beige overcoat. He looked like a beatnik from central casting. I introduced Sandy to Bob and could see the mismatch immediately. Sandy even tuned his small-combo drum set in a tight, jazzy sort of style. We played through two or three songs from our tour set list and Sandy tried a couple different approaches. Trying to be helpful, I went over to him between songs and confided: "Rule number one, don't swing. Never swing. Flighty fills and jazzy grooves don't work here. All that you've been studying in your music school needs to be left at home."

After a couple of run-throughs, Bob was ready to record. We rambled though a song called "She's Your Lover Now." Then another new tune, "Tell Me, Momma," with its salty punch line—"Baby, tell me, what's wrong with you *this time*?"

Sandy needed to quickly learn the arrangements of the songs we would play on tour. So he set up his drums in his room at the Irving Hotel and practiced around the clock. My room was two floors above Sandy's and I could hear him pounding away day and night. The hotel manager was outraged that anyone could be so insane as to be beating on drums in a hotel room. Sandy asked the manager if it was all right to practice during the day, explaining that it was really important for him to go over the music to get the job. The hotel manager replied, "You need to leave before I call the police."

At the beginning of February 1966, we hit the road again with Sandy on drums, starting in Louisville, Kentucky. We started using "Tell Me, Momma" as an opener, which meant not only were we going into hostile territory for our electric part of the show, but we were also starting the set with a funky, unfamiliar, aggressive, and not particularly melodic tune. Maybe it was a touch perverse, but I enjoyed coming out with a signpost song that said, *I don't need you to love me, I'm just going to play my damn music and maybe you'll dig it.*

Bob slipped off to Nashville for a few days at the request of his producer, Bob Johnston, and came back with a few songs that he had cut down there, beautiful new tunes that rang out with the precise arrangements and skilled musicianship of the Nashville studio cats. Bob seemed particularly proud of "Sad-Eyed Lady of the Lowlands." I think it might've been the longest song I'd ever heard, and it reminded me of his wife, Sara, though not completely. I loved the fictional, unobvious, personal yet impersonal side of Bob's writing.

As the tour rolled on, Sandy played reasonably well, but his persona still wasn't clicking for Bob. One day we were trying out some new songs at a sound check, and on the downbeat of a chorus in "One Too Many Mornings," Sandy did a backhanded crash on a cymbal in a jazzy way. Bob stopped the song abruptly. "Don't do that. Don't ever do that." The message was clear: We're playing rock 'n' roll here. Don't get schmazzy on me. Sandy turned red with embarrassment, but Bob was right: the drumming had to be solid and powerful, not flighty and groovy.

When we had a few days off, I moved from the Irving into a little suite at the Chelsea Hotel. This joint had a real aura to it, and all the legendary stories felt soaked into the wallpaper: Arthur Miller living there after he split with Marilyn Monroe; William Burroughs and Arthur C. Clarke pounding away at their respective masterpieces, *Naked Lunch* and *2001: A Space Odyssey*; Dylan Thomas writing and dying there at the age of thirty-nine.

Richard shared the suite with me. By this time Rick had moved in with his girlfriend, Robin, and Garth was back and forth a lot from London, Ontario, visiting old friends, which left Richard and me hanging loose. Richard was so easygoing, the perfect roommate, game for anything. Whatever I suggested we do—see a movie, catch a show—I'd ask Richard to come and the answer was always yes, and we always had a blast. Plus, I could talk to Richard about the big dream—getting a place where we could play and write, and where we could invent the sound, the music, we were meant to make. I could talk to Rick or Garth about it and they'd be excited too, but with Richard it was something more. Talking to him made the dream seem real.

Just down the hall at the Chelsea was a girl named Edie Sedgwick, a friend of Bobby Neuwirth's. She looked unique and gorgeous, had a starlike personality, and came from a wealthy socialite family in Santa Barbara, California. Edie and Bobby Neuwirth had some kind of a falling-out, and she came by my suite one day, ragging on him for his obnoxious behavior and asking if she could hang out for a while. I checked with Neuwirth to see if he was cool, but he acted indifferent and didn't want to talk about it.

Some nights I would go to Max's Kansas City and Edie would tag along. We'd have a bite to eat and hook up with some friends. She knew the members of the Velvet Underground and Andy Warhol. Andy adored Edie and always seemed to want her around. He was filming a series he'd conceived for her. Though she loved the attention he showered upon her, she sometimes felt she needed to escape.

Later one evening, the Velvets played a set and I couldn't take my eyes off a stunning, ghostly singer they had performing with them. Her name was Nico and I asked Edie to introduce me. After they finished their set, Nico came to sit with us. Edie took her hand. "I want you to meet someone really special and very, very talented. This is Robbie. He has a band called the Hawks that plays with Bobby Dylan."

Nico shook my hand, looked me over, and then whispered in Edie's ear. *All right!* I thought, *This is looking good.* We spoke briefly about her background in music, which struck me as minimal and a little vague. *Who cares, she looks enchanting.* But then Nico excused herself, got up, and went to say hello to some people at another table. "What happened to the angel in a white suit that I thought I was putting a move on?" I asked Edie.

She laughed and put her hands over her mouth. "By the way I passionately spoke of you, she thinks I'm in love with you. Sorry."

The Velvets played another set while Andy stood and applauded. One of the guys in the group, by the name of Lou Reed, had a strong street attitude to his vocals. No acrobatics, just straight grit. I liked a couple of the songs, but they had a bit of that "look, we got guitars for Christmas" approach. They didn't look new, but they sounded very new.

Before the night had gone too far, Edie grabbed my arm. "Can we go? I have a doctor's appointment early tomorrow," she said. "You should come with me: this is something you're really going to like a lot." When we got up to leave, Andy looked very disappointed and begged her to stay. She gave everybody a *La Dolce Vita* kiss good-bye, and we went back to my suite at the Chelsea for a little good-night puff on the hash pipe. Then she kissed me, thanked me for a beautiful night, and went to her room.

Ten minutes later there was a tapping on my door. I was half undressed and threw my shirt on to answer it. It was Edie in a change of clothes.

"I forgot something," she said.

I looked around. "Oh, what?"

"You. Do you want to come sleep in my room, or should I stay here? I don't want to be alone. You don't mind, do you?"

"Of course not," I said. "We'll stay here. You don't have to be alone."

In the morning Edie asked me again to join her at the doctor's office. On the way there we stopped at a drug store and she cashed a check, which she told me she did every day. I assumed it was from a trust fund. We caught a cab to the doctor's office, and as we were walking in, Robert Kennedy was walking out, his eyes pointed straight ahead like he was late and didn't want to be talked to.

When the nurse called Edie's name, she took my hand and pulled me to join her in the exam room. After a moment Dr. Max Jacobson came in, overjoyed to see Edie. "This is my friend Robbie," she told him. "He's been working so much that he's run down and needs some vitamins too. Please, just put it on my account."

"Dr. Feelgood," as he was known in some circles, gave Edie an injection of vitamin B_{12}. Her response was nearly instantaneous. "I feel better already."

Then he gave me a shot and a warm sensation ran through my body. Within moments I felt ready to take on the world. We left and I said, "I've never had a B_{12} shot before. You're right, it's quite a feeling." I wondered if Bobby Kennedy had gotten the same shot.

Edie winked at me. "They call it B_{12}, but it's a lot more than B_{12}, I can tell you that."

THE POET Gregory Corso was staying at the Chelsea too, and one day he told me about a bookshop on 47th Street called the Gotham Book Mart. Thanks to my uncle Natie, I knew that block: it was the center of the diamond district, with wall-to-wall diamond stores on both sides of the street and black-coated Orthodox Jewish men bustling about with briefcases handcuffed to their wrists. It did seem like an unusual place for a bookshop.

I went inside and was met by a guy who looked a bit disheveled, and you could tell by his glasses he read way too much. But he knew where to find whatever I asked for, and when he didn't, he'd call over to an older lady named Fanny who seemed to have a sixth sense for which pile of books it was buried in. Corso had told me this was the best place to buy poetry books, but as I browsed I noticed books of scripts too—French new-wave films, Italian stuff, Bergman. It intrigued me. When you've seen Fellini's 8½, you can't help but wonder how it all came together. And now—voilà!—here was the script. I bought the Fellini, and Truffaut's *400 Blows*, and more and more each time I went back.

Going through screenplays was a whole other kind of reading. It pulled back the curtain on how the moviemakers had made their decisions. To see what Bergman wrote, the descriptiveness in his writing, the dialogue, the difference between the page and the film, and the extraordinary contribution of the cinematography, the music, what the actors contributed—it really brought the movies to life in a new way. But what really came into focus for me was the storytelling. You didn't have to move straight forward, A to B to C. Storytelling could be like another way of hearing music, another way of mixing characters together and looking for the unexpected. It was freeing.

THE PHOTOGRAPHER Jerry Schatzberg had done a shoot with Bob and for a while became a regular part of the gang. He could take great candid pictures very discreetly or in a studio with full-on lights and production. I liked the way Jerry melted into the scene, doing his thing without too much noise. Bob and I went over to Jerry's studio to check out some shots he'd taken for the new LP Bob was working on, which would be a double album.

Jerry projected a bunch of slides he'd shot of Bob onto a white wall. He gave a running commentary with each photo. "Oh, there's a nice one. That's too dark. That's got nice composition but it's out of focus."

"Wait, go back," Bob said. "I like that slightly blurry one."

Jerry flipped back to it and laughed. "It looks like I don't know how to focus my camera, but it is a cool shot."

"I like it. Maybe that would be good for the cover," Bob said.

"We can crop it here," said Jerry, pointing to the middle of the shot. "Or block out the sides to make it fit the album format."

"Since it's going to be a double album," I offered, "why not print it sideways, the whole length of the front and back cover?" They thought about it and agreed it would be unique.

At Ondine with Jerry and Bobby Neuwirth, Bob told me he was going back to Nashville to finish his new record. "This time, you should come," he told me. "It's great down there." I mentioned I had been to Nashville with Ronnie Hawkins and found "they don't take well to outsiders." I asked if the other Hawks were coming, but Bob said it would be just me and Al Kooper. The studio was already booked, and we'd head there right after a mid-March show in Florida.

"Okay," I said, "but I'm telling you—they don't take kindly to strangers round those parts."

Bob lit a cigarette. "I'm a stranger down there, and they treated me just fine."

Bob and I had adjoining rooms at our hotel in Nashville, and I could hear his typewriter clacking away nearly all night. Al Kooper and I hung out a bit while Bob worked on song ideas. Al was a very humble guy, and said that Garth was a fantastic keyboard player. He thought the only reason Bob brought him was because nobody else would play such simple organ parts.

The next day, when we got to the Columbia studio, the musicians were already at their positions. You could see they had their system and everything was in order, microphones set, amplifiers baffled for sound separation. Bob Johnston, the producer, had this Nashville thing down, but I was a little suspicious of the "music factory" concept—the idea of a formula that was applied to most artists who passed through.

All the musicians greeted Bob like it was old home week. Al Kooper and I introduced ourselves, and although everybody was warm and inviting, you could tell the Nashville guys were hoping we were roadies. But as we were getting settled, I heard Bob Johnston telling the musicians that Al Kooper had come up with some catchy organ parts on Bob's last album. "And Robbie there," he added, "is a hell of a guitar player. He plays with the Hawks, the band that's backing Bob on tour."

Al and I sat out the first song, and I soon had a whole new appreciation for how the "new Nashville" studio scene felt. This crew was quick to come up with ideas and arrangements and to reset the baffles between them while Bob rewrote words on a music stand in the middle of the room. I really liked the way the different musicians passed around suggestions and ideas to one another, with Bob Johnston being the perfect filter.

The drummer Kenny Buttrey was very instrumental in helping to shape the arrangements. Joe South played bass or guitar, whatever was needed, and didn't seem too bothered by anything you put in front of him. His guitar work particularly caught my attention. They brought in a terrific piano player, "Pig" Robbins, who instinctively knew where and what to play. He was blind, and everybody sensed that he could hear with greater precision than any of us. Jerry Kennedy and Wayne Moss were coming up with beautiful guitar parts right and left. Henry Strzelecki was probably the main bass player, but it was hard to tell, they changed up so quickly and frequently.

While I was sitting in the control room, Bob said over the microphone, "Robbie, why don't you come play on this next one?" The studio went quiet and Johnston threw me a look that said, *Good luck, kid. Welcome to the lion's den.* They showed me where to set up and loaned me an amp. There was definitely a chill in the room as I plugged in and tuned up. It almost felt like my playing on a track might throw off their whole system.

I had no idea what song we were going to do, but I was at the starting gate and feeling restless. Bob stopped writing, looked up, and said, "Okay." The engineer asked what the name of this tune was. Bob answered, "Let's call it 'Five Believers' for now." We ran through a couple of verses, and then Charlie McCoy grabbed a harmonica and played a Roy Orbison "Candy Man" kind of lick and we kicked it off. The song broke meter in an interesting way, and Bob and I wailed like we were at a blues bar in Mississippi. By the time we'd finished the tune, the mood in the studio had completely changed. My extreme bending and quivering of notes wasn't in any of these guys' arsenals, so I wasn't taking anybody's job. They all came over and shook my hand after the playback. Bob Johnston said to the other musicians, "I told ya this cat could play! So what are you calling this song, Bob? 'Five Believers'?"

I said with a bit of flair, "*Obviously*, 'Five Believers'!"

Bob laughed, "Yeah, that's good—'Obviously Five Believers.'"

By the time we cut "Leopard-Skin Pill-Box Hat," I was settled in and had a blast tearing that one up. Sometimes it was hard to concentrate on playing while hearing the outrageous words Bob kept belting out. The images in the song were hilarious, which made me want to play even looser. By now, Kenny Buttrey and the boys were making me feel part of the gang. It felt good breaking down these barriers, kind of like the shows we were doing, steadily up against the odds and making our own rules.

DURING OUR NEXT TRIP to California for a run of shows, Bob and I stayed at a house called the Castle in the Los Feliz neighborhood of Los Angeles. It was a big, classic, Spanish-style house with a huge window that offered a view for miles, smog permitting. One fascinating thing about this place was that it sat right across the street from Ennis House, the classic Frank Lloyd Wright building that had been home to Bela Lugosi, the original Dracula in movies. He had a reputation for being a morphine addict, and you could imagine him holed up in this spooky fortress of a house for weeks at a time, peeking out the long, narrow windows to scan for police or intruders.

After getting settled in a downstairs bedroom that opened onto the garden, I went over to the Hyatt Hotel on Sunset, where the other guys were staying. We'd had word that Levon might be out in LA, and Richard asked me if I'd heard from him. I'd tried calling him the day before and again that morning, but no answer.

"If he wants to see us, he'll get in touch," Rick interjected. "Otherwise, I say leave it alone. Maybe he's not in a very social place right now."

Jim McGuinn of the Byrds came by to visit Bob and play a new track his group had just recorded called "Eight Miles High," which would be released as a single the next week. You could tell he was excited about it, and he certainly stirred up my curiosity with his space-age description of the song. He took off his little rectangle-frame shades, wiped them with his shirt, and put the disc on the record player. He was right—it was spacey, quite a departure from their earlier folk-rock sound. Bob didn't seem overly impressed.

"How'd you come up with that?" he asked Jim.

"Been listening to a lot of Coltrane. Trying to interpret that in my own way on the twelve-string guitar."

"Why?"

"I don't know," Jim answered. "Probably because I like it. Don't you like John Coltrane?"

Bob laughed. "Sure, but I don't try to copy his stuff."

Jim smiled. "Well, maybe you should. It's pretty good."

It wasn't uncommon at the Castle that over breakfast someone would offer you some grass or a hit of acid. I had tried LSD a couple times before and had some mind-opening experiences. We had a couple days off, and Rick and I thought, *What the hell, it caps breakfast off quite nicely.* We spent the morning playing a little music, looking at photographs, tripping and laughing. Later in the afternoon, Victor Maymudes, who had joined up with us as Bob's road manager, came out to the garden and asked me if I wanted to take a drive to the airport with him to pick up some equipment. I wasn't that keen to be tripping out in traffic, but Victor talked me into it.

As we drove along, the warm wind blowing in my face was a glorious sensation. The scenery going by started bending and weaving impressionistically. When we arrived at the airport, Victor drove to the cargo area where deliveries were picked up and found a parking spot right in front, where trucks were coming and going.

"Wait here," Victor said. "I'll go grab the packages."

It felt like I was sitting there for quite a while, but I couldn't be sure if it was five minutes or fifty. I looked over at some large containers being hoisted in and men carrying them to vehicles—seemed like quite a production. I stared and stared until suddenly I realized: these containers held the bodies of soldiers that were being shipped back from the war in Vietnam. I broke into a sweat, closed my eyes, and cringed and withered in the car seat.

As Victor climbed back into the car, I pointed to what I had witnessed. Stunned, he said, "Holy shit! I'm sorry, man, this is horrible." We peeled out of the lot. That night I reached out to my friend Ann Marshall for comfort. We both hated the idea of the war, and seeing the returning bodies had torn my guts out. We fell asleep in each other's arms.

WE HAD KNOWN it was going to come to this, but now it was upon us: Sandy Konikoff couldn't find his footing as a drummer for the Hawks. It had never really worked for Bob, and now we knew there was going to be a change. Sandy could feel it coming too and took comfort that Levon, one of his heroes, hadn't found his groove either.

Bob had seen a drummer from Texas playing with Johnny Rivers who he thought might fill the bill. We got together with Mickey Jones at Columbia Studios in Hollywood and played late into the night. Mickey was sturdy and powerful and had a right foot on the kick drum that could knock the lights out. It was hard filling Levon's shoes, a fact Mickey was well aware of. He could certainly play drums with us for the upcoming tour, but he knew he was a gun for hire. Eventually we embraced Mickey with open arms. Garth especially helped make him feel comfortable, and Garth being such a loner made that twice as surprising to see.

In the meantime, Levon had finally gotten in touch with us, and a get-together had been arranged. I couldn't wait to hear what he had going on out here in the City of Angels. The Hawks, including Sandy, caught up with Levon, and it was just like old times. I told him about some of our crazy adventures on tour and our new digs in New York City. Levon said that he and our friend Kirby Pennick had worked on an oil rig off the coast of New Orleans for a while, but they hadn't found it all that appealing. I thought, *I could have saved you boys some time on that one.*

As great as it was to see Levon, something had changed for the rest of us Hawks. Experience had opened our eyes. We had always been responsible with our work, but this advanced touring schedule called for a higher level of focus, being on our game at all times. And it showed on our faces.

The girl Levon had been seeing in New York, Bonnie, had rented a place in Hollywood and they were living together. Both of them looked tired and ghostly. I couldn't put my finger on it at first, but soon it became obvious: Levon was getting into some serious drug experimentation. Richard said he thought it was a shame to see Levon not really playing drums and wasting away. We all took pills here and there, but this was a whole other program, and it sure looked like it was taking a toll.

VICTOR MAYMUDES ASKED us to join him for a little spiritual getaway in Taos, New Mexico. I would've liked to go since it was part of Indian country, but Bob and I had things to do in LA. People from both the music and movie worlds of Los Angeles were continuously coming and going. Bob took me on a lot of his ventures and rendezvous, and he couldn't have had a more game comrade-in-arms.

We started hanging out with a savvy and gorgeous young actress named Pat Quinn, rumored to be Marlon Brando's girlfriend. She had dark hair and intense eyes, and her loose spirit gave the impression that you couldn't really cage this night bird. Pat was a few years older than me and gave off a vibe like she could handle herself and take care of you too. Bob invited her to accompany us on some of our rounds to clubs and get-togethers, and she fit right in. She knew the way in the front door and the way out the back.

One day Pat asked if Bob and I would like to go say hello to Marlon Brando, who was shooting a movie in town. So a couple of days later we went with Pat over to the set where they were shooting *The Appaloosa*. Pat took us through the guards and the gates with ease to where Brando was shooting a scene, and we were escorted up near the camera to watch.

"All quiet, okay, here we go," a man called through a megaphone. The director waited a moment, stood up from his chair, and yelled, "Action!" I had never been on a movie set before, and the whole scenario felt intoxicating. Marlon took a few steps, peeled off some dialogue, and patted a horse on the neck before the director yelled, "Cut!" Marlon's presence on the set was mesmerizing. After the scene ended, Pat waved to him and he started heading our way, but just then the film's producer approached him.

"Marlon," he moaned, "you act like you're bored in these scenes, like you don't mean a word you're saying. The director, the other actors, nobody feels that you're really committed. We can't have this."

Brando kept walking. "Who's saying these things?" he asked. "I want to know who's saying these things about me." Then he stopped and glared at the producer. "Look at you, the lenses of your glasses are all dusty. How do you even know you're talking to me?" The producer took off his glasses, shook his head, and walked away.

Pat threw her arms around Marlon's neck as he smiled. "You see what I have to deal with? People think this job is easy."

Pat laughed. "I know, baby, I know how hard you work. Here, I want you to meet Bob Dylan, and this is his guitar player, Robbie Robertson." Marlon gave us solid handshakes and invited us to join him in his trailer. As Pat led the way, Marlon admired her from behind, closing his eyes for half a second, as if to say, *God has surely blessed me . . .*

Inside the trailer I sat on the couch, Pat sat beside me. Bob kept standing, inquiring about the movie. Marlon pointed to the couch where Pat and I were sitting. "That's where I've been giving Anjanette Comer"—the lead actress in the movie—"massages for her back. She has a lot of tension. I'm trying to loosen her up." He smiled, then asked us if we wanted drinks. "What would you like to drink?" he asked Bob.

"Tea, some hot tea with honey and lemon."

"Nothing for me," Pat said.

I said, "I'll have a Coke, if you've got one." He looked at me and looked at Pat. Then he walked to a small fridge and took out a bottle of Coca-Cola, stood right in front of me, and opened the bottle with his back teeth. He stared deeply at Pat as he handed it to me. "I'll get the tea for Bob," Pat said. "Be right back."

What a charge, seeing Brando standing there in his cowboy costume, makeup on his face and hands. He asked Bob about writing songs and remarked that he'd always loved music and wished he had really devoted the time to learn to play guitar or piano well. He looked at my hands wrapped around the Coke bottle. "You play guitar?" I nodded. "Yeah, I wish I had learned properly. I can play a couple of chords or I can play 'Three Blind Mice,' but I'm mostly stuck pounding away on my bongo drums."

After we'd said good-bye to Brando and made our way off the set, I thanked Pat for arranging the meeting and confessed, "My jaw dropped when he opened that Coke with his teeth."

She laughed. "Yeah, he chipped a tooth doing that. But he don't care."

Pat had a nice little place in the Hollywood Hills where friends dropped by day or night. She invited Marlon and his buddy Wally Cox over one evening while Bob, Richard, Rick, and I were visiting. Wally, who had played the four-eyed, pickleberry type Mr. Peepers on TV for years, was the last person you would think of as Brando's running buddy, but he turned out to be cool and funny, even a bit salty. I chatted with him off and on while Bob and Marlon had a meeting of the minds, but I spent most of the time talking with Pat. I didn't know the terms of her relationship with Marlon and didn't want to get in the middle, but Pat's open, free-spirited personality didn't exactly help establish any boundaries. So I asked straight up what her situation was. She kissed me on the cheek and said, "I do what I want and he does what he wants. We are lovers, not prisoners."

A few nights later I was over at Pat's place with a couple of her friends when Marlon and Wally stopped by. When Marlon saw me there again, a look crossed his face that did not square with the description Pat had painted for me of their open-minded relationship. I tried to distance myself from Pat in the room, so as not to give Marlon the wrong impression. Hell, this was still the hot-tempered Stanley Kowalski from *A Streetcar Named Desire*.

All of a sudden Marlon said, "Hey, people, we're going to play a game. Come here, gather round this table."

I sat beside Wally, who whispered, "He likes games and mostly makes them up as he goes along. Hardly anybody ever gets killed." Pat sat beside Marlon across the table and looked at me with sympathetic eyes, as if she had gotten me into something I really didn't need.

"Okay," Marlon began, "if the . . . one, two . . . seven of us were lost at sea and then stranded on a small island, which of us would survive the longest? Simply, which one of us would outlive the rest?"

One person offered that they always carried a small Swiss Army knife, which was all you needed to survive. Someone else said they grew up fishing with their father, and if you could fish, you'd never starve. When my turn came, I mentioned my native heritage and said, "As a kid, I was taught how to make fire. I know how to make flames from sticks and stones, and as we know from human evolution, the key to life is fire."

"It can also be the key to death," Wally joked.

Pat said she was a great tree climber; even as a child, she never saw a tree she couldn't climb, so if there were any animals on this island, they couldn't catch her. Then Marlon looked around the table with his chin raised, like Fletcher Christian in *Mutiny on the Bounty*. "Well, you're all wrong, and you could never survive beyond me." He looked over at me. "You know why?"

I gently shook my head no.

Marlon rubbed his chin slowly with his thumb. "I'll tell you why. Because I'm the only one here who wouldn't feel bad about eating the rest of you."

Later, when I told Richard, Garth, and Rick about my Brando experiences, they fell apart laughing and pointed out that my hanging with Pat might not be the healthiest of pastimes. I related the story to Bob, and he said, "Yeah, Marlon's coming to the concert Sunday night." Bob had arranged for Marlon and his friends to come to our Santa Monica show. They were seated in the front row, and while we were playing, I couldn't help every once in a while glancing down at Brando sitting dead center, looking on bemused, as if studying lions devouring Christians. It was an odd feeling—as if he was the only one in the audience.

When they came backstage after the show to say hello, Bob asked Marlon right away what he thought. Marlon said he liked being able to hear the words clearly in the first part, the acoustic set. Then he grew more animated and said, "When I was a young man, about fifteen years old, one day I stood just a few feet away from a railroad track as a long freight train went roaring by. I made myself just stand there until it passed. That was the loudest thing I have ever witnessed, until tonight."

"Nah," said Bob. "This was an easy night. We usually play much harder than this."

TO CELEBRATE the end of the North American tour, we had a little party for the crew who wouldn't be going overseas with us, which included the Lodestar pilots who had flown us to every gig. About two or three hours into the party, our chief pilot, Tony, and his copilot came over to wish us good luck on the next leg of the tour. Tony shook our hands with a warm, teary smile on his face. He took a sip from his drink and pointed his finger at me and said, "Plenfo wifguy omsee mimfer sliba grevabebe."

"Sorry, Tony, I didn't catch that," I said.

He slapped himself on the cheek and grinned. "Imen lofla togar."

The copilot stepped in and said, "I think what he's trying to say is he's sorry for getting upset with you guys for smoking that stuff on the plane." I looked at Tony and he nodded his head in agreement. He was completely smashed and nearly tipped over. Rick grabbed him, held him up, and said, "Tony, I can't tell you how happy I am that you saved this debauchery till the end of the tour."

At the beginning of April, Bob, Albert Grossman, and I listened to a test pressing of Bob's new album, which he had named *Blonde on Blonde*. I told them that as much as I had thought "Visions of Johanna" would be my favorite song on the record, I was now leaning toward "Just Like a Woman."

Albert agreed. "There are so many artists that could do a great cover of that song."

"Like who?" Bob asked.

"I could hear Frank Sinatra doing it," Albert said gleefully.

I said, "You know who could sing the hell out of this and is my favorite singer in the world right now? Otis Redding." Bob and Albert both lit up. "You could also give it to Richie Havens," I added. "He'd do a beautiful job, but maybe get it to Otis first."

It just so happened that the night before we were scheduled to leave for Hawaii to kick off a new tour, Otis was playing the Whisky a Go Go nightclub on Sunset Boulevard. Victor made arrangements for us to catch his show. I hadn't seen Otis perform since the Buffalo show I went to with Levon, Connie B., and Mama Kosh. This time we were going to get to meet Otis as well. At around ten he took the stage and sang for an hour, and his performance knocked me out. After the show we hooked up with Otis and his manager, Phil Walden. Otis looked ageless—he could have been twenty-one or forty-one. He had a deep warmth in his eyes, and that voice—it had a shimmer to it even when he was just talking.

Bob played the acetate of "Just Like a Woman" and they absolutely loved it. Otis quietly sang, "and she aches . . . just like a woman." He broke into laughter and said, "Man, I dig that song!" I sat with Phil Walden for a few minutes talking about all kinds of music. "Who came up with the idea for Otis to do this song?" Phil asked.

I just winked at him and he hugged my shoulder.

Later I heard Otis went into the studio to record that song and couldn't get through it. When he got to the bridge and the part about "amphetamine and pearls," he couldn't get those words to come out of his mouth. It just didn't fit, and he had to scrap the idea. Richie Havens did a version of it, though, and it turned out to be a stunner.

SIXTEEN

Hawaii, Australia, Europe. *Marco Polo has nothing on us*, we thought. Bob's tour was taking us on our first venture out of North America to the other side of the world. Soundman Richard Alderson was joining us for this leg of the tour with a much cleaner, more powerful sound system. Richard was an outstanding sound mixer and thankfully very familiar with Bob's music.

We were all excited, but I especially got a kick out of how much Garth enjoyed traveling: his curiosity and enthusiasm were contagious. On landing in Honolulu, right away he asked, "Anybody want to go check out Pearl Harbor?" Richard, Rick, and I looked at one another, not quite knowing how to respond—it was hard to reconcile rock 'n' roll with sightseeing. Mickey Jones ended up going with him—the two made good sightseeing buddies. But for me the highlight of Hawaii was the people—such warmth, such unique style, although like in most places around the world, Europeans had dominated and overwhelmed the native culture. Here, in 1966, their music survived with the incorporation of lap steel and slack-key guitars and ukuleles side by side with indigenous instruments. Their island melodies and tender vocals were like a Maui breeze, and could there be a more dreamy, sensual dance than the hula?

We played a Saturday show at the International Center in downtown Honolulu. True to the laid-back vibe that pervaded Hawaii, the audience appeared somewhat neutral toward the Hawks' part of the show—and that was a relief. Plus, we didn't want to scare Mickey Jones away just yet.

The flight from Hawaii to Australia took fourteen hours. ("Garth slept the whole way!" Mickey told me with amazement. I smiled. He just didn't know Garth, who wasn't so much sleeping as dreaming and avoiding chitchat.) When we arrived it felt like landing on the moon, but a certain familiarity set in when I saw the Australian flag—British Commonwealth indeed. Sydney was an impressive city, and we all felt a bit renewed being such a great distance from the chaos of the last few months. Maybe the Australians would receive what we were doing with open minds and fresh ears.

The ground literally shifted beneath our feet when we performed for the first time in the round at Sydney Stadium on a rotating stage. The Australians didn't know if they liked what we were doing or not, but as confusing as it was for them, it was worse for Mickey Jones. He'd heard that things could get crazy on these tours, but this was his first real taste of standing before the firing squad.

The press in Sydney wasn't encouraging either. Headline: SEND THE BAND BACK TO AMERICA. But we forged on. Bob had a few press conferences lined up and, as he often did, he asked a couple of us Hawks to come along. I was always game for witnessing these odd sessions where journalists tried to get to the bottom of Bob's "ambitions." Very few artists have done more entertaining press conferences than Bob. Bizarre, quick, challenging answers were dished out faster than the reporters or music writers could digest. In the past he'd made entire rooms explode with laughter or frustration as he fielded pretentious questions:

"Do you think of yourself primarily as a singer or a poet?"

"I think of myself as a song and dance man."

"What poets do you admire?"

"Oh, you know . . . Rimbaud." He'd smile. "And W. C. Fields . . ."

I remember Bob once purchasing a ventriloquist's dummy and doing an entire conference with the dummy on his knee. Here in Australia the press seemed particularly naive—perfect for a ride on the Dylan express.

We'd heard ahead of time that Melbourne was more of an artistic center and that we'd probably enjoy it there most of all. Sure enough, you could sense a pretty hip feeling in the air. Scores of interesting characters passed through our hotel doorway, as if a medicine show was in town—musicians with didgeridoos, aboriginal poets, writers, ballerinas. We never lacked for company. Bob and I shared a two-bedroom suite with a living room where we could meet with friends or play music, and our road manager would automatically put out two guitars for us whenever we arrived. Bob never seemed to have much of an appetite, so playing music often took the place of room service, and we got by on cigarettes and tea. In those hotel rooms I also found that Bob probably knew more songs than anybody walking the earth.

Our bookers had arranged for us to play a television show in Melbourne, complete with a cheap set, corny flashing lights, the works. Afterward, we put together a little soiree at the hotel: Bill Avis rounded up some hashish and invited a few girls to come by. He gave Bob and me a big square chunk of hash and kept a nice stash for himself and the other guys.

I hit it off that night with a very attractive girl named Lynn, while Bob shared stories with a small group that included a local poet. We knocked back a couple of fat spliffs and at around two in the morning, when Lynn looked like she was starting to fade, we retired to my room. As we crawled into bed, I realized how beautiful she was, with a strong resemblance to Charlotte Rampling, the gorgeous star of the film *The Night Porter*. We melted into one another, and just before we fell into blissful sleep, she whispered in my ear that she was seventeen years old.

Too late, I thought as we drifted off. A couple hours later we were jolted awake. Three men in suits came busting into my room, scaring the hell out of Lynn and me. The first thing that flashed through my mind was that it was Lynn's father. *Holy shit*, I thought, *I'm busted for being with an underage girl.*

"Now get dressed and step out into the living room!"

When we came out of the bedroom, Bob was standing there with a groggy expression while detectives searched the place. We were all in a daze except for Albert, who kept up a constant stream berating the police for barging in like this and threatening to make a formal complaint. The cops asked to see our passports and IDs. When they looked at the girl's driver's license, I thought, *This is it. I'm screwed.* But they just looked at her, checked her ID, handed it back to her, and told us to sit on the couch while they searched the bedroom for drugs. So that was what they were after. I should've guessed. But now I had a new worry: What had happened to the chunk of hash Bill gave us? Visions of our trial back in Toronto flashed through my head. If we got busted for drugs half the world away, this could derail us completely. We waited while the police searched the other guys' rooms, with Albert hectoring them the whole time. This disturbance, he announced, was ruining the rest we sorely needed for our next performance. Albert was wearing a cap fit for a British gentleman: he looked sophisticated and properly outraged.

Finally the detectives left, taking Bill with them—they had found some hash in his room. We fretted, not knowing what would happen next or what charges would be brought against Bill. Lynn left a bit shaken, though relieved not to have gotten in real trouble. Albert, Bob, and I tried to make sense of everything.

"What happened to the chunk of hash we had?" I asked.

Albert smiled. He took off his British gentleman's hat to reveal the hash sitting on top of his head. I couldn't believe it! He'd coolly spent the whole time giving the detectives hell for busting in and harassing us.

We found out that Bill had slipped off with some guy's girlfriend at the party and the guy was so pissed off, he'd called the police, swearing we had drugs. Albert said he'd talk to the police about it, adding, "I think they'll let him go if we send him back to the U.S. or Canada." And that's exactly what happened. We felt terrible to see Bill go, but he said he understood completely and would see us back in Toronto. Exile was definitely preferable to jail.

Albert's humor sometimes had an edgier side. In Adelaide two days later, he and I went for a walk in the afternoon to check out the local scene. We were passing a butcher shop when Albert stopped suddenly, staring into the window. Hanging directly in front were three large pigs' heads, mottled, pink, and terrifying. I followed Albert into the shop as he announced that he wanted to buy one of them. Laughing, I asked what in the world he was going to do with a damn pig's head.

"I'm going to send it to Mickey Jones's room anonymously," Albert replied with an air of satisfaction. "Just let him figure it out." Hardly able to contain himself, he arranged with our hotel's room service to have the pig's head put on a tray, garnished with scattered greens and cherries in the eye holes, and delivered to Mickey's room while he was out.

When Mickey walked into his room and found the pig's-head presentation, he got very upset. He didn't think it was funny at all and racked his brain trying to figure out who had put it there and just what it was implying about him. "Are you saying I look like a pig?" he demanded. "Are you calling me a pig? Are you telling me I'm a joke? What the hell does this mean?" Albert said, "It only means what you want it to mean." Mickey kept posing these questions to all of us until eventually he became so upset that Albert finally admitted that he was just playing games with him and meant no harm.

PEOPLE IN THE more eastern Australian cities we'd played spoke of Perth like it was a no-man's-land, faraway and backward. Looking out the airplane window during the long flight across the continent, the openness and vast spaces reminded me of the American Southwest desert. *Only original peoples know what to do with this kind of terrain,* I thought.

In Perth, Garth and Mickey went on one of their discovery missions about town; Rick and Richard began searching, as usual, for where the fun might be; Albert and Victor amused themselves by harassing the staff at the hotel; and Bob and I played music, read, and hung out with aboriginal musicians. But just as we were settling in, Albert and Victor heard that the Australian government was sending more troops and personnel to Vietnam and had declared a military emergency. All international flights had been canceled out of Perth for five days. We had been scheduled to fly to London, where we could adjust to the time difference and catch our collective breath before starting the European leg of our tour in Sweden. Now we would have to cool our heels for five days in Perth, then fly directly to Stockholm. We'd practically be going onstage straight from the airport.

For the first couple of days stuck in Perth, I felt the angst of being tied down and trapped. Then, somehow, somewhere, I met two delightful twin sisters who dreamed of going to America someday. The idea totally occupied their imaginations and I was the closest thing they had found so far. They were about to turn twenty-one and looked identical, playing tricks on me to keep me guessing who was who. They had green eyes, red hair, and pale flawless skin and each stood about five and a half feet tall. The guys thought it amusing to see me traipsing around with the twins on my arms. They came to stay with me at our hotel and brought little overnight bags with them that held matching flannel pajamas. We went to dinner and took long walks, and they told me crazy stories about their family. In return I plied them with tales about New York City, Los Angeles, and Toronto. We even went to a drive-in movie in a taxicab, where we saw Michael Powell's incredible film *Peeping Tom* and endured a bit of *Door-to-Door Maniac* starring Johnny Cash—so much for being stranded in Perth.

Circumnavigating the globe, all the way from the west coast of Australia to Stockholm, in 1966 no less, deserves a world traveler's medal. We hopped from Perth to Singapore, then Malaysia, Thailand, Rangoon, and on to New Delhi, India, where we stopped at four in the morning to refuel. Crowds of people dressed in white milled around the air-conditioned airport. Outside it felt like a hundred degrees even in the dead of night. We were all completely exhausted, and we still had a stopover in Beirut. Talk about the joys of travel. We arrived in Stockholm red-eyed, tired, and dehydrated, with barely time to change clothes before a sound check at the Konserthuset, the elegant neoclassical hall where we'd be starting the European leg of the tour. Filmmaker D. A. Pennebaker, whom everyone called Penny, met us at the Flamingo Hotel along with his cameraman/editor Howard Alk and Howard's wife, Jones—known as Jonesy—who did sound. Pennebaker had filmed Bob's 1965 tour of England for his documentary *Dont Look Back*. Albert had recently made a deal with ABC Television to produce a music documentary special, and Penny was on board to shoot this tour as well. Bobby Neuwirth was part of the team too, along with our live-sound engineer, Richard Alderson. Of the film crew, the Hawks knew only Neuwirth and Alderson, but the smiling faces of the rest told us it would be a good time hanging with this bunch. There were cameras every time you turned around, and I thought it might be awkward to be filmed constantly, but Penny and company were so good at remaining unobtrusive and discreet that we all managed to stay relaxed.

Around the time the tour hit Belfast, I started getting concerned about Bob's health. We were working more and more and he was eating less and less. He kept losing weight and appeared to be subsisting exclusively on tea, honey, and lemon. I would order extra food for myself to see if I could tempt him into putting something in his stomach. He took a couple of bites here and there, but not enough to sustain him for the kind of energy he put out when we performed.

It became obvious that Bob was maintaining his performance level with the help of amphetamines. The boys and I were familiar with uppers—dexies, bennies, even black beauties—but these particular pills Bob had were said to be much smoother; you didn't get too wired or edgy. Half the pill was an upper and the other half a downer, so it was supposed to be more balanced. Nonetheless, in time all of this shit catches up with you.

I started feeling protective of Bob. This tour ran at a grueling pace, and though we were young enough to handle it, every day I saw him getting a little more run-down. It was upsetting, but beyond trying to get him to eat, there wasn't much I could do or say. In our circle we maintained a coolness about this sort of thing. You didn't express concern directly; you mostly walked and talked around it.

It didn't help that the disapproval of the audiences seemed to be growing with each show from Denmark to Ireland, Wales, and England. When we launched into "Just Like Tom Thumb's Blues" in Liverpool, a lot of the pain and frustration of touring came pouring out of my guitar. At one of the shows, where the stage wasn't much higher than the seating of the audience, a girl stormed the stage with scissors in her hand. Security grabbed her in time, but it was a close call. I couldn't tell whether she wanted to give Bob a trim or stab him. A kind of madness was percolating. We had to be constantly on alert. The whole atmosphere was heightened. I adjusted the strap on my Telecaster so I could release it with a quick thumb movement and use the guitar as a weapon. The concerts were starting to feel *that* unpredictable.

At the same time, the band was getting better and better. I remember listening to the tape of the Birmingham show and thinking Rick and Mickey had established a strong footing and a solid foundation, which allowed the rest of us to dance on top. Sometimes we could hear ourselves quite well because of the acoustics in a particular hall, and all the more so if Richard Alderson could find a sweet balance.

As we made our way through the British countryside, our wonderful driver, Tom Keylock—a World War II veteran who'd been driving the Rolling Stones for the last year and answered every request with "I'll look into it," which meant it was as good as done—stopped the bus at a beautiful old inn for lunch. He said this place was known for its tasty food, but this was 1966 and British cuisine left something to be desired. The restaurant staff looked wary of us before we even sat down. Our bizarre traveling roadshow, with film crew and all, had come to a place where weird had no limits: Pennebaker in his top hat, cameraman Howard with his British curved smoking pipe and black beard, Bob in his flowered shirt and shock-proof hair, Richard with his Adam's-apple goatee. I kept auditioning antique eyeglasses, each pair looking more old-mannish than the last. Rick, smoking some strange apparatus you might find in Timbuktu, ordered a bowl of umbrella soup.

The waiter asked if he wanted that plain or with carrots.

Rick implored, "For God's sake, man, plain! I want nothing to stand in the way of the pure umbrella flavor."

The waiter answered, "Oh, you said umbrella, sir. I thought you meant something else. We don't have that variety here."

"I thought this was England. How can you not have umbrella soup?"

Someone else interjected, "But you have sheep's-head soup, correct?"

"I'll check with the kitchen, sir."

WHEN WE PLAYED the Free Trade Hall in Manchester, our guns were fully loaded. We had no idea when we hit the stage that this would go on to become the most bootlegged show of the tour. Between songs the crowd would yell and holler insults about the music, and Bob would murmur and mumble into the microphone. I looked at Rick and was surprised to see him laughing, either out of embarrassment or simply because everything was so strange that all you could do was laugh. This was the concert where someone in the audience yelled, "Judas!" and Bob answered, "I don't believe you," which was the name of one of the songs we had played. Then he called out to us, "Play fucking loud!"—like we needed to be told. I don't know why, but that particular night I especially enjoyed playing. You never know when that muse is going to sneak up on you and spread her wings.

During the couple of days we had off in London, a lot of incredible musicians came calling at the Mayfair Hotel. The front desk got used to sending Brian Jones or Keith Richards up to the suite for a hello. I'd hung out with Brian in New York with Bob and found him to be a really sweet guy who loved American music with every bone in his body, and he played the part of an English rock star as well as anyone. One night there was word Johnny Cash was on his way to pay Bob a visit, and the film crew swung into action to capture the moment. Johnny showed up looking back over his shoulder as if someone was following him. He shut the door behind him like it needed to be double-bolted. He was trembling and smoking, as if on the back end of an all-nighter. Ronnie Hawkins knew Johnny, and we had crossed paths with him on the club circuit, so I knew what a tremendous presence and talent this man had. Bob and Johnny were on a wavelength that actually matched: "high-voltage madness." Suddenly, as Johnny flinched and twitched, there was a knock on the door. He bolted out of his chair. "If it's June, tell her I'm not here." And with that he disappeared into the other room and hid in the closet, yelling, "I'm not here!"

I answered the door, and it was room service. "Hey, John, the coast is clear!" we yelled. No answer. Neuwirth finally rescued him from the closet with the assurance that he wasn't in the doghouse, at least for now. Bob grabbed a guitar and started playing the chords to the Hank Williams song "I'm So Lonesome I Could Cry." Johnny started singing along, and within moments magic was stirring. Chill bumps: hearing that voice that could make you cry. I felt bad for Johnny when he left, knowing that he was probably going to get scolded later.

The next morning I walked through the streets of London Town, looking for things you couldn't find in the States or Canada. I found silk from India my mother might enjoy—a different kind of Indian. After a while I ran into Mickey Jones, out on his own mission. He pulled a hat out of a shopping bag and put it on his head. I swallowed hard as Mickey grinned at me, wearing a Nazi helmet. Mickey meant no harm; he just thought it was wild you could buy one here. He wore it proudly back at the hotel until Albert pulled him aside and said he didn't want anyone working with us wearing Nazi gear.

In Paris we stayed at the Georges V Hotel—by far the most glorious place that we'd stayed on the tour. The food, the style, and the service—everything was tremendously elegant. As was his custom, Albert took great pleasure in giving the Parisians a hard time, with some help from photographer Barry Feinstein. They started at the hotel, making impossible requests—hey, we all get our kicks in different ways. Local singers stopped by to greet Bob, starting with Hugues Aufray, a terrific guy who so appreciated Bob's lyricism that he'd translated his songs (quite an undertaking) and sang them in French. The breathtakingly beautiful singer Françoise Hardy also came by to say hello, statuesque, thin, with long brown hair and bangs drifting across her face.

"Don't you just love France?" I asked Bob. "They don't have singers in all of North America that look like her. She could be a world-class model. She can't be a good singer as well, can she?"

Bob answered, "She sounds fantastic. You should hear her."

THE NEXT DAY would be the start of something special that would change the course of my life. We were driving through the city and Bob and Albert had invited someone they knew to join us, a very good-looking French guy in a white suit. Then Neuwirth shouted, "Hey, stop! Look, there's Mason." The driver pulled over and Mason Hoffenberg, an American expat who'd cowritten the sexy bestselling novel *Candy* with Terry Southern, jumped into the car. He greeted everybody as he settled into the jump seat beside the guy in the white suit. After he shook hands with us, he looked at Mr. White Suit, leaned over, and gave him a big, long kiss on the mouth. "There," he said. "Now I feel better."

"Mason, what's happening over here?" Bob asked. "What are you doing?"

He replied, "I'm staying with Jimmy Baldwin, trying to see what trouble we can get in together."

The driver dropped us off and we rambled down the avenue, stopping to peer into various clothing stores and antique shops that piqued Albert's interest. Up ahead we saw a little crowd of people fussing about. We couldn't tell what was going on until the person at the center of this commotion started waving at Bob.

"Oh, it's Johnny Hallyday," Neuwirth said. " 'The French Elvis.' " Bob and Johnny greeted each other on the street and our little entourage traded "hellos" and "bonjours."

I immediately noticed in the group two fantastic-looking girls. *Damn*, I thought, *the French have got it going on*. While Bob and Johnny were chatting, I moseyed over to the girls, wondering if they spoke English, but they seemed distracted, taking it all in. Finally, I got their attention and asked what they were up to. They answered in broken English that they were journalists from Montreal, writing about the music world in France.

"Wow, you're from Canada?" I said. "I'm from Canada too—from

Toronto!" They didn't look very impressed, and then it hit me that English-speaking and French-speaking Canadians were on opposite sides of the wall during this period. One of the girls, Chantal, was blond and very pretty, with a beautiful sunny smile—immediately likable. But it was the other girl, Dominique, who completely intrigued me. With dark hair and a fire behind her dark eyes, she beamed a radiant energy. I couldn't help being drawn to her. Even her teeth fascinated me: they weren't perfect; they were a piece of art. There was nothing cutesy about Dominique's walk. She moved in a manner direct and determined, with an intelligent French motion that made me want to follow. Here we were, meeting on the street, in Paris, in the springtime, like a song—how could I resist? All this in thirty seconds. That's all it took.

I mustered up all the charm I could, offering to get them tickets to the show and inviting them to Bob's press conference the next day at the Georges V. The girls spoke to each other in French, then said, "Tomorrow, yes, see you. Merci." I realized that between them we might only be able to communicate in broken English, one sentence at a time at best. I didn't care. Just the chance to breathe in a little more of Dominique was worth it to me.

WE HAD BEEN transporting an enormous American flag with our equipment, and Albert had been waiting for just the right moment on tour to break it out. Now he suggested hanging it as the stage backdrop for our concert at Paris's Olympia theater—he thought this might stir things up with the Parisians. Bob seemed amused and went along with Albert's provocative idea.

The following day at the press conference, Bob decided to bring out a new ventriloquist dummy for the occasion. Quite hilarious watching these serious French journalists trying to get a handle on what this American provocateur was all about.

"Why do you have a puppet?" they asked.

"He followed me here," Bob responded.

Afterward, Bob and I invited Chantal and Dominique up to his suite. The girls were still going on about how bizarre the press conference had been with the dummy on Bob's knee. Bob picked up the puppet and said, "Here, do you want it? I don't need it anymore." Dominique wasn't sure how to respond to the gesture, but thought it was very funny. Chantal said, "Sure, we'll take it, why not?"

I invited them to stay for dinner. Bob tended to be a little uneasy about having journalists in our midst, so I took them to the suite I was sharing with Richard and Rick. Before too long Rick was joking and laughing with Chantal. I think Richard tried to ask them if they knew anybody with some pot or hash. When they finally understood what he was getting at, they laughed and said, "No, but we would like some too!" They'd decided that covering the next night's show and hanging out with us could be the makings of a good story for their newspaper. Dominique's fiery energy hypnotized me, and even though I'd just met her, I said they should come to the shows in London too. She and Chantal talked it over in their French-Canadian argot. "I don't know. Maybe," she said. "We'll have to see."

Rick jumped up. "That would be great! I hope it works out. And in London we will have *zee hashish*."

As they were leaving, Dominique and I shared a long, slow hug, which she later told me seemed to last forever. "*Bonsoir,*" I said, and when they turned to go I couldn't help notice what a strange sight it was to see the two of them walking out carrying a dummy in a tuxedo.

The next day—the day of the show—happened to be Bob's birthday. During our sound check at the Olympia, the crew hung up the huge American flag; it covered the whole back of the stage. At this point nothing seemed far-fetched or out of context. What else could happen? Well, that night we found out. Thanks to the big, glaring Stars and Stripes, the audience was already pissed off before Bob went out to do his acoustic set. We might as well have sent Mickey Jones out there in his Nazi helmet.

Because of the turmoil in the audience, Albert, Victor, and I walked with Bob to the side of the stage as he made his entrance. The crowd erupted, yelling every insult imaginable. Albert smiled at me like *So far, so good*. Bob launched into "She Belongs to Me," and after a couple songs he stopped to tune his guitar. But the more he tuned it, the worse it got. Then he thought it started to sound pretty close, but when he blew a note on the harmonica, the guitar was completely out of tune with it. Almost ten minutes had gone by, and the crowd was beyond impatient and restless. Bob kept tuning, but it wasn't coming together. Victor and Albert looked at me nervously, as if urging me to do something. I told Victor to get Bob to come to the side of the stage for a minute. He waved at Bob and led him over. I asked him to play a note on the harmonica and tuned the guitar quickly. He headed back out to the mic after this twenty-minute tuning break and played the rest of his set to jeers and a handful of cheers from the crowd.

By the time we went out for the electric set, it felt like the whole night had been laced with psychedelic mushrooms. Right then all I cared about was whether Bob was okay to get through the show. He looked drained and weary. After we played "Maggie's Farm," the crowd started yelling out scornful remarks in French and waving their arms in revolt. I stepped over and whispered to Bob, "Happy birthday, and many happy returns."

He laughed out loud. "Yeah, great birthday, isn't it?" Garth played a few quiet notes of "Happy Birthday." The guys all had a little chuckle and we launched into "One Too Many Mornings." Bob belted out the rest of the songs in a rage but looked like he was running on fumes.

At the end of this rough night, I again invited Dominique and Chantal to join us in London; they said that they would have to ask their boss to get the okay. "Please do," I said. "It would be great. It's the final shows of the tour, and I know we would have a terrific time."

Back at the Mayfair in London, Victor got a message that the Beatles wanted to come by. They asked if we had a good record player so they could play their new album for us, so he quickly arranged for a little hi-fi system to be sent up to Bob's suite.

The four Beatles and their road manager, Mal Evans, showed up full of humor and high spirits. Bob was acquainted with them; there was a story floating around that Bob and the journalist Al Aronowitz had turned the boys on to weed in New York at the Algonquin Hotel. The first thing I couldn't help noticing with the Fab Four was that they all wore the same boots: black, with a bit of a raised heel and a zipper down the inside. They actually called them "Beatle boots" and asked if we wanted to have some made for ourselves while we were in London. Their English accents were strongly Liverpudlian, so different from those in London. It was like when you first met someone from the South in the U.S.—there was a whole different rhythm to how they spoke, and they used it in a very humorous way.

John Lennon and Bob were quick to start throwing funny little jabs at each other. Bob teased them about playing for screaming girls and asked if that was still "going well."

"If you can't hear what you're doing," Paul McCartney responded, "it can frustrate the hell out of you."

"We're waiting until all this blows over," said John, adding that some of the tunes on their new record would be hard to scream to. "What about you, Bobby? The girls still screaming for you?"

"Oh yeah, the girls and the boys are screaming at what we're doing, but not in the same way as for you."

Watching the Beatles interact with one another was a sight. They were almost like characters in a Buster Keaton movie: their movements seemed sped up a touch, and playful. They had a cosmic energy that seemed to flow from Paul. John brought a sharp, edgy wit, and Ringo had a wonderful animated quality. George's engaging grace brought pure joy into the room. The group had a balance to it, with everyone playing their part. They had transitioned out of their early period, when they had seemed innocent and sweet, especially in comparison to the world we had come out of. But seeing them here, even seeing the artwork on their new record—it all added up to a new, powerful musical direction.

You could tell Paul was excited about their new album and eager to get it on the record player. What caught my ear immediately was the use of the recording studio as a musical instrument—incredible experimentation with sounds and effects, quite the opposite of a Bob Dylan record. The range of songwriting on this album went from pure British flavors like "Eleanor Rigby," with that indelible chorus of "all the lonely people, where do they all come from?" to "Taxman," which George said he wrote because their tax bracket in the U.K. was so extreme. The influence of East Indian music came through as well. Ringo said George kept showing up all the time with different Indian instruments until there was no way not to use them. The tune "Here, There and Everywhere" showed Paul's ability to go "classic standard songwriter" at the drop of a hat.

After "Tomorrow Never Knows," with all of its backward tapes and unusual effects, Bob said, "What's that? What's that supposed to be?"

"Something new, Bobby," John responded. "Gotta give the folks something new."

I could tell George hoped for a sign of approval for the record from Bob. He said they were calling it *Revolver*. John asked Bob if he was familiar with the *Tibetan Book of the Dead*.

"Sure," Bob replied. "Hey—I got an idea. Why don't you guys write a song and I'll record it, and I'll write a song for you to do? But I'll write a real good song, so don't write me no "Please Please Me" kind of thing," he said, laughing.

"Wait a minute, now. That was a long time ago," Paul said. "We've all grown since then."

John smiled. "Yes, that was back in our folk-music days."

"I'll be waiting for that song," Bob said as the guys got up to leave.

I asked John on their way out how they got that sound on the vocal for "Tomorrow Never Knows." George answered, "We put the vocal through a Hammond organ Leslie speaker. Love that effect. We're coming to the show tomorrow night, so play real good."

"We'll try," I said.

That evening, John Lennon and Mal Evans came back to the hotel for a little hang. Pennebaker wanted to get something with John on film. While filming in a limo, Neuwirth kept telling the driver to go slow because Bob was getting nauseous. As much as he wanted to engage in an interesting interplay between himself and John, Bob could hardly speak. This would become a scene in the documentary where John is shown razzing Bob, saying, "Pull yourself together. Another few dollars, eh? That'll get your head up. Come on, come on, money, money."

Back at the hotel, I dialed Paris, and Dominique's rich-toned voice came on the line. I told her that London was really happening—"but it would be much better if you guys were here too." She now sounded a bit more swayed by the idea of coming, and thought she and Chantal could get their air travel covered. I assured her that everything else would be taken care of, and that we'd have a wonderful time. I heard a hint of glee in her voice as she talked about when they might arrive in London the following day. I couldn't imagine a better way to end this tour than hanging out with her.

THE FINALE OF the European tour was upon us, and the promoters said they had saved the best for last. The crowd at our first night at the spectacular Royal Albert Hall was like a who's who of musicians and even included some royalty. And yet here, in the biggest venue we'd played on this tour, in the biggest city, we faced the harshest reaction to our music. On this night the hostility truly spewed toward the stage. We stood our ground and played with a "here it is, take it or leave it" attitude. Bob poured his soul out in those songs. A couple of times his balance wavered a bit. I didn't know where he was pulling the energy from, and I kept a watchful eye in his direction during the show. As thick as our skins had become throughout the tour, the negative reaction at the Albert Hall made us angry. Sometimes we'd been able to let it roll off our backs like a joke, but it wasn't funny anymore.

The following day, Bob gave another surreal press conference. The reporters and critics tried so hard to get under his skin, but he never took the bait. He left them with more questions than answers. I tried to follow suit whenever one of them came my way. A reporter from *Melody Maker* asked me to describe the mystery men playing in Bob Dylan's band. I told him we were just passing through and had no bones to pick with his people.

"My people?" he said.

"Yes, aren't these your people? They look like you."

He said, "What about the Hawks?"

"What about the doves?" I answered.

For the second night at Albert Hall, rock stars once again filled the balcony boxes, including the Beatles. We had made it to the last show of the tour and were feeling a sense of relief and survival.

"The last blast," I said to Bob. "You got one more show left in you?"

"Oh yeah," he said. "I'm just getting warmed up." His eyes looked dark and hollow, but his spirit was still rising.

As I watched the acoustic set from the wings, I thought of the several times on the tour that I'd overheard people preaching to Bob and Albert that they should fire the Hawks. "You gotta get rid of these guys. They're ruining the music. This band is not right. You hear the audience booing night after night? It's their fault." But Bob never budged. I knew Albert was on the fence sometimes, but some of the shows left him feeling elated too, full of praise for how we had played. Commendable, I thought, that Bob stood by us in the face of all these naysayers.

"Okay, fellas, it's showtime," Victor called out. "Let's hear some rock 'n' roll." For the final time we walked out on the stage to catcalls, hooting, cheering, and booing. Fire and ice, that's what it felt like as we charged into "Tell Me, Momma." The tempo and attitude were aggressive. We had nothing left to give back but a cold shoulder. It struck me as odd, playing in front of all these famous musicians from the British Isles—our peers, our brethren—*Bet you guys have never been through anything like this*, I thought.

During a barrage of hooting and hollering between songs, someone yelled to Bob that he should go back to playing only acoustic. "That was then, this is now," Bob shouted into the mic. For the final performance of the tour, we all stabbed away at the songs like there was no tomorrow. The amount of energy released into the air that night was somehow more than we had left. By the time we hit "Like a Rolling Stone," our final number, Bob looked like Jake LaMotta: he'd gone fifteen hard rounds, but he never went down.

As we jumped into the car after the show to escape back to the hotel, someone announced that the Beatles were coming over to Bob's suite. They'd said the show was really good and wanted to drop by with a message: "The booing didn't matter, the music did." Bob nodded his head slowly, tiredly, taking in the encouragement.

Rick and I were in our room changing clothes and freshening up when the phone rang. It was Albert, asking me to come to Bob's suite—"quickly, please." I had barely knocked on Bob's door when Albert yanked it open and waved me in. I went into the bedroom, and it seemed that Bob had fainted or was deliriously exhausted. I helped him loosen his collar. Albert reminded us that some people were coming by, but Bob could hardly react—he looked like he was passed out sitting up. I kept saying to him, "You okay? You okay, man?" He couldn't answer. Albert asked me to run a bath—maybe that would make him feel better—so I went and turned on the taps in the large English bathtub.

Just then, someone knocked on the door of the suite. As Albert started to help Bob take off his stage clothes I ran to answer the door. It was the Beatles with some friends and family.

"Bob's just freshening up," I told them. "He'll be out shortly."

I went into the bathroom to shut off the bathwater before it overflowed.

"Help me get him into the tub," Albert said. "I think that'll bring him around." We helped Bob into the bath and Albert went out and ordered tea for the guests. The whole situation seemed surreal, insane. The Beatles were outside, casually waiting to chat with Bob, and here in his room he was practically unconscious in the tub.

I tried talking to him. He answered me but sounded delirious, muttering about some stuff back home. Somebody knocked on the bedroom door, and I went out to see if perhaps room service had come for our guests.

"Sorry for the holdup," I said, trying to keep the worry from my face. "Bob's just pulling himself together."

I hurried back into the bathroom, only to find that Bob had sunk down into the water and was starting to bubble. My heart stopped for a moment. *Damn*, I thought, *he could really drown here.* I pulled him back up in the tub. There was a tapping again on the bedroom door. It was Albert.

"He's still in the bath, half passed out," I whispered, and sprinted back into the bathroom. Bob was again sinking down in the water.

"Look," I told Albert, "you've got to go out there and explain that Bob is too tired to get it together right now. He needs to get some sleep."

Albert nodded. "I'll take care of it."

I wrapped a big towel around Bob, and when Albert came back, he and I helped him into his bed. So strange, but now I saw a slight smile of contentment on his face. He slept peacefully, like he'd been though purgatory and back: safe at last . . .

This was rock 'n' roll, after all, and the show must go on. Relieved that Bob was now sleeping quietly, I went back to my room, where Rick, unaware of the drama that had taken place, had quite the party going. Some of our crew was there with a variety of libations and a promise of more in the pipeline. We had a long, wonderful night, and then Dominique and I and Chantal and Rick melted away and fell asleep.

The next day everybody was making plans to return to New York. To my surprise, Bob appeared, looking somewhat revived. I was relieved but mainly impressed.

"I'll see you in New York," he said. "Are you going to the Chelsea?"

"Yeah, I'll be there in a couple days." I felt as if we had been through a war together, and now I knew we had won the battle.

True to character, Garth and Mickey decided to take an ocean liner back to the U.S. I stayed on an extra day to spend more time with Dominique. Various friends and associates kept showing up at the hotel, bringing more goodies to experiment with. One of the guys came in with a bag of heroin, in case anybody needed some. "And here's another treat," he said, holding up a packet full of powder. "I think it's cocaine." Somebody else showed up with LSD, saying this particular form was really mellow and wouldn't keep you up for days. London was out of control. It seemed even crazier than New York, if that was possible.

Dominique and I tripped the light fantastic, and I told her how wonderful I thought our time together had been—she too seemed delighted about our adventure and my affection for her. I said I'd call her when I got settled in New York and hoped she'd come visit me at the Chelsea Hotel.

SEVENTEEN

The phone rang in my room at the Chelsea. It was Brian Jones, calling to say the Rolling Stones were in New York for a few days. "What are you guys up to? Is Bob around?" I told him I didn't know what Bob was doing, but that we could hook up a little later if he wanted. He said he'd come down to the Chelsea around nine that night.

Returning to New York and the Chelsea felt comforting, almost like going home. The manager of the hotel, Stanley Bard, had held my favorite little suite for me, room 410. It was a bedroom, a bathroom, and a good-sized living room with a small fridge area near the entrance, and that extra space kept me from feeling boxed in. Stanley—who was known to accept art pieces, which he displayed in the lobby, in lieu of rent—was kind enough to give me a break on occasion when money was tight.

The phone rang again a few minutes later, and it was John Hammond. He was playing that night at the Café Au Go Go and told me I needed to come check out his new band, which featured an incredible guitar player who'd played with Little Richard.

When Brian Jones got to the hotel that night, I told him I was going to the Village to catch John Hammond's set, and he decided to check it out with me. We got there as John was going on and snagged great seats just to the right of the stage. John wasn't kidding: his new band was hot. He sounded more powerful than I'd ever heard him before.

Then he introduced his new guitar player to do a song. "Please give a nice hand to an amazing guitarist, folks. This is Jimmy James." Jimmy played left-handed and his lanky body snaked around the instrument, like he was born with the guitar strapped on. He was young and good-looking, with hands and arms thrashing around like lightning. A bit of a show-off in the best sense. Holy smokes—this guy could wail! He sang, played the guitar behind his back, behind his head, with one hand. He ended the song playing with his teeth, which made me stand up and holler.

Brian Jones looked like a ray of light had just blinded him. "This chap should come to England," he said. "He would blow people's minds."

After the set, we said hello to John and his guitar man. "I gotta go crash," Brian whispered to me a few minutes later. "So jet-lagged, I can't hold my head up. Thanks, man. I'll give you a ring tomorrow." He jumped in a cab while Jimmy James and I talked about our big dreams and the songs that changed our lives, like Howlin' Wolf's "Forty Four."

The following week Jimmy and I grabbed a bite and talked a lot about songwriting. "Writing songs is a mysterious thing to me, man," he confessed. "I get an idea but I don't know where to go with it. I haven't cracked that yet."

"I wrote the original songs the Hawks have recorded," I told him, "and I love the songwriting process, but we're always on the road. I'm hoping to just concentrate on writing at some point."

"How does Dylan write?" Jimmy asked.

I smiled. "On a typewriter."

"What? No shit, on a typewriter? That's weird, man. I gotta try that someday."

As we wandered by Washington Square, we heard street musicians in the park, somebody preaching about the world coming to an end. "That cat you brought to the gig the other night, Brian Jones?" said Jimmy. "Well, he told somebody who must have told somebody and they want to bring me over to England, to London. Isn't that some wild shit?" He laughed. "Can't wait to check that out!"

"That's fantastic," I responded. "Brian seems to know everybody. He's like a goodwill ambassador. Hey, at the show last week you did some extreme bends on that tremolo bar. How in the world does your Strat not go way out of tune? That's one of the reasons I play a Telecaster—no tremolo bar to make it go out."

"Oh, man, I got to show you," said Jimmy. "I'm crashing over here at the Albert Hotel. Come on up and I'll show you my method."

We went up to his room and Jimmy took his Strat out of its case. "I need to change strings anyway. These are getting pretty rusted out." He knelt on the bed and put the headstock of the guitar between his legs. He replaced the big E string with a new one. But before he wound it into the tuning peg, he began massaging the string toward himself, giving it long slow pulls with both hands until it had no more give, then winding it into the peg. He did this with each string, like a ritual. A guitar always falls out of tune when you first change the strings as they adjust to being stretched but *this* was a solution.

After he tuned the guitar, Jimmy pushed the tremolo bar down, playing some crazy lick, then pulled it up. He played an A chord and it sat solidly in tune.

"See, it takes more time, but it's worth it," he said. "Then the only problem on a Strat is when you break a string, the springs in the tremolo bar throw the guitar way out of tune. You gotta change the string immediately while you tell the audience a joke, right?"

"I had a Strat when I was sixteen," I said, "but had to pawn it to get the money to go join Ronnie Hawkins and the Hawks in Arkansas."

"Ow! that's a shame," said Jimmy. "Did you ever get it back?"

I just shook my head.

Jimmy offered me a smoke and said, "Your first name is Jaime. I saw that in the credits for *Blonde on Blonde*."

"Yeah," I said. "They started calling me Robbie as a kid, you know, like if your last name is Smith, people would call you Smitty. What about you? Your parents called you Jimmy when your last name is James?"

He grinned as he lit my cigarette. "No, my last name is Hendrix and my first name is actually Johnny. Kind of crazy, right?" We both laughed at our evolving names and the idea that you could change them like you changed your clothes.

SOON RICK HAD to return to Canada under the terms of his probation from our pot bust. Richard, Garth, and I didn't want him to go back on his own, and besides that I had lost my wallet and needed to go back to get a new driver's license. I was frustrated because Dominique's number had also been in my wallet, and now I had no idea how to reach her. At first I was slightly apprehensive about going back to Toronto; I was still carrying around a bitter taste in my mouth from those two rough nights at Massey Hall. But it felt good to catch my breath for a minute at my mother's house. No matter what, Mama Kosh still made it feel like home. Old pals came by to say hello, and I made friends again with my hometown.

A few days in, a package arrived for me: it was my wallet. Someone had found it and sent it to the home address on my driver's license. Dominique's Paris number was still in it. I tried calling her a few times and finally reached her. She sounded genuinely happy to hear my voice, and I was thrilled to hear hers. I asked when she would be returning to Montreal. "In a few weeks," she told me in her beautiful broken English. I suggested she come through New York on her way back and visit me at the Chelsea. She seemed to like the idea but wasn't sure just yet if she could do it. I wondered if she was sizing up whether she felt comfortable joining forces with a bloody English-speaking Canadian. How would she explain that to her revolutionary, separatist, Québécois friends?

The next morning Albert Grossman called: Columbia Records wanted a stereo mix of *Blonde on Blonde*. Bob recognized that I cared a lot about the sound of records and asked if I would oversee the mixing. I had never mixed an album before, but I liked the idea of trying to make it shine in stereo. So I flew back to New York and the Chelsea. Bob came down from Woodstock, where he and Sara were now living, and told me I'd be working with an engineer at Columbia Studios. I asked if he was going to be there. He smiled and said, "Nah, I'll listen to it when it's done." Nobody was overthinking it. Everything was off the cuff, instinctual.

At Columbia I studied the track sheets to see how they had separated the instruments and vocal. There wasn't a lot of flexibility; back then there were only four-track machines. They would put the vocal and Bob's harmonica on one track, usually with the echo already printed. Bob's guitar, my guitar for the songs I played on, and all the other instruments with effects and echo were scattered over the other tracks. The mixing engineer assigned to work with me had pushed up the four tracks on the mixing console faders. There it was, take it or leave it.

I went through each track, judging whether each could use more or less bottom or top, or more echo—whatever slim variables could enhance the sound and give us some stereo separation. We tried different kinds of compressors and limiters, an assortment of tape delays, and a couple of live echo chambers. Not much was making it sound better. The stereo was subtle, but it sounded nice when opened up a bit. I gave the mixing engineer a list of cues and rides I wanted him to make as we were about to lay the first song down. In the middle of the mix, his head drooped, and he nodded off.

"Wait, wait, stop," I said. "Are you sleeping?"

"No, no," he said, snapping up. "I'm just resting my eyes. Here we go." But again he started nodding off, and again I roused him.

"What's going on? What's the problem? Is it the music? Is it me? You're not mixing, you're sleeping."

He confessed that he and his wife had a newborn and the baby's crying kept them up all night. His eyes looked blurry and red as he apologized for his exhaustion.

"Maybe you should go get some rest," I suggested. "We can get another engineer to do the mix." But he pleaded with me not to say anything—he could get in trouble, maybe fired.

I didn't have the heart to get this new dad canned, so for a week I wrestled him awake, trying to get through the mixes. When we got to the eleven-minute track "Sad-Eyed Lady of the Lowlands," I yelled the cues in his ear to keep him alert. We got through it by the skin of our teeth. On the acetate it sounded better than the experience warranted. It just showed how difficult it was to screw up a record that great.

A LITTLE WHILE LATER, Bob asked me to come up and stay at his house in Woodstock on Byrdcliffe Road. He talked about doing more touring. Albert was looking into arranging a show at Shea Stadium with Peter, Paul and Mary, and Bob's songwriting had struck a chord with Russian poets like Yevgeny Yevtushenko, which had even kindled the notion of touring in the U.S.S.R.—though the very idea of performing behind the Iron Curtain sounded outrageous at that time. After what we'd just been through on the last tour, I couldn't help but think he must be a glutton for punishment, but I guess you can't keep a good man down.

In my room at Bob's I started recording some chord changes and melodies on a tape machine. This was a new kind of experiment to see if I could find a flavor, a sound, a feel worth writing words to. I labeled this tape "Return of Luke the Drifter" after an alias of Hank Williams's from years back. The sound on the tape certainly didn't resemble anything of Hank's, or country music, for that matter, but it did have hints of some otherworldly roots music. All the musical strands that we'd picked up along the way were starting to weave together.

When I rode back into New York with Albert Grossman, he told me about a couple of sisters he was thinking about signing. "Actually," he said, "I think I'm going to sign *one* of the sisters." He asked if I would check her out and consider producing a couple of tracks. "She could do a great job singing some of Bob's songs," he said, "and I think it would be great to have the Hawks backing her up."

They set up a meeting at Albert's office for me to meet this young singer. As Albert walked me in the direction of his office, he said under his breath, "I think you'll like this girl. Could be something special." We went in and there she was. "Robbie," said Albert, "I'd like you to meet Carly. Carly Simon, this is Robbie Robertson."

She stood up and overwhelmed the room—tall, gorgeous, with a smile that went on forever. Albert smiled like the Cheshire cat. I told her the other guys in the Hawks would be back in New York in a day or two and it might be fun to cut a couple of tunes together. She said she liked that idea very much and gave me her phone number so we could set it up. Have to say, I was curious to hear the sound of her singing voice.

When the guys came back from Canada, we had a meeting at the hotel—our first concern was to discuss finding a place in the city where we could work on our own music. The idea had always been that we would do this thing with Bob for a while, but our ultimate goal was to write and record our own stuff. Our friend the photographer Barry Feinstein came through with a temporary fix: we could use his photo studio to make music at night. We were thrilled with that idea, and Garth said he would hook up a little mixer so we could record any ideas on a borrowed tape recorder. I played the guys my "Luke the Drifter" tape, and though the sound wasn't exactly what I was looking for, there was a clue in there that Richard and Garth could relate to. Rick played along with the tape on bass, giving it a rhythmic drive that made drums unnecessary—like what some bass players could accomplish on an acoustic bass.

I'd told the guys about Carly Simon, and a couple of days later I called her to see when would be a good time for our little studio experiment.

"Oh, I thought you'd probably forgot about it by now," she said.

"It's only been a week!"

Carly laughed. "I know, I'm just excited." Right then I noticed a slight stammer in her voice, as if maybe she had stuttered a bit when she was younger. It sounded so sweet and vulnerable.

The following week we went into a studio and tried out some Dylan songs. Carly looked way too beautiful for anyone to concentrate fully on the production. I even told her jokingly that she couldn't dress like that while making a record—no one would be able to follow the arrangement and look at her at the same time. She blushed and pushed my shoulder. Her voice was rich and full. She didn't sound like anybody else, and originality always caught my ear. It didn't take long before I could tell this girl wasn't interested in being a singer of Bob Dylan songs. She was going to be her own thing and just needed a little time to find it.

We hung out the next day and the day after. Every once in a while her slight stammer would sneak through, which got me every time. I don't know where we went, what we did, who we were with—our connection felt almost dreamlike.

I told Albert, "You're not gonna cage this cat."

Albert smiled knowingly. "Maybe you're right, but I think you're more interested in the artist than the art." That may have been true, but the last thing I was looking for at this point was anything too serious.

BARRY FEINSTEIN had asked a favor of us. He and Peter Yarrow of Peter, Paul and Mary were making a film called *You Are What You Eat*, and they had asked if we would play on the soundtrack with an interesting street musician by the name of Tiny Tim.

Tiny came to Barry's studio that night, overflowing with humbleness, dressed in a gray-checkered sport jacket and brown pants. His black shirt was buttoned to the neck, with dark curly hair hanging to his shoulders. He carried a little ukulele in one hand like a ventriloquist would carry his dummy. You couldn't help but like Tiny right away, with his gentleness and respect; he referred to everybody as "Mr." He spoke in a high-voice/low-voice, nursery-rhyme rhythm that sounded so strange at first but completely natural within minutes. Just to make him feel comfortable, I asked him to sing and play us a song that held a special place in his heart.

"Oh, Mr. Robbie," he said, "there are so many that I hold dear, but if I may, there is a particular song by the great Al Jolson that is one of my favorites." He picked up his ukulele, checked the tuning close to his ear, and broke into "Climb upon my knee, Sonny Boy." It was quite touching, and he sang and played the hell out of it. The other guys and I looked at one another, impressed, feeling we could do something with that.

Tiny flipped over the uke and played it left-handed as he ran through a couple more old Bing Crosby classics. "Let's give that 'Sonny Boy' song a go," I suggested. "We like that one." Tiny bowed with more appreciation than if we'd saved his cousin from drowning.

We set up a few mics for recording onto our little tape recorder, got a balance, and then Tiny suddenly excused himself. "I'm so sorry, Mr. Robbie, but nature calls and I have to use the restroom."

"Yeah, sure," I said. "Use the washroom right there in the hall."

Tiny looked apologetic. "Oh no, I couldn't do that. I have to go back to my place, my simple little place, use the facilities, and then shower. I could never do a good performance for you, knowing that I'm dirty."

It was clear that he wasn't fooling and that this wasn't debatable. Richard tried, saying he had used the facilities here and they were perfectly hygienic, and he felt cleansed inside and out. Tiny responded, "Thank you so much, Mr. Richard. I am so happy for your personal experience, but if you'll forgive me, I have to go home. I won't be long and I pray you'll have the patience to wait until I return."

I said, "Mr. Tiny Tim, by the time you get back, we will know this song and more. You go do your business and we will do ours." He bowed, threw kisses, and scurried out.

While we waited, a young singer named Eleanor from a girl group called the Cake stopped by with Peter Yarrow and Barry. They had come up with an idea of doing a duet of "I Got You Babe" with her and Tiny Tim. She would sing the boy's part and he would sing the girl's part. I liked Eleanor's voice and she had a cool little attitude too, for a seventeen-year-old.

When Tiny got back from his bathroom break, his hair was still wet and he looked fresh as a daisy. He could have won the *Good Housekeeping* seal of approval for being the cleanest street musician around. First we did the duet of "I Got You Babe," which turned out splendidly. Then we recorded "Sonny Boy." Garth knew how to accompany and highlight that tune like it was written yesterday. It sounded authentic and moving once you got used to Tiny's wild vocal vibrato from right out of the 1920s. Barry and Peter were knocked out by the recordings and said these songs were going to be a cornerstone of their movie.

What a brilliant and unusual experience. We felt like we had become honorary members of the street musician's association.

WHEN I GOT back to the hotel, I called Dominique again to see if she'd thought more about coming to visit me in New York, but I couldn't reach her. That night, Edie Sedgwick left me a message to meet her in the El Quijote restaurant downstairs. Her recent visit with her family in California had not been pleasant, and I'd already heard the whole sad story in my room as tears streamed through her mascara. Edie might have been easily dismissed as a "poor little rich girl," but I genuinely felt her pain. Her sorrow made me think that the coldness in her upbringing was terribly deep-rooted. Everybody hurts, but this was a lost soul.

At the El Quijote, though, I found her in better spirits, having a bite with Andy Warhol and a couple of friends. I told them about the session we'd just had with Tiny Tim. Andy and Edie thought it sounded bizarre and incredible, different worlds of music and film all coming together. Andy said, "I want to do something like that, with a musician who sings in the subway."

I knocked back an order of the fried bananas, one of the specialties of the house, and Andy made a suggestion. "Let's go over to Salvador Dalí's suite at the St. Regis Hotel for a nightcap." This sounded like a surreal idea to me. As we got in a taxi, I asked if they had seen the movie *Un Chien Andalou,* which Dalí had done with fellow Spaniard filmmaker Luis Buñuel. Andy said, "I know exactly what you're getting at. That opening scene of the eyeball and the straight razor slicing it in two."

"You never forget that," I said.

Edie squirmed. "I never *saw* it and I can't forget it—*ew.*"

Andy called up to Salvador's suite from the lobby. Dalí greeted us with grand gestures of welcome in his shiny maroon dressing gown. He looked tremendous with his slicked-back hair and curled, waxed mustache. Inside we found some other guests smoking and sipping drinks. A striking woman named Gala, whom I later learned was his wife, came into the room and spoke to Salvador in Spanish. He put his smoking cigarette holder into an ashtray and put his hands around his throat like he was choking. Then he pointed toward the woman and she waved him off, laughing, as he threw open a window to let some of the smoke out.

Andy and Edie introduced me, mentioning that I was a guitarist. Dalí gestured in the way a Spanish flamenco guitarist would play. I shook my head and said, "No, rock 'n' roll." He dropped his arms and smiled. "Too bad."

About an hour later Edie and I noticed a pencil sketch on a big piece of paper that was lying on the dining room table. Edie asked what it was.

Dalí answered, "Yes, yes, it is the beginning of an idea I am working on for a new masterpiece, but the horse has no head . . . yet." He laughed like he meant it.

Andy swirled it around for a moment. "Hmm, maybe I should do some horses," he said.

Dalí waved his arm. "What do you need horses for? You have soup cans and women's shoes!" Everyone laughed. You could tell Salvador really enjoyed teasing Andy. Andy stood up smiling and said, "Well, maybe I should be going." Everyone laughed again, and Dalí said, "No, no. You must never go."

Oh, what a night, and when it was finally time to leave, Dalí kissed Andy on both cheeks, then kissed Edie. He shook my hand and advised me, "Play some good music. Not that noise, I hope."

I said, "Okay, I'll do that." He said, "Good," and kissed me on both cheeks.

IN THE SUMMER of 1966, the city was overflowing with fascinating people and incredible culture. Meeting one person often led to meeting another, the world of art and music expanding at light speed before my eyes. I wasn't quite aware of it while it was happening, but every day somehow became more of a journey into the unknown. Bobby Neuwirth introduced me to a young up-and-coming artist named Brice

Marden. We felt like we were in the same boat, trying to make a mark. We both wanted to do something and have the world come to us, but that was a steep climb.

One day, while Edie was in my room rummaging through her purse, Brice came in with a piece of art under a cloth. He set the piece on the couch and unveiled it, saying, "I think it's dry. Here, look." I didn't know what to expect, which was exciting and a bit unnerving, because you wanted to be supportive of friends; if I'd played a piece of music for Brice, I would have wanted his support. As he showed his painting, Edie came over to take a peek. The painting was a deep, rich layer of brown.

"That's so pure," I said. "It's unconfused. It doesn't pretend."

Brice said, "That's it. That's what it is." He wrapped up the painting, shook my hand, and left. Edie closed her eyes for a moment and said, "You gotta talk to your friend. Nobody wants a brown painting that's just brown. God, tell him to try green or blue, but not brown. That's all I can say. I'm not an art expert, but brown is brown. It's like brown shoes, you know?"

Next time I ran into Brice, I said, "The chicks aren't digging on the brown painting. It's not coming from me, but Edie said, 'Tell him to try blue or green. Brown's not happening.'"

Brice looked at me. "Really, she doesn't like the brown? Well, maybe I'll do the green or blue. In fact, you can tell her I'm already doing a blue and green together."

"Okay," I said, "I'll pass that along."

(On a recent visit to the Museum of Modern Art, I stopped in front of that brown painting hanging there, along with the green and blue one, and reminisced about those days. Can't imagine what they're worth now. Brice is still a friend of mine, and we laugh about our strange backstories. And he still insists that Edie eventually liked the brown painting.)

EARLY ONE MORNING—too early—the phone stirred me awake. I mumbled into the receiver, "Yeah, hello?"

"Allo, Robbie. It's Dominique calling you from Paris. Hi, I hope it's not too early to call."

I sat right up, cleared my throat. "No, of course not. I was already up, thinking about going fishing."

She said, "Oh, really?"

"No, just kidding."

She laughed her joyful laugh. She said it would soon be time for her to return to Montreal, but she might be able to stop in New York on the way. All I could say was, "How soon can you come?"

"In about a week," came the reply.

When we hung up, I was elated. I told Richard, Rick, Edie—everybody I could—that the girl I had met on the street, in Paris, in the springtime, was coming to New York to see me.

In the meantime Garth took me to the Egyptian Gardens to hear some amazing bouzouki and oud players. These were musical instruments you would hear in Greek and some Middle Eastern groups, often accompanying a belly dancer who could do things with her hips that made your eyes roll around in your head. This particular group and this dancer were fantastic. It opened my ears a little wider to other musicalities. I was especially drawn to the sound of the oud—hard and soft at the same time, double gut strings slipping and sliding. The bouzouki player was amazing too, but to me the oud was as sexy as the dancer.

Rick and I would take in shows together too. One night we went downtown to the Village Gate and caught Charles Mingus and his full band. When the leader of the group plays stand-up bass and yells and hollers some fantastic vocables during songs while smoking a pipe, you want to have a good seat. Mingus had a stocky build and a powerful presence. The intensity in his eyes expressed every note he played. His arrangements and compositions were sensational, with a New Orleans looseness alongside remarkable precision. They did a song called "Better Git It in Your Soul" that lifted me off my chair. After the show Rick couldn't even speak. He just bobbed his head like he'd had a spiritual awakening.

Meanwhile, at Barry Feinstein's studio, something was starting to gel. Our sound was changing and becoming more dimensional. On one piece we worked on, we came in gradually, one at a time, on a chord progression that I was improvising. It lifted and swayed. Garth turned it into a spiritual right before my eyes. We didn't know where this was leading, but there was definitely a web being spun and a path spreading out before us.

Albert kept us on a modest retainer to live on while he worked out plans for our next tour with Bob. Once a week I'd go up to his office to pick up our money. They would always make me wait like I had nowhere to go, and each time when Albert finally wrote out the check, he would look pained at having to pay us.

"I've got an idea for you guys," he said one day. "Why don't you do a record of Bob Dylan's songs as instrumentals? All the songs with recognizable melodies, you know, like 'It Ain't Me, Babe' or 'Blowin' in the Wind.' Don't you think that's a good idea? Believe I could get you a record deal for that." He handed me the check, smiling at his brain wave. "Think about it."

I acted like I could see the idea lightbulb over his head and said I would talk to the boys. I realized in that moment that Albert knew the Hawks only through our playing behind Bob. He had never heard Richard sing or Garth's multi-instrumental brilliant musicianship or Rick's fantastic harmonies and killer voice. Albert knew I could play, but he didn't know I could write.

AT THE END of July, Albert called me at the hotel with a tremor in his voice. He said Bob had been in a bad accident on his motorcycle. Bob had flipped over on the bike and fractured his neck. I was shocked. "What hospital did they take him to?"

Albert explained that Bob had gone for treatment to a particular doctor in Middletown, New York, from whom he could receive private and intensive care. I asked the key question: "Is he going to be able to recover from this without permanent damage?"

"It's too early to say," Albert replied.

I tried calling Sara, but she was with Bob at the doctor's. Then I

told Garth, Rick, and Richard. We were all really worried, not knowing how badly Bob was hurt. When someone says "broken neck," you
can't help but think the worst. When Sara got back to me, she said
they thought Bob would heal in time, but it could be a slow process.
He would need some traction and then he would have to wear a neck
brace as long as necessary. She said, "I'm sure he'll check in when he's
recovered a bit more." In the meantime, Albert said, all touring would
be canceled indefinitely. We would remain on standby until we knew
how well and when Bob would recover.

ON THE NIGHT Dominique was arriving from Paris, Richard, Rick, and
I borrowed a car and headed for JFK. Perhaps we shouldn't have
smoked a joint on the way, because I got completely lost. I felt so terrible that Dominique would be waiting at the airport, not knowing
what was going on. When we finally arrived at the Air France terminal, I could see the exasperated look on her beautiful face. I jumped
out and hugged her, apologizing for my awful taxiing skills. She was a
bit freaked out, not knowing if I'd forgotten her or if she was stranded
there. Rick pulled out the rest of the joint and said, "Here, this will
settle your nerves." Dominique laughed, and even with a bit of a language barrier, we were back in a comfort zone almost immediately.

At the Chelsea, Dominique and Edie became fast friends. They
would go on Edie's daily run to the pharmacy to cash her check and
buy more makeup, over to Warhol's studio or Factory, as it was called,
and maybe a little stop at Dr. Feelgood's. Business as usual for the
summer of 1966. Sometimes Dominique and I would go down to musician Buzzy Linhart's loft, which he shared with his bandmate Serge.
It was way downtown in no-man's-land, where the streets were de-
serted and we could play music all night without bothering a soul.
Serge and Buzzy's pad was a musical sanctuary. You'd run into all
kinds of characters there, from Richie Havens to members of the
Lovin' Spoonful. When the sun started rising, it was our cue to wrap
things up. At dawn fruit and vegetable markets opened all along the

block, and stores and restaurants from all over would come to buy
their fresh produce. Once, as we were leaving, one of the vendors
yelled, "Hey, come on, don't stop the music now! I'll give you a dollar.
Keep playing."

"Make it two, and you got a deal," I yelled back.

If we got to sleep by 6:30 a.m., it was a good night; later than that,
the day could start to evaporate. Dominique fell right into the groove
and took this all in like it was meant to be. Everybody liked her, but no
one as much as me: ever since I'd met this girl in Paris she had been
stuck in my heart.

Dominique had planned to stay in New York for just a week, but
she ended up staying a lot longer. Eventually, she had to go to Montreal to see her parents and check in with the newspaper she wrote
for, *Le Photo Journal.* The boys and I were also going to Canada to see
the folks, and I asked if she and Chantal, who was already back there,
might enjoy coming to Toronto for a visit. I was eager to make plans
for our next rendezvous.

I called Bob from Toronto. We hadn't been able to speak since the
accident, and while he sounded a bit restrained, he still had electricity
running through his veins. It was so great to hear his voice. He'd been
staying with Dr. Ed Thaler in Middletown, New York, for the first part
of his recovery. Dr. Ed was a miracle worker, he said, getting him back
to normal as fast as possible. "This doctor's a genius. He's built these
speakers based on the human ear that sound as good underwater as
they do in your living room." Dr. Ed had ordered him a special neck
brace that he said would enable him to get back to the grind in no
time. As we kept talking, he sounded more and more like his salty old
self. "I can't turn my head," he said. "If anybody came up behind me,
I might not know they were there for hours." It was nice to hear him
joke about it. "Come up to Woodstock when you get back. That'll be
good timing."

I told the boys that Bob sounded pretty damn good, and he really
wanted to get back to work. Everybody breathed a sigh of relief.

On a hot Canadian summer day, I dropped Rick off with his family in Simcoe and drove over to the Six Nations Indian Reserve. I just wanted to feel this place under my skin again. On the banks of the Grand River I found a quiet spot and sat for a while, musical memories swirling around in my head. This was where it had all begun for me. Here I had learned my first G chord on a beginner's guitar with a picture of a cowboy on it, but an Indian showed me where to put my fingers.

The drive from Ohsweken to Hagersville felt shorter than I remembered. I also saw the place through another lens, not just in its personal resonance but from stories my mother had told me of her upbringing here. I saw the shack houses that had to endure tremendously harsh winters, many of them with no indoor plumbing. I knew my mother was one of the luckier ones, who'd had a chance to see what was on the other side of the mountain. Slowly I rode along Second Line trying to recognize all the little destinations from my childhood: where the wild strawberries grew, the railroad tracks, where we would wave at the train engineer going backward and tooting his lonesome whistle, the water pump that gushed out the coldest, best-tasting water into a tin cup. I pulled up to the little gray house where my aunt and uncle had lived with their twelve children. I sat in the car outside, wondering if some of the family still lived there. For some reason I couldn't muster up the courage to go knock on the door and say, "Hi, it's me, Jaime. I'm back." I wasn't *back*. I was just feeling my way through. *I'll come back here when I'm hopefully more successful or famous*, I thought, *and they can be proud of one of their native sons.*

While staying at my mother's, I wrote a note to my uncle Natie in prison. I couldn't imagine him behind bars, but I told him that my musical journey was full of extraordinary experiences and that pretty soon I was going to make a "real move." He would know what I meant. I missed his kids, David and Vicki, and my lovely aunt Fran, but I was like a moving target, never in one place too long.

DOMINIQUE HAD LEFT me the phone number of her parents' house in Montreal. I called and asked for her. *"Bonjour? Allo?"* was repeated. I said slowly, "Hello, could I please speak with Dominique?" A woman's voice told me to hold on a moment, then, "Louise, telephone." (I soon found out that "Louise" was Dominique's given name. She had changed it, another thing we had in common.) Dominique sounded jubilant, as if happy to be back on her home turf with family and friends. She said she had spoken to Chantal, and they could come visit us in Toronto after the weekend. She asked me where they would stay. I said we could all stay at my mother's.

"At your mother's?"

It was no problem, I assured her. Ma was like one of the gang. All the guys were camping out there right now.

Dominique laughed. "Well, they sure couldn't stay at my mother's, that's for sure."

Bill Avis came by for a visit and told me that the Beatles were going to be playing Maple Leaf Gardens in a few days. Though we'd met a couple months earlier in London, I didn't know them that well, but I said to Rick and Richard, "Let's get in touch with their road manager, Mal Evans, and see if we can say hello at the hotel after the show."

Rick and I went to pick up Dominique and Chantal at the train station. They looked beautiful, but I could see that they felt a little out of place—they were, after all, smack-dab in the middle of "English" Canada. They had grown up with English-speaking Canadians trying to dismiss their culture, and the good cheer of our welcoming committee wasn't going to erase that overnight. We told the girls that the Beatles were playing that night in town and we thought we could all try to meet up with them afterward.

I didn't want to arrive at the Beatles' hotel with too many people, so Rick, Richard, and I went ahead to see if the guys wanted to have some people over. We found Mal Evans and he ushered us past the big crowd gathered out front. In a huge suite upstairs we found a pretty mellow scene. Paul, John, and George were all engaged in different conversations, while Ringo read a magazine on the far side of the room. George stood up and glanced at Mal, as if to say, *Who the hell are these guys?*

"It's Bobby Dylan's band," Mal announced. "The guys we saw him with in London."

"Hello, guys." George waved as a look of recognition came across his face. "Visiting with some family here." John got up, came over, and shook our hands, laughing. "So you survived the tour with Bobby Dylan after all?"

"Oh yeah, we got through," I said, "but we've got the scars to show for it."

John talked a bit about their tour but didn't really seem to be loving the experience. Could have been too much screaming and not enough about the music. Suddenly he looked around the room with a sly smile and asked, "Would you like to join me in my office?" We got up and followed him into an adjoining bedroom and through to the bathroom.

"Let me show you a little trick," he said. He pulled the door to the bathroom closed behind him and reached into his pocket, retrieving a pack of Lark cigarettes. He took hold of the little plastic wrapper end and pulled it with a flick of the wrist. The three of us watched as if he were Merlin the magician. He peeled back the aluminum paper, ripped it off, and pounded the cigarette pack against his other hand, the way anybody would to remove the first cigarette. *Why the big ritual?* I wondered. *Sure, we're in show business, but is this really necessary?*

John flipped the Lark cigarette with its charcoal filter into his mouth and lit it. Immediately the smell of marijuana filled the room. He took a big puff and said, "Beatles have to take precautions." We all started giggling with delight and smoked the whole joint together. I could only conclude that John had someone make the cigarettes and package them exactly as they would in a factory. Must be good to be a Beatle.

When we got back to the house, we told the girls they weren't having a big after party. "We just said hello—and it got too late." You could see they were a little disappointed, but we knew that when you're on tour you have to catch your breath when you can, or it will take you down.

———

I ENJOYED BEING with Dominique more every day, but soon she and Chantal had to get back to Montreal, and the guys and I headed to New York. I had made a commitment to play on John Hammond's new record, which would be produced by Leiber and Stoller. And Barry was giving up his New York studio, so Rick, Richard, and Garth were looking to find us another place where we could rehearse.

Once we'd settled back into the city, I went up to the country to check in with Bob and see how his recovery was coming along. Albert Grossman's wife, Sally, was heading up too, so I hitched a ride with her. She asked what the Hawks were up to, and I told her that we were working at Barry's temporarily but it was tricky finding a stable place in the city where we could make music. She said Albert thought we could easily find a place in Woodstock where we could do whatever we needed without any bother. Sally made things sound natural and flowing, and the idea stuck with me.

After Bob saw the cut Pennebaker had done on the documentary from our European tour, he decided that he and Howard Alk would edit the footage themselves at his house in Woodstock. Bob said he wanted something more unexpected and experimental. Filmmakers like Federico Fellini had drawn a new line in the sand, and breaking the old mold was very inviting. The film, which Albert had already arranged for TV distribution with ABC, had become Bob's project as he recovered.

When I got to his house, I was hardly inside the front door when Bob, with his very stiff-looking upper body and hard-core neck brace, waved me into a side room where he and Howard Alk were working on the TV special. "You're not gonna believe this," he said. Smiling at each other, they sat me down in front of the little Moviola editing screen. Howard, still grinning, said, "Are you ready?"

I smiled back. "I think so."

They showed me the first eight minutes of the film, breaking into laughter every thirty seconds or so. I started laughing along with them without realizing it. What I saw was bold and incomprehensible, with surreal, disconnected editing that *was* kind of hilarious. Things were cut together to give a completely different meaning to what was actually going on: Bob and Albert having a phone conversation when they were really talking to other people. There would be a cut to one of our shows and we would play a big intro to a song; Bob would step up to the mic to start singing, and they would cut to some guy in Copenhagen talking about Hamlet. I liked that it wasn't taking itself too seriously. The editing was abstract and fun, once you took the ride.

Bob and Howard couldn't stop laughing. "Oh man," said Bob, reaching for the back of his neck brace, "this hurts, but it's getting better. So what did you think about the film so far?"

"I've never seen anything like it before," I said. "Let me see it again."

I liked this experiment; I liked them reaching outside the box. This was a stretch, and Bob Dylan—who was a master of stretching—was delivering. Albert thought this was a splendid rebuke to everything that the dumbness of TV represented. He had no problem sticking this in ABC's face.

A friend of Bob's and Howard's, someone I knew through them, was also staying at the house, and later that evening he asked me to come over to his room.

He said, "You wanna do some drugs? What are you into?"

"I've had some good and bad experiences on hallucinogenics. But mostly pot and hash."

He laughed like I was still a juvenile delinquent. He reached into a black bag and pulled out a "works"—a needle and syringe, a bag of heroin. "You never did H? You never got high?"

I said, "Yeah, I snorted it once by accident, and it made me throw up. I don't like shit that makes me puke."

He tied up on his arm, cooked up the scag on a spoon, shot up, and said, "You get over that real soon. *This* is getting high." I felt like a lightweight, but I thought Howard and Bob probably wouldn't even blink at this.

BACK IN THE CITY, the guys had struck out looking for a rehearsal space; everything they found was too expensive. And when I tried to get a room for Dominique and myself at the Chelsea, the manager said they were almost completely booked up: the only room left was on the main floor and looked out onto a dark alley. It would just be temporary, but I felt embarrassed in front of Dominique, who had come back to New York to stay with me. She thought the room was strange, but so what? We were together, and tomorrow was another day.

Right around this time, it became perfectly clear that Dominique and I were not in a casual relationship; we were a couple. I had never been involved with a girlfriend on this level before. She was different from anybody I had ever known: her sharp intellect and humor, her extensive knowledge of literature and international cinema, the sound of her accent, her blazing smile and fiery eyes. When I held her in my arms it was a perfect fit. She was stunningly beautiful inside and out. I couldn't imagine life without her.

Albert and Sally Grossman invited us over to their Gramercy Park house one afternoon. We had some gourmet delights, of which Albert was a champion.

"Oh, I almost forgot, "Sally said. She went into another room and came back with a tiny calico kitten to show Dominique, who melted immediately.

"We just had a couple of litters from our cats in Bearsville," said Albert.

"You can have this little girl if you want," said Sally.

Dominique couldn't resist. "Yes, please, can we take her?" she asked me. "She's so adorable." I gave in, wanting to make her happy. Sally then went back into the other room and returned with another kitten, fuzzy with black fur and cute as anything you've ever seen. "This one's a boy, and he's very funny. You know, sometimes animals aren't so lonely when they've got a friend to play with."

"That's a great idea," Dominique said. "Let's take them both! Come on, can we?" I should have known better, but I didn't.

We took the kittens back to our dungeon room at the Chelsea. You could step out of our window into an enclosed space where the hotel wrapped around itself, a black pit about twenty feet square that went all the way up to an opening at the roof. I watched the kittens go in and out of the window and play in the dirty pit.

"We gotta get out of here," I told Dominique. "This is too grim."

I thought if we found a little two-bedroom apartment in the Village, we could split the rent with Richard. We ended up getting a spot on the corner of Seventh Avenue and Bedford in the Village for eighty-nine bucks a month. So we moved with Richard and our two kittens, which we'd named Maybelle, after Mother Maybelle of the Carter Family, and Matt the Cat. It was on the first floor, and Dominique, Richard, and I instantly turned it into a cool pad. The location was brilliant—two blocks down from the Village Vanguard, great record stores, fantastic burger joint across the street. We were happening.

When I mentioned our problem finding a rehearsal space to Albert, he said, "I think you guys really should consider finding a place up in Woodstock." I hadn't forgotten that Sally had mentioned this a few weeks before, so when Bob asked me to come up to Woodstock again to see how the film was progressing, I figured I'd see what he thought about the idea. By now he and Howard Alk were halfway through the film, but looking a little weary. Their technique had produced interesting results, but it was extremely tedious and time-consuming. The good news was that Bob was recovering from his injury really well: he only had to wear the neck brace part-time now and could turn his head without turning his whole body. He suggested Richard, Rick, and Garth come up to Woodstock too and we could play some music and maybe do some more filming as well.

It felt good for us all to be together again, playing some tunes and having some laughs. Bob liked the idea of us moving up there, so Rick went on a mission to search out what we were looking for, usually dragging Richard along. The idea was to find a clubhouse—a place where the guys could live with a space for us to make music. Dominique and I were the only couple, so we would get a separate place.

Howard asked me to sit and look closely at the footage that he and Bob had cut so far, then to go through the scenes they had pulled to use in the second half. I took notes and absorbed as much as I could. After we'd run through it, Bob came in. He said he was burned out working on the film and was going to take the family to Jamaica for a little breather. "Why don't you and Howard finish up the second part?" he suggested. "It's all there, you just gotta put it together."

He knew I was a movie bug and thought I could help Howard with structure. Let's put together a sequence of the choices you've pulled and see what flows, I said. We'll juggle scenes around until it feels right. That simplicity appealed to Howard—he too felt the procedure for the first half had been grueling.

In a couple of weeks, with Bobby Neuwirth's help to keep us on the path, we had a rough cut of the second half. Bob came back from his vacation, put the finishing touches on the film, and it was done. There was a wild sense of humor to this film that we realized might fly over the heads of the public. The attitude was something like "We're not going to give you what you want. We're going to give you what you need." When Albert screened it for ABC Television, their response was "Are you crazy? We can't show this on television. It's too weird. Nobody will get it, and we don't get it." The film was called *Eat the Document* and that's exactly what ABC-TV did.

ONE DAY RICK came bounding into the "Red Room" at Bob's house, where we sometimes played music. "I think I found it!" said Rick. "It's very private. You wanna go see?" We drove to West Saugerties and up a remote side road to a long driveway. When we turned in, there it was: a pink ranch-style house in the middle of a hundred acres—a ridge of mountains, a good-sized pond, and nothing but space and wilderness all around.

The house was modestly furnished with essentials, just enough for a quick move-in, and ready to go. A large fireplace greeted us, and on the mantel was a decorative device put there by the landlords. Standing about eight inches tall and a foot wide was a picturesque lowlands scene with a river running through it to distant mountains. When Richard hit a little switch on the side of the device, the river lit up as if it were flowing. It told you quite a bit about the people we'd be renting from.

Richard rejoiced. "This could be just what we need."

I agreed. "Let's take it!" The slightly ugly pink house had four bed-rooms, a dining area, a kitchen, a living room, and a *basement*. That was my focus: turning that subterranean space into what we'd needed all along. The goal was to use whatever gear we could from our live show to create a setup that would let us discover our own musical path. Lay some rugs down and kill the sound reflection. Get an up-right piano in there with a mic for the soundboard and one for a vocal. Guitar amp and acoustic guitar mics. One mic over the drums—in case anybody played drums. Another few vocal mics for Rick, me, or Bob. Who knows! Garth had all this going through a little mixer with another mic for his Lowrey organ's Leslie speaker. I brought over the little quarter-inch tape machine I'd been using at Bob's house. The only effect was an Echorec tape delay, which was a bit noisy with hiss, but who cared? This was it! This was what I'd been looking for in my dreams.

I was drawn to the idea of the records that Les Paul made with his wife, Mary Ford, at his home studio in New Jersey, which I had heard was built into the side of a hill. Those records had a sound unlike any-thing the world had ever heard before. And I remembered the time we visited Hitsville, the legendary Motown studio. It had lit a spark in me—just how simple, how basic the place was, so underplayed, and yet the sound that came out couldn't have been more distinctive and special.

When I asked a recording engineer to take a look at the basement, he said the concrete walls, glass basement windows, and big metal furnace could make for the worst sound anybody ever used for re-cording music. To me, that was good news. This was all about break-ing the rules, and the more unacceptable the setting, the more it felt right. I was looking forward to discovering what this big pink house had in store for us.

EIGHTEEN

Sara Dylan had found a little gray house for Dominique and me on Glasgow Turnpike, several miles from the pink house. We moved in with our cats, Maybelle and Matt. Woodstock was a drastic change in lifestyle for us, and for the guys. We knew it could work for our musical needs, but there was a sense of isolation in the countryside. Everything seemed so far away. None of us had a vehicle. So we decided to go in together on a 1940 dark burgundy four-door Hupmobile with front suicide doors—pretty rare, and it ran real nice. We enjoyed cruising around town in it. But the car lived with the boys at their place, and Dominique and I quickly realized that if no one was around to pick us up, we were pretty much stranded. Our house was too far from town for walking. So every day the guys would swing by and bring me back to our new clubhouse, "Big Pink," as we started calling it.

Slowly but surely, the basement setup started coming together. Every day Garth and I tried moving equipment around and testing mics. We didn't have much to work with, so we had to beg, borrow, or steal whatever gear we could. We got half a dozen Norelco mics, also a couple little Altec mixers and two speakers for playback listening. Albert helped us with another mic or two, and Garth got a pair of headphones so he could adjust the levels on the mics through the mixer. We plugged the main vocal mic into my guitar Echorec machine. Surprisingly, it added just enough pizzazz to make the room feel like it had its own sound.

Our routine at Big Pink quickly took shape. Every morning, Rick or Richard would come by and get me and we would mess around with music ideas in the basement. Richard came up with some nice chord changes and was working on lyrics. He always wrote music first and then went in search of words that fit. I would sometimes start with a first line or title, maybe a rhythm, anything I could grab onto. Every couple of days we'd audition something for one another. On occasion we'd refer to a song or piece of music we'd shared in the past as a point of reference. "Remember that gospel song by the Caravans? Well, this is inspired by that." Or "Remember that break in 'Tossin' and Turnin'?" What we played rarely resembled the reference, but it was part of the creative process. No genre of music, no influence was off limits, and the sense of freedom this gave us was exhilarating.

I couldn't wait to take Bob out to West Saugerties to visit Big Pink. He picked me up in his blue station wagon. (Only a few years earlier he'd been using it to drive himself to gigs.) He had his dog, Hamlet, with him—a big black German shepherd/poodle mix with curly fur and a distinct funky smell. As we cruised toward Big Pink, I told him about our clubhouse music-factory concept, and that the boys and I thought we were onto something. Bob had recorded mostly in proper studios, and I didn't know yet if he could relate to this idea.

As we trailed up a long side road, I rolled down my window to let some of Hamlet's scent escape. "Where is this place?" Bob asked, amused. "Man, nobody's going to bother you out *here!*" He wasn't wrong, but I liked the sense of privacy and solitude.

Richard had a pot of coffee brewing when we arrived, and Rick was stocking the refrigerator. "Just like home," Garth remarked as he stood in the entrance with a screwdriver in hand. Bob looked the joint over like a sergeant appreciating a tidy barracks. When he saw the setup in the basement, he scratched his chin, looking pleased. "This is great. Can you record anything here?" In response, Garth played back some experimental taping we had done. Bob could feel our vibe

loud and clear. He said there were a couple of song ideas he had kickin'
around and it would be good to try them out with us at Big Pink.

For the next few months, we would convene there. Bob would usually pick me up in the blue station wagon with Hamlet in the back,
and we'd work from noon until about four thirty or five. For the first
couple of weeks, he brought his Martin acoustic guitar and small por-
table typewriter with him every day. Eventually he just left them there.
I usually got a ride home with one of the guys later so we could work
on music ideas of our own after Bob had left.

In the living room there were some coffee tables and side tables
scattered around. Checkerboards lived on two of the tables. Rick was
the champion checkers player, in which he took a certain pride, while
Richard was on a continuous challenge to win at solitaire without
cheating. On the other tables in the living room we kept two typewriters. Some lyrics were written with a song on one side of the paper and
another on the back. Drawing from Bob's custom, it became a ritual
for one of us to sit down at a typewriter and rattle off some lyrics or a
poem or just a train of thought, most likely with a bit of humor to it.

When I look back on that particular period, we never seemed to
have enough quarter-inch recording tape or typing paper. Pretty foolish, but it was what it was. I never saw Bob write out lyrics longhand;
he either typed them out or scratched a couple of words on a napkin
or something. His ability to improvise on a basic idea was truly exceptional and a lot of fun to witness.

OUR LONG HOURS at Big Pink meant Dominique was often alone at our
little house for most of the day. When I got back in the evening, it
was plain to see she was feeling a little trapped. Sometimes she would
go to Sara's and hang out with her, and on occasion she went antique
furniture scouting with Sally Grossman. Even if she came with me to
Big Pink, there wasn't a lot for her to do.

One day, on the way out to Big Pink, Bob said, "You and Dominique need some wheels. I'll sell you this blue station wagon for a

dollar. I got a new one coming." The boys and I were still just getting by, so his offer was a godsend. I reached into my pocket, pulled out a one-dollar bill, and handed it to him. He took it and said, "Sold!"

There was a real family feeling between Bob and the Hawks up in the Catskills. He was a very special friend and co-conspirator. We were already survivors from our year of living dangerously on one of the craziest tours in history. Now we had our feet back on the ground and sanity reigned—some of the time.

Bob continued, "You take the car and I'm going to see if Rick wants to take Hamlet. You know, that dog loves Rick. They seem to have a connection, ever notice that?" Rick did agree to take Hamlet. He groomed and freshened him up, and once Bob and Sara saw the dog looking so fine, they thought perhaps they should take him back. "No way!" Rick objected. "He belongs to me now." Hamlet became the Big Pink mascot. He would lie directly in front of our playback speakers. If he didn't care for a tune we had just cut, he'd go upstairs and lie on the rug in front of the fireplace, a good incentive for us to try to do better the next time.

At Big Pink we had a new realization about Bob. You could hardly name a song he didn't know all the words to, and you didn't have to ask twice. He was turning us on to some beautiful folk songs— "The Auld Triangle," "Ain't No More Cane," "Spanish Is the Loving Tongue," and on and on. There was always room for a few country gems thrown in—"You Win Again," "Waltzing with Sin," "I Don't Hurt Anymore"—and a good chance a couple of Johnny Cash tunes would slip in there too. I put in a request for "Big River" myself, and we tore up "Folsom Prison Blues."

But all these old songs and rare gems were a warm-up to the main event. After a quick game of checkers, a coffee, and a smoke, Bob would sit down behind the typewriter. Sometimes that was a signal for me to hit the basement and get a couple of guitar parts going, making sure there was tape on the machine. We were always afraid of running out of tape and were too poor to buy extra, so we recorded on a slow speed, seven and a half inches per second, or maybe three and three quarters if we were running really low. On this particular Ampex tape machine, you could record on both sides of the tape, which helped, even though it meant a sacrifice in quality.

Pretty soon Bob and the other guys would descend the stairs and take their positions behind whatever instrument they felt like playing. I might play drums or bass, Garth would start tickling the ivories, Rick would grab a trombone or guitar, Richard on lap steel or percussion and drums. It would be a starting place. Bob had a music stand in front of his chair where he would set fresh lyrics, maybe scratch out something with a pen, or add a couple words. He would strum a little intro on the acoustic guitar, and away we'd go. "Too much of nothing can make a man ill at ease, one man's temper might rise, while another man's temper might freeze." More often than not, we would have a tough time making it to the end of the song without breaking up laughing.

Nominally the logic behind these recordings was to put together a collection of new Bob Dylan tunes that other artists might cover. After we would lay down a cut like "Too Much of Nothing," Bob might comment, "Okay, that one would be good to send to Ferlin Husky." He was only half kidding. The clubhouse concept was in full effect, and we loved having a creative depot to gather in. It reminded me of a street gang or the Bowery Boys movies, but instead of fighting, we played music. When we would bring friends by to check it out, they could feel the vibe right away: the place smacked of music.

Meanwhile Dominique and I were looking to upgrade our own place. Soon after we arrived in Woodstock we noticed that our kittens were no longer kittens. They were full grown, with their own personalities and attitudes. Within no time at all, hell set in. Maybelle went into heat and began howling at all hours. Cats from the area gathered outside and joined her, a terrible chorus that kept us up all night. Then, a surprise: Matt the Cat became Matt-ilda. It turned out Matt was a female, and soon she began howling louder than Maybelle. Dominique and I agreed we just had to hold steady and not let them out, regardless of the sleepless nights and constant anxiety. But after four nights of no sleep we were losing our minds and finally said, "The hell with it," flinging the door open at 4:00 a.m. to preserve our sanity and get some shut-eye. The cats came in the next day like they had been to an all-night rage—haggard and bloody. They both scarfed down their food and fell asleep in their cat bed. Dominique and I looked at each other, knowing our troubles had just begun. Unsurprisingly, Maybelle and Matt-ilda soon were both pregnant, and we needed a bigger nest.

While Dominique went to Montreal for a family visit, I met with Norma Cross, the daughter of our old New York City landlord, and her friend Libby Titus. They showed me a cool, dark-wooded, two-story house on Larsen Lane between Woodstock and Bearsville. I liked the feel of the place much more than our pad on Glasgow Turnpike and said that I'd like to move in right away. In a room at the back of the house that you had to go out and around to enter, the guts of a baby grand piano lay on its side with its strings exposed, almost like a piece of art. I figured I might find some use for it.

I had started writing a song called "Caledonia Mission." There was a Canadian town called Caledonia we would drive by on the way to Six Nations, and something about that place conjured up strange images and a story of estrangement and solitude in my imagination. Mostly I just liked the name. I knew Rick's vocal sound would be good for this song. Even the town where he was born and raised wasn't far from Caledonia, so it felt like the right fit.

Richard had a tune in the works called "Katie's Been Gone." He had the chord progression and the first line. He asked me to finish the words and sort out the structure. I liked this kind of collaboration, in the tradition of classic composing pairs like Ira and George Gershwin or even Lennon and McCartney. It was a new method, writing with Richard. He wrote some beautiful melodies and changes and used piano chord inversions I didn't even know.

Right around this time, Bob typed out the words to "Tears of Rage." He handed it to Richard and said, "See if you can do something with this." Richard nailed the perfect melody and chords to go with those heart-wrenching lyrics. He played it for Bob, who thought it sounded just right—"Let's lay this down," he said. We grabbed our instruments and Garth pressed "record" on the tape machine. Bob sang it good and we ran through it a couple of times, but Richard's treatment and vocal made it his own. This was a breakthough for Richard's writing, and it set a high bar that I wanted to live up to.

Dominique got back from Montreal and announced that she liked the rustic feel of our new house. She moved things around and made it more modern and comfy at the same time. When Rick saw what she had done to the place, he said they could use her help at Big Pink too. "Too many men and not enough charm," he explained.

The next day Dominique, with our help, moved the furniture around at Big Pink and brought some of that charm that Rick was pining for. When Bob arrived, he immediately noticed the difference.

"Oh, this is much better. Now you can breathe in here."

Bob typed out the words to "You Ain't Goin' Nowhere," and we descended to the basement. We had all completely fallen under the spell of this atmosphere of devil-may-care creativity. Songs poured out of Bob and we tore through them; if lightning struck and you weren't around, the show went on without you. I had to run a couple of errands before the stores closed, and when I got back, they had re-corded "Yea! Heavy and a Bottle of Bread" and "Million Dollar Bash." We smoked a J and laughed ourselves to pieces at these recordings. Bob said, "Okay, who would be good to do those songs?" We suggested everybody from Brook Benton to Marty Robbins. "No . . . Little Jimmy Dickens, don't you think?" I offered. Garth made some toots and whistles come out of his organ.

Howard Alk and his wife, Jonesy, Albert and Sally Grossman, and Al Aronowitz all came out to Big Pink to see what was going on. They could tell we were having too much fun. We had just recorded "Quinn the Eskimo" with Anthony Quinn in mind—he'd portrayed a memorable character, Inuk the Eskimo, in the 1960 film *The Savage Innocents*. We'd already done "You Ain't Goin' Nowhere," so we had a nice cross section of material to play. Our guests were knocked out by these recordings.

Albert began seeing the Hawks in a different light—hearing Richard and Rick sing and getting a flavor of our kind of songwriting created a space for us in his mind independent of Bob. He called me the next day and said he wanted to pursue getting us a record deal right away. His first choice was either Columbia, Bob's record label, or War-ner Bros. This was music to my ears, and I couldn't wait to share the good news with the boys. For the first time, everybody had a sense that we were on track with our musical journey.

We made arrangements to go into a studio in the city the next week and record a song I had just written called "Chest Fever." It featured Garth's organ with Richard taking the lead vocal. Albert supervised the session and said we should record two songs while we were there, so we also cut a very bizarre tune of Richard's and mine called "Ruben Remus," inspired by the character of Uncle Remus in the movie *Song of the South*. Both these songs were in the basement-tapes mold of "anything goes," with boundaryless, surreal lyrics. We had a studio session drummer play on the tracks, and it was right then that I knew we needed to get in touch with Levon.

I wasn't happy with the finished recordings. They sounded dull, with no original sparkle, but Albert thought they would serve the pur-pose to land us a record deal. He had gone a little soft on the idea of the Hawks being on the same label as Bob; it got in the way of certain flex-ibilities, and he also thought we should have our own separate iden-tity. I very much agreed. He did feel an obligation to play the tracks for Columbia, but avoided the hard sell, hoping to make the deal with Mo Ostin at Warner Bros.

Back in Woodstock, I told the guys I wanted to call Levon. He still lived in our hearts and we hoped he would return. "I think he'll love our setup here, and it's time." Bob too was in such a different place now. Something had evolved with him since the accident, and after his son Jesse was born. He looked different and sounded different. I'd never seen him in a more relaxed, contented state, the polar opposite of what Levon had known in the past. These days Bob was a short-haired family man, he and Sara having kids quicker than you could shake a stick. We were off the manic treadmill of fame and madness, and it might have been lifesaving.

At the end of my spiel, Rick stood up and said, "Let me call Lee. I'd like to be the one to give him the news and invite him back. I'll also try to find out what condition he's in." The obvious and most natural thing would have been for me to make the call, but Rick's conviction and confidence struck me. In Levon's absence, Rick's playing had continued to bloom. He absolutely felt like he was holding his own, and I could tell that he wanted to make the call not just to bring Lee back but to let him know that he'd grown some too. This seemed a good way to smoke Levon out and see where he was really at. *Let little brother call him*, I figured. *That's gonna be good for both of them.*

The next couple of days in the basement were dedicated to Bob recalling some Ian and Sylvia Tyson tunes. When it came to folk music, I knew slightly more about the records of Gordon Lightfoot and Ian and Sylvia because of our Canadian connection. We ran over versions of "The French Girl," "Song for Canada," and "Four Strong Winds." Again the number of songs Bob had rolling around in his memory really impressed me. Amazing how he could remember all the words to *his* songs, let alone hundreds of other people's.

After a little break upstairs for coffee and a smoke with some frantic typing going on—two typewriters clacking away in stereo, Richard on one, grinning to himself, Bob on the other, same expression—we marched back down into our subterranean refuge and recorded "Get Your Rocks Off." Garth played some killer organ on this one. Bob could usually get through his hilarious lyrics, but after he sang "midmuscle creek," he cracked up, couldn't hold it in any longer. Richard's bass vocal raised the stakes—"Get 'em off!" Great fun, great mood, which set us loose that night after Bob left. We began recording a crazy collage of music called "Even If It's a Pig, Part 2." With Garth in the lead, paving the road to madness, the Hawks turned the basement into a laboratory of deranged noise.

Rick bounded downstairs, saying he had just spoken to Lee. "He sounded good—I think we got things worked out!" He came over and sat beside me. "Give him a call tomorrow too. He'd really like that. He's staying with a friend in Memphis but seemed ready to go." I couldn't wait to hear Levon's voice again, so we all called him the next day.

"Hey, boys. Hey, Duke. What's going on, baby?" Levon said.

"I'll tell you what's going on," I told him. "You need to get your skinny butt up here to the Catskills as quick as the wind will carry you." It was good to hear his fantastic chuckle. My heart jumped a beat. "When you get here, you should stay over at my house with me and my girlfriend, Dominique."

"Whoa, you got you a girlfriend, do you? Well, I'll look forward to meeting the sweet thing."

Then Garth, who never got too outwardly emotional, said, "I really look forward to seeing you, Levon," and I could hear he was touched by that.

Richard called out, "Come on, Lee, we already got your drums set up."

"I can get up there by Tuesday. How's that?"

"Perfect," I said. "See you then."

I told Dominique that Levon was the closest thing that I'd ever had to a real brother. He would be coming to stay over Tuesday night. She was genuinely happy for me. "He'll go stay with the boys at Big Pink after that," I added. "They're fixing up a room for him now. I hope he sticks around this time."

Bob too was happy to hear that Levon was going to join us at Big Pink. Nobody had any hard feelings from his sudden departure—that was all water under the bridge at this point.

I started writing out some abstract words on a typewriter at Big Pink: "The forefather pointed to kingdom come." Bob sat down and wrote the lyrics for "I Shall Be Released." A lot of the tunes coming out of the basement had deep humor, but "Tears of Rage" and "I Shall Be Released" were no joking matter. This material wasn't meant to reflect our lifestyle or the times we were living in. It was really just about trying to write an interesting song. In the Tin Pan Alley tradition, we were all just showing up every day at songwriting headquarters, doing our job, seeing if we could come up with anything of merit, and then going home. A big part of it was getting together and making music and discovering where we were really at during this stage in our own journey.

After we laid "I Shall Be Released" down on tape, I mentioned to Richard that I thought he could sing that one really well. "Maybe in a falsetto, like Curtis Mayfield might do it. In the same range as your harmony." I sang a couple lines of the chorus in falsetto, and Richard smiled. "Yeah, I can do that."

The boys and I drove down to pick up Levon at LaGuardia Airport in Richard's black 1947 four-door Oldsmobile, which was slightly roomier than our Hupmobile. There he was, with his suitcase in hand, looking good and healthier than the last time we had seen him. It felt great to see his "sorry ass" again, as he would say. First we cruised to Big Pink to show him the clubhouse, which we were feeling quite proud of. He took it all in with a look of wonderment. "Damn, boys. I like this," he said, laughing. Then, as Rick handed him a pipe of grass, "Hell, I'm liking this more and more all the time."

Anticipating Levon's return, I had written a tune called "Yazoo Street Scandal." Levon had once shown me a street in Helena, Arkansas, called Yazoo, and Yazoo was a pretty common name in the Mississippi Delta. The song had some of that voodoo southern mojo to it, which made it an obvious fit for Levon to sing. We congregated down in the basement and played it for him. I had sung the original recording into a tiny harmonica mic, or "conscious mic," as Rick called it. Extremely lo-fi, reminiscent of what your subconscious might sound like coming through an old-time radio. "Man, that feels good," Levon said. He turned to Richard. "Beak, is that you playing drums? Man, that's some good shit." We played a couple more tunes we were working on and a few things we'd done with Bob—I didn't want to barrage him with too much too quick. It felt so natural to have Levon back in the brotherhood, but I could tell he was taking it all in one step at a time.

Levon and I got into the blue station wagon Bob had given me and drove back into town so I could show him around. We ended up at my house, where I introduced him to Dominique. They hit it off right away, and we settled in for a bite to eat. There was so much to catch up on and no time to waste. Levon and I took some uppers and stayed up all night telling stories. He described how he and Bonnie had to take a break, that their lifestyle had gotten out of hand. "We had to cool it, or someone was going to get hurt," he said plainly. "So I went back to Arkansas." He confessed that he hadn't played much music in the past year. A little with sax player Bobby Keys and the cats from Oklahoma, Jim Keltner out in LA, a bit with the Cate Brothers in Arkansas. But music had somehow gotten lost in his day-to-day life. Then he ended up staying with a friend in Memphis. He explained it as a period of redemption, trying to get back on track. Rick's call came just in time. He was running out of options.

I filled Levon in on all of our crazy experiences playing around the world with Bob. "It all seems like a dream now, like it couldn't have happened." I knew Levon hadn't been thrilled working with Bob in the past, but I couldn't express strongly enough how I thought he would feel completely different at this stage. "Bob's been so supportive, and one of the best friends a guy could ask for. You'll see."

I saw a look in Levon's eyes that told me his concerns were set at ease. "Well, if you say so," he said, "I'm good with that. I'm in."

WITH THE HELP of the boys Levon got settled at Big Pink and became part of the family again in no time. He sat down at the drums, adjusted the height and position of everything, gave me a wink, and we kicked into a funky little riff like we hadn't missed a beat. The Hawks were a five-piece band, and now all the chairs were filled.

Bob came by the next day for our usual routine and greeted Levon like part of the gang. Rick and Levon were in a furious game of checkers as Bob took his place behind the typewriter. Garth passed around coffees as Richard did the brewing.

"You know what's missing here?" I said in Levon's direction. "A football. We need a football to toss around outside to limber up."

"Damn right," Levon answered. "Always need to limber up." I thought about when we used to toss around a ball down in Fayetteville, in an attempt at exercise.

Ding! Fresh words right out of the typewriter. Bob grabbed the sheet of paper and handed it to Rick. "Here," he said, "see if you can do something with this. It's called 'Wheels on Fire.'" Rick said he'd have something by tomorrow. I looked over at Levon, who had just lost to Rick at checkers, soaking it all in. In the basement Bob launched into a little rockabilly with "I Forgot to Remember to Forget." I mentioned John Lee Hooker, and in the blink of an eye Bob started singing Hooker's "Tupelo" and "I'm in the Mood." When he did the traditional song "Kickin' My Dog Around," it was hard to tell it from one of Bob's original basement songs.

Meanwhile, Hamlet had come into the room, wagging his tail, and wandered over to Levon, who looked unamused. He lifted his hands away from Hamlet. "Go on, get out of here." I had forgotten that in some kind of southern fashion, Levon had a strong aversion to dogs.

"No, Hamlet's okay," Rick said. "He's one of the boys. He used to be Bob's dog, but now I'm his master."

Levon answered, "Well, you can master him all you want. I don't need no shit-eating dog coming around me." Bob and I laughed at the geniune southernness of the remark.

As promised, the next day Rick had a melody and an unusual chord progression for "Wheels on Fire." It took Bob a few times through to get the hang of it, especially the diminished chord in the verse, but he sang it natural as can be. We stepped outside and threw the new football Levon had picked up until we needed a cigarette break. Meanwhile, Bob ripped off another gem on the typewriter called "Odds and Ends" and we tore that one up in the basement before Bob had to go home for dinner.

All these tunes were starting to mount up. The idea was to organize the tapes so they could be sent off to the song-administration people. Albert said they would only be heard by the publishers and select artists that the material might be appropriate for. Very private, very exclusive. That distinct concept gave us the looseness to experiment and have a good time.

Ever since we had hooked up with Bob, you would read in articles and reviews that he could write good songs but he wasn't much of a singer. Yet on our tours in 1965 and '66, I heard a vocal coming out of that skinny little body like a hurricane; incredible control and power. And when Bob and I had played music in our hotel rooms, I had started to hear different voices he had in his arsenal. When we were recording in New York or Nashville he wasn't precious about his vocals and never, ever overdubbed his voice, but boy, did he deliver. Still, there would be someone out there complaining about the sound of his voice. During the basement-tapes period, I witnessed some really unconventional, unique singing that was just killer. I came to the conclusion that this guy who had people whining about his vocal abilities had to be one of the greatest singers ever, and those naysayers were dead wrong.

Playing music in a circle in the basement or on an acoustic set in the living room was having a big effect on our musical approach: it was about a balance of vocals and instruments. If you couldn't hear properly, somebody was too loud and out of balance. This approach was as old as music but had very little to do with the way a lot of people were playing those days. Louder was becoming king, which we had been blamed for in our past, but we had evolved to a place where loud music was like greasy food, not really good for you.

Don't know if it was because we were living in the mountains, but mountain music started to find its way deep into our vocabulary. We might do the song "If I Lose" by the Stanley Brothers, or something by Johnnie & Jack or the Louvin Brothers. We weren't in the Blue Mountains, but it started to sound that way: Rick picking up a fiddle, Levon a mandolin, Richard a slide guitar, and Garth an accordion, and me slapping away high up on the neck of an acoustic guitar. Rick, Levon, and Richard would sing the three-part harmony, with me filling in on the low part. At the same time, the gospel harmonies of the Staple Singers and the Impressions were just as present. We ran over "Yazoo Street Scandal" with Levon singing, down and dirty.

Richard played a song that he thought could be sung by Rick, Levon, and him. Passing around the vocals like a basketball seemed to be at the core of what our sound could be. The song Richard was writing honestly reflected a stage in the Hawks' development. He sang out, "We can talk about it now, it's the same old riddle, only starting from the middle."

I loved watching Levon take in the carefree looseness of us laying down songs like "I'm Your Teenage Prayer" or "Crash on the Levee." He very quickly adapted. Some of the songs, like "Minstrel Boy" or "Sign on the Cross," never got the chance to be fully baked, but I underlined a few of those titles with Bob to look at later. They were worth finishing or revisiting, but songs were flying by so quickly that you couldn't hardly slow that train down.

At home, Dominique laid out blankets and towels for our cats, who were having kittens in every closet. I was so lost in the creative process at Big Pink that I responded as if we grew cats on trees around here. Just have to bring on the milk, right? But when Dominique said she had to go to Montreal for a week, that's when it finally hit me—we now had ten cats, and one of them was pregnant.

I was also building up quite a pile of classic movie scripts to read. Every time someone was headed into the city, I'd ask them to go to the Gotham Book Mart and grab some for me. I kept a list of movies: *Yojimbo*, *The Seven Samurai*, *Simon of the Desert*. Slowly, reading all these screenplays began to influence my songwriting. I was finally able to unlock the storehouse of images in the attic of my memory, all the characters and stories I'd absorbed from the time I was sixteen and arrived in the holy land of rock 'n' roll down south—at that age, everything pours into your mind in such rich color and detail. Between finally having a clubhouse and what I gathered from these scripts, I was able to tap into this imaginative, thematic material in my own writing.

Upstairs in the workroom across from my bedroom on Larsen Lane, I sat with a little typewriter, a pen and legal pad, and a Martin D-28 guitar that said NAZARETH, PENNSYLVANIA on the label inside the sound hole. I revisited memories and characters from my southern exposure and put them into a Luis Buñuel surreal setting. One of the themes that really stuck with me from Buñuel's films, like *Viridiana*, was the impossibility of sainthood—no good deed goes unpunished. I wrote "The Weight" in one sitting that night.

Levon could sing the hell out of that one, I thought. I knew his instrument, his talents so well, and I wanted to write a song that he could sing better than anybody. Then I put food, milk, and kitty litter out for our growing herd of seventeen cats and went to bed.

The following day I played the tune for the guys to see if it might be a contender. They reacted very strongly to the song's possibilities, but I mostly thought of it as a fallback tune in case one of the other songs didn't work out. I'd been thinking we should have something to show-case Garth's brilliant keyboard work, so I suggested he do an intro to "Chest Fever." We tried the song with Levon singing a harmony on the chorus and interjecting his laid-back drum feel during the riff section.

Halloween 1967. We heard it was Howard Alk's birthday, so we all grabbed Salvation Army band–type instruments, threw on some masks, and headed in his direction. He was finishing up work on Peter Yar-row's film *You Are What You Eat*—for which we had collaborated on the soundtrack with Tiny Tim—at his editing facility when we showed up hooting and honking outside. He and his wife, Jonesy, clapped and cheered and introduced us to a fellow named John Simon who was there helping with the film music. I had met John before, when I was record-ing with Charles Lloyd in 1965—he was the producer on the session. John was a staff producer with Columbia Records and had done an album featuring the Canadian philosopher Marshall McLuhan, called *The Medium Is the Message*, based on his mind-opening book. I thought the record was very unusual and wonderful in a crazy way. Some of it was along the lines of what we were doing in the basement with "Even If It's a Pig, Part 2."

Around the same time, Albert called me from Los Angeles saying he'd made a deal for us at Capitol Records, the same company that had the Beach Boys and the Beatles. He'd hoped to sign us to Warner Bros., but Mo Ostin was out of town and Albert wanted to get the deal done while he was in LA. I passed the news along to the guys, who thought, *Hallelujah! This is real, this is serious, and now we have to get down to it.*

In our pursuit of finding the right producer, I connected with John Simon. We hung out for a couple days before he finally said, "Are you guys going to play some music for me, or what?" He probably thought we were stalling, but we were still trying to get a bead on whether he was the man for the job. We played him some tunes from our basement tapes and then got behind our instruments and did "We Can Talk." The way we passed around vocals in the performance blew John's mind. He was nearly speechless. His face turned red. He stood up and paced.

"That was absolutely incredible," he said. We ran through a couple more songs, and he just shook his head. "Please, let me work on this with you. I think this is really special." John was the first and only producer we had met with, and his enthusiasm meant a lot. Most important, we felt comfortable with him and liked him.

ALBERT AND SALLY GROSSMAN had taken a trip to India, and upon their return to Woodstock, they claimed to have discovered an incredible group there. Allen Ginsberg had turned them on to some street musicians in Calcutta called the Bauls of Bengal. "If Ravi Shankar is *the* classical music guy of India," Albert told us, "then the Bauls are the Muddy Waters. They all sing and play instruments you've never seen before." Sally said Albert was making arrangements to bring them to Woodstock, where they would stay at the Grossmans' until Albert got them some gigs.

"This is going to be interesting," Sally smiled. "It's already getting cold here and I don't know if they've ever worn shoes."

When the Bauls arrived, Albert invited Dominique and me over to meet them. Really sweet, gentle people with a strong devotion to their spiritual calling, they seemed to be a family band, led by Purna Das and his younger brother Luxman. They were making breakfast when we arrived, and Albert said, "Check this out." The Bauls prepared some yogurt concoction and mixed marijuana and honey into it. Then, after they ate, they took out a large chillum and packed it with tobacco and hash. They wrapped a small, wet cloth at the bottom of the chillum, fired it up, and passed it among themselves. This was part of their cultural ritual. They picked up their instruments and sat in a circle around the living room in the guest quarters. Each member sang one song, and each performance raised the bar higher until they finished with Purna's almost operatic intensity. The rhythm coming from their instrument, called a khrmack, was intoxicating. It sounded like a combination of a gut-string guitar with only two strings and a tabla drum, melodic and percussive. This was chilling music, like funky East Indian opera raga.

I suggested the Bauls come out for a visit to Big Pink and meet the boys. And so the next day here they came, with coats and boots over their robes. A couple of them spoke some English, and we made a nice connection. They stood for long periods in front of the corny little picture on our fireplace mantel, transfixed by the revolving light on the back of the picture device that made it look like the river was flowing. They got a big kick out of that, and we got a big kick out of them watching it.

Charles Lloyd came up to visit with me in Woodstock while the Bauls were around, and I took him out to see our setup in the basement. He brought his sax, just in case we decided to jam a little. Some of the Bauls sat down at the checkerboards in the living room. They didn't know how to play and were making up crazy rules as they went along, jumping over one another's men in random directions and then calling out one another for cheating. At one of these tournaments, a couple of them got upset over the outcome of a game, and things grew heated. They stood abruptly and strutted downstairs to the basement in silent single file. Each of them took their instrument and tightened or tuned it in some fashion. Then—*bam*—they started playing their asses off, like they were letting off steam. "Wait a minute," we said, "let's record this," and we put some mics in front of them while Garth began to get a balance. While they played, they displayed a large picture of their father, an amazing-looking man, holding one of their original instruments, a kartaijulie, against the sky. The father was the high priest of the family and a founder of the Baul movement.

When we got the microphones all set up, Charles got out his horns, like maybe we could have an interesting world-music, East-meets-

West connection any moment now. He was into a lot of Asian mysticisms and musicalities, so he was at the ready. When the Bauls started playing, however, it became clear this was not a jam band; you might as well do yourself a favor and stay out of the way. I put my guitar back in its case, and Charles smiled and laid down his horn. They soared for close to an hour, and Garth recorded it all. No wonder we were always running out of tape. (The recording came out on Buddha Records a while later as *The Bengali Bauls at Big Pink*.)

ONE DAY WHEN Dominique was using our station wagon, Bob picked me up and we headed to Big Pink. He drove cautiously through the center of Woodstock and onto the highway that led to West Saugerties. We were only going about twenty-five miles per hour. Cars were passing us, some honking their horns. I noticed Bob was wearing glasses I hadn't seen before.

"How's your eyesight?" I asked, with images of Mr. Magoo, the shortsighted cartoon character, floating through my mind.

He answered, "Pretty good. I just got some new specs."

"Yeah, I noticed that, but why are you driving so slow? You're driving like an old lady," I joked.

He replied seriously, "You can't be too careful these days. Do you know how many people make a living by jumping out in front of cars and then suing you for everything you've got?"

I looked at him, a bit taken aback. "What? Who told you that?"

"Just look in the newspapers. Every day, there's somebody all bandaged up, suing a guy who was just driving along. But they pick their targets well. They're out there just waiting for you."

"If some fool is waiting to jump out in front of a car, wouldn't they be better off finding somebody not going too fast, so they wouldn't get terribly banged up?" I offered.

Bob pushed down on the accelerator a little. "Yeah, you see, they got you coming and going."

When we arrived in the basement, the boys were running over one of Richard's songs, called "Lonesome Suzie." It sounded quite lovely, and I was already thinking about a subtle guitar part that might blend right in. Bob went upstairs to get behind the typewriter, and Richard played through the tune again while I learned the changes. "This could be a contender," I said to the guys. Everybody agreed, so we decided to play it that evening for John Simon.

After a smoke break, Bob pulled a new lyric sheet out of the typewriter and we kicked into "Santa Fe," the beginning of a pretty good song possibility. Bob did some of his vibing vocables on words, and we played through it with Levon on drums. He was a bit rusty and tentative from just getting back, and still a little unfamiliar with the clubhouse groove. We had recorded a ton of songs with Bob already, and by the time Levon joined us we were winding down a little.

At the end of the afternoon it was already getting dark out, and Bob said, "Shall we head back?" When we got in the car, he looked concerned about something and drove a little more hastily than on the way out.

"I've had some weird shit happening at my house and I need to make sure everything's okay," he said.

"What's going on?" I asked.

"People. Strange people just show up at my door anytime—night or day. It's really upsetting for Sara, and I don't know who these people are or what they want. It makes me angry dealing with this shit all the time. You move up to the country for some quiet peace of mind, and they come like invaders on my doorstep."

This wasn't the first time we'd had this conversation. "When you're famous this comes with the dinner," I reminded him, "especially the kind of fame you've created. People think you've got some miraculous insight, and they want to be close to that magic."

"I don't have any fucking magic!" he blurted.

"Well obviously they think you do," I said. "Why don't you try what other 'famous' people do? Hire some security or build a gate. Or have your guy, Bernard, deal with them. He can send them away."

"He's tried, but they keep coming. He doesn't know how to deal with that. He's French. They don't have this kind of behavior in

France. Ask Dominique, she knows. French people don't act like that. Over here they don't even know what privacy means." He slapped the steering wheel. "I don't want to have to build a gate. I don't want to live like that."

THE NEXT DAY Garth and I put together a selection of Bob's basement songs for Albert to pass on to the music-publishing people, fourteen or so tracks that sounded like they could be covered by a variety of recording artists. The rest of these recordings would live underground and be for our ears only, especially a cut like "See You Later Allen Ginsberg," a takeoff on "See You Later, Alligator." Bob didn't want any of these humorous tunes to be taken the wrong way.

Timing was falling into place for the Hawks to work exclusively on our own music. Bob mentioned to me that he had made arrangements to go to Nashville again and cut some new songs, different kinds of songs, for his next release. Quite extraordinary, I thought, that Bob already had another batch of material in the works. Just showed what a clear mind and healthy body can do for you creatively. We all knew the stories about artists doing their best work while being addicted, insane, or drunk, but this period was pretty much on the "natch." We smoked a little weed here and there, but no more uppers or downers or hallucinogens, and nobody hardly ever drank. Once in a while Richard would have a few beers, but never enough to interfere with our work schedule. We had a clean dream machine, and it felt good for us all to work without any unnecessary baggage.

The boys and I sat down to review our own basement tapes and decide which tracks were real contenders for our album. We had a tape from Barry Feinstein's photo studio of Richard trying out the beginning of a song idea called "Beautiful Thing," just him playing a Wurlitzer electric piano and singing the words he had so far. It had a nice feel, but Richard couldn't figure what to do with it from there. During the earlier days of our basement tunes, Richard and Rick had recorded "Orange Juice Blues" (also called "Blues for Breakfast"), and

I liked some of the lyrics Richard came up with, like "I'm tired of everything being 'beautiful, beautiful,'" a touch of antihippie humor slipping in there. His piano playing impressed me most of all, but I didn't know if the song was a must.

"Tears of Rage" and "I Shall Be Released" were strong contenders, and we were working on a version of "Wheels on Fire." Rick felt quite strongly about "Caledonia Mission" and wanted to give that a go. We all agreed. I definitely thought "Yazoo Street Scandal" was right up Levon's alley, but I still wasn't sure about the flavor of it for our album. Even with Rick's unique bass playing on this track, the song sounded a bit like some of our older music, and this was a brand-new day.

One of the songs from the tapes that stood out was "Ain't No More Cane." We had learned it from Bob, but Levon had grown up with it and said his daddy used to sing it around the house. We each sang a verse, with a blend of harmonies, accompanied by Garth's soulful accordion—I might have had it somewhere in the back of my mind when I wrote "The Weight," which was also becoming a contender. "Chest Fever" too, with its crazy "basement" words, and Garth's new "Toccata and Fugue in D Minor" intro, borrowed from Bach. We had to choose between "Lonesome Suzie" and "Katie's Been Gone." Both had Richard's sympathetic sentiments. I liked that "Katie's Been Gone" had no intro and that Rick's harmony in the ending had a touch of "Pet Sounds" influence, but "Lonesome Suzie" was so moving. I suggested we let John Simon decide.

Levon and I pulled "Don't Ya Tell Henry" from the ashes of the tracks with Bob. We'd never gotten around to doing a refined version of it with him, but Levon gravitated toward the trippy, funny lyrics. I had a bit of an arrangement stirring, so Levon grabbed his mandolin, and we went to town. Richard sang a version of a prebasement song of Bob's called "Long Distance Operator," which we dug playing, but I thought it might be reverting back to our older, bluesier-rock style.

By the time John Simon came back up to Woodstock to finish working on the film *You Are What You Eat*, the Hawks were convinced: his taste, musicianship, and producing skills all felt like a strong fit. When he came over to Big Pink to hear what we had stored up in our arsenal, his choices matched ours to a T. His arrangement ideas also sounded inspired and worth trying. John had produced Leonard Cohen and Blood, Sweat & Tears. He had worked with Marshall McLuhan! How wrong could he be?

What we didn't have on tape we played through live for John. I loved seeing him shaking his head in admiration after we ran through Richard's beautiful lament "In a Station." "That's incredible," he rejoiced. "That's going to be truly great." I sang an acoustic version of "The Weight" for him that I was in the process of teaching to the guys. John started imagining drum parts with Levon and loved where we were going with the vocals. I thought Garth should play piano on this one, and Richard could sing harmony and play organ. I was in the midst of writing "To Kingdom Come," which I had started banging out on the typewriter a while back, and sang some of it for John and the boys. That seemed to push the needle over the mark; we were ready to head into the studio.

The idea of having a clubhouse recording facility was indeed extremely rare at this time, and we loved Big Pink for the creative freedom it afforded us. But we had never seen it as more than a writing workshop. John agreed that we'd have to take our sound to town and suggested A&R Studios in New York. Phil Ramone, the highly regarded engineer, had taken over the studio and turned the rooms into the best in the city. "I want to tell Albert we need to book A&R," John said. "We should get the room on top of the roof. It's the best."

THE NEXT AFTERNOON, we were hanging out in the living room of Big Pink when Rick glanced out the window and made an announcement: "Boys, we got company. Look who just pulled up. It's Allen Ginsberg and his boyfriend, Peter." He ducked back from the window. "Oh dear! He's got his harmonium with him." We absolutely enjoyed Allen and had great respect for his poetic brilliance, but when he started chanting and squeezing that harmonium, it could make you dizzy.

"I've got an idea," I said. When they came through the door I gave a warm greeting. "Hi, Allen. Hey, Peter. How's it going?" They shook hands with everybody.

"I brought my harmonium," said Allen, "in case we feel like getting into some music."

"Great. Oh! I nearly forgot. The Bauls of Bengal are looking for you. They kept asking, 'Where is Allen Ginsberg?' They looked a bit lonely."

"They did? That's what they're saying?" Allen asked, surprised. "I'm responsible for them being here, far away from their home. Where are they?"

"They're staying in the guest apartment at Albert and Sally's," I told him with a worried look in my eye.

Allen turned to Peter. "We better get over there. I'm sorry, fellas, but we need to go and check on the Bauls. They're such a long way from their culture and their people."

"Oh, don't worry, we completely understand," said Rick. "Tell them hello for us."

They scurried back to their car and took off. I looked around at the guys. "Well, it's true. I heard Purna Das say, 'Where's Allen Ginsberg?'"

Richard grinned. "No, you didn't."

Rick started singing "See You Later Allen Ginsberg."

Garth chuckled to himself and went "shhhh" with his finger in front of his lips.

NINETEEN

While we were still in the basement putting ideas together for our album, I kept harping to John Simon that it had to have a unique sound, a flavor of its own. I played particular records for him from my collection: tracks from Chess Studios in Chicago, Sun Records in Memphis, Cosimo's Studio in New Orleans, Muscle Shoals in Alabama, and Gold Star in Los Angeles. We listened to recordings by Otis Redding, Phil Spector, Howlin' Wolf, Lee Dorsey, the Beach Boys, Gene Vincent, Little Willie John, Elvis, and Sir Mack Rice. John completely understood that we were searching for our own sonic identity. Precisely how we would achieve the desired sound, though, was still very much up in the air.

Garth had been working on more advanced keyboard equipment and sounds. One of the new gizmos he had in the works was a blackbox, mini Leslie speaker. The box stood about two and a half feet square with sound vents on four sides. Inside sat a speaker and some kind of fan that made the sound coming out of it seem to "whirl" around. You activated the fan/Leslie effect with a foot switch. After Garth tried it out on a couple of his keyboards, we decided to plug my guitar amp into it and see how that sounded. I loved it—a lo-fi, raunchy swirl effect. The black box even sounded good without the Leslie fan turned on; it was something about the speaker Garth used, facing down inside the particular shape of that wooden box.

After months of being pounded down in the basement, the drums

Levon was using sounded pretty dull. He was putting on new heads one day while I worked on a chord progression on the piano, and as he tuned the heads, I noticed how deep and rich the drums now sounded. I asked him to leave the toms tuned low, so when you struck the head with a drumstick, it changed tonality and rang out with an ambiguous note. Levon somewhat reluctantly tuned the top and bottom skins of his toms much looser than normal, and when he played they rang out with a song of their own, as melodic as it was percussive. I repeated a few chords I'd been messing with, and Levon kicked in on the drums. It sounded fantastic, and Richard and Rick came downstairs to check it out. By then Levon was into it and stopped to fine-tune the toms even more. Pretty soon he was playing them like a stand-up bass, and the rest of us had to leave room for them to breathe throughout the arrangement of a song.

A couple of days later I joined Albert in his kitchen for edible delights and some business. "Capitol Records wants to know the name of our band for drawing up the contracts," he mentioned. "Are you still going to be called the Hawks?"

It was a good question. We both knew that "hawk" had taken on a different connotation in the growing antiwar movement, and our politics were at best Canadian, where they welcomed "draft dodgers" with open arms. Besides, "the Hawks" was left over from working with Ronnie. I told Albert the boys and I were talking about new names and we would have something for the record company soon. But when we did try to come up with a name for our band, it felt a bit absurd. We had been together for six years, and *now* we were going to figure out what to call ourselves?

At home, Dominique had shown me how to make a French filtered coffee. I got into it and started adding a hint of dark chocolate and cinnamon to the espresso flavor. Bob would stop by my house some mornings for a fresh brew. He would light a cigarette, sip on that big cup of java, and say, "This is tasty coffee. What's in it?" I would just look away with a grin: "There's some secrets we can't let out."

Bob was back from recording in Nashville, and he brought over an acetate along with his big Saint Bernard, Buster. I looked forward to hearing what he had stirred up this time in Music City. On most of the songs there was only bass and drums, with Bob's vocal, rhythm acoustic guitar, and harmonica—true to the nature of this straightforward storytelling material. "All Along the Watchtower" couldn't have been more satisfying, with its own mythology and those three chords that never wore out.

After our second cup of coffee and the end of the recordings, Bob said, "Well, that's the basic tracks. I thought you and Garth could overdub on all of these songs and make the whole thing sound full and complete."

The thought hadn't even crossed my mind while I was listening. I took a moment to digest the idea, then confessed, "I wouldn't know what to add to these songs." They sounded complete to me in their bold, minimalist way. Bob shrugged, as if to say, *Maybe you're right.*

He put on his coat, grabbed Buster's leash, and headed for the door. As he was leaving, I told him again how much I enjoyed the record just as it was. Soon as he stepped outside, Buster took off, tromping through the snow. Bob had the leash wrapped around his gloved hand. "Buster! Buster, stop!" he yelled, but Buster had not taken too well to his training yet, and galloped on down the driveway and through the snow with Bob tumbling behind.

A couple of days later Bob told me he was going to leave his new songs just the way they were. That was good to hear. He added that several different recording artists had heard the basement tapes and lots of people were going to cover them.

"Really, like who?"

"The list is too long to name them all," Bob said, "but you'll see. They're coming from everywhere."

JOHN SIMON HAD booked studio time for us in his favorite room at A&R Studios in the city. He suggested going in for just a few days at first to make sure it felt right. The boys and I were as nervous as we were excited. We had something to prove and were working on songs and music that didn't even remotely sound like stuff we had done in the past. The raging rockabilly from our apprenticeship with Ronnie; our rhythm-and-soul period as Levon and the Hawks, filled with "rave on" guitar blues; our explosive "electric" sacrilege with Bob; and finally our loose-as-a-goose, devil-may-care style of the basement tapes—toward all of this we had a subconscious rebellious attitude, even though all these musicalities and experiences added up to who we were at this point.

Packing up our gear at Big Pink to go into the city felt more than a little disconcerting. We had been holed up here for many months, sequestering ourselves from the world. Now we were going to reveal the goods and turn ourselves in. We loaded our equipment into A&R Studios with John's help. Don Hahn, the recording engineer, and his second, Shelly Yakus, showed us precisely where they wanted our instruments set up. They put out microphones and chairs where we would sit and arranged sound baffles between us. Don explained that this setup was what made this studio sound so good. "This is how we record everybody in this room. Tried and true, it works great." They gave us earphones because of the sound-isolation baffles and gobos to prevent leakage into one another's mics. They put blankets over the piano, set the bass amp behind a wall and mine facing away from me, and Garth's Leslie was padded and surrounded by glass. We followed all this protocol, wanting to be professional and get the best sound we could.

I talked to John Simon about what song we might start with. We thought "Tears of Rage" might be a good opener. I asked Richard how he felt about singing that first. He said his voice felt pretty good, and sure, we could give it a shot. Naturally we wanted to get off to a strong start and stir up our confidence.

I plugged in the black-box speaker Garth had made, which I thought would work really well on this song. They set up a vocal mic at the piano and another for Rick to do his harmony. John's voice came into our headphones from the control room.

"You guys ready?"

I looked over at the guys but couldn't see anybody for all the baffles. Richard answered into his vocal mic, "Yeah, I guess so."

"Let's run through it so you can get a balance in there and adjust our headphones," I said. "I can't hear the bass at all."

"There, is that better?" said Don, the engineer.

"Yeah," I answered. "Okay, let's run through it. Is everybody here? We might as well be in different rooms."

About halfway through the song, John stopped us, asking Garth about a noise coming from his organ output and for me to try switching the ground button on my amp. These were technical issues that would be sorted out. But musically there was something terribly wrong.

I put down my guitar on the floor and went into the control room. "This doesn't work, John. Sorry, but we can't record like this." John got up and we walked into the studio to join the other guys. They already knew where I was going with this. "We can't make music with an isolated setup," I explained. "We have to see one another. We have to read one another's signals. That's how we play—to each other."

Rick said, "I can't sing with Richard if I can't see his mouth moving."

"This ain't worth a damn," Levon chimed in. "I can't feel where to play fills, and it sounds like shit in these earphones."

John said, "Okay, what do you wanna do?"

I laid out the floor plan. "Rick needs to be right here, facing Richard. Take away all the baffles. I'm gonna sit here in front of Levon, and Garth will be between Rick and me."

John yelled into the control room at Don and Shelly, "Okay guys, new setup. We're moving everything around."

"The drums can stay where they are," I said, "and we'll all just move in. Piano, organ, everything."

The engineer complained that we would get too much spill—leakage in all the mics. It was going to sound really messy, probably terrible. Without blinking an eye, John said, "Then let's use mics that only pick up what's right in front of them. You know, those Electro-Voice RE15 mics. Do you have many of them?"

"We got loads of them," answered Shelly, the second engineer. "How many you want?"

"Let's put them on everything,"

"They're not high-quality microphones," Don cautioned. "I can't guarantee this is going to work very well."

"Let's see." John shrugged. "We have to make these guys feel comfortable. I've seen them play music in their basement and that's what works for them, so we've got to try."

As they started getting levels and a sound on each individual instrument, John looked reasonably confident about his decision. They tried some different mics on a couple of things, but it was mostly those RE15s.

Dominique and Sally showed up at the studio, our only audience and cheering squad. We started jamming a bit to loosen up and ran through the beginning of the song. When John felt comfortable with the sound in the control room, he came out into the studio and helped conduct Levon to where the fills should go. This way Levon could just play and not have to think too much about the arrangement. Now we could hear one another in the room and make eye contact. We were ready to go.

Richard quietly counted it off, and we set sail. We played through the song and felt warmed up. John ran into the control room to listen, made some adjustments. We were recording everybody live onto three tracks, with one track left to overdub horns. Final decisions in the sound and balances had to be made now. Richard remarked, "It sounds really good here in the room." I made some tone changes on my amp and agreed. Levon said he was still getting his part figured out and that John was helping a lot with his cues.

We recorded "Tears of Rage" two more times, back to back, and Don and Shelly said over the talk-back, "You guys should come in and hear this. It's sounding really good." I put my guitar down and looked into the control-room window. Dominique and Sally were waving their arms for us to come listen. When I walked through the door, Dominique started hugging and kissing me. "This music is incredible.

It makes me want to cry," she said, wiping away a tear. Sally just kept shaking her head and putting her hand over her heart, like, *This is going to blow Albert's mind.*

The guys and I thought we'd gotten through the last take well enough, but we hadn't heard a playback yet, so we didn't know what all the fuss was about. Then Don proudly hit "play" on the tape machine, and there it was. We all exhaled with joy. It was hard to believe that breaking the rules in the unusual way we had set up in the studio could produce something that sounded this magical. Richard's voice and piano were sterling. Rick's harmony vocal was loose and soaring, while his bass playing was like warm chocolate. Levon's tuned-down drums gave a thunderous heartbeat to the track. Garth's church organ could bring tears to your eyes. I found a new sound and guitar style with a subtlety to it that rebelled against all rock-raging guitar slingers across the land. I had to hold my breath at points playing like this, slipping in fills just in the nick of time. Then John overdubbed euphonium/high school horn and Garth played sax for our Salvation Army horn section effect. Beautifully sad. Now we were discovering what our new music could conjure up.

John was anxious for us to cut "We Can Talk," with its piano and organ gospel approach. Rick, Richard, and Levon passed the vocals around like the Harlem Globetrotters. It felt good the way it sounded in the studio with no headphones, and by the smiling look on John's face, I thought we might have something going on this one. When we listened to the playback, I knew we were making music unlike anybody else.

WE HAD A heightened sense of confidence as we regrouped in the studio the next day. I began singing the chorus to "The Weight" over and over to the guys, trying to convey the staggered vocal idea I had. "Levon, you go, 'aaand,' then Rick, 'aaand,' then Richard on top, 'aaand.' Levon, 'you put the load,' Rick, Richard, Levon, 'you put the load right on me.'" Garth's piano playing was dynamic and joyous in the key of A, a bit tricky for a piano man, but not for Garth. Levon would sing the first three verses, and I thought it would be interesting to have Rick, with his down-to-earth sound, sing the "Crazy Chester" verse. It might have seemed random at first, but when we ran it down, it sounded unexpected and refreshing. On the run-down keyboard parts between verses, I asked Richard to try a little falsetto turnaround melody to go with his organ part.

John Simon held a copy of the lyrics in his hand as we ran through the arrangement, working on the vocals. "These lyrics are fascinating," he said, "even though I have no idea what this song is about. Where did you come up with this?"

"I'm not too good at explaining song lyrics," I told him, "but basically, it was all I could think of at the time."

We took our positions behind our instruments and played through the tune a couple of times in order for the engineer and John to get a balance on everything. I asked, into my acoustic guitar mic, if the leakage from the live vocal mics and instruments was manageable. John said it wasn't too bad, and they were just going to make a couple of adjustments. Again he took his place in front of Levon to help signal what was coming next. I knew this song, but the other guys were still getting the hang of it, and John's signals helped. We never had music charts. Nothing but lyrics was ever written down.

We got through "The Weight" from beginning to end a couple times and decided to go into the control room and listen. Dominique and Sally sat breathlessly in the back of the room. Don, the engineer, was getting a deep, rich sound, and we heard what we needed to do to make it all come together—we had to get the vocals to fall just right at the end of the choruses. I also wanted to try a double turnaround before the last verse.

We headed back out into the studio while I rattled off some encouragement and cues. Everybody was a bit nervous about remembering all our parts in this delicate balancing act. We laid it down and nailed it. John said, "Let's do one more for good luck," and we aced it again. Dominique, Sally, and the engineers, Don and Shelly, were all on their feet in the control room, like Sputnik had just taken off.

As a songwriter, "The Weight" was something I had been working up to for years. I just heard what I was looking for. The images, the stories I had been putting away in my imagination's attic, had been brought out into the light. We'd aced this delicate performance, and I felt so proud of the guys, shining like this. I shook John's hand, knowing he had just grown a foot taller.

With our unconventional recording setup in the studio and the lower-quality mics we were using, Don and Shelly asked their boss and chief engineer, Phil Ramone, to come in and check out our discovery. They showed him how we were set up in a circle, with total eye contact. Some of our amps and speaker cabinets were a bit baffled, but the musicians were out in the open. Phil looked around and threw up his hands, like he couldn't believe this would work. They came into the control room and Phil said to John, "If it sounds okay, that's all that matters. Does it sound okay?" John smiled and pushed "play" on the tape machine.

Phil sat down and listened intently to a couple of the songs we'd recorded, then looked at his engineers, looked at John, stood up, and said, "That's incredible. That's really fucking incredible." Phil slapped Don on the back and went over to shake John's hand. John sincerely thanked him and introduced me, saying that I wrote the song he had just heard. "That's fucking incredible," he repeated, wagging his finger at me.

The other guys had stepped out for a bite, and I was disappointed they'd missed Phil Ramone's praise. Up to now, only Dominique and Sally had heard this music, and Phil's opinion, which I relayed to the guys word for word, meant a lot.

When we cut Richard's song "In a Station," Garth displayed his magic touch. I really enjoyed Richard sharing a piece of his heart in that tune. It sounded dreamy and distant, slightly psychedelic, I suppose. For some reason it reminded me of Alain Resnais's film *Last Year at Marienbad*, with its misty images and sense of loss. We all fell under its spell.

John asked if we could give my song "Chest Fever" a go. He had changed the arrangement in the verses from how I had written it, with the vocal coming in at a completely different place. A bit tricky, but by now we had a lot of faith in John's ideas and gave it our best. This song was right out of the basement-tapes program, surreal words and monkeyshine music. Garth kicked it off with that hint of J. S. Bach on a gravel back road. When my guitar riff came in, it made you want to rush a bit, but Levon's backbeat held everything at bay. We got to the bridge and everybody stopped except for Richard's vocal, while Levon kept time. When we came back in, Garth played an organ solo unlike anybody else on this planet, floating and soaring into space with a combination of musicalities that you would rarely, if ever, hear streamed together. Then we overdubbed our Salvation Army horn section in the bridge, in a similar style to when we went to serenade Howard Alk for his birthday on the night we first connected with John Simon. "Chest Fever" was definitely a fun track, though we could never play it with that arrangement again. Later we went back to the way I'd originally written it.

Just before we had started our recording sessions, Albert had arranged for the Hawks to meet with attorney David Braun to handle our contract with Capitol Records. We were unproven at this point, so there were no heavy negotiations going on. We also met with Marshall Gelfand, an accountant whom Albert recommended. Marshall said he would handle our U.S. taxes for free, and if we became successful, we would go with his accounting firm. I liked Marshall and appreciated his gesture.

Garth had brought a few of the basement tapes into the city with us, just in case we needed to refer to any songs we might record. Strong consideration was still going on for "I Shall Be Released."

"Oh, here's one I think we should do," Garth said. He cued up "I'm Your Teenage Prayer," a terrifically funny track from the basement tapes. Bob's vocal performance was classic.

John Simon said, "I love those background vocals. Who's doing that answer vocal to Bob? 'Come over here, baby'?"

Rick pointed at me. "It's our secret lead singer, Robbie.

"It's me doing the harmony and Rich doing the high part," Rick explained. "We did this before Lee came back."

"It's still one of my favorites," said Garth.

"Speaking of that, why don't we cut the song Robbie sings, 'To Kingdom Come'?" asked Levon. "That's what it's called, right, Duke?"

"Yeah, we need some guitar solos too," said Richard. "I'd like to do that one next." This song was more experimental to me, and I was still sorting it out, so I pleaded to hold off cutting that one. The guys insisted, so I plugged in Garth's black box and turned off the fan/Leslie effect and switched on my tremolo to see what it sounded like for the guitar solos.

"It sounds good in here," John said from the control room. "Let's go with it." Levon coached me through the vocal, when to hit it harder and when to pull back, and we laid it down in just a couple of takes.

I had a picture in my mind of what our musical group was, and the way "To Kingdom Come" shook out in the recording process was a little off-course for me. I wanted to stay away from an unbalanced form in our group. We had a special democratic arrangement among the five of us, and if I wrote the song, sang the song, arranged it, and played the solos, in my mind, that's not who we were. "Okay," I told myself, "we'll balance it out in other ways."

AGAIN THE RECORD company and management asked what the name of our group would be, and again we had trouble taking the question seriously. We laughed about calling ourselves "The Royal Canadians Except for Levon." Albert liked the idea of our not having a name. "Let them try and deal with that."

Richard liked "The Honkies" but knew nobody would go for it. He joked, "If we want to be up on the scene with today's kind of group names, we could go with 'The Marshmallow Overcoats' or 'The Chocolate Subway.' Levon related to being called "The Crackers" and no one vehemently disagreed, although we didn't know if they had true "crackers" in Canada. The record company thought that was a nice name, at first. They thought we meant soda crackers, Ritz, or honey ginger—not uneducated, country, bigoted, southern white trash.

Back in the studio, I was enjoying Rick's vocal on "Caledonia Mission." The texture of his voice sounded so honest, so natural. He was by far the best harmony singer in the group, which was extremely evident on the basement tapes.

We finished up our sessions at A&R Studios and returned to Woodstock. Winter had kicked in with full force in the Catskills, and we made steady calls to the Shultis family, the go-to people around there for firewood and snowplowing. When the long driveway and Pine Road leading to Big Pink got snowed in and kept us from getting anywhere, we faced a serious setback. With our limited recording budget, we had to figure out phase two of making the album. We had cut seven songs and had about five more contenders. There was a clause in our deal with Capitol that said if we used their studios at the Capitol Records Tower in LA, we could record free of charge. It would just be a matter of paying for travel and housing.

It was now so cold and snowy in Woodstock that I pushed to make the LA option work, and the boys and John Simon were more than sympathetic. John said he hoped that Capitol Studios could hold up to the sound we were getting at A&R. I pointed out that Bobbie Gentry's song "Ode to Billie Joe" had been recorded there, and it had a certain quality, a big sound and an earthiness at the same time.

"True," John said, "but Brian Wilson of the Beach Boys and Phil Spector use Gold Star Studios, not Capitol." He had a point. Some of the greatest Nat King Cole and Frank Sinatra recordings had been cut at Capitol Studios (famous for its underground echo chambers), but that was yesterday. This was early 1968, and maybe things had changed. While we were figuring this out, Bob came by my house in Woodstock one morning for one of our ritual coffees. He said there was a Woody Guthrie tribute coming up at Carnegie Hall, and he had agreed to perform three songs.

"That'll be terrific," I told him, "and they'll love you returning to an acoustic folk style for the event."

"No, I want to do it with you and the guys," Bob said. "You think they'll be into it?"

"I'll run it by the boys, but I'm sure they'll be up for it."

We were scheduled to go out to LA and start recording in about three weeks. That gave us time to run over some Woody Guthrie tunes with Bob and start to figure out what we would cut when we headed west.

When we got to Carnegie Hall and started to set up our instruments, you could see a worried look on the face of the concert producer, Harold Leventhal, a prominent folk-music manager. I suppose he was hoping we would leave the "electronics" behind this time. But what could anybody say? What could they do? Bob was going to do it his way, and that was that.

The Woody Guthrie tribute had the aura of a serious folk-music summit. I felt like a bit of an intruder in this setting. But the responsibility for inviting us along fell on Bob's shoulders, and I was ready to get in the trenches with him anywhere after all we'd been through.

Perhaps because we'd recently recorded in a mellower vein, not to mention the lingering effects of the basement-tapes vibe, we played those Woody Guthrie songs more subtly than we'd played Bob's songs on the tour. We took the stage with a rousing version of "I Ain't Got No Home," then did "Grand Coulee Dam" with a bit of a Muscle Shoals lilt. The audience and other folk artists on the show—Pete Seeger, Judy Collins, Odetta—watched us with trepidation in the beginning, but no one could resist Bob's passion for the songs. "Dear Mrs. Roosevelt" definitely won them over, such a pure Guthrie plea. The boys and I ended up enjoying the experience, even if we were venturing a little over the tracks. There's something dirty about rock 'n' roll and blues, and here at this Carnegie Hall folk tribute, things seemed pretty clean—even if they were dusty.

Back in Woodstock, Bob gave me a painting he had done of an American Indian looking straight ahead, while in the background an Indian woman, maybe *his* woman, rides away on the back of a horse with a cowboy. It was a rectangular canvas, and I liked how it hinted at a story. Without going into too much detail, I told Bob that the recording with the guys was going well and that we had some surprises for him. I mentioned that our name, "The Hawks," had come under fire, and we needed to come up with a new moniker. I said that our affiliation with him had made such an imprint, and if he had any ideas how we could solve this, to please enlighten us. Oh, and also, if he felt inspired to do a painting for our album cover, that would be good too.

We packed up and ventured west to the warmer climes of LA, moving into the infamous Castle in Los Feliz, where I had stayed with Bob before. From there we could aim straight for our hookup at the impressive Capitol Records Tower recording facilities. By now we felt that musically we were onto something, and we hoped to impress the Capitol staff and make them believers. Capitol had assigned A&R man John Palladino to help us get our recording schedule set up. There was a lot of variation among A&R men: some were very controlling, and others knew when to get out of the way. Thankfully, John Palladino was easygoing and didn't want to interfere. He let us do our own thing.

Union engineers worked the studios at Capitol, and the "union rules" meant John Simon wasn't allowed to so much as touch the mixing board or any of the equipment. An engineer named Rex Uptegraft was delegated to work with us in studio B. To get him familiar with our music, our sound, John Simon played him the songs we had recorded in New York. He listened, partially interested. After the playback all he had to say was "That's darn cute." It looked like this could be a tough one.

We showed Rex how we wanted to set up in the studio, and he went along with it, no particular skin off his ass. John tried to educate him on our process as best he could, without being able to touch anything.

I had a certain approach in mind for the great Lefty Frizzell record "Long Black Veil," more of an R&B treatment with a Wurlitzer electric piano and the drums playing in half time. I taught it to Rick, who was familiar with the tune from way back. We had come into a time where too many musicians thought they were songwriters, and the idea of doing one classic song that we could put a new spin on appealed to me out of pure respect for actual songsmiths. I thought we could try out "Long Black Veil" at Capitol Studios to see if we could find a groove with Rex "Darn Cute" Updegraft.

I showed Levon how I wanted to approach the song beatwise, and soon it started to come together. Rick sounded so authentic singing this song and telling the story. The studio didn't have all the mics John wanted, and it took a lot of trial and error before he gave us a thumbs-up. The sound here wasn't as vivid and shimmering as at A&R, but once we found our zone, magic started to flow. We got a take on "Long Black Veil," and I told John it might be worth considering our Salvation Army horn vibe on this song, just to go completely against the grain. Garth and John thought this could work and started messing around with a little horn part. I always enjoyed mixing musical worlds together and reinventing a song through experimentation.

When we recorded Richard's song "Lonesome Suzie," John was concerned that we had a lot of slow songs, and he suggested we try a more up-tempo shuffle version of the tune. We did, with John and Garth adding some horns to the track. But as we listened to the slow version and then the more up-tempo approach back to back, two things became very clear to me: the faster arrangement wasn't lonesome, and I wasn't concerned about the balance between slow songs and fast songs.

ALBERT AND SALLY came out to Los Angeles while we were recording, and one night the two of them, Dominique, and I went to the Shrine Auditorium to see the Jimi Hendrix Experience. Backstage, Albert greeted Mo Ostin, the president of Warner Bros. Records, whom I'd met briefly once when he came to Woodstock. You could tell in two seconds what a terrific gentleman he was. I told Mo we were finishing up our album at Capitol Studios. "You know," he said, smiling, "I started Reprise Records with Sinatra and that's where Frank recorded most of his best work." Mo and Albert were friends and had worked together for years. Mo was quick to point out that he was extremely disappointed with Albert for signing us to Capitol while he was out of town. "Just unfortunate timing," Albert said apologetically. We went out to catch Jimi's set, but we were positioned right in front of the PA; after a few fantastic songs our ears were bleeding. "I think we better go," said Albert. We all agreed, but I was sorry not to get a chance to say hello to my old guitar buddy, Jimmy James.

The work was getting done at Capitol Studios, but I couldn't shake the feeling that something was lacking. Just for the sake of contrast, John booked us a few hours at Gold Star Studios so we didn't feel so rigid and "unionized." We wanted to inject a little more looseness to keep things fresh. At Gold Star we completely switched musical gears and let go of the line, cutting a swampy version of "Yazoo Street Scandal." Some instrument switching too, with Richard taking over on drums and Levon grabbing his mandolin. That turned everything upside down.

Then Richard sang "Baby Lou," a tune we'd heard by a pretty obscure artist named Jimmy Drew. It had a Mose Allison flavor to it, which we dug. When we recorded "Long Distance Operator," it felt like a contender for the album. For the hell of it, we did a version of the bluegrass classic "If I Lose." Again Levon got out his beautiful Gibson mandolin, and Richard gave the track his clippity-clop drum style. We didn't labor over these recordings at Gold Star. This session was more of a party for the soul.

Back at Capitol Studios, we rounded things off with Rick singing "This Wheel's on Fire," the song he had written with Bob. Garth played some very unusual-sounding clavinet keyboard parts. Rick sang it how he felt it and we jumped on board and followed his lead. The arrangement was completely different from the way we did it in the basement with Bob—more of a drive and less of a lament.

With "I Shall Be Released" we brought this musical adventure to a conclusion. Richard gave it his heartbreaking falsetto, and I thought the harmonies on the chorus sounded unlike anybody else. I got so caught up recording this track that I wandered off for a moment rhythmically, and John Simon caught me on that. He also had Levon play something on the snares with his fingers for a backbeat. Levon wasn't too comfortable with this, but it sounded good, so he went along for the ride.

We had a tape recorder and some speakers set up in the big living room at the Castle. The room had a sweet reverb, which made the music sound like it had been around forever. When friends dropped by and we played a few unmixed songs from our sessions, some of them had a bit of a bewildered look on their faces—almost as if they found our music too distant.

Our old drummer friend Sandy Konikoff was in LA and stopped by for a visit. He seemed to have gotten over his rough experience with Bob and the Hawks, but he did say that playing on that tour was probably the most uncomfortable, devastating time of his life. We could laugh about it now, though, and that we did, after smoking a little weed. Sally and Dominique said we should play a few of our tracks for Sandy, so I threaded up a tape on the machine and turned up the volume. Sandy closed his eyes and sank into the music. I thought, *Look at that, he's spellbound.* After the tape ended, he opened his eyes and said, "Can I hear that again? I don't know what I just heard. It sounds beautiful, but I don't know what it is. Sorry, don't get me wrong, I think it's good, but I'm not sure I get it."

Oh, god, I thought, *maybe this music is too "inside," too much of its own thing.* There was a certain taste the five members of our group shared that explained why in the beginning we had been drawn to southern blues or sacred harp singing—we wanted to avoid the obvious, to reach out for rare musical gems. The less known some music was, the more appealing it could be to us. But had we pulled too far in that direction? I hoped we weren't making music that hollered out too severely against commercialism.

As Richard played the tape back again for Sandy, I left the room. When the music stopped, I went back in. Sandy came over to me, put his hand on my shoulder, and said, "I'm a damn fool. That's some of the best music I've ever heard. It just caught me so off guard the first time because I thought I knew what it would sound like. Man, was I wrong." I felt a sense of relief; I was so close to the music, I had no idea how it sounded to new ears.

John Simon and I were eager to get the songs we'd chosen for the record mixed, sequenced, and ready for presentation. It was kind of extraordinary how few people had heard what we were doing up to this point. Even Albert hadn't really listened. Dominique and Sally were actually the only people who had been through this recording process with us from beginning to end.

After the mixes were done at A&R in New York, we made an acetate for Albert. I very much wanted the powerful manager Albert Grossman to be proud of our efforts. The look on his face as he listened to it—I thought he was going to chew his nails to the bone, but there was pure glee in his eyes after each track. Everybody who came through his office or home for the next three months had to endure Albert playing some of our tracks. He liked making people guess who they were listening to.

We had a little listening session at Albert's house in Bearsville. Bob came over with Sara, and Al Aronowitz joined too. After some gourmet snacks, Albert put the acetate on for Bob, who was hearing it for the first time; we had all been busy and had wanted to finish the album before we shared it with him. "Tears of Rage" started the record, and as it played Bob looked at me like he barely recognized me. At the end of the song, he yelled out, "That was *incredible,* Richard!" Richard acted a little bit shy but thrilled. After each song, Bob looked at "his" band with proud eyes. When "The Weight" came on, he said, "This is fantastic. Who wrote that song?"

"Me," I answered.

He shook his head, slapped me on the arm, and said, "Damn! You wrote that song?" What a joy it was to push Bob's button.

At the end of "I Shall Be Released"—one of the most beautiful tunes Bob had written during our time in the basement—he stood up and said, "That was *so* good. You did it, man, you did it." Coming from a dear friend, one of the greatest songwriters ever, and our fearless leader, Bob's enthusiasm and words meant the world to the boys and me.

TWENTY

It was right around this time that Dominique and I started talking about getting married—or at least Dominique talked about it. I was twenty-four and truly didn't know if I had the wherewithal for getting hitched, especially since we were just launching into our new musical voyage—concerts, touring, writing, recording, serious road work up ahead. But I loved Dominique completely, and that's all I knew. If that made her happy and settled things for her family, then it felt like the right thing to do. So we set a date: March 24, 1968.

When I told the guys and Bob, nobody seemed that surprised or averse to the idea. Marriage looked good on the Dylans. Bob and Sara gave the impression in their relationship that a special contentment lived there. They were a few years older than Dominique and me, but their bond gave us something to aspire to—a certain rounded maturity.

Nobody else in our immediate circle had gotten married except for Levon when he had married Connie to avoid the draft, and good thing for that, because the war had heated up to a horrible bloodbath. There was a sick feeling in the souls of young people around North America and the world. From our little musical bubble in the Catskill Mountains, the view was devastating in terms of how many young men were coming back from this painful, pointless war in body bags or doomed to become homeless drug casualties. It was heartbreaking; you couldn't help but want to do whatever you could to stop this nightmare. Marches and be-ins or sit-ins had become stronger and more vital in the antiwar movement. Something big was stirring, and you could feel it all around.

Albert and Sally came back from a trip to the West Coast and said the vibe and the force of young people in San Francisco was unlike anything the world had ever seen before. The streets and the parks were lined with people from all over, sharing a voice, sharing food, sharing music, and the swell was growing larger every day. The revolution was on, and there was no turning back. Albert spoke of a vigilante group in San Francisco that robbed food distributors and vendors and fed runaway street kids or anybody who was hungry. He smiled broadly at this, like it was the return of Robin Hood. "The group is called the Diggers," he said, "and I've invited the head guy, Emmett Grogan, to come to Woodstock. I like him. I like what he's doing."

Meanwhile, Bob's station wagon was on its last legs, and with a little money coming in from our record-company advances, I was able to buy a copper-colored '67 Mustang convertible with a monster engine. I'd never seen one like this before, with a folding glass rear window. Fantastic ride.

One morning while I was running some errands in Woodstock at the hardware store, I overheard a couple saying, "That guy there is with the band. You know, they play with Bob Dylan and stuff." When I stopped into the Woodstock Bakery in Bearsville, where a grumpy old German woman and her husband made exquisite croissants and pastries, a patron in the shop referred to me as being in "the band." There weren't other bands around town at that time, so we got used to hearing ourselves described like this—on evenings when the boys and I were having a bite at Deanie's, the main restaurant in town, folks would stop by our table and ask, "You making any good music these days?"

We'd usually answer, "We're trying. Got an album coming out soon."

They'd walk away saying, "That's the band. They live up here."

I said to Rick, sitting across the table from me, "Everybody around here calls us 'the Band.'"

"That's what everybody's been calling us for nearly two years now," said Richard.

Rick laughed, "We *are* 'the Band,' simple as that. All those other silly names bug me. I don't even like thinking about it."

I passed the idea on to Albert. He thought it was perfect, almost like having no name at all.

One thing we did know for sure: we were a *real* band. Everybody played a major role in our balance of musicianship. We weren't a group with a cute lead singer who liked to take his shirt off, and his guitar man, who also liked being shirtless on occasion. In many bands the other players in the group remained in the shadows; they knew who the stars were. There was nothing wrong with that, but we were holding a different hand—like five-card stud. Nothing wild. Everything faceup.

When it came time to take some photos for our album artwork, we were getting all kinds of suggestions. "Why don't you get Irving Penn or Richard Avedon?" Or this guy from Paris, or that guy from London. Everybody at the record company and at Albert's office had an opinion on who was the best and who was the *very* best in New York. I felt crowded by all this talk. "Who's the worst?" I asked. "Who would be considered the worst photographer in New York City?" That shut everybody up for a moment, but to my surprise, they started coming back with suggestions as to who might actually be the worst. I certainly hadn't been serious about it, but now my curiosity was sparked. Information came in that there was an underground paper in New York called *Rat* that used a photographer named Elliott Landy. People said the pictures in *Rat* looked kind of fuzzy and were cropped funny. That, of course, could be the paper's fault and not the photographer's, but perhaps there was a chance he could be our man.

Albert got a kick out of the idea that I was pursuing the worst photographer we could find. I told him we had a contender and his name was Elliott Landy. "Oh, I know him," Albert responded. "He's a pain in the ass, but he can take good pictures."

Relieved, I said, "Good, let's book him."

First we wanted him to come up to Rick's family's farm outside

Simcoe, Ontario, to take a picture for the album with our parents and relatives that we called *Next of Kin*. During this period there was a lot of negativity toward parents going around. That wasn't our story, so we rebelled against the notion and said it loud. Elliott Landy took a wonderful shot of us with the folks and in the process became a trusted member of our gang. He was a kind and gentle soul, with bushy hair, a keen eye, and a warm smile. As we had with John Simon, we invited him into our world with open arms.

By nature the five of us were extremely private, and Levon especially didn't like having pictures taken. Elliott skillfully navigated those boundaries and made himself almost invisible. He hung out with us at Big Pink, and I liked looking through old photo books from the turn of the century with him. The rawness of that photography somehow connected with the music we were making.

Elliott took a classic shot of us with Overlook Mountain in the background. The way we were dressed and looked in that photo was pretty much the same as how we looked every day. Maybe we had a touch more "Sunday go to meetin'" style happening. Garth wore a string tie for the occasion, but that was about it. We put on our jackets and hats for the shot, but Elliott didn't want us to change a thing.

Then one morning Bob swung by, surprising me with a painting he had done for the Band's album cover. He propped it up, and as we looked at it we both started laughing, especially at the Indian in the back playing a stand-up bass with cutaways. The piano man hanging over the top of the upright reminded me of a character straight out of the basement tapes. And of course you have to have an elephant in there, right? "It's perfect!" I said, going over to the window to hold it up to the light. "You know, I've never seen anything like this for an album cover before."

"Oh good," Bob said, nodding.

"I wonder what the—"

"Okay, I gotta go, see you later." And he was gone.

Albert arranged for me to meet with his favorite album designer, Milt Glaser. He had a house in the country not far from Woodstock, so we met at Albert's. I brought Bob's painting, Elliott's photo of the

five of us, and our *Next of Kin* picture with the families. Milt licked
his chops over these visuals and asked the name of the album. "And
what's the name of the group?" I told him we were thinking of going
with the album title *Music from Big Pink*. He said, "What's Big Pink?"
I told him about our clubhouse, where the music we were making had
originated. "Can we get a photo of that house," he asked, "so we understand what Big Pink is?"

I said, "It's really kind of ugly, and the house *is* pink."

"That's okay," Milt said, "it may be good. What about the group's
name?"

"We don't have a fancy name. We're just called 'the Band.'"

Albert chuckled. "Isn't that great? A band with no name. Just 'the
Band.' No nonsense. I love it." Milt nodded in confused agreement.

John Simon suggested Dominique should write a little description of Big Pink and the music for the album notes. "She's a writer.
She should write something in her broken English. She's the only one
who's been here through it all with you guys." So Dominique wrote:
"A pink house seated in the sun of Overlook Mountain in West Saugerties, New York. Big Pink bore this music and these songs along its
way. It's the first witness of this album that's been thought and composed right there inside its walls."

"It's perfect," John said. "Like French prose in English."

Those were all the ingredients Milt Glaser needed to put together
the double-fold album cover design. Nobody had ever seen an album
package like it before, especially our record company. By then Alan
Livingston, the president of Capitol Records who had signed us, was
no longer there. The inmates were running the asylum, and they were
trying to figure out who the hell we were. They suggested getting an
elephant painted pink in front of Tower Records in LA for the release
of our record.

Albert and I flew to Los Angeles to get on the same page with Capitol's new president, Stanley Gortikov, and try to enlighten the company
as to what Big Pink and the Band represented, which most certainly
was *not* a pink elephant, nor a "name this band" contest, which Capitol had also suggested. Albert gave a fifteen-minute monologue to the

Capitol promo and advertising staff, but as I looked around the room at their faces I could see they had no idea what he was saying. Albert had a way of talking over your head in an almost condescending tone that made people embarrassed to admit they didn't follow. I enjoyed his performance much more than the staff, who were nodding their heads in agreement at what they didn't understand. When Albert finished, I ran down a list of what they shouldn't do to represent the Band, which was *everything* they wanted to do.

Since we'd first come together as the Hawks, part of the discovery process in making the group work was figuring out what each of us was good at. We all took on different responsibilities. When it came to dealing with the outside world—management, record company, art directors, the press—those tasks fell in my direction, probably because they came more naturally to me than to the other guys. Somewhere along the line I had found myself taking on more and more. It had gone that way slowly: Levon had become our leader when we left Ronnie; then he and I began to share that responsibility. When Bob first tried to hire me, I had convinced him and Albert that they needed our whole group—we all shared a loyalty that couldn't be betrayed— but because of our strong connection on both a musical and personal level, it seemed natural that I should step up and become the intermediary. When Levon left, all of those responsibilities fell on me; and when he came back he was comfortable with that because it was stuff he didn't want to do anyway. But I bristled when people said I was the leader of the Band. I was doing what needed to be done on behalf of the guys, but I didn't want to be called the leader any more than Richard wanted to be referred to as the lead singer. Ours was an equal playing field, with each person holding up his end and doing what he could for the sake of the group.

On the flight back east, Albert said he thought our trip had been very helpful to the record company. They had a much clearer understanding of the Band and our music. I said, "It looks different, sounds different, and doesn't fit into any of their ready-made categories. They think it's underground, which maybe it is."

"A lot of really good things start in the underground," Albert responded. "That's not a bad thing."

DOMINIQUE AND I decided to get married at the Church on the Mount in Woodstock. An archbishop presided over this shrine and parish, and Dominique thought that would impress her parents and sister. (Unfortunately, we heard at a later date that the archbishop, Father Francis Brothers, had gotten in some hot water with the Church over skirt chasing, so Dominique's family wasn't quite as impressed as we had hoped.) I wasn't that particular about the religious affiliation for the ceremony, but I knew it had meaning for Dominique and her family.

My mother came down from Toronto for the occasion. Just our immediate families and the gang were on hand. Levon served as best man, and Albert and Sally held a reception at their place after the service. I was awkward and out of sorts on the day, I have to admit. Sure, you just put one foot in front of the other, but I kept tripping over my own feet and wandering off with the guys. Bob and Sara helped me feel more grounded as the day wore on. I felt bad for Dominique that I was having trouble adjusting to the altitude. I absolutely wanted to be with her, but the ritual at the Church on the Mount turned my head inside out.

Finally that night, when it was just Dominique and me on our own, I tried to explain that something about this process knocked me off balance and made me feel unsure of myself. Was it because of my strange upbringing? The way my parents broke up? My father situation? That this whole ceremony felt so conventional? That I'd been on the road since I was sixteen, and married life seemed like an oxymoron? My partner, my bride, my darling Dominique, comforted me and helped me find a little serenity.

And on that special night, we got pregnant.

Glory be.

TWENTY-ONE

A few days after the wedding, I accompanied my mother back to Toronto to help her move into a new apartment. When I flew back to New York, Dominique, Richard, and Levon all came to pick me up at the Albany Airport. Immediately I knew something was wrong. I could feel a sullen mood among them. "What's the matter?" I asked. Richard spoke first. "Well, I've got some bad news. Last night I totaled your Mustang." My mouth dropped open.

The story was: Levon and his old girlfriend Bonnie had met up with Dominique and Richard at the Café Espresso. They decided to head out to Big Pink, and Richard asked Dominique if he could drive the Mustang. As they sped out of town on the two-lane blacktop toward West Saugerties, Richard, with a few drinks under his belt, decided to see what this muscle car was made of. It was very dark up ahead and Dominique asked if he could see okay. He said, "I see like a lynx." But then they flew around a curve way too fast, and the car skidded off the shoulder and smashed violently into a line of cement posts meant to prevent vehicles from going over the side. They eventually ended up sideways in a ditch. Dominique was completely flipped out and terrified. And all Richard could say was "Total fuckup." He lit a match to check the damage. "Put that out! You're going to blow us up!" Dominique yelled. "Get out! Get out!"

As they crawled through the driver's-side door, a police car came along; it stopped in the road and the cops put on their lights to investigate. Richard told Dominique that he didn't have his license with him, and she should say that she was driving. When the police looked at her license, they said, "This is from Quebec, and it's expired." Dominique said that she didn't speak very good English and had misunderstood, and that actually Richard had been driving.

Just then, Levon and Bonnie came screeching around the curve in her Corvette. They slammed on the brakes, missing the cop car by inches, and the policemen dove into the ditch in fear for their lives. Crawling back onto the road, the cops were fuming. They yanked Levon out of the car, threw him on the hood, and cuffed him. Then they took everybody to the courthouse. Albert had to come bail them out. He showed up with a bundle of cash, and the judge and police kept referring to him as Mr. Goldman. Freed on bail, Dominique, Richard, Levon, and Bonnie then went to Big Pink to meet up with Rick, Garth, and John Simon. While they were there John backed into one of their cars, which made it a "three strikes and you're out" evening, and on top of that, it happened to be April Fools' day.

As I tried to absorb this story, of course I was upset to hear my new car was destroyed, but what really tore me up inside was that Dominique could have been killed. I kept visualizing that Mustang careening off the road and pounding into the cement posts—over and over, like a nightmare.

This was turning out to be a life-changing period of time. After my wedding and my car getting totaled, on April 3, Martin Luther King Jr. made a speech that turned the nation inside out, the "mountaintop" sermon. Only a great orator, a great leader, could have made that speech. The following day he was shot dead on a motel balcony in Memphis, Tennessee. The country wept. The anger, the sadness, the hurt spilled out into the streets of cities and towns across the land: "a good man gone down." Two months later, on June 5, Robert Kennedy was assassinated in Los Angeles, while running for president. Our generation felt he was one of us, somebody we could fully relate to, somebody we could support with unabashed conviction. His death crushed a tremendous amount of hope. We were tore down, and again the country was in mourning. When our album came out four weeks later, it almost felt like a reflection of the sadness and disillusionment that hung low over the nation.

MUSIC FROM BIG PINK was released a few days before my birthday in July 1968. Naturally we were anxious to see how our music would be accepted out in the world, especially since our sound no longer resembled anything we had done in the past. As it turned out, it was extremely well received, particularly among music people. The Hawks had long been called "musicians' musicians," and it was always a good feeling when our peers sounded the trumpet. Word got back to us in Woodstock that George Harrison had scored an advance copy and was singing our praises. Pretty soon we heard that Eric Clapton was on a mission to convert all ears he came in contact with to the sound of the Band. The enthusiastic review in Jann Wenner's groundbreaking new magazine, *Rolling Stone*, was even written by a fellow musician, Al Kooper, whom I had played with on Bob's album *Blonde on Blonde*. This kind of approbation reached deep in our souls. I started feeling like anything else would just be a bonus.

Albert had scheduled more meetings with Capitol Records in Los Angeles, so he and I flew out and checked into the Chateau Marmont. Our friend and photographer du jour, Barry Feinstein, brought us up to Alan Pariser's house in the Hollywood Hills, a mecca for music people and art directors. Alan was a serious music person and was managing a new group called Delaney & Bonnie that featured a rich pool of talent. He loved holding listening sessions for major new records. He had the coolest-sounding home stereo system and the best weed in LA. Alan introduced me to Eric Clapton, who was there with his Cream bandmate Ginger Baker. Eric confirmed his deep regard for *Music from Big Pink* and then confided that he was on his last run with Cream—*Big Pink* had turned him around with its subtleties and laid-back feeling. Cream played with a much more bombastic approach and he wanted a change. That was a huge compliment coming from Eric, but I liked some of Cream's songs and wasn't sure how I felt about our record being partially responsible for their demise.

Capitol was delighted with the attention *Big Pink* was getting, and the record-company execs now had a better fix on who our music spoke to. They hoped we'd be able to go out and do shows in support of the record, and Albert told them we were considering live dates. *Rolling Stone* reached out as well, wanting to do a cover story on us. I felt very appreciative of the offer, but I was hesitant. We had trouble letting go of the whole mystique of the Band. All anyone knew of us was that we were affiliated with Bob Dylan and that we lived somewhere up in the mountains. Coming out into the open would pull back a veil that we thought suited us, so we decided to postpone the *Rolling Stone* article for the time being.

At a music-business event in New York, Ahmet Ertegun, the president of Atlantic Records, approached me, grinning like a cat that just caught a mouse. He must've had a few, because I could only make out half of what he was saying, but the gist was that Atlantic owned some of our earlier Hawks recordings, and he intended to release them, with or without our approval. Just then, his right-hand guy and ace record producer, Jerry Wexler, came over and shook my hand, saying he'd known about the Hawks for a long time and really liked our new record.

"Yeah," Ahmet said, "we have some of their music in our vaults that I want to release. It's great when some other company does all the work and pays for everything, and we get to piggyback on their success!" He took a sip of his drink and a puff on his cigarette, and nodded at me: *Live and learn, kid.*

Jerry laughed. "Well here's some good news: I'm going to Muscle Shoals to record 'The Weight' with Aretha Franklin, and I got Duane Allman on guitar."

"That's unbelievable!" I said. "I just heard a couple other people are cutting it, too, the Staples and Jackie DeShannon."

"Jerry will blow their versions away with Aretha, trust me," Ahmet said as he started to walk away. "Nice being in business with you."

Albert and his people were discussing plans to set up our tour, but I wasn't anxious to hit the road just yet. We only had the songs from our album to go out with and still needed to put together a full repertoire.

Privately I had a certain admiration for Brian Wilson of the Beach Boys, who didn't tour and concentrated instead on songwriting and making interestingly produced records. Same thing for the Beatles—they were a music-making machine around this time. And I had been on the road since I was sixteen, so I didn't feel that appetite needed to be served just yet.

WITH DOMINIQUE'S PREGNANCY, we looked for a house in Woodstock that had more of a family feel to it. We found a place on the other side of town, up Boggs Hill Road, fully furnished and ready to go. John Simon decided to rent the house right next door, which made it even better. And after the record came out with pictures of Big Pink on the jacket, the guys and I knew we had to get out of there if we wanted to preserve our privacy. So when the lease ran out, we let the place go, though not without a certain amount of sentimentality.

Not long after, Eric Clapton called from England and asked if he could come pay us a visit in Woodstock with his girlfriend. John Simon said they could stay at his house. Eric was such a gentleman when he arrived, and pleased to be in our surroundings. It seemed he wanted to witness the magic of this place where the basement tapes had come from and *Big Pink* was created. The other guys in the Band, Albert, Bob—all of us—lived quite privately, and I hoped Eric wouldn't find it too low-key and boring. I took him around town and showed him the millstream that they said the song "Down by the Old Mill Stream" was written about. I might have even taken him over to see Clarence Schmidt's place, a dwelling built on the side of a hill out of junk and trash. It looked like a big garbage heap, or perhaps even a sculpture. Beside his house was an abandoned car onto which he had built four stories that you entered by getting into the car. At one point Schmidt had covered his entire house with aluminum foil, but the air force had him remove it because it was causing problems with their radar. He had also set up memorials in his yard to people who were still alive. He had a nice one for Joan Baez.

I could tell Eric wanted to make some music with us, but when I confessed that we didn't jam, he looked around like, *Well, what do you do up here?* I didn't know how to explain that these days we just worked on songs and didn't do much jamming. He took it in stride, but I don't know if he found his visit very fulfilling. (Many years later, when Eric inducted the Band into the Rock and Roll Hall of Fame, he admitted for the first time that when he came to visit us in Woodstock, he was really coming to ask if he could become a member of the Band but never worked up the nerve to ask. I jokingly asked if he was suggesting that we could have two guitar players, or did he want to take my job? He never answered.)

A few weeks later George Harrison and his wife, Pattie, came to Woodstock. George had been increasingly outspoken in regard to our music, and we got the impression that he was keen to see what we were up to in this neck of the woods. I think he was the biggest fan among the Beatles of Bob's writing, and he seemed to have a curiosity about what was happening out in the world, whether in India with the Maharishi, in Haight-Ashbury, or here with us. I asked Albert if they could stay at his place, but for some reason Albert wasn't that into the idea. Come to think of it, I never did see him play a Beatles record. George and Pattie had Mal Evans, the Beatles' trusty road manager, with them, and I wanted them to feel welcome and comfortable, so Albert finally agreed. During this period Bob was keeping a very low profile, and when I asked him if he wanted to see George while he was in town, he too was a little iffy at first. *What a bunch of grumps we are up here in the Catskills*, I thought.

But George was one of the most open people I'd ever met, and Pattie was one of the prettiest and sweetest. George spoke incredibly candidly about the problems within the Beatles. John, he said, was far out on a limb, testing his balance. "Kinda crazy," he laughed. And our dear Ringo was following in the tradition of many a hard-drinking Brit—apparently he had threatened to quit the band at one point. George was quick to admit there were serious tensions between Paul and him. "Whenever I present a tune, the Lennon and McCartney songwriting team will ignore it as long as they can," he said. "Sometimes I even have to fight for my guitar parts. Paul has such a clear idea of how the song should go that he tells me what to play, or he wants to play it himself." I felt bad hearing of their struggles, but with that kind of phenomenal success, insanity couldn't be lurking too far behind. Hearing George's inside story gave us even more confidence that our "under the radar" method might be wise. The Band had been together for several years already and had witnessed Bob's success close up, so we felt a little immune to the obvious pitfalls of the music business. But we would soon learn that no one is bulletproof when it comes to fame and success.

I was very curious about recording techniques the Beatles had discovered. George described their process as extremely experimental and sometimes accidental. I could definitely relate to that. When George inquired about the Band's recording methods, I could barely keep up with him. For every question I posed to him, he asked me two about *Big Pink* and *The Basement Tapes*: "How did you get that guitar sound on 'Tears of Rage'?" I told him about Garth's black box. "Speaking of Garth, how does he bend the notes on his organ?" To that I just gave him a wink. George smiled. "I love the sound of Levon's drums. It reminds me a little of Ringo's on 'A Day in the Life.'"

Eric and George may have enjoyed their visits to Woodstock, but at our house on Boggs Hill, a rural reality soon set in for Dominique and me that we were *so* not ready for. There was a large storage area by the house, and during the night our cats would get into knock-down, drag-out fights in there with other cats from around the neighborhood. We'd wake up to howling and squalling and I'd have to run down with a broom and chase the other cats away, but they'd be back the very next night. And every week when I put the trash out for pickup, it would be scattered all over the yard by raccoons. One morning I looked outside and saw four raccoons enjoying leftovers from the cans. I ran out and charged them, hollering and waving my arms, but they just stared at me with their bandit-masked faces and hissed back aggressively. It stopped me dead in my tracks. I said, "*Bon appétit*," and walked back in the house.

One evening in our bedroom, with Dominique asleep and me up watching TV, I was startled by a bird flying manically around the room. After a moment I realized it wasn't a bird at all—it was a bat. I'd duck every time it flew over the bed, trying to figure out what to do. Eventually I crawled along the floor to the wall and opened a window, and it flew right out. The next day I asked David Boyle, the local Mr. Fix-it, to come by. We went together into an attic area off the bedroom. Inside, there were about twenty bats hanging upside down from the rafters. I was totally creeped out. Dominique cried, "You have to get rid of them. I can't live like this!" David grinned and removed them in glass jars, one by one.

The other guys seemed to manage this stuff a little better. Rick and Richard were cruising Ohayo Mountain Road one night when they hit and killed a deer. Rick insisted on carting the dead animal back to his place. Leaving it on the road wasn't an option—he used to be a butcher and couldn't relate to letting it go to waste. So they sent for Garth, Levon, and me to come help out. Once we got the carcass back to Rick's, Dominique and I had to excuse ourselves. We couldn't imagine taking part in the skinning procedure or the feast. I asked Dominique if she knew the expression "city slicker." She laughed. "I didn't, but I do now. This country living is driving me crazy."

I DON'T KNOW if you would call it a celebration, exactly, but after *Big Pink* was released, all hell broke loose among the boys. The accident in my Mustang was only the beginning. Rick and Richard were on a rampage of destruction around Woodstock, with Levon coming up on the inside. Richard's relationship with alcohol started growing new roots. Prescription pills were being passed around, and Rick liked to be at the front of the line—anything goes. All seemed in good fun, but some of the classic old cars the boys had acquired, like the Hupmobile, were being found upside down on various side roads around town. Car wrecks with Richard, Rick, and Levon became a regular occurrence. All Garth and I could do was get out of the way.

After one crash, Rick went ahead and bought himself a sweetheart of a classic automobile. I don't recall the make, but it was a beauty. He looked sharp sporting around town in that baby. Then we got a call in the middle of the night that he'd wrapped his pretty little car around a tree and been rushed to the hospital in Kingston, New York, in critical condition. This wasn't funny anymore. We were terrified that this could be fatal.

We went to visit him as soon as we were allowed to and were shocked at the sight. They had shaved his head and drilled two holes in his skull, one on each side. There were tongs inserted in the holes for traction. He had broken his neck badly and this was the only way he could heal properly. He also had a laceration and stitches on one cheek under his eye. The doctor said he was lucky. I thought to myself, *Lucky?* But he was right. Rick had almost lost an eye, and his neck fracture could have killed him.

He obviously couldn't move his head, so I leaned over him and asked, "How are you doing, brother?"

"My neck hurts bad," Rick said in a dry rasp. "This cut on my face is sore, but surprisingly, the holes in my skull don't hurt hardly at all." As medicated and out of it as he was, I could see terrible sadness and remorse in his eyes. He trembled as he spoke. "I'm sorry, guys. I *really* fucked up and I'm so sorry. This screws up our plans, but I'm gonna heal quick as I can and I won't slow us down ever again."

I felt terrible for him. A high-intensity guy with energy to spare, he looked trapped in this setting. I squeezed his hand and said, "Just get better."

The doctor told us Rick would have to stay in the hospital for a month to six weeks. Knowing how restless and fidgety he could be made me wonder how he would be able to lie still for so long, but we were just relieved that he hadn't been killed and that in time he would recover. Rick was seeing an attractive local girl named Grace, who sat quietly beside his hospital bed crocheting or knitting, looking calm and devoted.

Rick's situation meant we couldn't go out and play concerts in support of *Big Pink*. As the designated spokesperson for the Band, I didn't want to talk about the accident with the press, so I made a conscious decision not to do interviews for the album—a decision that came off as extremely unusual. Here a record had come out with big buzz around it, by a group called simply "the Band." The very people who were booed continuously with Bob Dylan? With their music now being covered by a slew of artists. What an opener! And then . . . silence. The mystique around us grew even deeper.

We were biding our time until Rick was back on his feet, but in the meantime Woodstock itself was slowly taking on a legendary status, with a powerful magnetic effect on other artists. Musicians and showbiz people suddenly seemed to be flocking to the area. Comedian Henny Youngman and the actor Lee Marvin had lived here for years, but you'd also run into actors like Michael J. Pollard and musicians like Tim Hardin and Fred Neil around town.

One day, I was over at Levon's when Tim Hardin and his young son stopped by for a little visit. Tim seemed to be a bit unsteady on his feet. It was no secret that he used heroin, and he looked pretty groggy. Levon said he was going to make some coffee and went into the kitchen. We had a big record collection in the living room, beside the phonograph player. Stacks and stacks of LPs and 45s were piled high on a table. Tim started looking through the LPs, commenting on certain records. His kid stood by his side, looking around the place.

I went to help Levon bring in the coffee and cookies when I heard a thunderous crash. I looked back to see that most of the records had fallen off the table to the floor, and Tim was pulling himself up from the table. Levon and I hurried over to see if he and the boy were okay and to assess the damage.

Tim straightened his jacket and gathered himself. He sternly eyed his son and said, "Look at this mess! You've knocked all these records on the floor. Come on, we've got to pick them up and put them back the way they were."

The boy looked confused and upset and leaned down to pick up the discs. I told him not to worry about them; we were going to move them anyway. Then I turned to Tim. "I saw what happened. I can't believe you're laying this on the kid, man. This is some weird shit."

Levon abruptly told Tim that we'd better have coffee some other time. Tim took his kid by the shoulder and started leading him toward the door.

"Do you need a ride?" I called after him. "I really don't think you should be driving."

He yelled back, "The hell with you! I can do anything I damn well feel like," and slammed the door behind him.

Tim had written some wonderful songs, and at that moment he was at the top of his game with "If I Were a Carpenter." It made this incident even more disturbing—to see that his problems could totally overshadow his gift.

THE RECORD COLLECTION over at my house was changing more and more. Dominique brought her LPs from Montreal: Léo Ferré, Gilbert Bécaud, Georges Brassens, Félix Leclerc, Jacques Brel, Nana Mouskouri, and Charles Aznavour filled the air. This music helped Dominique feel connected to her culture and language here in the Catskills, where it was rare for her to speak French. Albert would always tease Dominique about French recording artists in a dismissive but funny way, and she came right back at him, saying the French had long been putting poetry in their music, and thank goodness somebody like Bob had finally come along to give American lyrics a deeper imagination and meaning.

Carnegie Hall in New York was presenting Jacques Brel, and Dominique insisted we go. She had hyped me about his powerful, passionate performances, and he didn't disappoint. It was extraordinary. When he sang "Amsterdam," the hall exploded with emotion, people standing with one arm in the air, belting out the words to the song in French. It was all very different from the concerts I was used to. Dominique whispered to me the meaning of the words he was singing.

After that, when she played her records around the house, she would occasionally translate the lyrics for me. From this, and from seeing Jacques Brel, I gained a whole new awareness of how poetic the music was. These songwriters were inspired by Rimbaud and Verlaine, Balzac, Louis Aragon, and Victor Hugo, and so many European, Russian, and Asian writers and artists. Musically, a bit of American inspiration was thrown in there too, but this music was more classic and ageless. It reached back to a place and tradition we didn't have in the New World. This music, like the foreign film scripts I was reading, made a connection for me. It influenced my writing in a unique way that I figured most North American songwriters didn't have access to.

One afternoon, a couple of the guys and I were over at Albert's house in Bearsville, talking about upcoming possibilities for when Rick was back to full strength. Albert said that promoters all over the country were inquiring about booking the Band but that the number one concert promoter, Bill Graham, had asked if he could come up to Woodstock to meet with us personally. We knew that when we were ready for our debut performances, Bill was the man who could present us in the proper light. Albert asked me to meet with him. "He'll drive up next week and tell you his ideas if you're cool with that."

"Sure," I said. "It would be good to hear what he's got in mind."

Albert then asked if I wanted to check out a young road manager by the name of Jon Taplin. Albert said Jon's goal was to work with the Band, to be our official road manager. He seemed to think Jon had potential—he had been working with the Jim Kweskin Jug Band while he was still studying at Princeton. So I agreed to see him.

The following week, Bill Graham showed up at Albert's house, and we sat out back under a big tree with the pool in view. Bill had style and grace. He complimented you on everything but your shoes, and you felt sure he was just about to get around to that. You could tell he had the chops for dealing with musicians and truly loved what he did. He told me a short version of his story about escaping Nazi Germany and making it over to America to fulfill his dreams. He was a fascinating, vital character, all the more so when he got down to business.

Somehow Bill was under the impression that we weren't planning to play live at all. "You've got to show up," he implored. "You've got to come out and be there for 'the people,' for the kids that worship your music. It's the right thing to do. You can't disappoint 'the people,'" he went on. "It means so much to them. I can't express strongly enough how much this means." After that moving sermonette I didn't want to admit that the Band fully intended to give concerts. But I also didn't want to go into detail on Rick's accident and recovery, so I thought the best thing to do was to let Bill give his speech and do his dance, and then act converted. I told him and Albert that we would give them dates when we could play Bill's venue Winterland in San Francisco and his recently created Fillmore East on Second Avenue in New York. These would be our first shows as "the Band." Bill got up and bowed like this was a holy moment in his mission to Woodstock.

When he left, Albert looked pleased. "Bill Graham is unquestionably the P. T. Barnum of rock 'n' roll," he said. "You can put up with all the hot air because the guy really believes his own bullshit . . . and that's a big part of being good at what you do. By the way, can you meet soon with Jon Taplin? He's driving me crazy—calling and leaving messages. I'll tell you, you're not going to find anybody who wants the job more than him. I think he's got some free guitars for you too." Albert smiled. "At least meet with him and get him off my back."

Not long after, Jon Taplin showed up at my house with two guitars in his hands. Now, if guitar players have a soft spot, being offered unusual, free guitars is one of them. He handed me one. "Here, you want to try this out?" The instrument was called a Melobar—basically a slide guitar that you could play standing up. It did feel good, and kind of sporty with its modern design. Jon seemed like a very ambitious, smart, dedicated person. He was just about to graduate from Princeton on a film he'd made and claimed that *Music from Big Pink* had had a profound effect on his life and his view of music. There was nothing he wanted more than to be affiliated with the Band and work as our road manager. Shortly after that, we hired him.

VISITING RICK in the hospital was encouraging. As his hair grew back, like Samson's, so did his strength. He was from tough, hardworking stock, and it showed in how quickly he was recovering. His doctor advised, "You can't cheat the system, and the healing process will take its own time, especially with a broken neck," but there was a chance he would be out of traction and able to go home a little earlier than estimated. He had decided to marry his girlfriend, Grace, when he got back on his feet. She had been there for him through the whole ordeal and they had grown very close.

I had started writing a couple of songs for our next album and asked Richard to join me. I had some chord changes that I played for him on guitar, and he had the beginning of a chord progression that I liked, but they were in different keys. Rather than change the key on one of our ideas to accommodate the other, we tried the chords I had in the key of E for the verse and B section and went to the key of C for Richard's part in the chorus. After the third chorus, I made up an outro section back in E. When we were happy with the structure, I asked him if he had any ideas for words. But he said that lyrics just weren't coming to him lately, and he would leave that in my corner. I asked him, "What do you think about 'When you awake, you will remember everything'?" He gave me a thumbs-up.

Sometimes I would get together with just Garth or Levon to see if we could stir something up songwise. Levon would groove along on drums or mandolin, but he was much more comfortable accompanying. Making up a tune made him restless and uneasy, so I didn't want to push it. With Garth, every time we sat down it was like a musical journey into the cosmos, a lesson in improvisation. Beautiful stuff came out of it, but no defined structures, nothing I could repeat or build upon.

Before we released *Big Pink*, Albert had asked me how we wanted to handle the song publishing. A mystery loomed around music publishing—like electricity, you needed it but you didn't know where it came from. Some of this was left over from the song-plugging days when publishing houses would go out and try to get artists to record material they represented. Albert said it was standard for his management company to get a piece of the publishing. The song royalties were typically split 50 percent to the songwriter and 50 percent to publishing. Often in the past songwriters were lucky if they got any of the publishing. That was just one more way artists could get taken advantage of. Hell, it had been much worse in the fifties, when record execs, DJs, or publishers would even steal some of the songwriter's portion. The record would come out and you'd see someone else's name as cowriter, much like I had with Morris Levy and Roulette Records when I was fifteen.

I told Albert that, as with our record royalties, I wanted to share the publishing equally with the other guys. He said, "You can if you want, but you certainly don't have to." I understood that, but sharing it just felt right. Also, I told him that I'd like to publish all our *Big Pink* and basement songs with Bob's publishing company, Dwarf Music. The gesture seemed appropriate given how supportive Bob had been of the Band. Albert said it sounded fine to him, but he reiterated that it was very generous. He didn't want me coming back later saying, "Why did you let me do something I didn't have to do?"

When I told the guys I thought we should share the song publishing five ways, they were in total agreement and very appreciative. The idea of publishing our first record and the basement tunes with Dwarf Music was a harder sell. They thought it might be an unnecessary measure. Richard and I, the two main songwriters in the group, pushed for it. Garth wasn't really objecting; he'd go with the consensus. Rick and Levon took convincing but came around after a couple of meetings. Soon after, while Bob and I were riding along in his automobile, I told him about the gesture we wanted to make, to him and to Dwarf Music. He was genuinely surprised and grateful.

DOMINIQUE, WHO WAS four months into her pregnancy, decided she wanted to do natural childbirth and that we needed to start Lamaze exercises daily. I was very proud of her desire to be a super-healthy mom and deliver the healthiest baby possible. We started a serious regimen of exercise, macrobiotic diet, breathing program—the works. Dominique had always been in good shape, but now—look out! Our marriage and the pregnancy were helping us mature into family mode quite beautifully. She insisted on having the baby in Montreal. It was unimaginable to her not to give birth in her own language, in her own country. And if being there made her feel totally covered, that was all that mattered to me. So she went up to find the right doctor and make arrangements with her parents so we could stay with them when she was due.

I knew it would be tough to get much songwriting done at her folks' apartment, and there was pressure coming from all around now: if we couldn't go out and do concerts, we needed to make a new record. Our friend Al Aronowitz said he had been contacted by *Rolling Stone* to write the cover story on the Band, and he asked us if we would please finally consent. He was a good buddy of ours and a good rock journalist, and if we were going to do it with anybody, it would be Al. I asked him not to write about Rick's accident, and not to reveal too much about us personally, and said that we'd give it a shot.

In late August the article hit the newsstands, with an Elliott Landy photo on the cover. It showed the Band, shot from behind, sitting on a bench with not quite enough room for all five of us. Elliott had come around the back of the bench and photographed us from behind to match a shot he'd taken from the front. I thought it was bold of Jann Wenner and *Rolling Stone* to use the back shot, which didn't show our faces. And Al Aronowitz wrote a nice story without blowing our cover.

Around this time, there was a chord progression and melody rumbling through my head, but I didn't know yet what the song was about. I played it on the piano one day for Levon. He liked the way it stopped and started, free of tempo. I flashed back to when he first took me to meet his parents in Marvell, Arkansas, and his daddy said, "Don't worry, Robin—the South is going to rise again." I told Levon I wanted to write lyrics about the Civil War from a southern family's point of view. "Don't mention Abraham Lincoln in the lyrics" was his only advice. "That won't go down too well." I asked him to drive me to the Woodstock library so I could do a little research on the Confederacy. They didn't teach that stuff in Canadian schools.

When I conjured up a story about Virgil Caine and his kin against this historical backdrop, the song came to life for me. Though I did stop and wonder, *Can I get away with this? You call this rock 'n' roll? Maybe!*

The next day I sang the chorus of "The Night They Drove Old Dixie

Down" to Richard and Levon. I still had to shape the lyrics in the verses, but I thought I was on the right track.

Writing "To Kingdom Come" and "The Weight" for *Big Pink* had felt like a real breakthough and opened a door, but now I felt as if I was entering a whole new realm. The songs that were starting to filter through me rang with a darker mood and an earthiness that offered the clue I was searching for. This new material was more raw. As I wrote, I started thinking about where we should record these songs. If we could find a unique setting, something unexpected might come from it, and I asked Jon Taplin to look into spaces we might convert into a place to record.

Rick was finally out of traction, and we all went to pick him up at the hospital. Hallelujah! Of course, he would have to take it slow and easy for a while, and he walked unsteadily and cautiously, but you could see the joy in his eyes at being set free. He talked immediately about getting a guitar and a bass to start hardening up the calluses on his fingers. At home, I played him some of the song ideas I had cooking. He tried to play along, but we were getting a bit ahead of ourselves and he needed to rest.

True to his word, Rick set a date for his wedding to Grace. When that day arrived, we dressed up to see him down the aisle. He was walking very stiffly; he couldn't turn his head, and you could see in his hairline where the traction tongs had been. *What a trouper*, I thought. I didn't know if I could have pulled it off in that condition.

Now it also looked like Richard and his girlfriend, Jane, might soon take the plunge. You would think from this that we were all growing up and settling down. But not quite. One day I heard Richard spinning a story to Levon about another rent-a-car mishap: "Somebody must have come along in the middle of the night and banged it all up." He claimed that at Hertz in Kingston they no longer lied to him about not having any vehicles to rent. Instead they would simply lock the door and hide when they saw him coming.

In December, Dominique and I got settled in her parents' apartment in the Côte-des-Neiges area of Montreal. By then we were deep into the Lamaze breathing exercises, and Dominique was solid as a rock, in great shape for natural childbirth. But soon after we arrived my stomach started bothering me, and Dominique's father, Georges, made arrangements for me to go see his MD. The doctor felt all over my abdomen and examined me thoroughly. He asked if I was working in Montreal. I told him my wife and I were here to have our baby. "We've chosen natural childbirth," I added proudly.

The doctor looked concerned. "You have a swollen spleen, and a natural birth is very intense. You should not be there for the delivery."

"I have to be there," I said. "My wife and I have a whole routine of Lamaze practices, and it's a partnership. The breathing, the pushing, the communication, the whole works."

The doctor leaned over his desk and said, "I cannot recommend you do this. You need to remain very calm. No exertion, no strain or stress. If you go through with this, your spleen could rupture and explode."

I stood up. "Explode? My spleen could explode? I never heard of such a thing."

"I don't think this is how you want to find out," the doctor said.

This talk of exploding spleens scared the hell out of me. I went back to the apartment and told Dominique what the doctor had said and that he had advised me not to participate in the natural childbirth.

She thought it all sounded preposterous. "If anybody's going to explode, it's me if I don't have this baby soon."

On Boxing Day in Canada, the day after Christmas, we turned in for the night. Suddenly Dominique sat up and said, "My water broke!" We leaped into action. Dominique's father grabbed her suitcase and ran out the door, forgetting his daughter. He came charging back in, and we all carefully headed for the car through ice and snow. I was trying to project my best Zen attitude, even if this was the most exciting moment of our lives.

As we settled in at the hospital, everything was in French, just as Dominique had wanted. Sometimes I didn't know what was going on, but my job was to go with the flow, stay calm, hold Dominique's hand,

and start the breathing exercises. Smooth rhythm, hours passing, everything going like clockwork, then *kaboom*! Dominique crushed my fingers in her hand and screamed blue murder.

"Holy fucking hell, I can't! I can't, it's killing me!"

I said, "Breathe . . . harder, faster . . . keep breathing"—as I breathed with her—"just do it!"

She screamed, "I can't, you fucking bastard! Look what you've done. Ahhhh!"

The nurse said in French and English, "Push. Push. *Pousser* . . . It's coming."

"Keep breathing! Keep pushing!" I yelled, thinking, *My spleen better not explode now. Oh shit.* "Breathe . . . breathe. Push . . . push."

The doctor cried, "*Oui! Parfait!* Here we go. Yes. Yes! You have a beautiful . . . *petite fille.*"

Calmness settled over Dominique immediately, and she cooed at the sound of our baby daughter having a good little cry. What a feeling—something so chilling and so thrilling. I had never seen Dominique this happy, this content, or this glowing before.

Alexandra Fanny Robertson lifted our lives up and forward. Dominique and I spent a couple of days just mesmerized by the fact that now there were three of us. As soon as we got our wits about us, though, the first thing we had to do was to get out of this freezing weather. We had decided to go get "healthed up" in Hawaii and rented a house on the water in Waikiki. It's a long haul from Quebec to the Hawaiian Islands, and we worried about the baby the whole way. Alexandra sneezed once on the flight over and we panicked. Landing in Hawaii, we went straight to the nearest hospital. Of course she was perfectly fine. Her parents were just new, nervous nellies.

I had made arrangements for John Simon and his wife, Brooke, to meet us in Waikiki so John and I could start going over material for our new record. They settled nicely into our pad as Dominique and I started learning how to become Mom and Pop. John kindly agreed to become Alexandra's godfather, and we felt that everything was falling into place.

I played John a song I was writing in a new guitar tuning I'd found by accident. I called the song "Unfaithful Servant." John thought it had a cinematic quality and asked who I had in mind to sing it.

"Rick. For sure, Rick," I said. "Now that he's back in action, I believe he'll do it splendid justice." I felt strongly that one of my jobs in the band was to write parts that suited the individual voices of my bandmates.

In the meantime, Jon Taplin found us a house up on Sunset Plaza in the Hollywood Hills where we could do some recording. It was a place Sammy Davis Jr. had owned. Our plan was to turn Sammy's pool house into a makeshift studio; we'd record our album there, rather than booking time in a professional studio. Nobody was thinking along these lines back then, and Capitol Records thought we were crazy. But my theory was that the Band could do something truly original if we had *our* own atmosphere, a music machine that ran on our course of time and creativity. We asked Capitol to find us a little recording console, an eight-track machine, some mics, and monitor speakers and amps. Easier said than done, but our A&R man, John Palladino, had faith that we knew what we were doing and put the plan in motion.

Bringing our musical equipment across the country from upstate New York to LA would be a chore in itself. Jon Taplin brought on Lindsay Holland, a friend of his from school, and Bill Scheele, a rough and ready guy who could handle things the rest of us couldn't dream of. They drove out to California through ice storms and wicked weather that wasn't for the meek-hearted. Dominique and I flew to LA from Hawaii with Alexandra and met up with Garth, Rick and Gracie, Richard and Jane, and Levon at the Sammy Davis Jr. house. We even brought Mama Kosh out to help with the baby and do some cooking. Having our whole crew with us in this temporary homestead gave us a good feeling, but turning the pool house into a studio was a much bigger undertaking than I had imagined. We had to soundproof the place from the outside, which made it look like some kind of a military bunker. Inside, carpet was laid everywhere to help the sound and to ensure that we could work at all hours without bothering the neighbors. Getting the electronic equipment in and wired seemed to take forever. We carried one upright piano down the hill into the pool house and brought another down to the little apartment area where Dominique and I were staying with the baby.

Levon decided he would bunk in the bedroom area of the pool house—that way, he could just roll down the stairs and be ready to rock. The only problem was that we were using the pool-house bathroom as an echo chamber, so he had to move a speaker when he wanted to take a shower.

One of my favorite musicians around this time was Van Morrison. His album *Astral Weeks* was one of those records you could just leave on repeat. Beautiful images in the lyrics, and that *voice*. Van liked *Music from Big Pink* too, and he dropped by the Sammy Davis Jr. house to say hello one afternoon as we were putting the studio together. I dug him right off the bat. His abrupt, straight-arrow Irish temperament tickled me. When he spoke of music-business people he deplored, it cracked me up, which made him have a good laugh too. As we were talking, I picked up my guitar and started noodling around, and he said, "Wait a minute. Where did you learn to play like that?"

"I don't know," I said, "it's just what I picked up along the way."

He said, "No, seriously, where'd you get that kind of playing from?"

I had no real answer, so I tossed it off like I was just messing around. "No, it's nothing, man, just a more understated approach. You know . . ."

He looked at me like I was keeping secrets and didn't want to tell him the truth. With that, he got up and walked out. I was a bit confused for a moment, then thought, *I guess he's just ornery.* But I liked it.

My songwriting schedule those days was morning, noon, and night, some songs coming easier than others. With our newborn, I couldn't be thumping around our room too recklessly. I had to pick my spots, and Jon Taplin and his team were still busy putting the studio together, so I couldn't use that area. I tried to encourage the other guys to write with me, but I couldn't get a rise out of anybody. Even Richard felt uncomfortable trying to get something going when it just wasn't happening.

Once we got our studio set up, John Simon started giving me

recording-engineer lessons. I had certain sounds in mind for the songs I was writing, and in some cases it was easier to just do it myself than to try to describe it. I was enjoying the woody, thuddy sound we were getting out of this room—it matched the nature of the music, not bright and shiny, but rather having a dark, dry quality that most artists would have run from. After we recorded "The Night They Drove Old Dixie Down," "King Harvest (Has Surely Come)," and "Across the Great Divide," I felt we were making some kind of magic, regardless of our unorthodox method.

We had Altec 604E speakers hanging from the ceiling above the recording console, but our main listening playback speakers were on the floor up in Levon's bedroom. You had to sit on the foot of his bed to get the full percussive effect. We played Jon Taplin a few of the songs we had cut, and his eyes welled up. He said, "I can't fucking believe it." That was a good sign. That's what I was looking for. Once in a while everybody would come down to the studio from the main house to hear what we were coming up with. The close family vibe influenced some of my songwriting along the way, especially on tunes like "Rockin' Chair" and "When You Awake."

Here and there we had bumps in the road. Some days I pleaded with Richard not to drink until we finished recording. Alcohol completely disabled his performing abilities. He couldn't play in time, couldn't sing in tune, and would constantly mess up the lyrics. There are hundreds of recordings where artists have done amazing versions of songs drunk or intoxicated. Not the case here.

Typically we all refrained from mind-altering influences until we had a song in the bag. We'd tried it the other way, and it mostly interfered with the process. Richard would insist sometimes on sipping on a beer, just to steady his nerves and lubricate his throat, but even that could be touch and go. I finished the words on a new song called "Up on Cripple Creek" with this in mind, the punch line being "A drunkard's dream if I ever did see one." Garth used a clavinet with a wah-wah pedal on this track that sounded like an electric Jew's harp. Levon played and sang the hell out of this song like he just couldn't help himself.

With each track we cut, the vocal harmonies soared higher and higher. John Simon had studied harmony and was brilliant in helping solve some musical mysteries. We were working to all hours of the night, whatever it took to get the best we could out of a song. I was also sharing parenting duties, getting up with the baby, which made for very little sleep.

I had a new song to spring on the boys with a whole different approach in mind. It got sparked when we recorded "Rockin' Chair" with Garth's moving accordion and Levon's mandolin. I had mentioned the word "ragtime" in the lyrics and wanted to go deeper in that direction, to get my hands on a modern version of that sound. I suggested that Rick could play fiddle on this new tune, with Garth on piano. It was perfect for Richard's funky drum style, but with Rick on violin and Levon on mandolin, we'd have no one holding down the bass. Knowing John Simon had pretty good chops on the high-school horn, I asked if he thought he could handle the bass part on tuba. Even though his head nearly exploded getting through the whole song, he did a terrific job, and we had a track unlike anything I'd ever heard before. Levon's vocal with Rick's harmony and Garth's amazing piano tore the roof off. And we were all in awe of Richard's drumming, especially Levon, who cracked up every time we listened back to our favorite take.

When we recorded "The Unfaithful Servant," which I'd written in Hawaii, Rick killed it. Man, what a vocal. It made me want to play some guitar. Not since we cut "King Harvest (Has Surely Come)" a few weeks before had I been compelled to make a guitar statement like this. I chose to play my solos at the end of these songs and stories, almost like a movie-score finale.

About halfway through our recording adventure, Barry Feinstein came by and said that Dennis Hopper was directing a film called *Easy Rider* and wanted to talk to us about doing the music. It would star Dennis and Peter Fonda, who was also producing, and a new guy named Jack Nicholson. We were in the middle of making our record and it wasn't possible for us to do the music, but I was curious. They set up a screening for me, and there was a strong antisouthern bent to the movie that would have been a hard sell to the boys anyway. Then they asked to use "The Weight" in the movie, along with many other popular songs of the time. This was a fresh idea in 1969. There are different accounts of the specific origin of the idea for the soundtrack, but it was clear in any case that Peter and Dennis made an indelible mark on the culture with *Easy Rider*.

John Palladino came by to see how we were making progress. We brought him up to Levon's bedroom and sat him in front of the play-back speakers. He listened intently, trying to decide whether the folks back at Capitol would understand what we were doing. He was both baffled and blown away by what he heard, but I could tell he had no idea how to convey this bizarre experiment to the company heads. I thought, *That's okay. I like it when nobody gets it, too.*

Our West Coast musical extravaganza was winding down. I was running out of songs, but I told Rick there was something in the works that had his name all over it. I called it "Look Out Cleveland," and it had yet another flavor of North Americana stamped on it. Richard and I also had a cowrite in the works, called "Jawbone," that used several different time signatures. Some of it was in 7/4, some in 6/8, some in 2/4—God, we didn't know what to do with that. The song was a throwback lyrically to our times in the streets, when our best friends were gangsters and thieves.

Our management office called. Michelangelo Antonioni, the renowned director of *Blowup* (and *L'Avventura*, starring the stunning Monica Vitti), was putting together his next movie, *Zabriskie Point*, and wanted to come and hear some of our new music. He and his girlfriend and coscreenwriter, Clare Peploe, would stop by the next afternoon to meet up and have a little listening session. *Now we're talking*, I said to myself. It didn't mean as much to the other guys, but I was stoked. It was Antonioni!

Michelangelo and Clare looked so cool and beautiful when they arrived. I escorted them to Levon's room for a playback of some of our tracks. They didn't seem to mind sitting at the foot of the bed and taking in what they could of this Americana sound. Clare translated some of my comments and details of the songs for Michelangelo. I could see him trying to fit this music onto pictures in his head. He had a little nervous tic in his eyes, and they were flickering pretty good. It's interesting listening to your music through somebody else's ears, especially when it's someone like Antonioni who comes from a whole other world. I could sense that our music was a deep corner for what he had in mind. He and Clare were definitely moved, but it wouldn't have been that much different for him to be listening to Muddy Waters, Johnny Cash, or Hank Snow. We wouldn't go on to work on the music for Mr. Antonioni's next movie, but somehow Michelangelo and I would remain friends for many, many years to come.

WHILE WORKING ON the album and having our sweet little Alexandra in our lives, I had given very little thought to our upcoming live debut as the Band. We were booked into Bill Graham's Winterland Ballroom in San Francisco in two weeks. We ran through some tunes from *Big Pink* and were thinking about what else we could throw into the mix, but our heads were in a different zone, and I desperately wanted to get as much recording done as possible before we had to leave. It was almost unimaginable that at this juncture we also needed to put together a live show.

Dominique wanted to get organized with the baby back in Woodstock, so she decided to head home while the Band prepared for our Winterland gigs. I hadn't really slept for a month and started to get weak in the knees as we rehearsed. I had spent all my energy writing, recording, and helping Dominique look after our little one. I had let all the air out of the balloon. Excitement and exhaustion mixed together in a wicked combination, and as we headed up to San Francisco, my immune system shut down.

I had come down with a vicious case of stomach flu. I felt like I was dying while also panicking about our first gig. When we got to the hotel in San Francisco, Albert, John Simon, Jon Taplin, and the guys gathered in my room to assess my condition. I couldn't go to sound check and rehearse. I couldn't move. Albert told Bill Graham we might have to cancel, but Bill was adamant. "We can't," he insisted.

" 'The people' have been waiting for this like a religious experience. It's impossible to cancel. The show must go on."

Albert said, "Well, I don't know what we're going to do. Robbie's *really* not well." I think John Simon had a doctor friend come by. Bill Graham was calling witch doctors. Everybody was pulling out all the stops to get me feeling better. The guys went and did the sound check, but going on without me wasn't even a consideration: they flatly refused, and I didn't know what to suggest in my nauseous delirium.

The next day I still couldn't hold any food down, so gaining back strength just wasn't happening. I looked in the bathroom mirror at my drawn, haggard, pale face and asked myself, *Is this stage fright? Is this all in my head? What the hell is happening?*

Albert and Bill came to my room. "How do you feel about trying a hypnotist? There's a renowned French hypnotist by the name of Pierre Clement we can get."

"I'll try anything," I said, sweating and shivering. "I'm game. Let's get him."

A little while later, an older gentleman with white hair showed up dressed in a black suit like an undertaker. Mr. Pierre Clement had a confident air about him, suffused with the power of his special gift. His eyes were mesmerizing, and he spoke with a gentle command in his voice that made me listen to every syllable he uttered. John Simon and photographer Elliott Landy hung around trying to feel out if he was a quack or not, but soon I was aware only of Mr. Clement's presence. I asked him if he thought my condition might be psychosomatic. "You look very ill, and it doesn't matter," he said. "We are going to address each of your symptoms one at a time and make you feel stronger." He put his hand on my forehead and said, "You have fever. First we are going to take that down." He held his hand there for a few minutes and told me to close my eyes. Then, "There, that's better." Amazingly, I felt less feverish.

He concentrated on the achiness in my body, then worked on settling my stomach. I felt a hint of strength. Slowly some color came back into my face. He asked if I could tolerate a little soup and helped me rise out of the bed and move around, all the while telling me that

I was starting to feel stronger. After a little soup, I got dressed and we drove to Winterland Ballroom. On the way, he told me I would be okay to play but that if I got tired or felt faint I should look over at him in the wings; when I did, he would say, "Grow," and with that I would become steady again.

At Winterland, Bill Graham was back to his P. T. Barnum self, now that this hypnotist experiment was in full swing. The guys and our whole gang looked at me skeptically, like I was a space alien, which was exactly how I felt with Pierre Clement on my arm. Levon pulled me aside for a moment. "Hey, partner, how we feeling?"

"I'm gonna do my best not to let you down," I said.

He smiled. "I know that. Let's just take it one song at a time."

I vaguely remember Bill Graham introducing us with great fanfare, and we launched into our first song. The audience was incredibly enthusiastic, but in my dazed state of mind it was like looking out onto a psychedelic purgatory. We got through a couple of songs— then I turned and looked at the backdrop on the stage behind us: they were projecting gobs of mush and goo onto the screen. Maybe it was the "Joshua Light Show" or the "Haight-Ashbury" look for groups out here, but it was a bad fit for us. It made me nauseated. I looked over at Pierre Clement on the side of the stage. His darting eyes looked back at me and he mouthed the word "grow." Somehow I could hear him over the volume of the music, the sound system, and the crowd. It was spooky and supernatural; I just went with it the best I could.

The rest of our set was vaguely unconscious for me, and after about forty minutes the hypnotist looked at me and nodded his head as if to signal, *That's enough. You shouldn't do any more.* We left the stage knowing it was too short a set, but I didn't have any more in the tank. I walked directly over to Pierre, and he patted me on the back approvingly, but without any hoopla. We walked to a dark corner away from the lights, and his silhouette reached out and shook my hand, and he quietly said, "I'll see you in the stars."

And I never saw him again.

TWENTY-TWO

The Winterland shows formally marked our reemergence as a live act, but we had a ways to go. We had a fuller repertoire now, with songs from both *Big Pink* and *The Band*, but we needed to find what would work best in a live setting. After our shaky debut in San Francisco, we came back strong for Bill Graham during a run at the Fillmore East in New York, and then played a strange show at the Toronto Pop Festival. Our old tailor in Toronto, Lou Myles, insisted on dressing us for the show. He was a dear friend and we wanted to be respectful, but times had changed. Lou made us all fancy clothes that we would never wear under normal circumstances. We laughed at one another in our new duds, but when we stepped out on the stage at the open-aired Varsity Stadium in midtown Toronto, some people started hissing at us, probably because we looked like we should be sipping martinis with the Great Gatsby. Then it started raining, which made us now look like homeless socialites. It was so contrary to our sound and how the audience viewed us. In those threads we couldn't recognize ourselves or our music.

We got in a few songs between the June downpours, and when we finished I yelled, "Somebody's got to do something. This is going to be a disaster." Dr. John, the Night Tripper, was also on the two-day festival, and he heard me as we headed into the wings. In his gris-gris New Orleans drawl he said, "I think we can do something about this rain. Might have something in my satchel." He and his band kicked into their set, defying the downpour, and sounded fantastic—voodoo rising into the night sky. As they finished their first song, Dr. John released his guitar and raised a shaker above his head. And just like that, the rains came to a halt. Now, I'm not making any comment about black magic, but the damn rain just stopped.

Next we were asked to play the Mississippi Riverboat Festival—and the name sounded so cool I asked Bob if he wanted to come and sing a couple of tunes with us. He said, "Sure, what would you want to do?"

"Whatever you feel like singing. You want to do something from your last record, the basement, one of the older tunes? You name 'em, and we'll play 'em. In the words of Jimmy Reed."

He nodded. "Okay, we'll figure it out on the way there." He knew by now we could tackle any of these tunes on a moment's notice. It felt so natural playing with Bob again, and together we gave that crowd an unexpected finale that included Woody Guthrie's "I Ain't Got No Home," Little Richard's "Slippin' and Slidin'," and an old mountain song called "In the Pines."

Albert told me that a 150-year-old stone house straight through the woods from his place had come on the market. The property also had a beautiful, large wooden artist's studio and a very big swimming pool. Albert said the "Hood House" had previously been owned by Evelyn Hood, a concert violinist. He'd heard stories that she would go into the snow-covered woods and play her violin wearing nothing but a fur coat. I told Albert it was highly unlikely I could afford it. "Yes, you can," he said. "I'll help you work it out."

FOR DOMINIQUE AND ME, it was our first real home together, though it needed a lot of fixing up and painting. Our road crew, Jon Taplin, Bill Scheele, and sometimes his brother John, along with Lindsay Holland, helped get the place in shape. Dominique and Alexandra and I stayed in Albert and Sally's guest house while our new home was being prepared. One day, while I was over at Richard's working on a new song called

With Rick Danko

Garth hot-
rodding his
Lowrey organ
in Woodstock

Running over a song with Levon, who had hung a portrait of
Freddy McNulty on the wall

Going over lyrics in Levon's room upstairs in Sammy Davis Jr.'s pool house

Playing a new song for Rick, downstairs at Sammy Davis Jr.'s house

The Band's Salvation Army horn section, including John Simon

The Band
out behind
Big Pink

On an elevator with John Simon as
Albert Grossman and Bill Graham
discuss the possibility of having to
cancel the Band's first performance

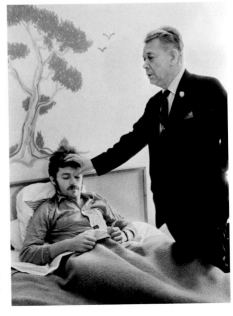

With hypnotist Pierre Clement
before the Winterland show

With Richard and Levon, recording "Daniel and the Sacred Harp"

Richard holding a gold record after crashing another car

With Elliot
Roberts, Bob, and
David Geffen,
Tour '74

With my daughters, Alexandra
and Delphine, in Montreal

Bob with Alexandra at one
of our last shows of Tour '74,
at the Forum, Los Angeles

Dominique with
our son, Sebastian

The Last Waltz concert

With the Hawk at the Last Waltz

Muddy Waters performing "Mannish Boy" at the Last Waltz

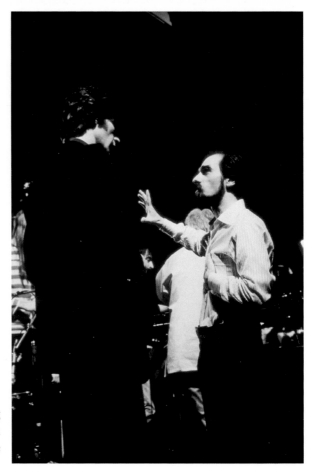

Martin Scorsese explaining
the next shot of the Band on
the MGM soundstage

"Whispering Pines," Dominique wanted to get a new crib for the baby and Garth offered to take her to Kingston to pick one up. She told me that when she and Garth got back to the guesthouse, there were some strange people lounging around inside, eating our food. Albert and Sally weren't around, and not knowing who these people were, Garth went in and kicked them out while Dominique stayed with the baby. It turned out that it was Ken Kesey and his Merry Pranksters. They got back into their psychedelic-painted bus and drove off.

WE WENT BACK into New York to record a few more tracks to finish our album at Jerry Ragovoy's Hit Factory studio on West 48th Street. Jerry, who had written "Time Is on My Side and "Piece of My Heart," said the place used to be Cecil B. DeMille's old headquarters, and there were still some artifacts left in a storage room from *The Ten Commandments* and *The Greatest Show on Earth*. Jerry liked to use the stairwell in the building as an echo chamber, but the reverb was too long and echo-ey for the flavor of music we were making. So we changed the type of speaker in the stairwell and moved the microphone closer to it, which shortened the reverb.

I had a new song called "Jemima Surrender" that I tried to get Levon to work on with me—I had a feeling he might enjoy getting his hooks into this one. And though he did come up with a guitar riff for the intro and turnarounds, he couldn't get into words or structure. But I was just happy to have him involved. We tried recording it with Levon singing while playing guitar, kick drum, and high hat, all at the same time—a one-man band—but that didn't fly. So Richard took over on drums and Garth moved to piano while Levon and I riffed on guitar. Levon and Richard's vocals gave a straightforward and humorous spin to the words. Sometimes I couldn't be sure if a lyrical idea really worked until I heard it sung just right. "Sweet Jemima won't you come out tonight, the ground is so warm and the moon is so bright." We finished off by recording "Whispering Pines." This mood, this performance, was different from everything else we'd cut. I really liked the haunting quality of the track, the distance and loneliness of Richard's vocal.

When it came time to mix the album, we went back to A&R Studios. Tony May was the assigned mixing engineer; he had done an outstanding job on the Isley Brothers' recording "It's Your Thing." But when he heard our recordings he wasn't thrilled with my and John Simon's engineering abilities. He kept saying he was going to have to fix this or fix that. At one point Rick asked Tony if he was adding reverb to the bass. "Don't worry about what I'm doing," Tony replied. "Let's just see if I can make these tracks sound any good." That pissed me off.

He mixed two songs and I didn't like his idea of what this music should sound like at all. He tried to shine it up but made it sound ordinary. I wanted to go back to the Hit Factory and work with their recording engineer, Joe Zagarino, who I felt had an understanding of what we were looking for. So we returned to our subtle stairwell-echo-chamber setup, brought in our own monitors, and mixed the record precisely how we thought it should sound. We all had our hands on the faders of the mixing console, getting the moves just right.

Next John Simon and I went to the highly regarded mastering engineer Bob Ludwig at Sterling Sound. Mastering is the process where they fine-tune the tonality and cut the master disc from which all the records are pressed. Bob listened to our mixes and told us that he thought mastering this record was going to be problematic because the mixes were so dense and heavy. But leave the tapes with him, he said, and he'd see what he could do. I left there feeling let down and worried that our recording experiment might have failed—Bob Ludwig had mastered many, many great records and he knew his stuff. I told the other guys and no one knew what to say. Making a record, you get so close to the music that after a while you realize that your perspective is definitely questionable. Still, I didn't understand how I could be so wrong.

A couple of days later Bob Ludwig called me, his words punctuated with nervous laughter; it turned out he was calling to apologize profusely for his misjudgment of the sonic quality of our record. He'd realized that the album had a depth and richness, with a unique character that he couldn't even describe. He finished off by saying that it was also one of the best records he'd ever heard. Well, that was certainly a tremendous relief to hear.

IN THE SPRING we'd got word that some promoters wanted to put on a huge music festival in Woodstock. *Why Woodstock? Why this simple little art colony in upstate New York?* "It's the mystique of the Band and Dylan," said Albert, "and the way other musicians are converging on the town." He said he had met with Michael Lang and Artie Kornfeld, two of the concert organizers, and he liked them. Albert embraced the idea of Woodstock becoming a cultural mecca because he had ambitions of making Bearsville his own center of the universe. I was of two minds: the festival might make the place more interesting, or it could ruin its charm.

Michael Lang had approached Albert about the Band performing, saying he thought it would be appropriate if we closed things out at midnight on the festival's final night. The Band would be the only act in the three-day event that actually lived in Woodstock. It all sounded nice on paper, so we agreed.

The show promoters couldn't find a site around Woodstock, so they settled on a big farm in Bethel, New York—quite a distance from Woodstock, but they wanted to stick with the name. The festival was set for August 15, 16, and 17, and as it grew nearer, we kept hearing about all kinds of problems cropping up. First, the townspeople of Woodstock were annoyed that the event was being called *The Woodstock Festival: 3 Days of Peace and Music.* Too much hippiedom in that title for their liking, and, worse, hordes of people would likely descend on Woodstock itself in search of the festival. Meanwhile, the town of Bethel was panicked about how to supply enough water and food, let alone restroom facilities, for a few hundred thousand people. There was nothing there to start with but an empty field.

With the stories growing wilder each day, Dominique decided not to attend the festival, and I didn't feel that much different myself. By the third day of the event, we heard that all roads were closed coming and going around Bethel. Someone said there were now close to half a million people at the site. We had to be flown in by helicopter. Our pilot circled over the crowd on the way in, and it was astonishing. None of us had seen an audience of 500,000 people before, and it was hard to comprehend this vast gathering, with people packed together as far as the eye could see in every direction. On the one hand it was an incredible accomplishment, and on the other, somewhat frightening.

The helicopter landed in a backstage area that looked like a village unto itself, and as we disembarked, various attendees and staff greeted us like we were entering the gates of Eden. They offered a stream of insights into this *eighth* wonder of the world, as well as brownies laced with everything under the sun. One of the greeters was someone we'd met before, Hugh Romney, better known as Wavy Gravy, a sight to be seen here in white overalls with purple-stained pockets. We soon learned that the stains were from Owsley Stanley's special LSD pills, which Hugh was handing out like cough drops for anything that might ail you. Experimenting with hallucinogens wasn't on the menu for us; we had to be on our game for this extravaganza.

As we were settling in to our little camp area, Michael Lang came over and whispered to me, "We have a slight problem." *How could we not?* I thought to myself. "Jimi Hendrix claims he was promised that he could close the show," Michael said, "and he won't perform unless he can go on last. I know I said you guys should close, but he's making a big stink over it. I'm sorry, but would you mind going on at nine, when it gets dark?" I thought if we could do our thing earlier and get out of here unscathed, so much the better. All of it felt a bit out of our comfort zone; that the whole thing was called "Woodstock" made it even more suspect.

With hours left before we went on, a parade of backstage personnel and musicians kept stopping by to see if we wanted to partake in various intoxicants. I'd never turned down so many offers to get stoned in one day, ever. Albert helped bat away these stoner flies while reading the riot act to the camera crew filming the concert about what they shouldn't do during our performance: "No cameras on the stage. No running around with handheld cameras." The film director, Michael

Wadleigh, objected to these restrictions, but Albert was exceptionally good at saying no.

When Jimi Hendrix arrived, I was told he wanted to explain why he insisted on closing the show. I relayed that we were cool, no explanation necessary, but he wanted to say hello anyway. We hadn't really caught up in years, since back in my Chelsea Hotel days, and it was great to see him. He looked like a different person in his rock-star British garb. And so did I, he remarked. We just stood there for a moment, looking each other over and laughing.

"Man," he said, "I wanted to tell you I covered that song you did with Dylan, 'Crawl Out Your Window,' and I copied your guitar lick. I borrowed it. I didn't steal it."

"It's yours. It's a gift from the old days."

He gave me a hug. "Your record *Big Pink* has changed the musical landscape. It's like you turned the music world on its head. I dig it." I appreciated Jimi's endorsement, especially because our record underplayed lengthy guitar solos. Then he reminded me of when we were hanging out in the Village together, and how badly he had wanted to learn to write songs. "I'm still working on it, baby. Don't know if I'm getting any better, but I'm trying." He smiled. "And hey, I'm sorry about this mix-up with who's going on last. I'm not doing some ego bullshit. They just told me if I agreed to be on the show, I could go on whenever I want." I assured him it wasn't in any way an issue with us.

As the evening wore on, the guys and I took a moment to gauge how everyone was feeling. "I might have to do some dancing during our set," Rick joked. "You have to keep them entertained, boys."

"Well, do you think I should stand on the piano to sing?" Richard joked. "You know, so the people in the back can see." We all agreed—*Oh, yeah, absolutely!* These showbiz antics couldn't have been more adverse to anything we would ever do.

The show was running way behind, but eventually it came time for us to hit the stage. Albert and Sally were right there to protect and comfort us, knowing how virginal we were to this kind of experience. Michael Lang kept telling us that this was now the largest festival audience in the world; there'd been two babies born, and the gathering now qualified as one of the biggest cities in the tristate area.

The audience looked and felt manic as we took the stage, a sea of faces and bodies and colors stretching out beyond the horizon. We sensed them wanting to rock, to go crazy. If that was the case, boy, did they dial a wrong number putting us on in the peak hour of the festival's final night. Most performers on the show wanted to "take you higher," but we took the stage at 10:00 p.m. and proceeded to play a set that we might have done in the living room at Big Pink . . . talk about settling things down. Some folks in the crowd were still jumping up and down wanting to go wild, but many sat down and were swaying to the music—taking it in like a spiritual missive. What else could they do? It was overwhelming; I could hardly look out at the crowd. I got so lost inside my guitar that I barely knew where I was.

When the helicopter flew us out of there around one in the morning, it felt like a relief. As exciting as the event was, it came with a sense of chaos, the feeling that anything could go very wrong at any moment. Looking down at the crowd, you could already see an exodus of people, even though we'd been told by one of the promoters that it looked like the show probably wouldn't end until dawn. *Thank heavens Jimi insisted on playing last,* I thought. We would have been like zombies come sunup.

Back home, there was a chill in the air. Woodstock had suddenly become the most famous small town in the world, and as far as the locals were concerned, that wasn't good news. They were not keen on the festival at all, and the Band's participation sent the wrong message. Word got back to us that some of the townspeople felt betrayed that we had in any way encouraged this parade of tourists from hell. They saw it as the attack of the hippie monster. I started noticing that no one would wait on me when I went to the stores. When I asked questions, the clerks just shrugged.

I understood how the Woodstock folks felt about this invasion of their privacy. At the same time, we were having an invasion of privacy all our own. We heard that quite a few songs from the basement tapes had been released on a bootleg album called *Great White Wonder.* It might have been naive on our part to think the public would never hear these songs—only certain recording artists and publishers. This was private, personal music being made for us by us, and only a few tracks were meant to be shared with the outside world. This bootleg was becoming a phenomenon, the biggest bootleg record of all time. Lawyers and record companies and publishers all went after the boot-leggers, but it was too late. The tornado had come and gone, but more bootleggers were lying in wait. The whole thing pissed Bob off; it was like someone listening in on your phone conversation and stealing from you at the same time.

We had made a commitment to play at the Isle of Wight Festival in England with Bob just eleven days after the Woodstock event. This would be Bob's first full live concert since his motorcycle accident. I asked him if I should coordinate things with Albert. But Bob said that he and Al were having some differences these days. I had never heard Bob refer to Albert as "Al" before. It sounded strange, and I was disheartened to hear that they were at odds. Bob and Albert had always seemed to be a great team and a powerful duo. It could have been that Bob saw Albert's involvement as specific to setting up tours or getting a record deal, but beyond the Isle of Wight there were no plans for him to go back on the road and tour in the near future. And anyway, Albert was more focused these days on building his empire in Bearsville.

The arrangement for the Isle of Wight was that we would play a set with Bob and one on our own. We didn't have much time to run over songs for the show, so we decided to fly over a few days early and rehearse. The Isle of Wight is an island off the south coast of England that had been a home of the poet Alfred, Lord Tennyson. Bob rented a house in the small town of Bembridge, with a building where we could work out some material, while the Band stayed at a nearby hotel.

John, George, and Ringo came down for a visit with their better halves to catch some of the show. John appeared thinner with his shoulder-length hair. He and Yoko were looking similar in spirit as well as physically, and they sat quietly in the corner smiling and hold-ing hands as we rehearsed. George and Pattie cheered us on and made song requests like "Everybody Must Get Stoned" and "To Kingdom Come." And Ringo made Levon's day as he marched around the room peering through his sunglasses yelling, "Turn up the drums! We need more drums!"

Before we hit the stage, we heard that the police were having problems with the crowd. Of course, at such an event there's going to be some unruly suspects—especially in the British Isles, where they have rivers of beer flowing and lochs of scotch whiskey and gin. But the promoters said the police had German shepherds attacking people who were trying to crash the gates. Not what you wanted to hear before you go on. It sounded ugly and disturbing.

Since Bob had hardly played live in almost three years, I hoped the craziness wouldn't throw him off his game. Before we went out there, I said, "Okay, captain, let's go get 'em." He nodded and threw his guitar strap over his shoulder. There was something about these huge events that sent me into a vacuum, into a zone between a dream state and nightmare. The only grounding I had was looking down into a private section in front of the stage and seeing the Beatles sitting there, and I couldn't even be sure *that* was real. We couldn't hear one another very well on the stage, so I just put my head down and plowed straight ahead, recalling Bob's earliest instruction: "Just don't stop." There was no longer much booing like in '66, but there were some catcalls and hoots.

We were supposed to head to London the next day, but Ringo said he had a private plane if I wanted to go that night. I was a little bit wary. "What kind of plane?"

John Lennon laughed. "Oh, don't be worried. Ringo is much too lucky to be in any bloody plane disaster." George gave me a push and said, "Yeah, yeah, it's perfectly okay. Go on. I'll see you in London."

On the way, I asked Ringo where their incredible bass player, Paul, was. He answered, "Why, I don't know what the bass player's up to this weekend. Think he might be having some girlfriend problems, but hopefully he's just off writing some good songs for me to sing." The airplane pilot let out a hearty laugh.

In London the guys caught a connecting flight back to New York while I lingered for a couple of days for some meetings at Capitol's parent company, EMI. George had invited me to his house in Surrey to play me the Beatles' new album and for me to play him the Band's new record. He put *Abbey Road* on the turntable, and it came blasting out of his big Tannoy speakers. After the first two songs, "Come Together" and "Something," I thought, *These bastards just get better all the time.* Pattie seemed to be particularly proud of George's song "Something," as it could very well have been a reflection of her. I thought George would play the *Let It Be* recordings they had been working on, but he shook his head no; he said the Beatles were having some serious internal differences on that record and had decided to put it on hold.

I played our new album, simply called *The Band*, for them, and it sounded rustic and a bit homemade after *Abbey Road*. As the songs went by, George would jump up, puffing on a smoke, yelling, "That's fucking amazing! Nobody can do that; only you guys can do that. Have you played this for Bob yet?" George continued, "Did you see our little film performing 'Hey Jude' on the Smothers Brothers TV show, where Paul starts singing, 'Take a load off, Fanny,' in the outro section? Can't wait to play your new record for the boys. Can I keep this acetate?" I said yes, even though it was the only copy we had at the time. He handed me his acetate of *Abbey Road* and I left his house flying high.

WE RELEASED *The Band* (or *The Brown Album*) a month later on September 22. It had a different look, sound, and feel from *Big Pink*. Elliott Landy photographed us for the album cover. We didn't want to show up looking the same as we had on *Big Pink*. That look had become a signature, and we didn't want to play that note again. Elliott had a spot picked out where he wanted to shoot. When we showed up, it was raining, and Levon was hoping to call it off. I was drawn to the idea of the photo being taken while we were standing in the rain. It gave a darker, more dangerous feeling to the picture, and you can't beat that.

I asked art director Bob Cato to design the album. He'd done a cover for Thelonious Monk that I really liked, and I felt he was our man. Cato said he'd listened to the record twenty times before he understood what it should look like. Garth suggested using words from the old song "The Darktown Strutters' Ball" on the back of the sleeve: "I'll be down to get you in a taxi, honey, better be ready by half-past eight, now honey, don't be late, I want to be there when the band starts playing."

The record company released "Up on Cripple Creek" as a single. Then there was a demand from EMI to release "Rag Mama Rag" in Britain. Among the five of us, we had an unusual attitude regarding singles and popularity. Naturally we wanted to share our music with as many people as possible, but that was matched by a suspicion of being trendy, too well known, or corny in our own eyes. Part of that came from our already having been together for eight years and having a keen bullshit meter; the other part was that a lot of the music we admired could be somewhat obscure, like hidden treasures.

A movie and music journalist from *Time* magazine named Jay Cocks contacted us, saying that he wanted to convince the magazine to do a cover story on the Band. Jay came up to Woodstock to talk it through. I told him the Band mostly operated from behind a curtain; publicity was a delicate balance in our circle. Levon hated doing interviews. "They always turn things around and try to fuck you," he'd say. Jay was very understanding, but he stressed that *Time* didn't typically put music groups on the cover—we'd be the first North American rock 'n' roll band ever to appear there. "That's how unique we think your music and your story is," he emphasized. Jay turned out to be such a fantastic guy and made us feel much more at ease with the cover-story idea. We decided to cooperate.

After Dominique and I settled into the Hood House, Bearsville started to feel quite homey. One day Dominique came back from a doctor's appointment and said, "Guess what? I'm pregnant again!" Alexandra wasn't even walking yet, so we were both a bit stunned but totally thrilled. Dominique immediately started talking about going to Montreal to see her family, share the news, and have a visit with her own obstetrician.

When we got there a week later, the *Time* magazine cover story on the Band had just hit the newsstands. The story had a nice edge to it. Jay Cocks and two other writers who usually wrote about classical music contributed to the article. The editors at *Time* wanted them to classify the music the Band made, but nobody could figure out what to call our gumbo of sounds. Was it "roots rock"? "modern ragtime"? "Canadian Delta R&B"? "cinema rock"? "Americana from Canada"? Jay asked me how I would describe it in a headline for their readers, but I shrugged. "I don't care what they call it. Just don't call after midnight."

Time settled on the subtitle THE NEW SOUND OF COUNTRY ROCK. We never thought of ourselves in those terms, but I guess that's what happens when you write a song about the American Civil War from a southern point of view. And "The Night They Drove Old Dixie Down" had become a hit when Joan Baez covered it, though she did a much happier, bouncier version of the song than our recording. Dominique thought her version completely fucked up the song, that it was totally out of context. Our friend the songwriter Bobby Charles, who wrote "See You Later, Alligator" and "Walking to New Orleans," commented, "Yeah, she fucked it up all the way to number one."

WHILE DOMINIQUE AND I were in Montreal, a friend of mine, Gordon Sheppard, told me about a talented American singer-songwriter who was holed up in the basement of a monastery up in Ottawa, hiding out from the draft. We took the train to go check him out. At the monastery a monsignor escorted us down into dungeonlike hallways, and in one of the rooms sat a lone figure. Gordon and the monsignor introduced me to Jesse James Winchester from Memphis, Tennessee. "Originally from Louisiana," Jesse added. He had a sad, withdrawn face but a spark in his eyes. He knew the music of the Band and my songwriting. We had a little tea and then he took out his guitar and sang me a couple of songs, "Yankee Lady" and "Brand New Tennessee Waltz." There was a powerful melancholy sweetness to his music that really impressed me. I said that I'd try to help him get a record deal and, time permitting, I'd produce his record myself. He glowed with that encouragement and looked like he was being rescued from a lost island, which in a way he was.

He had a few of his songs on a reel-to-reel tape, which I took with me, and when Dominique and I got back home I played it for Albert immediately. He thought the music had real potential and said he could sign Jesse to his new record company, Bearsville, which was affiliated with Ampex and Warner Bros. distribution. He thought it was a great idea for me to produce the record. I said there were some fantastic musicians in Toronto I'd like to work with, but I wanted to bring my own engineer. Albert suggested a young musician and engineer he was starting to work with named Todd Rundgren. He said Todd was a whiz in the studio with progressive ideas, and he could play, sing—whatever you needed.

I connected with Todd right away. He had a youthful, no-bullshit approach, and I needed to move swiftly. We made plans to make an album with Jesse in Toronto and headed up north together. When Jesse showed up at the studio, I noticed right away he had a cold. I was concerned about his voice, but Jesse didn't fret. I decided to start out with a couple of his songs that I thought might sound good with a bit of a nasal quality in his voice, like "Payday" and "The Nudge." The musicians in Toronto did a great job on Jesse's songs—Bob Boucher on bass, Dave Lewis on drums, Ken Pearson on keyboards. I played on a couple of tracks too, and I even got Levon to sit in on some songs. "Yankee Lady," "Biloxi," and "The Brand New Tennessee Waltz" were all beautiful tunes of Jesse's, and we did fine versions of them, although I might have recorded "Yankee Lady" a bit too slow. It felt really good at the time, but it might have had wider appeal had I done it a little brighter.

During the recording of the album, I came to understand that Jesse was a bit of a haunted soul, and a certain bitterness lingered within him. Being uprooted from your home, family, and friends over a war you didn't believe in was really tough. If I'd had to dodge the draft, I might have been bitter too.

I was very satisfied with the work we did together. But after the album came out, I read an interview that Jesse gave where he said that the record wasn't *his* record, "it was Robbie's record." That wasn't true, and it bothered me that he would say such a thing. I had done my best to give strong direction to the songs and help make a terrific record in every way I could, but Jesse had the final say on everything. He became a bit of a dark shadow after that, and I never saw him much again. His talent, though, was never, ever in question. To this day some of his vocal performances still send shivers down my spine.

BACK IN BEARSVILLE, I got an unexpected call from the Czech film director Miloš Forman—I had seen his movies *Loves of a Blonde* and *The Firemen's Ball*. He'd read about us in *Time* magazine and asked if he and his girlfriend, the actress Bibi Andersson, could come up for a visit. He had a project he wanted to discuss with me. *My God, Bibi Andersson?* I admired her so much in Ingmar Bergman's movies *The Seventh Seal* and *Persona. Yes, Milos, come right up.*

They stayed in one of the cabins between Albert's house and mine— rustic but nicely put together. You couldn't help but like Miloš. He was charming and vibrantly intelligent. He said he'd been listening to the Band's music and then read the *Time* story, and asked if we'd be interested in developing a movie script based on the article. It was flattering to hear of his interest, but when it came to Milos telling the Band's story, I felt a little confused—as he described images and particular scenes he envisioned, it sounded original but distant from our reality. Perhaps his Czechoslovakian accent added to the distance even more.

At the same time I couldn't help asking Bibi about Ingmar Bergman's style of writing and directing. She made it sound like they operated in creative seclusion around Sweden. Ingmar had his own little committees of actors and technicians he liked to work with, not an unusual method, but Ingmar's group felt still more remote and mysterious. It reminded me of theatrical groups that would trade roles from story to story. Given the Band's working relationship in Woodstock, I related to this scenario musically. It often felt as if Rick, Levon, and Richard were playing different characters in the stories I was writing, and Garth was providing a sonic counterpoint to the settings—a *real* workshop. Miloš and I pushed around ideas on making a music film until I think we talked ourselves out of it. It was really a bold challenge, and so many things could come off as hokey or lame.

In the meantime, Dominique and I were getting ready to have our second child. Her pregnancy was progressing smoothly, and we were back on Lamaze duty. We weren't as filled with anxiety this time, because having our sweet Alexandra gave us the ability to embrace the experience with more confidence. I asked Dominique if she was sure she wanted to do totally natural childbirth again. "Absolutely," she answered. "Don't let them give me anything, no matter what I say." We laughed, remembering when Alexandra was being born and she nearly ripped my arm off and beat me over the head with it.

Around this time I heard that Van Morrison had rented Richard's old house and was becoming a Woodstock resident. I invited him over to Albert's one day to play him *The Band* album. After each song he pushed back his ruffled red hair and let out a hearty "Yeah!" When we came to the last song on the record, "King Harvest (Has Surely Come)," he said, "I don't know if I get that one. I'll have to hear it again." Then he got up and left. *There he goes again*, I thought.

Van was in the midst of making a new record of his own. One day he played me "And It Stoned Me" and "Caravan." We were convinced there was a musical thread between us. So for a show at Symphony Hall in Boston, when the promoters asked who we'd like to have open for us, "New England, hmm, Irish? How about Van Morrison?" I suggested. When we got to the gig, I didn't get a chance to see Van before the concert started, but in the middle of Van's set, the promoter came into our dressing room looking concerned. "I think Mr. Morrison's been drinking. He's lying down on the stage, singing."

Richard piped up, "I think we should all lie down and sing tonight. It's different!"

But the promoter was insistent. "Somebody's got to do something, please. This is too weird." I put on a hooded jacket and slipped out to the front of the stage, and sure enough, Van was lying there, singing his heart out. "Pssst! Van!" I whispered, and winked at him, gesturing up with my chin. I don't know if he heard me, but he rose to his feet and cried out, "Say good-bye, say good-bye to Madame George." He threw his acoustic guitar on, hit a rhythm, and belted out a couple of vocal lines, and I saw in that moment one of the greatest music artists of our time. The fire in his eyes, the bulging veins in his neck, his powerful hand beating mercilessly on that guitar, a little giant.

After we got back home, I went for a checkup with Dr. Ed Thaler. I'd experienced a harsh bout of pneumonia some months earlier, and my breathing still felt tight. He told me the hay fever I had as a kid had developed into an asthmatic condition. I had known for quite a while that my breathing was compromised; it was another reason I preferred the other guys do most of the singing. Dr. Ed prescribed an inhaler for me to use. It's strange now to think that he never mentioned quitting smoking. We all smoked like chimneys then, so I guess the suggestion was unimaginable.

I wrote two new songs, "Time to Kill" and "The Shape I'm In," and played them for Rick. He got up, paced around a bit, and said, "You should sing those songs. That's the way they're meant to sound."

I took out my inhaler, took a puff, and said, "I think I'll leave that up to you boys."

ONE DAY ALBERT gave me a ring. "*The Ed Sullivan Show* wants to book the Band a week from Sunday," he said. "It would be good promotion for the single 'Up on Cripple Creek.' It's climbing nicely up the charts." This was news—we never paid much attention to "the charts." We just weren't into that. If we heard our music on the radio, we figured everything must be copacetic.

At the sound check, Ed Sullivan sat on a stool at the side of the stage, observing. He was eating an Eskimo Pie and looked a bit like an alien. He had grown sideburns, which looked stiff and out of place. As a matter of fact, *he* looked stiff and out of place. Sullivan was very cordial, but disconnected at the same time, maybe even a bit ghostly or robotic. But he had the biggest and most entertaining show on TV. Pearl Bailey, who was a huge star at the time and my mom's favorite, was also on the bill that night, as was comedian Rodney Dangerfield. When we passed him backstage, he called out, "Hey, boys! Who's got the reefer? I'm nervous, you know what I mean? I'm nervous!"

The showbiz glitziness of Sullivan's show wasn't a perfect fit, but we played well enough against the corny, rustic set they had built for us. The stage manager and producers told us that if Ed liked your performance he'd call you over to the center of the stage. Sure enough, he waved us over with a big smile on his face and raised our hands in the air like we had just won the middleweight boxing championship.

We finished out 1969 playing December 26 and 27 at Madison Square Garden's Felt Forum. The promoter, Ron Delsener, thought we were "cookin' with gas." Ron was a terrific character, and his opinion meant a lot to me. He saw many great bands coming and going, but for his personal taste you could tell he truly enjoyed our show. I felt like the Band was experiencing a high point in our live shows—we were locked in and feeding off one another's performances in a powerful way.

There would be some rough roads ahead, though. Our drug experimentation was still going strong, and at one gig we played in Chicago, Rick and I hit a wall. Our sound check at the concert hall took place in the early afternoon, and everybody decided to stick around and rest until the gig that night. But Rick and I got restless and drove back to our hotel for a little break. Somebody had given me a little chunk of tar called DMT. You smoked it like hashish, but it had a psychedelic effect to it like a short LSD trip. With a few hours to go before the show, we thought we could kill a little time and have a few trippy laughs. But the effect was much stronger than either of us had imagined, and it didn't seem to be wearing off. As time went by and the show crept closer, we started hoping just to come down.

With an hour left before showtime, we knew we had to head back to the hall, regardless of how we were feeling. Rick got behind the wheel and drove for about fifteen or twenty minutes in silence, confidently retracing his footsteps back to the venue. Suddenly he blurted out, "I don't know where in the fuck we are! I thought I had it, I thought the hall was up here, past this park, but I must have gone the wrong way."

We pulled into a gas station and asked for directions, but the guy had a strong accent that made him hard to understand. His directions kept getting more and more vague until Rick just stepped on the gas and roared out of there.

Finally, we pulled up next to some cops in a patrol car. By now we were running very late; even if the police could tell we were stoned, we were desperate. They led us to the stage door of the auditorium, and we ran in. The guys were standing in the wings, ready to go on. They shook their heads, looking at us like the idiots we were. I'm not sure how we played that night because I don't remember a damn thing—and maybe it's for the best.

Capitol wanted a new record from us as soon as possible after the success of *The Band* album. We considered the idea of recording our next album at the Woodstock Playhouse. The building had nice acoustics and a warm, woodsy feel to it. It was mainly a summer-stock theater, and availability didn't seem to be a problem.

Rick didn't want John Simon to produce our next album, and the other guys thought it would be good to produce it ourselves. It was partially a financial issue and also just wanting to try something new. To me John was like family, and he'd played a vital role in our discovering our musical path. But I could see how strongly the boys felt, and if producing ourselves would get everybody more involved I was all for it. So I asked Todd Rundgren if he would do some engineering, and he agreed.

But before we got set up at the Playhouse, a dark cloud rolled overhead. Levon, Richard, and Rick had started some serious "chippying" around with heroin. You could feel it: out of reach, out of touch, a cold and dark disconnect. I tried to engage them with ideas and possibilities we might try on the new record, different instrumentation and vocal stylings, but things kept getting worse by the day.

This wasn't completely new. Some months earlier I had seen a certain strain of medicated madness in Levon's eyes. He had been seeing an African American girl who was a knockout and decided he wanted to, as he put it, "take her down home with me and see what those fuckers think about that. Those ignorant sons of bitches will fall by the wayside when they see us together. I'll show them that my country ass ain't the same as it used to be." It was like some demon had crawled inside my friend's soul and pushed a crazy, angry button.

I said, "Why would you want to submit this girl to such a terrible, uncomfortable situation?"

He just waved it off. "Nah, she'll like it. I'll show her something she ain't never seen before. We'll blow everybody's damn mind." He was looking at me with one eye closed, and I could tell that something he was taking was bringing this behavior to the surface.

A couple of months later, after that relationship had unsurprisingly ended, Levon hooked up with our singer friend and local beauty Libby Titus. Libby had a very smart, street-savvy side and I thought she might be able to pull Levon back on track. I complained to Rick and Richard about their messing around with scag and how it was affecting Levon—and them, and our working relationship. I got through to Rick a little bit at times, but he drifted in and out.

It did surprise me some that Levon, Rick, or Rich never offered me *any* heroin. Over the years we had shared just about everything, but with this, not a peep. They probably knew I would condemn this hardcore interference with our work, so I didn't really expect an invitation, but hell, I was no angel. I didn't know if they asked Garth into the fold either, but I suspected not. Garth was all too familiar with the drug-fueled downfall of many a jazz great that he admired.

At one time, there was talk that if you wanted to play like the angels, you had to dance with the devil—that heroin was a gateway to music supremacy. That myth was yesterday, but the power of addiction was still in full force. It hit me hard that in a band like ours, if we weren't operating on all cylinders, it threw the whole machine off course.

This was the first time that writing songs was painful for me. In some cases I couldn't help but reflect on what was happening behind the curtain. I wrote "The Shape I'm In" for Richard to sing, "Stage Fright" for Rick, and "The W. S. Walcott Medicine Show" for Levon— all with undertones of madness and self-destruction. While watching

Richard pound out the rhythm on the clavichord, I couldn't help but
see the irony as he sang out, "Oh, you don't know, the shape I'm in."

Garth and I showed up every day on time, hoping the other guys
would follow suit. When Levon returned from another trip home to
Arkansas, he said he might have the beginnings of a little blues tune. I
was thrilled to see him making an effort in the songwriting direction
and, without even hearing what he had, said I'd help him finish it.
He called it "Strawberry Wine," and I treasured this rare songwriting
collaboration.

But back at the Playhouse, Todd Rundgren didn't know what the
hell was going on. He wasn't acquainted with the world of hard drugs
and didn't understand why the guys were showing up late or maybe
not at all. On a couple of occasions he spoke his mind about it, and
Levon chased him around the Woodstock Playhouse threatening to
kick his ass. Levon had just totaled his new Corvette after nodding off
at the wheel, which might have contributed to his being a little short-
tempered.

While we were working at the Playhouse, Jon Taplin brought me
a new green BMW CS2800 coupe that had just been delivered from
Germany. I had ordered this sweet baby a month earlier and looked
forward to getting my hands on it. The car handled like a dream on
these mountain roads and looked pretty sharp. One afternoon, during
a break from recording, Levon said he needed to make a run back to
his house and asked if he could use my car, winking around the room
at everybody. I wanted to show faith in our brotherhood and belief
in better days ahead. I wouldn't be bluffed, even if it wasn't the wis-
est decision. I immediately, defiantly threw him the keys. He grinned
back at me with his one lazy eye. "Don't you worry, Duke. I'll bring
her back all in one piece." He did, but I also knew I would never do
that again.

After we recorded "Stage Fright," I thought we'd finally started to
hit our stride. Garth and the guys played strong and determined. In
a completely different vein I wrote a tune reflecting on fatherhood
called "All La Glory" (a slight *français* tinge in there for my wife and

daughter) and thought it might be inspired to see if Levon could handle the vocal in his present state of mind. Levon's performance on it was extremely touching. The sound of his voice and his superb phrasing—pure talent. Next Levon and Libby announced that they were expecting a little one.

I invited John Simon to stop by the Playhouse to see how we were coming along and maybe to play horns on a track with Garth. I missed working with John, and I didn't want him to feel shut out. He listened to some of our tracks approvingly, but you could tell he didn't like seeing Todd sitting behind the recording console. I could also feel that John sensed something dark and heavy in the atmosphere. The smell of drugs and dust lingered in the air, and the volatile behavior of Richard, Rick, and Levon said it all. John looked around, looked at me, and shrugged his shoulders. He didn't have to say anything. Garth, meanwhile, kept busy, working on his instruments and experimenting with electronics. He knew better than to try to make sense of what was happening with our brothers in the band.

One day between setups, Levon got a mat, a cushion, and a blanket and lay down and went to sleep. Todd, who was doing a superb job engineering, said to me in dismay, "I really don't get it. I don't understand how you guys work. How can he go lay down on the floor and go to sleep in the middle of the recording session?" I felt somewhat ashamed and didn't have an answer.

That evening when we finished working, I told Levon that I would drive him home. On the way I said how horrible it was watching Rich, Rick, and him on this drug binge. I confessed how helpless I felt in the midst of this monster. "It's destroying us. It's tearing our band apart. You are my brother, my best friend, and I can't stand watching this happen."

I pulled the car up in front of Levon's house and shut the motor off. He turned to me and began a ten-minute rant. "No, baby. What do you think? I'm strung out? I wouldn't do that shit. No, man, I'd tell you if I was sick, you know that. I got it under control. You don't need to worry about me. You wanna see my arms? You wanna check for needle marks? Here, let me show you." He took off his jacket and rolled up his sleeves. "Look. Clean. Just a couple of old bruises. Sure, I did a little skin popping a while back, but I'm cool now."

For the first time, Levon had looked me straight in the eye, patted me on the shoulder, and lied. We had never lied to each other. It made me terribly sad. He opened the car door and said, "If you want, I'll talk to Rick and Richard tomorrow and make sure they ain't getting in deeper than they need to be. But you don't need to worry none about me. This ship ain't going down on my account." He stepped out of the car, waved at me with a wink, and walked away.

Things changed in that moment. A distance grew between Levon and me that I don't know if we were ever able to mend. It wasn't about the drugs; whatever he wanted to do, that was his business. It was about the betrayal. About disrespecting the brotherhood and our partnership.

When I got to my house, I shared with Dominique my painful exchange with Levon. She helped clear the air and grounded the situation. "Everything can't revolve around drugs and insanity," she said. "I'm having a baby and that's reality. This other shit is imitation life."

WE FINISHED OUR stretch at the Woodstock Playhouse, but I had one more song for which I needed to finish the words. I wrote about a traveling medicine show I had heard Levon speak of years earlier, something between a carnival sideshow and the African American origins of rock and roll. We recorded "The W. S. Walcott Medicine Show" and another take of "Daniel and the Sacred Harp" with Todd at a studio in the city, and these turned out to be a couple of our favorite tracks. That put the finishing touches on what we could pull out of the hat for this record. I was worn out from this process and trying to maintain a stable family life with my baby daughter and pregnant wife.

As the recording was wrapping up, we accepted an unusual offer to play a train tour across Canada called the Festival Express. It sounded like a fun idea and included Janis Joplin, the Grateful Dead, and others. But the whole thing was ill-fated from the start. Local authorities in Montreal pulled the plug on the planned first show, and instead the tour kicked off a few days later in Toronto.

Before the show in Winnipeg, Garth said that Don Docker was here—the Mountie who had been one of the arresting officers in our Toronto pot bust. I couldn't believe that tough-ass RCMP was here at this rock 'n' roll event. Garth smiled. "Yeah, he's here, and he wants to say hello." We brought him backstage and Levon introduced him to Jerry Garcia of the Dead and Janis Joplin. People were smoking grass all over the place. "You see," I said to Don, "we were just ahead of our time."

"Oh, you don't know what happened," Don replied. He explained that after our bust was basically dismissed, all the arresting police came under investigation. Their superiors in the police department believed there was some kind of hanky-panky going on, and they paid the price. Don claimed some of the cops were reassigned to Nova Scotia and British Columbia, and he'd been sent to Manitoba.

As the Festival Express chugged westward, it turned into more of a fiasco. All the musicians on board drank the train dry, and the promoters had to stop and reload the express with booze. Rick knew how to roll, and I heard he was the king of entertainment on board. I had to slip back to New York to do more work on the record, and I talked Levon into joining me. We were doing mixes with Todd, and at the same time Levon made arrangements to send multitrack tapes to London, England, for engineer/producer Glyn Johns to take a crack at mixing. We thought a fresh perspective on this material could be helpful, and though Todd was doing his own mixes, he didn't seem to mind at all. He knew and respected Glyn's work.

The train tour made it to Calgary, Alberta, before the whole thing imploded. What had started out as a romantic notion of traveling across wide-open spaces turned into a ballyhoo of danger and destruction. The initial plan was to wrap up the tour in Vancouver, but the city wouldn't approve the permit. Then we heard that the promoter and the Calgary mayor had gotten in a fight at the show. Musicians who actually rode the train across Canada looked haggard and beaten by the time they finished up. Nobody died, but that was probably just luck.

We returned to Woodstock to catch our breath and compare Glyn's and Todd's mixes. Art director Bob Cato said he had a new photographer from South Africa we should try. He was just arriving in the U.S., and Cato sent him directly up to Woodstock to shoot us for the album cover. The photographer arrived like a phantom and set up in the studio building at my house. He had kind of a wiry frame and blond hair. He looked a bit jetlagged, and scared. I never spoke to him, just got out of the way. When the guys came over for the shoot, we had no idea what to expect. I could tell the photographer was very nervous; he tried to situate us in a particular way but could see we weren't picture-friendly at all. He spent a very short period of time placing his flash and getting what he could. I wanted to thank him for coming to Woodstock to take the shot and venturing from South Africa, but I hadn't caught his name. He politely shook my hand and said, "Norman, my name is Norman Seeff." Later, two shots were anonymously delivered. I had never seen this texture, the style of art, in photography before. It was soft and stark at the same time, in a modernistic sepia tone. We ended up using one of his shots for the cover. Norman went on to become one of the most celebrated and sought-after photographers in the whole country. Once again I said to Bob Cato, "Good eye."

I ended up sequencing the songs on the album, which we had decided to call *Stage Fright*. I know it probably sounds a bit odd now, but I wanted any cowrites with the guys to be presented up front, even if it meant some of the best songs ended up on the second side of the LP.

Capitol put the machine in motion to get this album on record-store shelves before you could blink an eye. They had just hired and fired another president and had no comments, no feedback, nothing. It felt like an empty pit, a vacuum. But maybe there was nothing anyone could say about an album called *Stage Fright*. I was just trying to do the best we could under these dark, drugged-out circumstances. It is what it is. One thing I knew: some of my favorite songs that I'd ever written were contained on this album, so I could live with that.

TWENTY-THREE

On July 30, 1970, Delphine Kateri Robertson was born in Montreal. She favored my mother a little, and looked like a little Indian in her blanket. We were living temporarily in a little apartment near Dominique's folks in Côte-des-Neiges when she was born. This was a thrilling time for us. We were growing into a new stage of true parenthood. Having two daughters can bring out a protective side in a father that you didn't even know you had. Dominique was right: *This* was real. Everything else in my world was balancing on a wire.

We took Alexandra and Delphine back to our house in the Catskill Mountains and put both cribs in the bedroom next to ours. Quick, easy access was our goal—until the girls would start crying in stereo in the middle of the night. Dominique was nursing, so she would pick up Delphine and I would get Alexandra, and we would walk them in circles while we were half asleep, praying for slumber before we all keeled over.

In the beginning, Dominique wouldn't consider hiring any help, but I tried to encourage the idea of getting a nanny. The Band had a concert schedule, and I really wanted Dominique and the kids to be covered. Dominique, however, would only agree to French-speaking help, which was fine so long as we could find people who wouldn't mind living in the mountains, a hundred miles north of New York City. As one might imagine, we went through an interesting array of characters in search of someone Dominique trusted and who didn't drive us crazy, like the flying squirrels that had taken up in our roof.

I HAD BARELY recuperated from finishing the album and the Festival Express tour when we were booked for several concerts around the country. We ran over some of the new songs to see what felt good live and to see if everybody was road ready. We all showed up, though some days were extremely encouraging and others were borderline. For an upcoming date at the Hollywood Bowl, Albert asked us our thoughts on the opening act. I looked at the list of possibilities and saw only one name: Miles Davis. What a night of music this could be for the audience at the Bowl, I thought. Miles had extraordinary musicians playing with him at all times, but they were really exceptional during this period: Chick Corea, Jack DeJohnette, and Keith Jarrett. I shared my enthusiasm with the other guys and hoped this would encourage everyone to be on top of their game.

While Rick usually rose to the occasion, my biggest concern was Richard, who walked the most vulnerable tightrope with his health and keeping his voice in shape. During these particular days, Levon too was struggling with his drugs of choice. It seemed to me that he was trying not to get caught in a heroin web, so he took pills to help soften withdrawal. A whole lot of Valium might ease the pain, but it could also make you groggy and crazed.

At the hotel the night before the show, Levon fell in his room and cut open his forehead. When we did our sound check at the Bowl the next day, it quickly became clear what a hard time he was having. He seemed unsteady and sluggish. I pulled him aside, and he said that he'd be fine in time for the show. He looked rough but said he just needed a little nap. That night he showed up wearing a Confederate flag shirt, a straw cowboy hat, a bandage on his face, and sunglasses to cover his blurry eyes. He acted pissed off at the world. Again I pulled him aside to ask if he was going to be able to play, but he didn't answer me. Instead he went on a tirade about our accountant, lawyer, and management, venting his fury. Trying to calm him down, I changed the subject and asked if he wanted to go check out some of Miles Davis's set. He just complained about our even *having* an opening act.

From the side of the stage, I watched Miles and his array of powerhouse musicians. Miles Davis looked like an alien that night. He wore round, bulging, ball-like sunglasses and a space-age black and red leather jacket. He wasn't playing any of his earlier material, the modal jazz from *Kind of Blue* or *Sketches of Spain*. This was all about new, experimental music. *Bitches Brew*, his jazz-rock fusion record, had come out a few months earlier, and he was putting it out here in full force. The music was quite abrasive and cluttered at times, with Miles often playing with his back to the audience or even leaving the stage. Miles was more than modern, more than hip; he was futuristic.

Still, the majority of the audience were fans of the Band, and I could feel a pronounced lack of appreciation for him. As Miles's set went on, the crowd began hissing like snakes in a pit. It occurred to me that when our group went out there, we'd have to chill everybody out and get them back on our side.

Backstage I thanked Miles for playing the show with us. He seemed quite unfazed by the audience's reaction, except for a quiet, raspy "Kind of tough crowd out there . . . but they're okay."

Garth, Rick, and Richard knew what we were up against with the crowd, but Levon had been back in a dressing room with some friends. The lights went out, and we took the stage. The audience seemed relieved and excited, cheering and whistling in the dark. When the lights came up, Levon began stomping his foot on the drum riser to kick us into "Stage Fright." But his tempo was too slow, so I nodded a little faster with my head, and he began stomping to that tempo. The audience clapped along to the beat, with Levon's foot vibrating through the mics on the drum riser. The energy was building until suddenly Levon shook his head, stopped, and said into the vocal mic, "Hey—I'll keep the goddamn beat." The place froze.

I turned my back to the crowd. "Easy does it, Lee. Let's just play some music."

As I looked at him with his Confederate flag shirt and bandaged face, I knew this was going to be a rough night. During every song we played, Levon would start slowing down at a certain point. I wanted to have his back the best I could, so I would either swing my guitar neck to the right tempo, tap my foot so he could see it, or nod my head in time. After each song Levon looked away, embarrassed. We got through the show, but just barely. The audience watched us like they were at the zoo—pointing and waving. They could tell something was off-kilter.

After our encore, I put my arm over Levon's shoulder and whispered in his ear, "Well, old buddy, I ain't gonna do that ever again. I'm done."

He answered in a direct and apologetic tone. "You won't have to, 'cause I promise you, I ain't gonna do that no more—ever. You can count on it."

Rick was particularly upset by how embarrassing the show had been, and he confronted Levon backstage. "If someone is unable to hold up their end on a gig, say so. I don't wanna go out there and make a fool of myself because someone else can't do their part. If any of us can't play a show, let's cancel. Are we in agreement on this?"

Levon really didn't want to be chewed out by Rick, whom he still thought of as the little brother in the group. For him, that was humiliating enough. Levon had a lot of pride, and he vowed never to let anything even close to this happen again.

WE WERE on the road pretty regularly in those days. We played in New Orleans at a great big funky club called the Warehouse, a bit of an unusual venue for us, but I liked the ambience—less formal and more bare-bones. A cool-looking crowd roamed the joint. They had their own dance styles, their own costumes—they even sounded different in their reaction to our music, which made us play looser and rougher. After the show we met up with some local musicians and an interesting group of artists and hustlers. They insisted we go with them to an after party in an industrial part of town, where there was an incredible place like we'd never seen before.

We entered a concrete and brick building where the setting was somewhere between modern industrial and voodoo ceremonial, with masks and top hats hanging on the wall. In the middle of the living area, there was an open pit in the floor with a fire burning below. This wasn't just a party; this was an experience. Local New Orleans funk, like Jessie Hill's "Ooh Poo Pah Doo" and Lee Dorsey's "Ya Ya," played over the sound system. Quite a few people were pouring in from the hall we had just played. They grabbed glass cups and scooped up a drink concoction from large bowls that had been set out on a table. I asked one of the show promoters if it was sangria.

"Hell, no," he laughed. "That's devil juice. Try it. It'll make you get down on all fours."

Richard sampled it and said it was like a combination of white lightning and peach. "I wouldn't light a match near this."

Soon the guy who owned the establishment came over and welcomed us to his "inner sanctum." He wore a purple shirt open to his waist, loose pants, and no shoes. He looked rumpled, like he'd just had sex, and stared at us with eyes darker than black. You couldn't help but imagine what this guy did for kicks.

It seemed like we were going to find out right quick. People started gathering on the floor around the fire pit, and our host gestured for us to join. He threw a screened wire basket down into the fire and picked up two hoselike attachments. He handed one of the hoses to people sitting on the left side of the pit and the other hose to people on the right. The basket crackled and sparked in the fire. He peered down into the pit, then said, "Okay, it's ready."

Everybody started taking big puffs on the hoses and passing them around. The smoke smelled like marijuana, but mixed with some other scent I didn't recognize. We all took a puff on this hoodoo mixture, and pretty soon everyone was laughing and moaning. Our host started howling and dancing around to the jungle beat of the Meters. Others joined him and two or three of the girls took their tops off. Somehow it all seemed quite normal in this scenario. I asked someone, "What was that stuff we were smoking?"

"It's some kind of pot from Africa," he told me. "Imported through Haiti. There's a hothouse out in the bayou where this cat gets it."

In all of North America, only in New Orleans would you find this kind of black-magic partying going down. People danced and moved like they were under a spell, and we looked on in wonder. The host threw another basket of ganja down into the fire, and I thought *that* was my cue to get up and leave while I still could. The guys smiled at me and at one another. They knew that if we stayed any longer it would be trouble. So we stole away into the night.

At the Warwick Hotel in New York, I received a message that Elton John and his songwriting partner, Bernie Taupin, wanted to come by for a visit. Elton's album had come out the year before, and we admired his singing and playing. When they showed up, Levon and I were hanging out in my suite. They seemed a little nervous but terribly sweet. Bernie explained that their new album was very "inspired" by the Band, and they wanted to give us the first acetate. They didn't want us to think anybody was ripping anybody off. Elton said the album was called *Tumbleweed Connection*, and right away I knew they had nothing to be worried about. Levon was distracted, rolling a joint, and asked Bernie and Elton if they wanted to go in the bathroom and smoke it. At that, Elton and Bernie got up, bumping into each other awkwardly like they were interrupting Frank Sinatra shooting up in *The Man with the Golden Arm*. They shook our hands and scurried out the door.

BETWEEN SHOWS and travel dates, it felt so good to get back home and see Dominique, Alexandra, and Delphine. Being with them made me feel sane and warmed my heart. I started taking serious Polaroid portraits of the girls. I just couldn't help myself; they wore hats and painted their faces and reminded me of classic vaudeville characters. I had to capture it.

Dominique thought our house and the setup in Woodstock were beautiful, but she also believed that small-town living had extreme limitations. I had an escape, going to play gigs, so I didn't feel it as severely, but for Dominique our trips to Montreal or into the city were too infrequent, and she was getting a bit stir-crazy out in the woods. It was also important to her to have her language spoken around the kids, and not to leave her Canadienne culture behind. We decided on our next trip to Montreal that we would see if we could find a second home there. Thanks to the Band's live dates and record sales, an idea like this was financially feasible.

Albert was on the opposite track. He kept buying more properties in Bearsville. He was originally from Chicago, so with the combination of the Bears football team, living in Bearsville, New York, and to some extent his own appearance, *everything* began revolving around "the sign of the bear." He bought a house down on the main road and turned it into a three-star-type French restaurant called the Bear, with offices upstairs. He brought in a French chef, so the food was marvelous, as were the design and ambience, with beautiful, comfortable chairs and a full bar in the back. Classical music piped softly through speakers, nothing later than Brahms, as attractive female servers in black tights explained the menu. The place was incredible but totally out of context to the area.

Albert's empire grew from there to include a Chinese restaurant over by the creek. Then, next door to that, a great burger place that also served breakfast. The biggest news, though, was the building of Bearsville Recording Studios just up the hill from my house. This was a major project, undertaken with Albert's full confidence that he could single-handedly turn this small town into a worldly crossroads. The actual junction of Bearsville was made up of a little post office and convenience shop—that's it. This man had balls, and he was digging the challenge. He even built a theater next to the restaurants, where acts from all over could come and perform.

I often dropped by Albert's house for one of his infamous BLT sandwiches, made with the best aromatic lightly toasted whole-grain bread, homemade mayonnaise, imported lean bacon, and organic tomatoes homegrown in special soil he had shipped in. Albert said he wanted to invent a delicious sandwich glue so nothing would ever slip out.

At the beginning of October 1970, I called Albert to ask his advice on an addition I wanted to build on my writing studio. When he answered, his voice sounded distant and quiet, and then he said, "Janis is gone, Janis died, so upsetting, I thought the world of her. This is unbelievably sad. She was so fabulous, such a wonderful soul." I had never heard this tone in Albert's voice before, over anything. Janis would sometimes come to Woodstock and stay with Albert and Sally. She did seem incredibly down-to-earth and a wonderful soul, like he said. We had done the Festival Express train tour together, where I think she and Rick had an especially good time. Janis's death knocked the wind out of me. I had seen her just weeks before in Albert's kitchen, helping with the cooking and looking full of love and life. How could this be?

It had only been about three weeks since we got word that my old guitar buddy Jimi Hendrix had died in London. What a horrible loss. I couldn't get over it. And a year earlier, our friend Brian Jones had died as well. The eerie thing about it was that Janis, Jimi, and Brian were all twenty-seven years old when they died, and now I was twenty-seven too. And then, the following year, Jim Morrison would also die at the age of twenty-seven. All four of their deaths were drug related. It shined a harsh light on our own condition with the Band. Life can be fleeting, especially when you're playing with fire.

AT THE END of 1970, the Band had a few upcoming dates, and the boys were in reasonably good shape. Heading to a show in Madison, Wisconsin, we ran into some tricky timing and bad weather and ended up riding a chartered prop plane to make the gig. It was just big enough to hold six of us and the pilot. We flew for what seemed like way too long with zero visibility and constant turbulence. The pilot looked extremely busy and focused, navigating through endless clouds and rough winds. We were all hardly breathing, with eyes closed much of the time. Levon blurted out at one point, "Maybe we should turn this son of a bitch around and get back on the ground. This is horrible!"

"It feels worse than it is," replied the pilot. "We should be fine."

So we white-knuckled it until we started our descent into the Madison airport. As we broke through the clouds, it was snowing heavily and we were getting tossed around, but at least now we could see lights on the ground. The pilot was talking loudly to the tower, pushing and pulling levers and buttons with hands tight on the yoke, fighting those winds. We sat breathless in the back with a prayer in our hearts. As we came in for a landing, I watched wide-eyed as the runway came up fast on this flying machine. When we touched down, a gust of wind spun the plane sideways, and we skidded on the ice and snow for what seemed like forever. With clenched teeth I cried out, "Not now!" Finally we slid to a halt with one wing scraping the ground. I opened my eyes to see that we were sitting crosswise on the runway.

The pilot apologized for the near-death experience. "Hey, all's well that ends well," he said. We scrambled out of that plane angry, upset, and scared, mumbling about never ever doing this shit again. I started developing some serious reservations about this whole "being on the road" thing.

I played with a vengeance at that show in Madison, thinking, *You gotta play every show like it may be your last.*

DOMINIQUE AND I brought the girls to Montreal for the Christmas holidays. We looked at homes in Westmount, up on the mountain, and in various neighborhoods. Finally we found a place in Notre-Dame-de-Grâce that had been a convent. It was a beautiful old stone four-story building with a fully finished basement. From the top floor you could see across the Saint Lawrence River into Vermont. I asked my mother if she would like to live there and take care of it.

While we were in Montreal, Dominique and I spent more time with her friend Louise Latraverse and Louise's husband, Emmett Grogan, a writer and founder of the activist group the Diggers. I'd first met Emmett when he was up in Woodstock visiting Albert after doing press for his book, *Ringolevio*, which I had really enjoyed reading. The protagonist, Kenny Wisdom (Emmett's alter ego), was my kind of guy: he balanced between being a cat burglar and working with the outrageous Italian movie director Pier Paolo Pasolini, known far and wide for his powerful religious indignations.

In Montreal, Emmett told me about a new novel he was writing called *Final Score*, about a heist with a serial-killer twist. I told Emmett I was trying to write new material for the Band but that times had changed. We no longer had our old clubhouse/private-street-gang mentality. We were all married with kids or in serious relationships. A distance had grown among us, and our drug use and the boys messing around with heroin was taking a toll. Emmett knew all about that, having had his own issues with "H." I confessed to Emmett that I was struggling trying to write music for a wounded beast. A certain gloom hung over me, and I couldn't help feeling unenthusiastic about rising to the occasion fully when I didn't know what the occasion might be.

My songwriting in Montreal felt labored and flat. I missed my studio in Woodstock, where I had a proper setup and relative isolation. Also, being disconnected from the other guys bothered me. "Out of sight, out of mind" was not what we needed.

For reasons I wasn't consciously aware of, the songs I began writing at this time had a strong theme about things becoming extinct: railroads ("how can you get to sleep when the whistle don't blow"), blacksmiths, traveling carnivals, the old ways of the North American Indians. There was a despair to it, and a reflection of the world shifting inside the Band.

RICK AND LEVON came over to my studio in Woodstock one day, and I played them a song I was just finishing called "Life Is a Carnival," which grew out of my time working at a ragtime carnival and midway sideshow in Toronto. I wanted to get a different rhythmic feel in the choruses, and Rick jumped right in and started to play along. Levon got behind the drums and worked on an unusual pattern to go along with my guitar and vocal. There was no getting around the fact that when we made music, sparks flew. We were back in the circle, and it felt so good that I ended up sharing the songwriting credit on the tune with Rick and Levon.

Albert was in the final stages of getting Bearsville Recording Studios up and going. He was anxious for us to come in and check it out, which was tantalizing. He hired a talented recording engineer, Mark Harman, and we went in and started messing around. The place wasn't entirely set up yet, but we weren't new at makeshift studios. If technical problems and sound issues bogged us down, we pushed on through the distractions. There was a feeling in the air that had us unbound.

One afternoon, Van Morrison stopped by my home studio while I was working a chord progression on the piano. I offered him a puff on a joint, but he said, "No, if I have any of that, I might start barking." Then he said, "Play those chords again. I've got an idea for some words."

As I played, he started improvising lyrics about how merciless our managers and agents were about touring schedules, then started singing words directly to Richard (who wasn't there), as if Richard would understand his plight. I sang back, answering, "Oh Belfast cowboy, tell me, is it poker, oh Belfast cowboy, is it poker, and who's got the joker." Van scratched down a few more words about Johnnie Walker Red and asked if the guys were around. He thought maybe we could go up to the Bearsville studio and record that night.

We gathered at Bearsville around 8:00 p.m. that evening. Van had a bottle of whiskey, maybe Johnnie Walker Red, and Richard brought a six-pack of beer, knowing the whiskey would put him out of commission. I made up a rough structure for the song and taught it to the guys. As we went along, Van refined the words. As he sipped on the whiskey jug and Richard gulped away on beers, I knew the clock was ticking before the lights went out. We ran it down once, and I yelled to Mark Harman, "Let's cut it."

We recorded it one way, and then Richard and Van swapped verses, just to see what might happen. It was fantastic and hilarious, Van moving up and down, arms wailing in the air, Richard pounding on the piano, singing right back at him, like two angry barflies quizzing each other on the madness of the world. When Van got to the lyric about smashing a bottle of Johnnie Walker Red on a rock, I knew we were done. I ended up calling the song "4% Pantomime": "4%" because that's the difference in alcohol level between Johnnie Walker Red and Johnnie Walker Black, and "pantomime" because of Van's body language when we recorded the song—like he was acting out the story play by play.

I offered to drive Van home, but Richard claimed that was *his* responsibility. Van now lived in Richard's old house, and Richard insisted he knew how to get there with his eyes closed. I just hoped he wouldn't put that challenge into effect. I teased Van that those notches on Richard's belt weren't from girls he had loved but from cars he'd sent to the wrecking yard.

Van fell back laughing. "Are you kidding? Richard drives like an old geezer. I fear not!" Still, it was snowing and icy outside, so I gave Richard a look. He gave me a look back to assure me he was completely fine.

Later Richard told us that he'd driven Van back to his house safely and without incident. They said good night, and Van got out of the car. Richard waited a moment, put the car in reverse, and started to back out of the driveway. Suddenly he heard Van yelling and swearing at him, so he jammed on the brakes. Just in time—Van had slipped in the heavy snow behind the car, and Richard was starting to back over him.

Van stumbled to his feet and stomped up to his front door. "Jesus!" he yelled at Richard. "You nearly killed me!"

Richard swore he didn't know Van had fallen and that he had no reason to want to run him over. "Dying is easy," he hollered back. "Comedy is hard!"

AFTER WE RECORDED "Life Is a Carnival," I was jonesing for a horn arrangement on it, but not the Salvation Army/funeral-style horns we'd done in the past. Lately I'd been listening to a Lee Dorsey album called *Yes We Can*, written and arranged by Allen Toussaint. The incredible New Orleans horn charts Toussaint did seemed like they could be a good fit for our track in that "Carn-i-vale"/Big Easy mode.

Spur-of-the-moment, I called Allen Toussaint, asking if he'd be interested in doing horns for the song. I wasn't even sure if he'd ever listened to the Band's records. Over the phone, though, he had an air of southern sophistication and seemed very aware of our music. I sent him the track, and he agreed to meet me in New York City in five days and asked me to pick the studio and musicians—he said he wanted seven horns.

I ventured into the city with Jon Taplin, a multitrack tape, and a bit of nervousness inside wondering if this idea was going to fly. Allen showed up at the studio looking early-1970s cool, and younger than I would have imagined for someone so experienced. When I found out that he'd had his first hit song, "Mother-in-Law" by Ernie K-Doe, when he was eighteen years old, it all made sense. He was still making notes on his horn charts as we settled in to work, and showed me a section he still might want to change. I had to admit that I didn't read or write music.

He looked at me and smiled. "That's okay. We'll decide when you hear it. By the way, for the intro could you count it in for me? The guitarist is playing a strange figure there, and I'm not sure where 'one' is."

I said, "I'm the guitar player."

He laughed. "Well, you play some far-out timing."

The musicians arrived and tuned up their horns, and Allen put the horn charts in front of them. These were seasoned, hard-nosed instrumentalists who had been around and seen it all. One of them looked at his chart, looked at the next guy's chart, and frowned. He played a phrase from the page and said, "This part here at the beginning isn't going to work. Maybe it's a mistake."

Allen didn't even look down at the music. He just said, "Play what's written. Thank you." The horn player just shrugged his New York shoulders.

"Bar twenty-four," Toussaint called out. "Two, three, four . . ."

They played it, and afterward Allen instructed them to slide to certain notes. They made marks on their music charts and the playback came over the headphones. As they started getting familiar with the arrangement, you could see the musicians looking at one another with slight grins, almost as if they had discovered something sneaky. Horn players were used to playing parts in harmony, together, or against a countermelody, not one or two at a time, voicing in full-on rhythmic patterns. Like call-and-response, rarely all playing together at the same time. This was N'awlins gumbo horn styling, quite rare up here in Gotham. "I apologize, man," said the skeptical horn player to Allen. "This is very cool. Some of it shouldn't work, but it does."

I couldn't wait to get back to the studio in Bearsville so the guys could hear the horn arrangement Toussaint had done. When I played it, the expression on everybody's face was one part trying to adjust to space travel and another part hearing ourselves in a whole new light, like having a new funk master in the group.

A few days later, Bob Dylan came by my studio and we listened to some records. I put on the turntable an acetate I'd just received from Elton John and Bernie Taupin of a song called "Levon." Bob smiled to himself as he listened to it. I told him that I had played it for Levon yesterday, and it bugged the hell out of him. The Christian stuff in the lyrics prompted him to say that "Englishmen shouldn't fuck with Americanisms." Levon could have taken the song as a compliment, but that wasn't happening. Bob found the whole episode pretty amusing.

I told Bob I had written some songs for the new Band album, but that we needed one more. I didn't go into too much detail but I implied that it was a bit rough going with the boys these days. He got it. He knew the chemistry of success and destruction in the rock 'n' roll world. He thought for a moment and said, "There's a tune, might be good for you guys." He picked up my guitar and sang what he had so far on "When I Paint My Masterpiece."

What a song! What an idea! I thought. I asked him if he wanted a Coke from the small fridge I had in my studio, and he came up with a bridge, "Sailing around the world in a dirty gondola, oh, to be back in the land of Coca-Cola." I wrote down the words and the guys and I recorded the song the next day. With everything we brought to the table—Garth's soul-stirring Italian accordion, Levon's vocal, Richard's drumming, Rick's and my pure, rhythmic churning—I thought we aced it. I couldn't wait to play it for Bob. When I did, he just said, "That's great. What a vocal from Levon. Is that Garth on accordion? Beautiful, like an Italian concertina. Makes me want to have spaghetti."

To finish off our experiment at the unfinished Bearsville studio, I wrote a song called "The River Hymn" on the piano. I had imagined Garth playing an official-sounding church piano intro, along with his majestic keyboards. The song had a southern flavor to it—I had discussed with Levon the setting I was trying to evoke in the words. He related to it as being similar to an "all-day singing and dinner on the ground" gathering. Like most songs I wrote, it was a combination of the real and the mythical. That gave room for imagination and personalizing, along with vivid life experiences. Levon sang the hell out of it, and I asked him if Libby, his girlfriend, could do some background vocals. Libby had a lovely singing voice and took direction very well. Garth helped her with some choir voicings, and she did a wonderful job. Putting the finishing touches on that song gave me a sense of completion for the record.

IN MAY, we were scheduled to do a European tour starting in Germany. Albert asked, "Are the guys up for it?" hoping everybody was in good enough shape.

"That might be just the medicine we need," I told him. We shipped off for Europe: nowhere to go, nowhere to hide, just show up and play our music as good as we possibly could. These foreign cities were majestic and inspiring. The crowds were different too, overwhelmingly enthusiastic. The old world felt new and fresh. We started out in Hamburg, where they made us feel we were long overdue for an appearance. Same thing in Munich and Frankfurt—such appreciation for our North Americana sound—and Vienna and Paris, with all of their incredible musical history; now we felt a little part of that tradition.

Albert was very proud of how we were playing and joined us for much of the tour. The European concert promoter he worked with was headquartered in Copenhagen. When we arrived in Denmark, the promoter decided to throw us a party on our day off with lots of traditional Danish food, pretty women, and an interesting group of his friends. He asked Albert if he had ever been to a *show* in Denmark.

"It depends on what you mean by 'a show,'" said Albert.

The promoter asked me the same question. When I shook my head no, he called to his secretary across the room. "Come, come. You must take Robbie and the fellas to a show. They've never seen one."

So after dinner we all piled into vehicles and headed to the heart of Copenhagen. We entered a building with bleachers surrounding what looked like a dance floor. The place could hold about a hundred people; on this night it was about half full. Nobody would give us a clue as to what we were about to witness. Someone in our crew, having done their own detective work, asked the secretary if this was going to be some kind of transvestite parade.

"Shhhhh," she said. "Just watch."

The lights dimmed, and spotlights shone on the middle of the floor. A woman appeared with a man, who was carrying a chair. When they walked into the spotlight, the man set down the chair and they both disrobed, but not like a striptease—they just took all their clothes off abruptly, matter-of-fact. The man had a gigantic dong. I laughed and looked at Richard sitting next to me; he raised one eyebrow. The music in the background made no statement at all; it just blocked out some of the weird noises coming from the audience. With no messing around, the woman dropped to her knees and started performing oral sex on the man's huge dong. Then he got up from the chair and screwed her every which way known to man. The audience looked like they could have been watching a fashion show—appreciative, but no big deal.

Next, two women appeared, one carrying a bullwhip, the other with some chains wrapped around her naked body. They strutted around the floor area, sizing up members of the crowd. Round and round they went until the one with the whip stopped right in front of Albert, put the whip around his neck, and started to pull. Albert laughed. "No, no thank you." But the girl was determined to get him onto the floor. He pulled back on the whip with his hand and said, more strenuously this time, "No, really, I'm not into it." But the girl thought he was just playing shy or hard to get. Then the other girl came over and tried to help her. We were all cracking up, yelling, "Go, Albert! Show 'em what you got!" Both girls were tugging on Albert and begging him to join them in the middle of the floor. Finally he said with great force, "Stop! This is not my thing! It's not for me!" as he unraveled the whip from around his neck.

The girls didn't even blink. They moved on and pulled a more willing gentleman onto the floor. They ripped his shirt open and pulled down his pants to reveal his bare ass. They fondled him every way possible, whipped him, and rode on his back, yelping like cowboys.

I whispered to Albert, "Now I bet you're sorry. See, you could have been enjoying all that fun."

He laughed helplessly, like, *Can you even imagine?* The show went on with several other acts for another *hour*. It was exhausting and intimidating but not really sensual, like watching circus sex on a trapeze. It was a relief when it was over. The audience filed out, looking as if they had just finished a heavy meal.

"Did you enjoy the show?" the promoter's secretary asked me.

What do you say? *Oh yes, quite invigorating, thank you.*

She escorted us back to our hotel. When we arrived, she whispered in my ear, "Would you like me to come up and tuck you in?" I thanked her for the thoughtfulness, and told her I was married. But at the same time, I was thinking, *How in the world could anyone follow an act like that?* The show would make King Kong feel inadequate.

RETURNING TO PLAY Royal Albert Hall in London was a major experience. We played two nights there, our first time since we'd played with Bob in 1966. The audience was now rippling with enthusiasm and tremendously familiar with our music. What a wonderful relief to not be booed or have to duck flying objects! Standing ovations after certain songs made us sing and play our hearts out. Jack Nicholson, whom we'd met a few times before, came to both shows. At an after party on the second night, he commented on the difference between the vocal harmonies in the two shows. "On night two," he said, "they sounded tighter and stronger, and soared over the heads of the audience." He was absolutely correct. I was impressed.

The tour concluded with two shows in Holland, the first in Amsterdam. At a lot of our concerts you could smell marijuana in the air, but here the pot smoke outweighed tobacco ten to one. We were either playing good, or the crowd was simply lifting us higher. We loosened up and wailed the night away. For our final show we drove through the city of Haarlem to Rotterdam. The concert promoter told us that the audiences here *loved* their music. He promised that the crowd's enthusiasm would make this one of the most exciting concerts of the whole tour. He was right. They stomped and rejoiced, and because it was our last show of the tour, we pulled out all the stops. During the encore, on "Loving You Is Sweeter Than Ever," I broke two strings, and *that* was during Garth's solos.

I had missed Dominique and the girls on this European tour, but it was necessary for the Band to feel our oats, to show ourselves that we could rise to the occasion and knock it out of the park. Richard had a challenge not letting his drinking interfere with his singing and playing. As far back as the Woodstock festival, whenever Richard was having trouble with his vocals, I would help out by doubling his part—on the other guys' songs I would either sing a low part or the melody as I'd written it. Fortunately, at these shows Richard avoided any big bumps in the road. I felt renewed and positive about this phase and hoped we could hold it steady and carry it forward.

SUMMERTIME IN WOODSTOCK, and Dominique and the girls were putting our big swimming pool to good use. Delphine had grown some and was getting around pretty well. Alexandra kept a cautious eye on her, though, careful not to let any harm come her way, which completely melted my heart.

Our friend the writer Mason Hoffenberg came by one afternoon for a visit. Mason and Libby were old friends and they were hilarious together—both brilliant comic minds. Mason was telling us that he'd driven Libby to the bus depot in the middle of Woodstock for her to make a trip into the city. As Libby waved to him from her bus seat window, he yelled out to her, "Good luck with your sodomy trial!"

Libby stopped waving and looked around. *Who could this crazy man be talking to?*

Our new album, which we had decided to call *Cahoots*, was released on September 15, 1971. There were a few gems on it, but we knew it wasn't all our best work. Some of it was a test to try out the new studio, and some of it was real album material. Deep down I wished we could have made the record after our tour, so we could have all been in our clubhouse mode.

Toward the end of the year, while the Band was on a roll of playing some pretty damn good concerts, I made a suggestion. "Why don't we do a live album while our chops are in good shape? I'll see if we can get Allen Toussaint to write horn charts for the appropriate songs." The guys liked the idea. We happened to have a request to play the last four days of the year at the Academy of Music in New York City, so I called Toussaint in New Orleans and asked him what he thought of the idea. "Yes, I believe that could work out just fine," he responded in his southern-gentlemanly fashion. I cautioned him that he would have to come up and work with us in Woodstock over Christmas. "That will be fine," he said again. "I don't believe in Santa Claus anymore."

We made a plan that I would send him songs I felt might work with a horn arrangement, and that in December he would come to Woodstock and work with us, refining the parts and rehearsing before the shows leading up to New Year's. John Simon and I got in touch with our friend Howard Johnson, who was the master of the low-register horns, about putting a solid section together. Allen thought a five-piece would do the trick.

He would call once a week to go over details. We talked about all different horn arrangers, from W. C. Handy to Willie Mitchell, and their styles and flavors. Allen had a wide-open imagination and was into exploring all sorts of interesting possibilities. After every conversation I felt better about this concept.

When it came time for Allen to join us up in Woodstock, we were in the middle of a major snowstorm. He arrived looking flustered and upset, and explained that when he got off the plane in New York, someone had stolen his briefcase while he was gathering his luggage. In that briefcase were all the horn charts he had written over the last few weeks.

I was stunned. We had ten days before the show. *What the heck are we going to do?* I wondered.

"Maybe someone had a mix-up of briefcases and will return the charts," Allen said, trying to stay hopeful.

I scoffed. "In New York? Fat chance."

"Yeah, I forgot where I was." He thought for a moment. "Well, we really don't have a choice. I'll just start over."

I had made arrangements for him to stay in one of the cabins between Albert's house and mine, and we had a little phonograph player and an electric piano put in his cabin so he could work there. When I drove him over, he admitted he had never seen snow like this before: a full-on winter wonderland. As I helped him inside with his bags, I thought he must be feeling there were probably no black people in this area for a hundred miles.

The first couple of nights, we brought Allen to the Bear for dinner. But after a couple of days he announced that he was having a slow start on the music. From now on, he wanted to stay in the cabin working, so we arranged to have food and whatever else he needed brought in daily. When I would stop by to see how the charts were coming along, he looked a bit discouraged. He claimed that he was having some kind of writer's block and hoped that he would have a breakthrough soon. It even crossed my mind that maybe he never wrote the charts in New Orleans and didn't want to admit it. Could it be that our music didn't fit his writing style—that our luck with "Life Is a Carnival" was a one-off? I asked him point-blank whether he thought this whole thing would work; the days were going by, and we were running out of time.

"No," he said, "the music is great. I need to pull it together. Give me another day."

The following day when I went by, Allen answered the door looking terrible. Disheveled, worried, and sickly. He pointed at his ears. He said in a loud voice, "*I lost my hearing!*"

I said, "You can't—"

"What? Speak up! My ears are closed!"

Oh, no, I thought. *We're doomed.*

I called a local doctor we knew and brought him to Allen's cabin later that night.

"My goodness!" said the doctor. "You have a bad infection in both ears. They're red, swollen, and feverish—very unusual." He gave Allen strong antibiotics and some other medicines to take immediately. I looked out the cabin window at the four feet of snow and the woodsy wilderness and thought, *We've put poor Allen Toussaint in this foreign setting, and under all this pressure, and it's made him go deaf.*

In the morning, I went back to Allen's cabin and wrote on a piece of paper, "I understand if you want to go home. Don't worry. We'll figure out the concert." But when he responded to it, he was speaking almost normally, and told me he felt much better. The medicine was working and he had already written two more horn charts. I thought, *Well I'll be damned. Beethoven's deafness worked for him. Why not Mr. Toussaint?* Garth looked over some of Allen's charts and smiled, like he could already smell that jambalaya cooking.

With each day, Allen's condition improved. Even better, he was tearing away at those horn charts. Electricity filled the air as he wrote day and night. Papers flying, running out of pencils and ink, all while the rest of us had a lovely little Christmas with the kids. Allen didn't want to be disturbed.

Driving into New York the day after Christmas to start rehearsals with the horn section, Allen was still writing and refining charts in the backseat, humming quietly to himself. John Simon and Howard Johnson had put together a fantastic horn section. We would have Howard himself on baritone sax, tuba, and euphonium, the legendary Snooky Young on trumpet and flugelhorn, Joe Farrell on tenor, soprano sax, and English horn, Earl McIntyre, trombone, and J. D. Parron, alto sax and clarinet. John Simon said these cats could handle anything that Toussaint was putting down. *Well, step right up,* I thought, *'cause Allen's got "Creole style" all his own.*

That night, we all met up to rehearse at Ultra Sonic Studios in Long Island. We needed everybody to get this music under their skin quickly. There was no guarantee these charts were going to work, or that the Band's sound would mesh with this horn section. When everyone was in place, Allen tapped on his music stand. "Let's try 'Caledonia Mission.'" We scrambled through it two times, making adjustments. Then, on the third run-through, we heard for the first time what it was really supposed to sound like. *Very promising,* I thought. Just a touch of Macon, Georgia, below the surface. Next we ran through "Life Is a Carnival," knowing that horn part was tried and true. "The Unfaithful Servant" wasn't ready to take out of the oven just yet, and Allen wanted to make some changes on it. By the time we got to "Don't Do It," the horn section was getting relaxed and accustomed to Toussaint's flavor—extra cayenne pepper.

Allen had worked on these charts up in Woodstock, but we started from scratch in the rehearsal hall on one old song I wanted to take a shot at, Chuck Willis's "Hang Up My Rock and Roll Shoes." Our friend Bobby Charles, who was from Louisiana, had come by and he loved the idea. He promenaded around with a big ol' alligator smile as we ran through it.

By the time we wrapped up at Ultra Sonic, there were signs we could win this battle, but we still had a ways to go and very little time. Half the songs were still out on the ledge. Allen calmly said, "I've got work to do, but we'll do better tomorrow."

"We've only *got* tomorrow," I reminded him. "We rehearse onstage at the theater, and the next night is our first show."

We loaded in and set up our equipment on December 27 at the Academy of Music on 14th Street. The Academy was a very large, beautiful old theater, warm and inviting. We'd been told it was one of the best-sounding venues around. At the same time, recording engineer extraordinaire Phil Ramone and Bearsville Studios' Mark Harman were setting up mics and a couple of sound baffles to start getting some levels on the mobile recording equipment.

John Simon kept an eye and ear out for the changes Allen was making with the horn section. Everything was getting better, but not better enough. There were sections in a few songs that weren't blending well. Everyone pitched in—the horn players made suggestions, Garth had ideas, and Allen felt convinced he knew what to do. Allen decided he was going to sit with the horn section so he could help them with signals and reminders, and he would also be able to hear any rough spots that still needed work.

On Tuesday, December 28, we played the first of our four shows. We finally came up with a song list for everybody just before the curtain went up. We all felt a stir of confidence around us. Everyone was in shape to play our asses off. The five of us got in a huddle and said, "Come on, let's make some noise."

As we took the stage, the audience erupted in a roar. It was as if they could sense something was going down tonight. I looked at each of the guys, and they all seemed salty and ready to dig in. We pounded out "Up on Cripple Creek" and "The Shape I'm In" and steamed through the first half of the show with our engines revving. Before the second half of the show I announced, "We are going to do something we've never done before," and introduced Allen Toussaint and the horn section to wild cheers from the audience, like they were privy to an exclusive revival. We hit "Life Is a Carnival" with lightning force. We got through the set with high spirits, rough spots and all. Allen was still making some changes with the horns and said, "It's only gonna get better." Phil Ramone agreed and said he only had a few screw-ups, but now they were ready and able.

Before the rehearsals, I had asked Bob if he'd like to come and do a few songs with us on New Year's Eve. He still wasn't playing live during this period, so I knew he'd want a little time to think it over. Now I called him from the city to see if he was up for it. He said he liked the idea and would come to the theater in the afternoon before the show on New Year's Eve, and we could figure out what songs to do. We had been so distracted with getting the horns in shape and the recording that rehearsing with Bob had never really come into play. We had made so much music together over the years I thought we could probably wing it.

Each night there were high points for the Band's performance, or the horn section, or the sound of the recording, and it was wonderful to have four nights to get our message across. It was great too having friends witness the process. Bobby Charles was spreading good cheer, and Dr. John showed up at one point. But first he came by the Gramercy Park Hotel, where we were staying, and sprinkled some gris-gris powder in the corners of my suite—just for good measure.

For the next show they wheeled our dear old friend Doc Pomus, who was now in a wheelchair, down to the front row. We hadn't seen him in several years, but in that time his songwriting reputation had expanded to truly legendary status. Doc looked very much the same, with his "light up the room" smile and only a few more gray hairs. If you wanna play better, all you gotta do is put Doc Pomus in the front row. We played much of that show directly to Doc.

On the third night, filmmakers Howard Alk and Murray Lerner shot a few songs of the show, really just for preservation and the archives. The next afternoon, when we were running over a few tunes with Bob, some union reps showed up at the hall and said if we did any more filming without going through them, they would destroy the cameras. "Somebody could have an accident." We got the message loud and clear and promised no more filming. Their interruption put a crimp in our rehearsal, but we played through a couple of songs of Bob's we had recorded in the basement days, like "Crash on the Levee" (also called "Down in the Flood"). We ran through the songs just enough to refresh our memory but hardly to the point of having a down-pat arrangement. Ragged but fun, just the way we rolled with Bob.

Well, this was it: New Year's Eve, the last night of this joyful experience. We went on a little later in the evening, so we could hit that magic chord at the stroke of midnight. Our families and friends were there, and we were all pumped to bring in the New Year with a bang. We played hard and tight, with a sense of abandon, like the last round of a championship heavyweight fight. What a feeling of elation and pride to see all the guys at the top of their game. When Garth played the intro to "Chest Fever," which he called "The Genetic Method," I was reminded there was no other keyboard player in rock 'n' roll who had his improvisational abilities and imagination. At ten seconds to midnight, I started the countdown. Garth flew into "Auld Lang Syne" as the clock struck twelve, and the audience went wild.

We ended our set with "(I Don't Wanna) Hang Up My Rock and Roll Shoes," and no one in the house wanted to hang them up either. We went out for the encore with a sixth member in the group. The lights were low, so the crowd didn't know yet what we had in store. Bob was using a Gibson electric guitar that was way out of tune, so I gave him my Tele and took the Gibson, tuning it up quickly. Then the lights came on, and Bob stepped to the mic. The audience thought they were visiting rock 'n' roll heaven. We did "Down in the Flood," "When I Paint My Masterpiece," and "Don't Ya Tell Henry," and it felt loose and magical.

I turned my back to the audience and asked Bob, "You wanna do one more?"

"Okay," he said. "What do you wanna do?"

Rick jumped in. "Let's do 'Like a Rolling Stone.'"

Bob said into the mic, "We haven't played *this* one in six years."

I said, "Six*teen* years!"

Bob repeated, "Six*teen* years!" and kicked into the intro. Playing that song was like riding a bicycle for us. It came back in a flash.

WHAT A NIGHT. What a show. What a New Year's Eve! It was fantastic to have Bob there with us to celebrate. Allen Toussaint said this had been one of the highlights of his life. The horn players were thrilled, and Phil Ramone felt he'd captured it beautifully. Everybody was on a high, probably nobody more so than me. It was a perfect way to start the New Year.

I told Bob Cato that we wanted to call the album *Rock of Ages*. There was an old-timey hymn of that name. Cato told me that his son, Eric, had just photographed the face of a tiny statue that looked ancient and gold. He showed it to me, and I said, "Let's use it for the cover." When the album came out that summer, one of the best music journalists in the world, Ralph J. Gleason, reviewed it for *Rolling Stone*. He compared the album to some of the best live records ever: *Mingus at Monterey*, *Ray Charles in Person*, *Duke Ellington's Seattle Concert*, *Miles at the Blackhawk*, and more. Certainly we wanted people to enjoy our efforts on this live album, but Mr. Gleason's affirmation had already made it all worthwhile to me.

TWENTY-FOUR

Nineteen seventy-two was an extraordinary year for cinema. When you got Coppola's *The Godfather*, Buñuel's *The Discreet Charm of the Bourgeoisie*, Bergman's *Cries and Whispers*, Elaine May's *Heartbreak Kid*, Herzog's *Aguirre, the Wrath of God*, Fosse's *Cabaret*, Boorman's *Deliverance*, Perry Henzell's *The Harder They Come*, Fassbinder's *The Bitter Tears of Petra von Kant*, and John Huston's *Fat City* as the tip of the iceberg, you knew you were in a golden age. Dominique and I took in as much as we could at the "artsy" Woodstock Cinema, and sometimes we would drive to neighboring towns like Kingston or Saugerties for a fix, but going into New York City and bingeing on new releases was not unheard of.

Several people had gotten in touch to see if the Band would be interested in doing music for their films. I wanted to find a movie we could sink our teeth into, but it hadn't come our way. We had been asked about creating the music for Sydney Pollack's *Jeremiah Johnson* with Robert Redford. I read the script but didn't think it was our calling. Photographer Jerry Schatzberg had just directed a movie called *Scarecrow* with Al Pacino and Gene Hackman, but again, not the right fit. The other guys didn't care that much about movies to begin with, so I knew we would have to find just the right thing.

Then I received a script from the Japanese director Hiroshi Teshigahara. He had directed a black-and-white film called *Woman in the Dunes* that haunted me. The script was titled *Summer Soldiers*, and it took place during the Vietnam War. It centered on deserters from the war in the underground of Japanese society. Reading the script, somehow, something didn't gel. I couldn't tell if the story was getting lost in translation or what was missing. I sent a message back saying it wasn't right for us.

If I can't even find the right material with Hiroshi Teshigahara, I thought, *I give up.*

DURING OUR LAST ROUND of live dates leading up to the Academy of Music, Jon Taplin had struggled to gather us together. He was doing a really good job as road manager but no doubt feeling frustrated. One day, when he was pushing hard to get everybody ready so we wouldn't miss our flight, Levon threw him up against the wall and pressed his arm into his neck, yelling and threatening him. Levon was edgy from something he had taken, and reasoning with him wasn't working.

After the tour ended, Jon came to me and said that he was thinking of moving on and getting into producing movies. He spoke of how tough it had become to do his job, wrangling this bunch of cats. I'd had a special relationship with Jon from the beginning, and I have to say it hurt to see him go.

For me, the only upside to Jon's leaving was his new ambition to produce movies. We were both film buffs, and I found his new direction extremely exciting. A few weeks later, Jon called me, thrilled about a project he had mentioned before he left. "You remember the movie I told you might come together with this very talented Italian American director? Well, it looks like it's going to happen, and I'll produce. It's tentatively called *Season of the Witch,* and it stars this young actor Robert De Niro, who is amazing. I think the director is the real thing too. His name is Martin Scorsese, and he was the assistant director on the Woodstock movie."

IN THE NEW YEAR, we took a breather while finishing up the *Rock of Ages* album. I spent more time in Montreal, and Levon went up to Boston to take some drum classes at the Berklee College of Music. Spending time with family was important too: by then Rick, Richard, Levon, and I all had young kids, and we wanted to be there for these precious years. During this downtime, our accountant, Marshall Gelfand, came up to my studio in Woodstock for a business meeting with us all. I had always had a good feeling about Marshall. I could tell he was honest and trustworthy. He would make the trek up to Woodstock every so often when there were tax issues to discuss or investments for business that were necessary. Over a period of years, as these meetings went on, things became more informal. Levon would take out a bag of grass and use Marshall's tax papers to remove some of the sticks and seeds. He would then proceed to roll a beautiful joint, light it, and hand it to Marshall, who would laugh and politely refuse. On one occasion Marshall claimed he would take a puff when Levon had a million bucks in his account.

That spring, during one of these meetings, Levon insisted we all invest in shopping centers in Arkansas. The other guys and I didn't know if this was a wise move, so we left it up to our business manager. Marshall thought it was an obscure idea, but said he would look into it. He came back saying that he couldn't recommend it. After that Levon never felt the same about Marshall. I spent a lot of time trying to convince him that Marshall wasn't screwing us, and that neither were the concert promoters, nor our lawyer, David Braun, nor Bob Dylan over our publishing. Albert always made sure the concert promoters weren't taking too much under the table—"You gotta give them a little room to get the best out of them," he'd say. With Albert, whatever the deal was, he was right up front about it, more straightforward than most management companies at that time, yet Levon was suspicious of *him* as well.

I knew what Levon was getting at. Recording artists always got taken advantage of, and we'd seen it happen with some of our friends. We were lucky to have fallen in with a group of fair-minded associates in a business that was infamous for its cheating ways. I wasn't quite sure exactly why Levon was so caught up in thinking all businesspeople around him had their hands in his pockets. Sometimes it felt like his paranoia was drug induced; other times it seemed like a country-boy inferiority complex. I tried everything I could to help him not obsess about something that wasn't happening. It was painful to be around. He harped on it, over and over, until it drove all the guys crazy. Finally Rick and Richard told him that if he could show them one example of anybody stealing a nickel from us, "we'll start a revolt."

Around this same time, Dominique kept expressing that she felt the Woodstock scene was becoming a darker place, more drug infested. She heard stories from a hundred years ago about how native people from around here would avoid this area—bad juju. This was the Band's headquarters, for better or worse, and I couldn't just scrub it. Still, she did open my eyes to the idea that something else— somewhere else—might work. But where? Getting everybody to move to Montreal wasn't going to happen. Going back into New York City just felt obnoxious now that we had kids and families. I also sensed that those years I'd spent living in the city at the Chelsea Hotel were a golden age. I'd tasted the honey, and it don't get much sweeter than that.

It had also started to become more and more noticeable that cocaine was gaining popularity. At random moments people you'd least expect would offer you a little dab on a teensy, tiny little spoon—like one might offer a pinch of snuff in the old days. For all of us who smoked cigarettes, it made the experience more rewarding. Smoking and speed, I think, were born on the same day. A well-worn phrase was "This drug's nonaddictive. You know, like a good cup of espresso."

VARIOUS MAGAZINES were calling Albert's office, wanting to do articles on the Band. Curiosity was growing in our absence, and they said we needed some current photos, "just to show you're still kicking."

I said, "There's an interesting photographer I heard about recently. He captures shadows and auras and reflections. Maybe that would be suitable for a situation like this."

We got in touch with the photographer and he came to Woodstock to scout for locations. Rick suggested some places that had some mystery to them. We all gathered at one setting, but the photographer didn't feel the light was quite right there. He suggested going to another area where a stream led into a pond. "We may have to remove our shoes there to get the right image in the water," he said.

I thought this was getting interesting, the way he was visualizing different shots, with sunlight bouncing off the water and casting shadows. Garth took off his shoes and splashed through the shallow stream; he found a stafflike stick and waved it in the air like Moses. Rick was quick to follow, playing mountain man as he fought the current. Our photographer and his assistant meticulously studied the angle of the sun and placed cameras accordingly. They found the perfect spot where an image reflecting in the water was vivid and clear. He asked us to stand in a specific spot at the edge of the pond to get the right angle. The camera was facing down to catch our image off the water. "Yes. Yes, that's it," he said as he finished adjusting our positions.

He walked back to the camera as the assistant wiped the lens. He looked through the viewfinder, looked up at us, looked back through the lens, turned the focus, looked at his assistant, turned his eyes to the sky, and looked back through the camera, twisting and turning, zooming and focusing. We didn't know what the hell he was doing, but we stood there patiently. As all this unfolded, he seemed to be growing increasingly agitated. He put a different lens on the camera, made his assistant look through it, then pushed him aside so he could adjust it himself. He looked up at us almost angrily. He lifted the camera off the tripod and moved around with it, scurrying along the water's edge back and forth. Finally he said to his assistant, "Okay, that's enough! Let's get out of here."

"Did you get what you wanted?" I called out. "Did you get the shot?"

"I got nothing," he fumed. "There's nothing to get. I have to go."

"Wait," I said, "what's going on? What's the problem?"

He abruptly threw his equipment in his bag. "No reflection! There is absolutely no reflection. I don't know what to tell you. I don't know what it is with you people, but you have no reflection, and I can't deal with this. I'm sorry. I have to go."

And with that, he and his assistant turned and left. The boys and I looked at one another for a moment and then we all cracked up.

"I should have warned him beforehand about our lack of reflections," Garth joked, "but I got hung up watching the birds mating."

"I didn't like his aura," added Richard.

Levon waved it off. "You know how I feel about taking pictures. He's a weird son of a bitch, anyway."

"Look, Lee! I can see your reflection right there." Richard pointed down at the water. "I can see everybody's reflection. Look! That moron was set up on the wrong side of the pond. I guess we're not vampires after all." It was considered a perfect disaster among the members of the Band—*it almost felt like home.*

But in the weeks leading up to the release of *Rock of Ages*, whenever I called for a meeting with the boys, I could tell something was wrong. Richard rarely showed up, and the other guys seemed to be there in body but not in spirit. Sometimes I would go over to Levon and Libby's house to watch the Arkansas Razorbacks while Levon whipped up some popcorn. One afternoon, I talked about our making a new record and some different musical approaches, about working on some tracks together and seeing if anything might turn into a song.

"Throw it! Throw it! Oh, hell . . . he got sacked," Levon yelled at the TV.

I called Rick to see if he wanted to get together and talk about some ideas for new songs. He said that he was going to Florida with Fred Neil to work on the Dolphin Research Project, Fred's organization focused on protecting dolphins. I respected Rick's ambition to support him, and we made plans to get together, soon as Rick got back. But he didn't know when that would be just yet.

Garth came by my studio and I played him some of my tapes of nocturnal creature sounds. We talked about my idea for a piece called "The Works"—maybe we could do it in conjunction with the National Film Board of Canada? I waited for a response, but when I sat up and looked over at Garth, he had dozed off. He wasn't making a statement by falling asleep; Garth's narcolepsy caused him to doze at random times, day or night. Still, I would have liked a little volleying on these ideas. When Garth finally did open his eyes, he started talking about a new instrument modification he was working on. I didn't have any idea what he was describing, but had no doubt it would sound great.

When I stopped by Richard's house, the drapes were closed. Richard hadn't written much in a couple years, and I hoped to stir him up a bit. I think he was caught off guard. He looked drawn and glassy-eyed. He scrambled to throw on a shirt and clear stuff off his living room coffee table as I said hello to Jane, who was busy in the kitchen.

"What's been happening, Rich?" I asked once we'd sat down. "What have you been up to?"

"Aw, not too much," he said. "Mostly just feeding the cats. Yeah, I gotta change that kitty litter."

I asked if he'd be up for setting a writing schedule; see if we could come up with material for a new record. But he said that he hadn't been feeling too good lately. "Kinda achy all over. Sometimes I get the chills. No energy."

"You ought to go see Dr. Ed in Middletown," I told him. "Let him fix you up. You do look unhealthy, to be honest."

He nodded. "Yeah, I need to do that."

As I got up to leave, I called to Jane, "Make sure Rich goes to Dr. Ed. He needs some medicine, get him back on his feet."

Instead of going right back to my place, I drove up on the mountain. I thought, *Well, I've made the rounds. Knocked on everybody's door and came away with nothing.* I used to be able to rev everybody up—get the blood flowing in the right direction. Either I was losing my touch, or there was nobody home. *What the hell are we going to do next?* I wondered. I didn't like being affected by the negative energy around me. I didn't want to be a victim of these circumstances, but damn, it was hard to be in a band and not feel torn down at a time like this. It doesn't pull you in, it pushes you away.

When Rick got back from Florida, I called a meeting. It got postponed twice, and the third time Richard still didn't show. And when Levon and Rick arrived, they looked incredibly stoned.

"Guys—level with me," I said. "What's happening?"

Levon started to speak. "Well, we've run into . . ." He stopped and closed one eye, like he'd lost his train of thought.

Rick lit a cigarette. "Some guys we know laid a bunch of China White on us, and we didn't have the nerve to say, 'No, thank you.'" *Oh, man, here we go again,* I thought. *Fucking heroin.* Rick continued, "Personally, I'm just checking it out and letting it go before I get in too deep. Lee, how you feeling about it?"

Levon opened his eyes and lifted his head. "No, man, I ain't gonna fuck with that shit too much, but I can't say the same for brother Rich. I believe ol' Beak's done bit off more than he can chew already."

I looked over at Garth. He had a deep sadness in his eyes at this news about Richard. None of us knew a damn thing about rehab or finding help for addicts and alcoholics. I had brought up the name Alcoholics Anonymous with Richard a couple of times in the past, but he wouldn't hear it. Somebody we knew had mentioned a clinic in Switzerland, but Switzerland was far enough away that nobody took the suggestion seriously.

Levon and Rick came back a week later, looking more clear-eyed and concerned about what we were going to do with our future. But again, Rich wasn't able to show up. We called him daily. We pleaded with him. We yelled at him. There were offers coming in to play concerts and Albert kept asking for answers, but we didn't have many. We even discussed having to replace Richard in the group and went over to his house to give him an ultimatum. He looked haggard and broken inside. He swore he'd pull it together with everything he had, immediately. We said we'd be back in two days to hear his thoughts and how he planned to get better. This was it, we told him—the end of the line for excuses.

As we left Richard's house, I said, "Well, if nothing else, we could put out a book of excuses."

Rick smirked. "Yeah, I got the first two chapters written already."

God, we wanted to help Richard, but we were so ill equipped. All we had was a bunch of love and anger for the guy—and a pocketful of threats.

When we returned, he had a crazy positive look in his eye. "I've got it," he said enthusiastically. "Right here in these two old medical journals. It's written right here, from during the time of Freud and Huxley. My problem, which you have obviously figured out, is that I have a severe habit. Totally strung out on this China White, and I'm terrified of kicking. Withdrawal could send me into shock and even kill me." His hands were shaking as he took a sip of coffee. "According to Sigmund Freud and other doctors, the way to kick a major addiction to shooting heroin is to replace it with injecting high-quality cocaine. No withdrawal symptoms. And cocaine is not addictive, so I can stop as soon as I'm over the hump! Isn't that incredible? And they knew that back in the twenties!"

Garth, Rick, Levon, and I looked at one another like we had just been told the world was flat. Richard continued, "I've already scored the coke. I'm getting rid of the junk, and I should be up and at 'em in a week or two, ready to go to work." He seemed so hopeful and determined. I didn't know whether to congratulate and hug him or call the loony wagon. We left scratching our heads. His plan sounded crazy, but if it worked, we'd take it.

Our next visit to Richard's, though, was tremendously alarming. He looked wired to the hilt, trembling all over. My heart sank. He explained to Levon and Rick that he thought he was almost past the heroin withdrawal, but shooting coke was really strange. Suddenly he jumped up and smacked the wall with his open hand. "Did you see that?" he murmured. "Goddamn bugs everywhere." I asked Richard what the marks were all over the walls. He said that's where he'd had to burn the bugs that were crawling around. Shooting cocaine had given Rich the DTs, and seeing him in the midst of this madness brought tears to my eyes.

Over the next couple of weeks, we managed to get the needles and cocaine away from Richard, and he started slowly to gain some strength and confidence. But the craziest part was, while seeing this terrible, disturbing thing that cocaine did to Richard, the rest of us found it totally sane to continue snorting it. None of us were angels. We all had our own personal demons to chase, and the race was on.

Around this same time, one night Dominique and our nanny, Nicóle, said they were going down to the bar at the Bear for a glass of wine. I watched the kids and caught up on a little reading while they were gone. When they got back to the house, I could hear them giggling downstairs and I came down to see what was so amusing. They both looked happy—whispering and laughing so much I couldn't tell what was so funny. Finally Dominique said, "I've made a wonderful discovery. We were going for a glass of wine, and instead we decided to order a drink. A 'cocktail' you call it . . . right?" And they both broke out laughing again. "Well, we ordered a drink with vodka, which I've never done in my life before! It was so great we couldn't believe it . . . and then we had one more, and we haven't stopped laughing—it was like the first time you smoke grass. So much fun!"

When Dominique and I went upstairs, she said, "Have you ever had any vodka drinks?"

"No, I don't think so," I said. "I drank some scotch years ago, but you know, mostly just some wine with dinner."

"You should try vodka. It's really fun."

ALBERT HAD BEEN doubling down on Bearsville. He bought another piece of land up Ricks Road called Turtle Creek, with accommodations where visiting musicians could stay. The land also held a barn, which he converted into another recording facility. I started meeting the guys there every morning, trying to get something going. The idea was to work on new material and to try to get everybody involved. For a few weeks, we tried all kinds of different approaches to discovering new songs. It made Richard feel discouraged, not being able to write, and he stopped coming. Everybody else was game. But nothing was going anywhere. It took about a month before I finally got it through my thick skull, once and for all, that some people write and some people don't.

Still, I wanted to think of a way we could have some enjoyment in the recording studio. So I asked the guys what they thought of cutting some of the tunes we used to play in clubs back in our days as the Hawks. Everybody seemed up for that, knowing it would mean a lower level of pressure. As quickly as I made the suggestion, though, it occurred to me that the original recordings of songs are usually my faves. And going "back" could feel tired or strained too. Almost immediately I started imagining other songs besides our old repertoire that we could tackle with a new challenge.

I took a trip to LA to feel out the record company on the concept. Albert thought it was a good idea to show up anyway, because we'd been MIA for several months. It seemed like every time I went to the Capitol tower for a meeting, the company had a new president. This time I met Bhaskar Menon, an executive from India via London, where he had held a special position at EMI. There was something very likable about Bhaskar. No hustle, no jive—just down-to-earth and classy. I told him what we wanted to do for our next album.

"There is no question what your fans and the public would most like from you," he replied. "They would wish for a stunning album of new songs. We know that. But sometimes it's healthy to throw them a curve. If you do a record of cover songs that you choose and do it very well, which I'm sure you will, I applaud the idea."

While I was in LA, I got messages from Jon Taplin and our lawyer, David Braun, saying that the head of Asylum Records, David Geffen, wanted to meet with me. I didn't know much about David's background, but they strongly encouraged me to check him out. They both said the same thing: "He's a fascinating character."

So one day, late in the afternoon, I stopped by the Asylum Records building on Sunset. This sure didn't look like any record-company offices I'd seen before. Things here seemed much more relaxed and informal. Inside they pointed me to David Geffen's office. The door was open and there was no "He's on a call, take a seat, would you like some water?" No pretense. Just a warm welcome: "Hi! Come on in. Nice to meet you, I'm a huge, huge fan." Within ten minutes, David was telling me about a conversation he'd had with his therapist that day.

"You go to a shrink?" I asked. "Does it help?"

He laughed. "I hope so. I go five days a week, so it better! I want to be happy, if I can, and I'm willing to work on it. Don't you want to be happy?"

"Sure," I said. "But maybe I should stop watching all those depressing Ingmar Bergman movies."

"Yeah," he replied. "But sometimes watching depressing things can make you feel better about yourself." Then he added, "Your fellow Canadian Joni Mitchell is living with me. We're housemates. She's a genius. It's not easy living with a genius, but I love her."

I had never met anybody this open, this candid. David was the extreme opposite of most people from my background, who kept their inner thoughts closely concealed, but he made me feel totally comfortable. Before long, David knew the Band's deal with Capitol, how many records we owed them, practically my Social Security number. Something clicked for us, and I liked him right away. David was just a few months older than me, and before I left his office, I felt like I had known him for years. As I got up to leave, he invited me to his house for dinner that night. "I'll ask some friends over, and you can say hello to Joni," he said. "Come—we'll have a terrific time."

So that night I put on my new blue suede jacket and headed to Beverly Hills. The place was beautiful; it was Blake Edwards and Julie Andrews's old house and just the kind of place a movie star like Julie Andrews should live. David's idea of a few friends dropping by for dinner was screenwriter Robert Towne, who was in the process of writing *Chinatown*; Jack Nicholson, who was always a joy to run into; and Warren Beatty, very funny and smart but way too good-looking. I think the brilliant writer Buck Henry was in and out as well. Then there was Joni Mitchell, who looked angelic, like a translucent blond Indian. When we sat down for dinner, I realized David was right. This wasn't a party—just a Tuesday night with interesting friends. But I soon noticed that everybody here was on a mission. Everyone was relaxed but working. All eyes in the room were casting about for what might be right for their next project. That electricity was intoxicating, and my battery was in need of a jolt.

After dinner, Joni told me she had a new song almost finished.

There were a couple of acoustic guitars in the living room, and she picked one up, changed the tuning, and motioned for me to pick up the other. Then she soared off into the cosmos with her angelic voice. I tried to follow her on guitar, but between her unusual tunings and obscure fingering, I was a man in search of the lost chords. When she got to the part where she hadn't finished all the words, she just started scatting and broke up laughing. Everybody had gathered around and cheered, urging her to sing another one.

David sat with me through the dinner; we traded stories and had a great time. He asked about Albert and told me they had an old working relationship, which I hadn't known. He asked, "What's Bob Dylan doing these days?"

"He's very involved with his family," I told him. "He keeps having kids, so all you can do is get out of the way."

As I said good night to everyone, David walked me outside. "We have to find a way to work together." He said he would call David Braun, our attorney, to try to figure something out. I started to tell him where I was staying, but he cut me off. "Oh don't worry, I'll find you."

BACK IN WOODSTOCK, I couldn't wait to tell the guys about this blast of fresh air I had just met. I didn't know yet what we could do with David businesswise, but he sure conveyed a confidence that he could make things happen. At Albert's, I mentioned my meeting and the dinner and what a strong, positive impression I'd gotten of David.

Albert nibbled on his thumbnail a moment. "I can't say that I feel the same way about him at all."

I was taken aback by the stern tone in his voice. I instantly thrashed through all the ways they might have been competitive with each other—management, record company, publishing, past business dealings that had gone sour. I had no idea. "He seems like such an open, nice person to me," I said. "What's your take on him?"

Albert answered abruptly. "He's just not the kind of person I choose to do business with. It doesn't work for me, that's all. I much prefer dealing with someone like Mo Ostin. At least I know when Mo says something, he means it, and he's not trying to change the rules to benefit himself. I find it very questionable what David did with Laura Nyro in selling her publishing."

I said, "Really? I heard it made both of them pretty rich."

"What can I say? I don't agree with the way he does business." Albert cut a paper-thin slice off a block of cheddar cheese.

Around this same time, Levon started pushing for us to leave Albert's management company, as Bob had done earlier. Rick and Richard didn't disagree with Levon, but Garth hadn't expressed how he felt about it yet. Since Janis had died, Albert had been slowing down in the management field anyway, so I didn't think it was a pressing issue. His interest now lay much more with building his record company and all the Bearsville entities. I'd always been closer to Albert than the other guys—I'd learned a lot from him and had a deep appreciation for that. I always found him to be a great character and friend, maybe even a bit of a father figure.

David Geffen and I began chatting a couple times a week, sometimes just to talk about new music we'd heard. He mentioned that he had business in New York City and was thinking about driving up to Woodstock. I said it would be good for him to meet the guys and we could talk about some future possibilities. Meanwhile, my bandmates started coming by my studio so we could listen to old records that might be worth covering for a new album. If some of those tracks were a little more unknown, it could help. We'd be taking more of a risk with a famous classic that had already been chiseled in stone. Sometimes it felt like you shouldn't mess with the *Mona Lisa*, but once in a while it could be a wonderful homage or a worthwhile variation. It was a thin line, and we were having a good time throwing these ideas against the wall to see what would stick.

The following week, David Geffen came to Woodstock for a visit. I welcomed him and started showing him the place. He had a bemused look on his face, as if he had just crossed the Mojave Desert into no-man's-land. "Wow, all you guys actually live up here, year round?"

"Well, it's not so bad when it's not grizzly bear season," I joked. "Oh, did I tell you? This town is called Bearsville."

"I know, I heard . . ."

David and Dominique connected right away. I made reservations at a nice French-American restaurant in a nearby town for dinner, lest David think we were completely out in the sticks. I invited Levon to join us, but for some reason he didn't want to. I was disappointed that he didn't want to check out this young dynamo I had told him about.

The next day, the guys came over to my studio to meet David. The meeting had a pleasant, friendly vibe. David told us of business possibilities we could explore. He claimed that the record companies' "status quo" was due for an overhaul, and he wanted to be instrumental in updating the way it worked. The guys enjoyed David's enthusiasm and his anything-can-be-done attitude. He finished the meeting saying that, with our permission, he'd like to discuss some ideas with our attorney. He even agreed to talk to Albert about our future.

"That won't be necessary," Levon interjected. "We're winding down with Mr. Grossman." After a while the boys left, and David and I talked for hours. I thought to myself, *What other head of a record company would fly across the country, drive a hundred miles, stay over at your house, and leave with no guarantees of anything?*

The Band went into Bearsville studios with a short list of songs to record. Not surprisingly, the list was R&B heavy, with a good dash of New Orleans delights mixed in, and there were now only a couple tunes that we used to do as the Hawks. I thought it might be a kick to see if Levon would be into singing Clarence "Frogman" Henry's "Ain't Got No Home," an offbeat choice in its humor and playfulness. He laughed. "Hell, I'll give it a whirl." He crushed it, as did Rick singing Lee Dorsey's "Holy Cow." For the little guitar solos I did on that one, Richard insisted on working my wah-wah pedal by hand, which made it sound like a talking guitar. He was looking a little better all the time, although I still couldn't help but worry about him.

The biggest challenge was doing "Mystery Train," written by Sam Phillips and Little Junior Parker. The most well-known version was Elvis Presley's, which Sam Phillips had produced on Sun Records. We wanted to come up with a whole new take on the song, so I wrote additional words for it, which I had to get permission to do. We decided to try both Levon and Richard playing drums, with Garth's clavinet and my guitar dictating the chord structure. Levon sang lead, and his vocals made the new lyrics I wrote sound like they had always been there, like we'd just never noticed them before. While Lee went to Arkansas for a few days, the other guys and I recorded a version of "The Third Man Theme." It was from the 1949 Carol Reed noir film of Graham Greene's screenplay *The Third Man*, starring Joseph Cotten, Alida Valli, and Orson Welles. The score was written and performed by Anton Karas on zither. Impossible to forget and perfectly unique.

DAVID GEFFEN CALLED: he and Joni were going to Paris for a holiday and wanted Dominique and me to join them. "It's on me—I'll set everything up," he said. "Come on, it'll do you good to get away. We'll have a great time."

"You know," I said, "that's where I met Dominique—on the street, in Paris, in the springtime. She can translate for us." Needless to say, Dominique loved the idea. I thought this would be a good opportunity to see what David really had in mind for the Band. We still owed Capitol three records and that could take a while, but I knew he was a man with a vivid imagination.

Dominique and I met up with David and Joni at the historic Ritz Hotel in Place Vendôme. David had made reservations for us to have dinner at La Tour d'Argent overlooking Notre Dame Cathedral. When we arrived, an elevator operated by a teenage boy in uniform lifted us to the elegant dining room. Dominique and I had never experienced anything quite on this level. They brought the wine list to David and he chose a Château Margaux 1928. "You only live once," he said.

The next day we strolled the streets, lapping up the architecture. The four of us had nowhere we had to be, nothing we had to do, no one to see—complete freedom. When we got back to the hotel, Joni, as usual, picked up a guitar and began humming and strumming different chord changes and melodies. I hadn't brought a guitar, thinking this was a chance to get away from it all.

I mentioned to David that I was going to try to find an old friend of mine, Mort Shuman, Doc Pomus's old songwriting partner. As the story went, Mort's wife had run off with the chauffeur and emptied their bank account. In his depression Mort left New York and his partnership with Doc for France, where he ended up creating a tremendously successful show called "Jacques Brel Is Alive and Well and Living in Paris." With that and his own popular recordings, he had become an enormous celebrity in France.

I tracked him down, and he and David and I decided to meet up for dinner. I asked Mort to pick his favorite restaurant, so he led us to Le Grand Véfour, one of the oldest and very best in France. "Don't we need a reservation?" I asked.

Mort looked at me with a slight smirk, and a moment later the maître d' approached him, bowed, shook his hand, and led us to a center booth. Mort didn't even have to speak or smile. The restaurant was spectacular with its ancient moldings and tile work—so French, so classic. Mort told us that Napoleon and Joséphine ate here, and that it was a favorite of Victor Hugo and Jean Cocteau.

"Same chef?" I asked.

Mort laughed. "And he looks good for his age!"

We had a fascinating time exchanging stories. I reminded Mort of the first time I had met him and Doc, at the Brill Building when I was only sixteen years old. "Yeah," he said, smiling, "you were that greasy little punk with Ronnie Hawkins, looking for songs. Doc and I didn't know what the hell to make of you. It did seem like everybody thought you had talent, though, so I guess that's how we ended up here." He slapped me on the arm. "Try the sweetbreads."

When David and I got back to the hotel, Dominique and Joni seemed to be slightly toasted and in a mischievous mood, and we joined right in. I had started to tell them about our dinner with Mort when Joni picked up her guitar again and began playing and singing. Dominique stood up. "Wait, wait, wait. Can you *please* not sing and play right now? We just want to talk for a while."

Joni smiled a little to herself and put the guitar back in its case. Then we all burst out laughing. I thought, *When was the last time somebody told Joni Mitchell to stop singing and playing her guitar?*

After some more wine and drinks, apparently someone in our group threw up on the room service table in the hallway, but afterward no one knew which of us had done it. Joni wasn't sure if it was her, Dominique thought she had done it, and David was sure it was him. One more reason for Parisians to look harshly at the ugly Americans, even if three of us were Canadians.

Have to say, there was relief in being away from the trials and tribulations of the Band. All four of us felt like we were off the grid and having a deserved getaway. David suggested we go to Cannes the next day—the film festival was in full swing, and he could get us rooms. *Sounds like a fun idea,* I thought.

As soon as we arrived, we strolled over to the lobby of the Carlton Hotel, the festival's main social hub. As David made the rounds, saying hello to friends and acquaintances, he ran into comedian Richard Pryor. They knew each other, and David invited him to come join us at our table. He introduced us, but Richard looked tired and a bit edgy. David whispered to me, "I think maybe the necessary drugs are missing."

David tried to keep the conversation light and lively. Just then, an elderly couple stopped by the table. "Mr. Pryor," said the gentleman, "I just wanted to say my wife here and I saw your show last month in Vegas." He paused, looked around the table and then to his wife, and continued, "We very much enjoyed the show and thought you did an excellent job, so I just wanted to stop and say how much my wife and I really had a wonderful time seeing you."

Richard looked them over quickly, turned away, and said, "Well, your wife's a pig."

It took a couple of seconds for any of us to process what he had just said. As we gulped and looked at one another in shock, the elderly couple headed off looking confused and disturbed. David asked Richard why he was so angry. "Oh, I'm not angry," Richard fumed. "No. I'm not angry . . . yet!" This was our cue to head to dinner.

Later that night as we strolled along the main drag in Cannes, David turned to me and said, "You know what? I think you and Dominique should move to LA. You should move to the beach in Malibu.

You'll love it. It'd be great for your kids. Dominique has made it quite clear she thinks Woodstock is not good for you guys anymore. Why don't you do it?"

I could see he was dead serious, and it rumbled around in my head for a moment. "Malibu? That never crossed my mind. Let me think on it."

Back in Paris for another couple of days, Joni seemed to be writing a song for David about our trip. She said she had never seen him so relaxed, so "off the clock" before. Meanwhile, David kept encouraging me to move the family to Malibu, specifically to the Malibu Colony. "It's a private road with a private beach—it'll be heaven for the kids," he said. "Try it, and I'll help Marshall Gelfand and your people find a place. Once you're out there, we'll figure out something great for the Band. I'm already talking about things with David Braun."

With that he got up and said, "I'm going downstairs to take care of the hotel bill." A few minutes later he rushed back into the room with a look of panic on his face. "They don't take credit cards," he said. "Who carries this much cash? And we can't leave until we pay the bill. I don't know what I'm going to do."

I hadn't witnessed David so ruffled before. Seeing how upset he was, I tried to lighten the mood. "How many dishes would we have to wash to pay this baby off?"

David tried to reach someone who might be able to bail us out and finally got Prince Rupert Loewenstein, who managed the Rolling Stones, to vouch for him so we could leave. He took a deep breath. "Thank god."

It was such a joy spending this time with Joni and David in France. I knew the experience would stay with us forever. Dominique and I thanked him for this exquisite trip, and felt our friendship with David was deepening. Joni finished her song "Free Man in Paris," and it turned out to be a beauty. When David heard it, he was a bit embarrassed, but there was no denying it was a true statement and a great record.

SOON AS I got back to Woodstock, we went right into the studio. I felt revived from the trip and couldn't wait to make some noise with the guys. To get warmed up, we did a quick version of the gospel classic "Didn't It Rain," but once you've heard Mahalia Jackson wrap her voice around that one, it almost becomes sacred territory. We tried a somewhat obscure gospel tune Leiber and Stoller had written called "Saved," and it was ironic to hear Richard sing, "I used to drink, I used to smoke, I used to drink, smoke, and dance the hoochie koo."

We flew out to Capitol Studios to record the last few songs we wanted to tackle. A highlight there was revisiting one of our old Hawks standbys, Bobby "Blue" Bland's "Share Your Love with Me." Richard's vocal gave me the shivers, it was so moving. Right after we recorded it, out of nowhere George Harrison walked into the studio. "I'm sorry to barge in like this," he said. "Well, no, actually I'm not, because I wanted to ask you a favor. Ringo is making an album. I wrote a song he's going to record and I wanted to see if you guys would play on it. It's quite simple and won't take up much of your time." We said we'd be happy to help out. Now that the Beatles had broken up and they were all making solo albums, you couldn't help but be reminded how hard it is to keep a band together.

We showed up the next evening and recorded "Sunshine Life for Me (Sail Away Raymond)" at Sunset Sound. It was a bit of a haze because we were in midstream of doing our own record. After George sang us the tune, we immediately went into our mountain-music mode, with Rick on fiddle, Garth on accordion, Levon on mandolin, and George and me on guitars. It was fun to hear these Brits doing a real shit-kicker kind of song. George, Ringo, and the producer, Richard Perry, were in flight, and we were clouds streaming by—one of those dreamlike experiences.

We ended up having a hell of a good time making our own record, which we decided to call *Moondog Matinee* after Alan Freed's old radio show. For the cover Bob Cato wanted me to meet with an artist who did paintings and photography for *Sports Illustrated*. He thought Edward Kasper could capture this vision of the Band revisiting a place in our past. I gave him some of our backstory, and he took it and ran.

He conjured up pieces of this music built around a hangout—half street gang, half rock 'n' roll musicians.

DOMINIQUE AND I seriously discussed selling our house in Woodstock as we considered David Geffen's suggestion that we move to Malibu. I talked it over with the guys to see if a change of scenery had any appeal for them, but nobody knew what this world of Malibu even meant. I thought if I went and checked it out to see if it could be musically inspiring for us, and a healthier atmosphere, I could report back.

I told Albert that I was thinking about selling my house and moving west. That was disappointing news to the person who was building a music mecca here. Albert was no longer managing us or hardly anyone else at this point, but I could see the letdown in his eyes. I knew I would miss him and Sally, but the feeling in Woodstock had become stale and confining to me, and especially to Dominique. I did feel a bit like I was abandoning ship, leaving Bearsville behind—and the guys too—but I felt the need to search for a new frontier. Between finishing the *Rock of Ages* record and recording *Moondog Matinee*, the Band hadn't played any gigs in over a year, and things had begun to get pretty ragged again among the boys.

Then we got a request from Bill Graham, who was putting together a show "just up the highway from us" at the Watkins Glen Raceway. We'd be performing with the Allman Brothers and the Grateful Dead. Playing some gigs could help us get "back on the stick," as they say.

We went up to Watkins Glen the day before the show for the sound check. Bill Graham said that the Dead would go on first and play for three or four hours—that was part of their thing, giving the audience their money's worth. "Until the drugs wear off," said Bill, laughing. We'd go on in the late afternoon, and the Allmans would take over at sundown. As we were leaving the sound check, it looked like cars were heading toward the racetrack from every direction. Bill said he expected maybe a hundred thousand or more.

When we came back the next day, we couldn't believe our eyes. Hundreds of thousands of people had showed up, and more just kept coming and coming. The crowds mowed down the high chain-link fences around the racetrack and filled the area as far as the eye could see. Bill was running around trying to make people pay admission, but the mobs were out of control.

When it came time for the Band to take the stage, it started pouring. As we waited, hoping it was going to let up, Bill came over. "They've determined there are 650,000 people here. It's the biggest concert in history." The news was somewhere between an incredible accomplishment and a huge disaster.

The rain started letting up, and Garth played some churchy, rainy-day keyboard sounds out over the crowd. When it was safe to go on, we decided to start our set with Chuck Berry's "Back to Memphis." And wouldn't you know, as Levon sang that baby, the sun came out.

After our next song, I looked upward at the vanishing clouds and was surprised to see something descending from the sky. It was a sky-diver parachuting into the midst of the crowd. He lit two flares in midair to really put on a show, but the wind whipped the sparks and set his clothes on fire. There was a flaming man spiraling down into the crowd, and the audience thought it was part of our show. They started cheering and applauding as we yelled over the PA system, "No, no—this is bad! Please get help!" The man on fire landed in the crowd and was taken away by paramedics. We were told that miraculously he survived the fall, though he was burned up a little, so we continued to play. (Later we heard that wasn't true and that he had died.) Then, a few more songs into our set, some young guys decided to climb the scaffolding that the stage was built on, and this was the highest stage I'd ever seen. As they reached the top with their fingers, Bill Graham ran over and stepped on their hands, yelling at them for being such idiots as they fell back into the crowd.

I hollered at Bill for his cruel behavior. "Not during our set! Do not do *that* while we're playing."

Bill flashed a grin and adjusted his fedora. "You can't smother them with love all the time, Robbie."

DOMINIQUE AND I got an offer on our place in Woodstock, and we took it. Marshall Gelfand and David Geffen found a house for us to rent in the Malibu Colony, and we moved there, sight unseen—we had a lot of faith that David wouldn't steer us wrong. We showed up with our suitcases and the clothes on our back at 97 Malibu Colony, known as the Sam Peckinpah House. This could be good, bad, or ugly, just like "The Wild Bunch" or "Straw Dogs." It was the end of September, and in the early evening the sky turned purple orange. The girls ran on the beach—our backyard—and dipped their toes in the Pacific. *Okay*, we thought, *life feels pretty good here in paradise.*

As evening settled in, we got the girls cleaned up and put to bed. Dominique and I were relaxing in the living room, taking in our new surroundings and smiling to ourselves. Then, out of nowhere, we heard an ungodly shrieking. It was a woman, screaming her brains out. We panicked. We ran out the front, grabbed the phone, and went out on the sundeck, confused and alarmed. Could we help? Call the police? Moments later the screaming started to sound wrong. It was too constant, almost like a vocal exercise. It turned out to be our next-door neighbor, the actress Dyan Cannon, practicing primal scream therapy. When David Geffen showed up later to check on us, I told him the story and he laughed. Maybe we should get into primal scream too, he suggested, and when Dyan started screaming, we could scream back.

David and I went out that night to grab a bite, and as we cruised down the Pacific Coast Highway, he pointed out where some of his friends and certain celebrities lived. This felt so fresh to me, and I was lapping it up. When he drove me back to the Colony, we sat in the car and chatted.

"I think, after you're settled," he said, "you should get the other guys to come and join you out here. We should put something together with Bob Dylan and the Band. It could be historic. It could be the biggest thing to happen to music in a long, long time. And I'll help put it together. You guys could make a lot of money."

David had struck me as a very open and generous person, and I appreciated that. But I also knew that Bob and the other guys in the Band could be hard-edged. I told David to be careful of getting ahead of himself, that the guys in the Band were not like these West Coast "sweetheart of the rodeo" types. "They're different from the LA 'put a flower in your hair and everything is brotherly and groovy' kind of folks," I told him. "They're from the streets and live by the code of the road. And Bob's a good guy, but he's tough, man. He comes from the streets too. You might want to go slowly and be careful what you wish for."

David stared at me through the tops of his eyes. "Robbie, please. Don't worry, I know how to take care of myself. I'm a big boy. Go get some sleep, you're gonna love it here. I'll call you tomorrow."

TWENTY-FIVE

Waking up to the roll of the ocean was a new sensation, and at first the rhythm of the crashing waves just outside our back door was slightly alarming. The next morning, I strolled out to the private road inside the Colony just to stretch my legs. As I came upon the mailbox for our house, I heard someone call out, "Top of the morning!" I looked up. It was Cary Grant, retrieving his morning newspaper. He smiled broadly and waved the paper in the air.

We already knew that Dyan Cannon lived on one side of our house; actor Bruce Dern lived on the other, and Cary was on the other side of Bruce. We heard that Cary was gay, though with the help of LSD he had tried a heterosexual relationship with Dyan. They had married and had a baby girl, but apparently it didn't last. Now he lived close by to be near his daughter.

Dominique and I took the girls and hit the local food market to stock up. We filled two big carts, the most food we had ever bought at one time in our lives. On our drive back into the Colony, I saw a man walking briskly along the road. As we got closer, I saw that it was actor Burt Lancaster. When I let out a breath of amazement, my two little girls said, "Who's Blurt Ranfaster?"

We heard that Bob and his family were in the area too, feeling out the Malibu vibe. It was great to know we had friends on the same wavelength here, and when we got together I didn't feel as much like a stranger in a strange land. Bob and I were so used to living up north that we were still in the habit of wearing wintry clothes. Our wives chided us that we looked out of focus for this tropical weather. I told Bob I hoped I could convince the other guys to come west too, to transport our Woodstock clubhouse routine out here for a while and see how that shoe fit.

WHEN THE final artwork for *Moondog Matinee* was presented to me at Capitol Records in the fall of 1973, one of the execs at the company pulled me into his office and offered me a little bottle of cocaine with a tiny spoon attached. He said it was part of the celebration of launching a new album. *What a pleasant surprise,* I thought. We returned to the outer office area to find John Lennon there, wearing an olive green military jacket, studying the cover painting. He said he was doing an album of classic songs too with Phil Spector. We talked about all kinds of older rock 'n' roll tunes we loved that were part of our musical background. John looked like he hadn't been to bed, so we made plans to catch up another time. These days he seemed a little dazed and confused. He and Yoko were on the outs, and I'd heard he'd become hard to reach. When you had to go through Harry Nilsson to get to John, you knew you were in trouble.

Artie Mogull, an old friend of Albert's from the music-publishing business, now an executive at Capitol, was there too. He was a terrific character, blunt and pugnacious, and it was great to see him. He asked me if they could hang the original big painting of the cover on the wall of their conference room for a while to remind the staff that *Moondog Matinee* was a priority. "Sure," I said. "If that helps, of course."

My transportation was still a rent-a-car, so after I left the Capitol offices, I stopped into a nearby car dealership. I'd had my eye on a certain set of wheels and finally decided to take the plunge on a new, chocolate-brown 1974 Citroen Maserati. It was a strange-looking beast, with an air-ride suspension unlike anything around. It flew around those Malibu Canyon hills like a spaceship. I got a speeding ticket the first day I drove it.

When I called Levon to tell him about the wonderland out here by the Pacific Ocean, he sounded really upbeat. I missed Levon and wanted to convince him to come share in this discovery with me. I think all the guys were feeling a little staleness in the Catskills. One after the other I called them, trying to stir them up. When I told everybody that Bob was already out here, it added a layer of comfort.

Meanwhile, I told Bob about David Geffen and what an interesting and smart guy I thought he was. I mentioned that he wanted to get together with us to discuss some ideas he had. We set up a meeting, and as I expected, David made Bob feel pretty relaxed in no time, and wanted to be helpful to the Dylans and the Robertsons in any way he could while we acclimated to the Malibu setting. Obviously we knew he wasn't going so far out of his way just to get a good seat in heaven.

He invited us to the opening of the Roxy, a club he was starting on the Sunset Strip with Lou Adler, Elmer Valentine, Peter Asher, and his ex-management partner Elliot Roberts. Bob, Sara, Dominique, David, and I got to the club about half an hour before Neil Young and his band were going on. Someone asked David if Cher could join us at our table—I think Bob had met Sonny and Cher before, but none of the rest of us knew her. She turned out to be funny, sharp, and very warm. I could tell David was fond of her right away, but since he had told me he was gay when I first met him, I didn't think much more about it.

Then a road manager came to our table and said, "Neil Young wants to invite you guys backstage to say hello."

Bob answered immediately: "Oh no, we can't. We just ate." Dominique poked me in the ribs, trying not to laugh out loud.

The Roxy was rockin'. Nils Lofgren played guitar with Neil Young, and he had a small trampoline set up onstage. Every couple of songs he would jump on the trampoline and do a backflip in the air while playing lead guitar. I had never seen that before, and I leaned over to Bob. "I'm surprised we never incorporated that into our act."

He shrugged. "It's never too late."

I shrugged back. "It might be."

Later that week, David invited Dominique and me to join him and Cher for dinner. Cher and Sonny had broken up, and when we got to her place, we found out that she was living in one wing of the house while Sonny lived in the other, with a new girl. David led us to Cher's boudoir area where she was getting ready. A TV and videotape machine was playing the movie *Deep Throat* in the background, which struck Dominique and me as hilarious, but David and Cher were oblivious to it as they talked about not taking any guff from Sonny. At dinner, you could tell David was totally smitten with Cher. He kept offering helpful ideas and advice, as if he wanted to take care of her and protect her. She seemed very touched and was falling for David moment by moment. I found their relationship fascinating and very loving.

Not long after Joni Mitchell finished recording "Free Man in Paris," she asked me to play on a song called "Raised on Robbery," which referred to places and people from our common ground in Toronto. I wasn't much of a "session guy" who could show up at the studio and go after some sweet little hooks for your tune. My move was more to come in the back door in search of a diamond in the rough. But I loved much of Joni's music and wanted to bring *something* to the table for her, if I could.

In the studio, they played me the song over my earphones, and right away I felt an urge to toughen this track up with a rhythmic attitude and then wail a bit, but not too much. I played it two or three times and thought, *There, how's that for you?* I didn't know if Joni or her producer liked what I did, but I packed up my ax and hugged Joni good-bye. Later she told me when she properly listened to what I did, it slayed her, and that guitar rhythm had changed the whole feel of the song. She held my hand and thanked me deeply. I was moved and told her I would play guitar with her anyplace, anytime.

Then Richard Perry, whom I had worked with on the Ringo Starr song, called to ask if I would play guitar on a session with my old friend Carly Simon and her husband, the extremely talented James Taylor. When I showed up at the studio, I saw Richard had put together a terrific cast of musicians, including Dr. John on piano and Jim Keltner on drums. James and Carly were very sweet and said they wanted to cut the classic Inez & Charlie Foxx song "Mockingbird," which sounded like a great idea. I didn't act like Carly and I were acquaintances from the past, and she barely let on that we knew each other. This was probably best all around; different time, different place. I liked the way Richard quickly herded all of us to our positions to get an arrangement under way. We played through the tune a couple of times, trying out various structure ideas, and as Levon would say, "it was rough as a cob." Amazing how a studio full of such talent could sound so mediocre. I could see James might be having second thoughts about cutting the tune, and Richard, who had probably chosen this song, was scrambling for suggestions. I pulled James and Richard aside in the control room and offered up some thoughts on the arrangement. I suggested a much more laid-back feel, because everybody was pushing too hard. "We should play it with more of a lope, churning instead of burning. More open and spare." Richard gave those instructions to the musicians. Jim Keltner got it right away and we headed back into the studio for another take. I whispered something to Dr. John about trying a Huey "Piano" Smith rhythm approach. He grinned wide and nodded his head, like I was speaking his language. Everything was starting to click, and now Richard couldn't even sit down in the control room. Carly and James sang it beautifully and I played a nice little solo. Listening to the final take, there was a lot of backslapping and hand shaking. I drove back to Malibu feeling my oats.

SOON I GOT the good news from my bandmates that they wanted to join us out west and were looking for houses to rent in the Malibu area. I couldn't wait for them to get a taste of this vibe. It seemed the total opposite of where we had been the last seven years. The timing could be good too, as Bob and David were spending more time together and had begun to discuss the possibility of doing a Dylan/Band tour. Bob's recording deal with Columbia was ending, and the Band had a clause in its contract with Capitol that gave us the freedom to record or play with him anytime, for any record company he was with. For David to sign Dylan and then the Band to Asylum, and to have a hand in reuniting Bob and the Band, would be a major coup.

One day, Dominique came back to the house with a distracted look on her face. She grabbed my arm and said, "I think I'm pregnant. I do, I really think I'm pregnant!" She was half laughing and half crying out of excitement. I gave her a big hug and held her for a long time, thinking this was splendid news and the right place and right time. "I'm going to see a doctor in Santa Monica to find out for sure," she told me, "but I've got that feeling I get when I'm pregnant." Later that week she came back from the doctor and said, "I was right! Isn't that wonderful? We're going to have another baby. And I bet it's a boy—you'll see."

By the time everyone in the Band had found houses in Malibu, the plans for our tour were in full swing. David was willing to help put the tour together for free, if he thought he could get the live album or a new record on Asylum. "If you're going to go out and play all these dates in the U.S. and Canada, you should have a new record to go with it," he said. Bob thought he might be able to come up with songs for a new album to come out on Asylum. The Band had just released *Moondog Matinee*, so we reckoned playing with Bob on *his* record would be a good solution for what to do next.

I thought a new ax for the tour might be in order. I had heard about a guy named Norman Harris who specialized in selling rare guitars. Boy—what a collection he had. He brought guitars by my house that just made me drool. I couldn't afford to go crazy, but he had a red '59 Stratocaster that I couldn't resist. He also showed me a Telecaster with a V-shaped neck that I called Bob about immediately, and he ended up buying it for the tour. What a beauty.

We found an off-season camp by Mulholland Highway, north of Malibu, where we could rehearse for the tour and run over any new songs Bob had written for the album. The camp became our solitary, temporary clubhouse, even more remote than our old pink house in Saugerties. As we played through some of Bob's classics, you couldn't help but be reminded of the last time we had done these songs on tour and wonder if the audiences would still be unaccepting of us. Bob hadn't toured in eight years, and it was interesting to see him start to get back in shape, physically and mentally. As we rehearsed, he poured a lot into singing these songs, like he was starting out on nine and raising the power to eleven. Amazing that his vocal cords held up, let alone his energy. I wanted to try to play some of the tunes with a less aggressive approach, but soon we were a driving wheel all over again. It was an automatic reaction. There would be no pulling back.

To cut Bob's new album, we found the closest fully equipped recording studio to Malibu, the Village Recorder in West Los Angeles, and booked some days in the first two weeks of November. The studio was founded and owned by Geordie Hormel, an eccentric, almost Howard Hughes type who turned out to be a terrific guy. He was heir to the Hormel food products company (famous for its mystery meat, Spam) and was a musician himself. The studio was run by a gentleman named Dick LaPalm, an absolute sweetheart of a guy. Dick had worked for Chess Records in Chicago and before that with the great Nat King Cole, and boy, did he know his blues and jazz.

Bob wrote throughout the recording process, pulling together enough material for an album to come out on Asylum in conjunction with the tour starting in January. Rob Fraboni was the engineer at the Village, and I liked working with him right away. He was fast and deliberate, and gave off a good vibe in the studio. Once we were set up, each song Bob pulled out of his satchel was a new challenge. On "Going, Going, Gone" I got to try out my new red Strat's whammy bar, pushing it down so far the strings looked like they were hanging off the body of the guitar. We were rollin' and tumblin' with Levon's wicked beat on "Tough Mama." Bob had a gem of a song up his sleeve called "Forever Young," and he wanted to try it in a couple of different ways. When we played it straight, though, Bob just sang it to pieces—it gave you goose bumps. We also did an up-tempo version of it, but Rob Fraboni kept pushing for the emotional take of "Forever Young," and we ended up using both versions on the record.

The days and the music flew by. All I knew was we were having a rare old time. When we sailed through "Something There Is About You" my feet weren't even touching the ground. As Rob and I were setting up to mix the album, Bob came into the control room and asked me to play on one more song. He sat at the piano and I picked up an acoustic Martin D-28. He played through one verse to give me the flavor and then we cut it. This was "Dirge for Martha," and I think we only did one take. That session reminded me of late nights eight years earlier, Bob and me playing music in our hotel rooms.

After we mixed the album, Bob said he wanted to call the record *Ceremonies of the Horsemen*. Then he did a couple of paintings for the cover and decided *Planet Waves* worked better. I didn't worry about how this album stacked up against Bob's other records or what we had done together in the past. This was a pure reflection of where we were at during this particular period—that's it. Sure, there was some pressure to get a record out in time for the tour, but to me it was an accurate document of those couple of weeks at the end of 1973.

FOR OUR first Christmas in Malibu, it was 80 degrees Fahrenheit, and it felt as magical as it did unreal. David and Cher bought a stuffed animal for my kids so big we had to force it through the doorway, and David gave me my first VCR, a beast of a machine, with big three-quarter-inch tapes that lasted just an hour. Dominique was going into full pregnancy mode: exercise, healthy diet, no smoking or drinking of any kind. She would check the I Ching and pendulums regarding our unborn child. All indications were it would be a boy.

The holiday break that year was a short one. David Geffen had brought in Bill Graham and his partner, Barry Imhoff, to produce the Dylan/Band tour, and right after Christmas we went to the Los Angeles Forum for a run-through. We were testing out ideas on the run, and David was trying to give us feedback. There were different elements to the performance—Bob and the Band playing together, Bob doing some acoustic songs on his own, the Band playing on its own, and the finale. But in what order, and who should be where, and when?

By this time, Bob had stopped smoking and was doing exercises to get in shape for the road. Sometimes I'd walk into the dressing room and he would be standing on his head up against the wall. I wished that I had the courage to stop smoking for this tour too. The definitive word on how truly bad cigarettes were for you hadn't come down full force yet. An unfunny joke went around that tobacco was the revenge of the red man against the white man, but ironically my first puffs of tobacco were on the Six Nations Indian Reserve, where it grew wild and my cousins rolled it in newspaper.

The day after New Year's 1974, the Band and Bob boarded a leased 727 for our first show in Chicago, with David Geffen, Elliot Roberts, and company, and Barry Imhoff and his crew on hand to help us launch the tour into orbit. Barry Feinstein was the personal photographer for the tour, and Bob's old friend Louis Kemp came along for the ride as well, helping out when he could.

The whole affair was big news. *Newsweek* magazine was doing a cover story, and I had to laugh when David told me about their interview with Bob. David said he had warned the reporter not to ask Bob any political questions—he didn't like to talk about politics. But when they brought the reporter into Bob's suite, Bob was sitting on the bed with a sheet on his head, and the first question the reporter asked was about politics and President Nixon. "I'm not really into presidents," Bob answered. "I prefer kings and queens."

Our first concert in Chicago revealed a lot about the structure of the show. David gave us very good advice, helping us to improve the timing of the different segments and to remove unnecessary moments, like Bob standing over to the side and playing rhythm guitar during the Band's set. We started kicking off the show with a ripping version of "Most Likely You Go Your Way (and I'll Go Mine)." Then Bob suggested we end the show with it as well, like bookends. I'd never heard of that before, so we gave it a shot.

We played two nights at Maple Leaf Gardens in Toronto, and a lot of our old friends came by to give their regards. Uncle Natie had been released from prison, and he brought the family and semiretired Toronto mob boss Paul Volpe with him to the concert and after party. I was especially happy to see my cousins David and Vicki, who were all grown up and very cool. Paul Volpe, in great humor, took in the success of our whole setup. "Jaime, you guys are cleaning up! What are you, printing money? Come on, how do your uncle and I get in on this?" The audience reception in Toronto was fantastic, it was as if our concert fiasco at Massey Hall in '65 had never happened.

At our show at the Omni in Atlanta, Otis Redding's former manager, Phil Walden, came to see us and brought along Chip Carter, son of Georgia governor Jimmy Carter. After the concert, Phil and Chip invited us back to the governor's mansion for an after party, where we met Governor Carter and his lovely wife, Rosalynn—they were so welcoming and friendly, you couldn't help but think he had to be the coolest governor in the country. Later that night, Phil and I sat over in a corner and talked about the tremendous loss of Otis Redding. I told Phil that I thought Otis was unquestionably one of the greatest singers God had ever put on this earth. He nodded. "Here's something I bet you didn't know," he said. "Duane Allman told me you were his favorite guitar player. After your first couple albums came out back in 1970, that's what he said." That news completely made my night, tinged as it was by the thought of Duane's tragic death a few years after Otis's.

Just then, Governor Carter came over to me and said, "Let's take a picture together." We went into the front foyer and stood in front of a painting of George Washington with his hand inside his coat. I put my hand inside my T-shirt, Washington style, and so did the governor. We had a good laugh taking the photo. A few moments later, I saw Gregg Allman and Buddy Miles coming out of a bathroom together. I looked at Chip Carter and he just winked at me.

I said to Phil Walden, "This has to be the hippest governor's mansion ever."

He put his arm over my shoulder. "I'm in the process of talking Jimmy into running for president."

When we played Madison Square Garden, with the crowd standing and cheering us on, I was very conscious of how on our last tour with Bob, in 1966, the audience had booed us most nights. All around Europe, Australia, and North America, they'd condemned the music we were making together. Now here we were, playing Bob's songs hard and direct, the same as before, and the world was accepting it with open arms. We hadn't given up. We didn't come around. The world had come around. All we had were those tape recordings from the 1966 tour to go on—we knew that music was real when there were many nonbelievers. We fought a good battle in '66, but we won the war in '74.

The tour wrapped up on Valentine's Day at the LA Forum with

an early show where our kids and families could come and see what we actually did for a living. Barry Imhoff had the dressing rooms all suited out for the children to play. Bob pulled my daughter Alexandra up on his knee and Barry Feinstein took a photo. As we had in New York, we recorded the shows at the Forum for the live album. Knowing this was the last round of this heavyweight fight, we played our hearts out. Bob took no prisoners, and the Band floated like a butterfly and stung like a bee. There'd been no slack on this tour. Everybody rose to the occasion and gave their all.

At the end of our last show, Bob thanked Bill Graham and Barry Imhoff and the whole crew for doing such a great job. The only problem was he didn't thank David Geffen, who was in the audience with a bunch of his friends. This tour had been David's idea, and he had overseen all the important elements of making it such a success. Bob hadn't meant to overlook his contribution; he was just specifically thanking the road crew and everybody who was in the trenches day in and day out. But not thanking David was unfortunate, and very hurtful to him.

I knew how upset he was, so I called Bob the next morning and said we should go over to David's office and tell him how appreciative we were, and that not thanking him hadn't been purposeful or meant as a slight. Bob agreed, we drove over, and the three of us talked it through until, I think, David felt a little better. Cher suggested we throw David a special birthday party. We agreed, and Bob helped organize a crazy carnival bash for him where we played and sang with Cher, hoping it would ease his disappointment.

A FEW WEEKS after the tour wrapped up, I called Artie Mogull at Capitol Records and told him I was going to send someone to pick up the painting we had used on the cover of *Moondog Matinee*.

"I think somebody already picked it up," he said.

I hadn't sent anybody, so I didn't understand. He said he'd look into it. A little while later he called me back with strange news: one of the executives at Capitol had taken the painting, claiming it was his.

"What?" I said, shocked. "Who took it?"

"Rupert Perry," he replied. "He's from England."

I'd never heard of this Rupert guy, but I called him and told him that Edward Kasper, the artist who'd painted the cover, had given it to me. It was my vision, and I'd been loaning it to Capitol at Artie's request. Rupert Perry gave me some horseshit legal explanation, but in my view he basically stole the painting. Bob Cato wrote a letter, as did Edward Kasper. But Perry ended up sending the painting to England like a thief in the night, and I was never able to retrieve it. I pondered revenge.

With some money in my pocket from the tour, I called Norman Harris to check out some more guitars. Over the next few months, I purchased a 1919 Martin 00 45K (one of a kind), a 1960 Gibson Les Paul Black Beauty, a 1928 Martin 000 45 gut-string (a gem), a 1920 Gibson Model O, a Martin 1901 1-42, a 1951 Martin D-28, a 1961 Gibson Double Neck Mandolina (very rare), a 1951 Fender Broadcaster, a Martin 5K Ukulele, and a 1938 Rickenbacker Lap Steel. On one of Norman's visits he mentioned a singer-songwriter he thought I might like to hear named Hirth Martinez, who played under the name Hirth from Earth and sang about UFOs and sci-fi stuff. I listened to some of Hirth's material and thought he was one of a kind. I hoped at some point we could find a way to work together.

First, though, came the work of putting together a live album from the tour. I went through all the rough mixes of the recordings with Bob and the guys to see what we had. The LA shows were the best, and Rob Fraboni and his assistants had captured it well. As I started mixing the album with Rob and Nat Jeffreys, the excitement and subtleties of the performances really stayed with me. Some of Bob's vocals had unusual nuances to them. On different performances he would change the words on "Knockin' on Heaven's Door" and "Rainy Day Women #12 & 35." After I got four or five songs mixed, I went to play them for Bob. They sounded hot, and he laughed out loud at some of our "power drill" performances. At the same time, I could see he was bothered about something. I didn't know if it was personal, so I didn't want to ask. The next time we got together for a listening session, I played the version of "Knockin' on Heaven's Door" from the Madison Square Garden show that Phil Ramone had recorded, which had a certain vibe that I preferred. But Bob seemed distracted. This time I asked what was on his mind.

"I don't think I want to do this Asylum Records deal with Geffen," he said. "It doesn't feel right to me." This came out of nowhere and caught me off guard.

"But I thought we'd already agreed to do it with Asylum," I said. "David's already made the arrangements with Capitol for the Band. I don't understand. What's not working for you?"

Bob couldn't explain. He just repeated that it didn't feel right to him. I tried to imagine what could have turned him around. *Planet Waves* had gone to number one on Asylum. Was it that he had been on Columbia Records since the beginning and felt like that's where he belonged? Was it an "LA vibe" he couldn't relate to? Was it that he didn't want to be another feather in David Geffen's cap?

I had a closer friendship with David than Bob or the other guys in the Band did, and felt a bit torn by this change of heart. I told the guys what Bob had said and that David had put this tour together with the belief he would get the live album. But the guys were indifferent as to whether the record was on Asylum or Columbia—they didn't feel any particular sense of loyalty either way. This was exactly what I had been afraid of when David and I sat in his car on my first night in Malibu. I had tried my best to explain that "street" element, the "chill" that could surface with the Band and with Bob, like a freeze-out.

I called David Braun, who was also Bob's lawyer, to ask if it was wrong or unethical to bail out of this deal. He said he had already spoken with Bob about it and that "a man has a right to change his mind. I'm going to call Geffen now and tell him."

About an hour later, David Geffen called me, stunned by the news. He couldn't believe this was happening. I told him I really didn't know why Bob was having second thoughts. He said David Braun was setting up a meeting where we would all get together and settle the issue.

The meeting took place at Rick's house out at Broad Beach. It was awkward to begin with and then grew terribly uncomfortable when

David Braun suggested that he, Bob, and the Band would go into the next room and decide yes or no on whether the live album would go to Asylum. When we adjourned to the next room I asked everyone, "Haven't we basically given our word to David Geffen that he would get the record?"

"I haven't given my word to nobody," said Levon.

"I want to go with whatever's the best deal," stated Rick.

"I know we can make a better deal with Columbia," David Braun interjected. It seemed that Bob had pretty much made up his mind not to go with Asylum.

"This tour wouldn't even have happened without David," I declared.

"Whose side are you on, anyway?" Richard asked.

That stung. I'd had enough. "Okay, fuck it! Don't give it to him. Don't give him nothing," I blurted.

David Braun called us together. "Okay, let's take a vote."

Everybody said no. What could I do? This was my band, my brothers. Bob and I had been playing music together for nine years and were like family. But David Geffen had become a good friend, and I felt he hadn't done anything wrong. So I didn't vote, not that it would have mattered anyway.

We rejoined David Geffen in the main room and David Braun tried to explain the reasoning behind the "no" consensus. When he got to the part about how "it was like he was taking food out of the mouths of our children," David Geffen couldn't take it anymore. He got up and walked out.

But he had a lot at stake with the live album. It was already assumed in the industry and beyond that David had the record. So now he had to match Columbia's offer to convince Bob and the Band to let him release it on Asylum.

Afterward he called me, furious that I had betrayed him. "You're the only one of those guys smart enough to have come up with this scheme," he said.

Stunned, I fired back. "What are you talking about? I stood up for you. I told them this tour wouldn't have existed without you." But he was too upset. He said he'd heard me in the next room saying, "Don't give it to him." He thought I'd gone along with the whole thing over money, even though my end wasn't all that significant, just one fifth of half of the deal, and I would never have jeopardized our friendship over it. But it would take some time for those wounds to heal.

THE LIVE ALBUM *Before the Flood* came out on June 20, 1974, on Asylum Records. Rock journalist Robert Christgau reviewed it, saying, "Without qualification, this is the craziest and strongest rock and roll ever recorded. All analogous live albums fall flat." Elliot Roberts put together some gigs for the Band in the beginning of summer, but as soon as they were over, I needed to get back to Dominique and the girls. We had a baby coming, and nobody was more excited than Alexandra and Delphine.

On July 18, 1974, Sebastian Barnaby Robertson was born at Saint John's Hospital in Santa Monica—our first child not born in Montreal. Once again, Dominique was a real mercenary giving birth. She brought Sebastian into this world with the gusto of Joan of Arc. Holding Sebastian was different from holding the girls. When he stretched or pushed, you could feel his strength. His little noggin was tough too, as he banged it against my arm or chest. Dominique insisted on having a real nest for our growing family. We ended up purchasing the largest house in the Malibu Colony, number 34, where Carole King, Shelley Winters, and Lee Marvin had all lived before. Dominique eventually found a couple from Montreal, Jacques and Rosemary, to move in, since she was still persistent in wanting to have French-speaking help.

One day, while Bob was over visiting, he said he liked the sound of French being spoken in our house. He suggested he and I take French lessons. I told him that the actor Donald Sutherland, who was married to a Frenchwoman, had told me about a great language teacher named Michel Thomas who worked with a lot of actors. So Bob and I started taking regular lessons from Michel in the tearoom at my house. Jacques would bring in little French sandwiches and snacks, and after Michel had left Bob and I would practice a few phrases together, but our conversations soon turned to a different subject. Bob confided that things were becoming a bit strained between him and Sara. He said he needed to go to New York for a while and let things settle down. I was sorry to hear this. Bob and Sara had been an inspiration to us. Hell, I had stood up for them when they got married. Bob seemed confused about what was happening, and every time the subject came up it sounded a little worse.

The guys and I were in search of a new clubhouse, a place where we could gather and write and record songs but that offered a higher level of recording possibilities than we'd had at Big Pink. Our search led us to a strange ranch-type place off the Pacific Coast Highway, across from Zuma Beach. The more we found out about it, the more we liked it. It was called Shangri-La and consisted of a large house with little motel-like rooms built on the end. The walls were covered in velvet, and just outside were corrals for horses. No one could figure out quite why a house would need a little motel attached to the back of it, until we learned that it used to be a whorehouse for cowboys who worked in the area. *If those walls could talk.*

We turned a big playroom area into a full-on recording studio. Our soundman, Ed Anderson, was in charge of making it work, and Rob Fraboni helped figure out how to get the most professional setup and what gear we needed. Soon it was starting to feel like the real thing—a little music factory.

While the studio was coming together, the Band went out on the road to finish the dates Elliot Roberts had set up for us, but Richard wasn't doing so well. The bottle and drugs were sneaking up on him and wearing him down, night after night. He tried to not let it affect his performing, but he often complained about losing his voice or feeling sick. We grew more worried. In Cleveland, toward the end of the show he collapsed, and we had to get the paramedics. As they carried Richard past us on a stretcher, Levon called out, "Get up and walk like a man!" Richard looked over at him with a shocked expression on his face.

Levon had reached his limit with Richard not holding up his end and always making excuses. We were all fed up, but it surprised us that he chose to voice his opinion at such a sensitive moment. Eventually the doctors confirmed that Richard was terribly run down from alcohol and drug abuse and needed time to recover, so we canceled the remaining dates of the tour.

Still, we weren't off the road for long, and by the middle of September we were at Wembley Stadium in London. Elliot had put together a show there with Crosby, Stills, Nash, & Young, Joni Mitchell, and us. The day before the gig I found myself on a little stage somewhere blowing the roof off the joint in a jam session with Jimmy Page, John Bonham, Neil Young, and others. Jimmy and I traded licks back and forth, just messing around. Neil tried to turn something into a song, but it was a bit too loose for that. John Bonham wasn't bashing and crashing but floating, scaling the surface like a seagull on the hunt.

London felt alive and stirring, and bringing our North American sound over fit in nicely there. Our collective forces, though, brought out the most wicked rock 'n' roll behavior, with Stephen Stills and David Crosby leading the charge. London, for whatever reason, cried out for pure madness. Trouble was brewing, and we couldn't wait to grab hold of it: first the drugs, then the whiskey, then the rock 'n' roll. There were so many crazies hanging out, it felt like we could have elected Keith Moon as prime minister. Rick gathered up Bianca Jagger and Britt Ekland from the side of the stage and pulled them into our web. I don't remember what happened that night, but when I saw Rick the next day, he was clean-shaven. I hadn't seen him clean-shaven in years.

"What happened?" I said.

"Who knows?" said Rick. "Someone didn't want whisker burn. But it's like the glass slipper in Cinderella. To find her we'd have to search the kingdom and see who has the most sensitive skin."

I remember vividly the day I got home to Malibu and walked in the front door. Delphine wrapped herself around one of my legs, and Alexandra around the other. Sebastian was bouncing in a Jolly Jumper device at the end of the hall. Best feeling in the world. Dominique made the girls let go of my legs after a few steps, knowing I must be feeling like a zombie after flying for twelve hours.

I STARTED PUSHING to get our new clubhouse studio, Shangri-La, sounding great and ready for action. Soon as I could, I got in there and started making an album with Hirth Martinez. Notwithstanding his "Hirth from Earth" moniker, he truly was a musical alien, and his diverse style of songwriting gave me an opportunity to study and explore different ways of producing. I asked Hirth if he did any live gigs around town. "Oh yes," he said. "I sometimes play at a Laundromat in Hollywood. And on occasion I go to a mental hospital and do a set or two. They completely get my music—good crowd."

On one of the songs I told Hirth, "We need a girl to sing background."

"I know someone who sings with me at the hospital who'd be great," he said. Soon a beautiful girl named Maud showed up, and her voice blended wonderfully with Hirth's. She ended up becoming Garth's girlfriend, and then his wife. Right on, Hirth.

One day I invited Bob over to check out how the Shangri-La studio was coming along. While we were chatting, he mentioned another bootleg of our basement tapes coming out, and how it really annoyed him and Columbia. I suggested going back to the original tapes to see if there were some tracks we could release properly. We didn't want to put out music that was sonically unacceptable, but with the technology of the time, I thought maybe Rob Fraboni and I could reduce some of the hiss and improve the sound quality. Bob agreed to see what we could do.

As Garth, Rob, and I experimented with different devices, the guys would stop in and make suggestions. On one song Rick thought that the bass got lost in the original mix, and he wanted to redo it. Richard might want to add a tambourine, just trying to upscale a bit. All of the music originated in the Big Pink basement, but not all of its recordings were finished there. We would choose some of the best songs that had the best sound quality. Anyway, we did all that was possible at the time to make the music sound more presentable and less like a field recording. We didn't want the public to feel ripped off. When we looked back on it later, though, we realized we liked field recordings.

A friend of Rick's named Larry Samuels had come aboard to help the Band out in any way he could. His disclaimer was that he didn't want to be paid—he had a trust fund of some kind and didn't need the money—but he would manage Shangri-La and take care of any business we needed just because he wanted to be part of our world. Too good to be true? Of course. Rick took in this sweetheart of a mad dog. Larry fit right into the mold, and we liked him, for better or for worse. He was enthusiastic and protective, and the timing was right—we'd had no real management since we left Albert. Elliot Roberts was mainly just getting us gigs here and there—he probably knew better than to get in deeper, plus he had his hands full with Crosby, Stills, Nash, & Young and Joni. Since Tour '74 Elliot had become a friend, and though we only saw each other on occasion it was always a great time. One of the most classic moments happened when he and I were out getting dinner at a restaurant.

"You wanna go in the restroom and do a bump?" he asked.

"Sure," I said. "Let's go."

In the bathroom Elliot poured some cocaine out on the sink. After he mushed it and made some lines, he took out a crisp dollar bill, rolled it up, and started to snort it. Just then, while he was in mid-snorting motion, someone opened the door and walked into the bathroom. Without missing a beat, Elliot stood up and said to the person, "It's not what you think."

WITH SHANGRI-LA in full bloom, I was itching to get in there and start recording. Given all the other projects and gigs we had going, I hadn't been in much of a writing mode in the last couple of years, since *Cahoots*. But something changed for me in the next period of time. I started writing without the strain of what was happening with the motor, or under the hood, of the Band. I wrote a song called "It Makes

No Difference," and it sent a signal that I needed to get back in the studio and make some noise.

At Shangri-La, I sat at the piano and played a new song for the guys called "Twilight." Rick said, "Boys, if you don't mind, I'd like to stake a claim on that one. I gotta sing this baby. Love that sentiment. 'Don't leave me alone in the twilight, 'cause twilight is the loneliest time of day.'"

Richard grinned. "I'll flip you for it," he said. "Heads, I win. Tails . . . well, you know."

Garth was reaching a higher plateau with his electronic sound experimentations. On the one hand he had very traditional organic flavors and at the same time cosmic sounds I had never heard before. I wanted to write some songs where he could really flaunt his magic. I had just finished writing a tune called "Forbidden Fruit" that felt like holding a mirror up to our current state of affairs, kind of a "check yourself before you wreck yourself" reminder. I could hear Levon singing this one with real authority. We had a good time cutting the track; everybody showed up in force and it set a standard for what I was hoping to get out of the record. I didn't try to push the other guys to participate in the writing, which took pressure off everybody. I just assumed my position and dug in.

After we recorded the master take on "It Makes No Difference" and Rick sang his heart out, I thought it was a classic. That was forever. Garth and I played some sweet solos. His tone on the soprano sax sounded like Rick's voice being squeezed through a miniature saxophone—sad and sexy.

By now I was in the zone. I grabbed an acoustic guitar, tuned it to an open D, and sang for the guys my first draft of "Acadian Driftwood." The song was inspired by a documentary I had seen in Montreal a while back called L'Acadie, l'Acadie, where for the first time I understood that the name "Cajun" was a southern country slurring of the word "Acadian." The documentary told a very powerful story about the eighteenth-century expulsion by the British of the Acadians: French settlers in eastern Canada. Thousands of homeless Acadians moved to the area around Lafayette, Louisiana. When I finished playing the song through, Levon patted me on the back and said, "Now that's some songwritin' right there, son." I was proud that he felt so strongly about it.

"We've got to find the sound of Acadian-Canadian-Cajun gumbo on this one," I told the guys. "We have to pass the vocal around like a story in an opera. There has to be the slightly out-of-tune quality of a French accordion and fiddle, the depth of a washtub bass—all blending around these open tuning chords on my guitar like a primitive symphony." When we were recording the song, it felt as authentic as anything we'd ever done.

Coincidentally, around this same time some French-Canadian music people were visiting the Malibu Colony. The actress Geneviève Bujold had moved in a few houses down from us, and between her place and ours we housed songwriters Luc Plamondon and François Cousineau, with singer Diane Dufresne. I wanted a little singsongy vocal riff for the outro of "Acadian Driftwood," so I asked Luc and François what a French Acadian phrase for this would be. They helped me find a lovely little farewell for Rick to sing in the end fade.

There was another tune I was anxious to spring on Levon because I thought it had his name written all over it. The song dealt with the mysterious disappearance of Ophelia, and I had an old-timey-type chord progression to go with a whole new spin on the story. I liked having a modern-day Shakespearean character that Hamlet couldn't get, and neither could I. Ophelia—they don't have names like that anymore, or maybe they do in Denmark. I loved the way the track felt after we cut it. The combination of horns and keyboards Garth overdubbed on this song was one of the very best things I'd ever heard him do. It was definitely the cherry on the cake, and completed this musical odyssey. "Ophelia" became my favorite track on the album, even if it didn't have the depth of some of my other songs. The pure, jubilant pleasure of that tune swayed me.

The creative energy at Shangri-La felt productive, and we thought we now had the technology and staff to mix the album there. All the guys were involved, and it was good to have the gang back in a circle. We called on Reid Miles, the photographer who'd shot the cover for the official release of *The Basement Tapes*, to shoot this cover too. We built a fire out behind my house on the beach and Reid shot us by the firelight in the twilight hour.

With the album, called *Northern Lights–Southern Cross*, finished, the boys and I sat down to listen to a test pressing. We felt better about this record of new songs than anything the Band had done in a while. It felt so good to get this record under my belt; before writing these new songs, I hadn't been sure whether a new record from the Band would be in the cards.

A couple of days later, Richard told me he was really sorry that he hadn't contributed to the Band's songwriting for such a long time. "I just didn't live up to my part of the deal." He reminded me that in the early days we had even talked about becoming a songwriting team in the tradition of Pomus and Shuman, Bacharach and David, or Rodgers and Hammerstein. I held no resentment for that; I knew you can only create when you feel the spirit. But Richard said, "The plan in the beginning was that we would all write, and that's why you insisted that we share the publishing equally." He felt bad about it, and offered for me to buy out his end of the publishing. I disagreed. "They say never give up your publishing." But he said he didn't want to have this burden hanging over him and he could use the money now. Rick overheard the conversation and said he also thought he hadn't come through on his end of the bargain. If I could afford it, he'd like to be bought out too. I didn't know quite how to process this. I had been writing all of our songs for a long time and realized that wasn't about to change, but I had no idea whether I had the means to buy them out. When I discussed this with Garth and Levon, Garth was quick to say he had something he wanted to buy and could use the cash. Levon was hesitant, and I reminded him what they say about publishing and asked him to hang onto it. If at a later date he wanted to sell it to me, I'd see if I could manage it. "Fair enough," he said. "I'll let you know."

I called Marshall Gelfand and asked if I could afford to purchase Richard's, Rick's, and Garth's publishing. He said he would look into it and thought I might have to take out a loan, but that it wasn't a bad idea since I had written most of the songs anyway. He asked, "Why don't you buy Levon's end too?" But I told him I didn't want to pursue it unless Levon insisted.

I HADN'T SEEN Bob in a couple of months when he called to say he had done some recording in New York. I was curious to hear what he'd cut, and he played me an early version of *Blood on the Tracks*. It was tough, bold, and dark, more powerfully personal than anything I'd heard him do in a long time. I really enjoyed it. Bob's friend Louis Kemp kept nodding at me after some key biting lines, as if to say, *You know what that's about.* "Wait till you hear the one called 'Idiot Wind,'" he said. Some months later Bob told me, "I recut the record up in Minnesota. You wanna hear it now? It's much better." This new version was more up-tempo and energetic, but the first recordings he had played for me still stuck in my mind.

Living in Malibu with so many creative people around, you never knew quite what each day would bring. One afternoon I swung by Rick's house out on Broad Beach for a little smokeski. When I got there, he seemed nervous. "Man, I'm gonna need your help. I saw something pretty weird from my upstairs window. We have to go down by the water." We trudged over the sand toward the shoreline, and as we got closer to the water I could see someone lying where the tide was coming in. Concerned, we started half running toward the surf.

"Grab his leg," said Rick when we reached the body, "and we'll pull him up further on the sand." As I picked up a leg, I realized I was looking down at Keith Moon, drummer of the Who. He was dressed in a Nazi uniform and completely passed out, with the waves lapping over him. As we dragged him up on the bank, we saw someone who appeared to be looking for him, and Rick yelled out that he was okay. "You better get him inside, though." He pointed down. "He looks pretty sunburnt on one side of his face."

David Braun called me. "I'd like to introduce you to someone else I represent, Neil Diamond. He's your neighbor in the Colony, and he'd like to talk to you about producing his new record." This caught me completely off guard. I mumbled something about not necessarily being the right person for the job, but David told me what a great guy Neil was and that I should at least meet him. I said it would be a pleasure. I liked a lot of songs he'd written: "Solitary Man," "Cracklin' Rosie," "I'm a Believer," "Red, Red Wine."

I ended up digging Neil right away—he was a real New York City songwriter from the classic Tin Pan Alley tradition. He still had the classic good looks that had led some people to refer to him as the Jewish Elvis. His kind and open manner made my family take to him right away. But I still wasn't sure producing this record was right for me. I gave Neil the typical excuses for not being available—my obligations to the Band, my newborn son, et cetera. Neil was cool about it. "Okay, just keep it in mind."

But David Braun must have thought I was holding out for more money, which wasn't the case at all. Every couple of weeks he would come back with another offer, and Neil would check in to see if my schedule might be permitting. In the meantime, friends and music associates kept telling me, "This is ridiculous. You can't do a Neil Diamond record. That's just wrong." But the more I heard that, the more I wanted to rebel, and thought, *Don't tell* me *what to do.*

One day, Neil and I were having coffee, hanging out, and we stumbled upon the thought that our common crossroads was the Brill Building in New York City. We had both gone there at a young age with a dream: if you could write songs like those Brill Building guys and send them out into the world—man, that would be the best. We talked about that scene, that story, and the legacy of Tin Pan Alley— how we were part of the generation that had watched that tradition fade into the distance.

Finally I said, "Hell, yeah—let's do it. You got any songs?"

Over the next couple of months, Neil and I put together an impressive assortment of musicians, from Dr. John to Bob James, and we had a blast making the record, which was called *Beautiful Noise*. The theme centered around New York City and a young man learning the hard way about the trials and tribulations of making it in the music business during the midsixties. Neil and I wrote one song together called "Dry Your Eyes" about how *many* people felt after the assassination of Martin Luther King Jr. As a whole, the songs on the album had a cinematic quality, and I could even imagine it as a Broadway musical.

Neil had a tour of Australia booked in the middle of making the record, which allowed me time to experiment with production ideas and to play a little guitar on it. When Neil returned, he took delivery of a new BMW motorcycle with all the trimmings. Soon after, he showed up at the studio all battered and taped up. He'd taken his new bike up into the Malibu Hills for a spin and two Doberman dogs had charged and chased him, gnawing at his boots and his pant legs; then, as he returned to the Colony, the guard accidentally put the gate down on him, landing it on his face and cutting his nose open. He joked to me about his bandaged face, saying, "It's only my livelihood." I told him to stick to his singing—joining the Hells Angels wasn't his calling.

When the album came out, Neil put my producing credit on the front cover as part of the artwork, something I had never seen before. I told him that it *really* wasn't necessary, but he insisted. Neil was so dedicated to his art while making this record and so devoted to his songwriting craft that I ended up profoundly impressed by the whole experience. The record was tremendously well received, which Neil truly deserved. I was grateful to have had another terrific musical experience while pulling off something that most people thought went totally against the grain.

TWENTY-SIX

Life inside the Malibu Colony was a scene unto itself. There was the movie director Hal Ashby, Paul Newman, Linda Ronstadt, Burgess Meredith, Larry Hagman, Ronnie Wood, and my old friend Charles Lloyd; but there were also folks who just liked living there. Directly across from our house two attractive girls lived in a funky bungalow on an overgrown lot. I don't know what they did for a living, but Dennis Hopper visited them on occasion. Whenever I ran into him, he looked happy to be there and a bit stoned, with a mischievous smirk on his face like Dennis the Menace on a motorcycle.

A few houses down from us on the ocean side lived a friend of Dominique's named Barbara Linson. She was into healthy foods, supplements, and seeds and would sometimes take Dominique up to Ojai to meet with certain spiritual leaders. Barbara's husband, Art, drove a Rolls-Royce. Through our wives, Art and I ended up spending time together, and I found out that he was a lawyer who had turned his back on the profession and gone to work for the music entrepreneur Lou Adler. He was now producing movies, which may or may not have explained the Rolls-Royce. Hey, we were in the Malibu Colony—where excess was the order of the day. Hell, I had just purchased a Mercedes-Benz 600 Ambassador model with curtains in the back window. Who was I to talk?

Art turned out to have a sharp sense of humor, and we both liked a lot of the same things, drugs and all. One day I was over at his house and he was listening to the Bob Seger song "Night Moves." "There's something about this guy I really like," he said. "Obviously his voice is really good, but take a look at the picture on the album of this fellow. He looks like a werewolf, and he's singing about his sexual maneuvers. It's kind of hilarious and great!"

Up at the clubhouse, Larry Samuels was a doing a fine job running Shangri-La and helping with the Band's business affairs. The only major problem was his vicious temper. On occasion I would hear him screaming on the phone in an ugly manner that I wasn't comfortable with from someone representing the Band. He promised me he would cool it.

Larry made the studio available for some of our friends. Eric Clapton booked time to cut his new album. He and Richard had a special bond, and they did some writing and recording together. They were also grand drinking buddies, both speaking the same language during this period. Rick got in on the action too, working on some songs with them called "Beautiful Thing" and "All Our Past Times." Crazy as things were then, they did some pretty damn good work.

Bob would stop by Shangri-La on occasion, and Eric asked if he had any songs kickin' around that he could cut. Bob laid a funny tune on Eric called "Sign Language." They recorded the song, and then Eric asked me to play on it at the Village Recorder. I set up out in the studio with Eric; my old friend from Oklahoma, Jesse "Indian Ed" Davis; and the engineers in the control room. They played the track for me and I did a take on the guitar. When I looked up, Eric and Jesse were in stitches. *What the hell's so funny?* I wondered. Then I realized it was the deep dive-bomb whammy-bar maneuvers I was playing. I tried another take, and they fell apart laughing again. I went into the control room, where they were both getting their drink on, and they were really enjoying my guitar acrobatics. "Nobody plays like that," they said. "Incredible! You play guitar like it's an East Indian tabla drum." It was a beautiful compliment coming from Eric Clapton and Jesse Ed Davis.

One of Dominique's heroes, the American author Henry Miller, lived in the Pacific Palisades and had recruited her to help with a book he was writing in French. Henry spoke French after living in France for many years, but it's one thing to speak the language and another to write it. Dominique asked me to accompany her to weekly Thursday-night dinners at Henry's. It was usually just him, us, and his assistant, the lovely Twinka, a model who had recently become known for posing nude in a Judy Dater photograph that appeared in *Life* magazine. Henry said he had a thing for women with one name. Every Thursday he told breathtaking stories about how he had struggled to get his books published, about his affairs with Anaïs Nin and so many other lovers. His friend D. H. Lawrence had delved into the sexual revolution, but Henry threw down the gauntlet.

Henry was now in his eighties and came to the dining-room table in his pajamas and dressing gown. His age was mild in comparison to his experiences. With every meeting I understood and appreciated him more. Dominique worked diligently on the book, making his written French sound more sophisticated, as he'd requested. As time went on, I could see Henry was becoming infatuated with her, but somehow, from a man in his eighties, this was excusable to me. His character and his stories held me in a spell.

As Dominique was finishing work on the book, the publishers decided they preferred Henry's broken French with its innocence and charm. I think she felt a sense of rejection, and she stopped going to the Thursday dinners, but I continued for a while. Henry and I would watch wrestling matches on TV together. When I'd declare that professional wrestling was a circus act and it was fixed, Henry would get very upset. He didn't want to admit that it was a sham. He preferred this world of make-believe and the bad guy sometimes winning.

One night at Henry's, it was just the two of us, with Twinka serving the food. He asked if I knew any Asian women. I thought for a moment and said, "I know these girls at one of my favorite Japanese restaurants in Santa Monica."

He grinned out of one side of his mouth. "Can you invite them over here sometime?"

One of the girls had heard of Henry and said he was quite famous in Japan. I convinced them to stop by his place and say hello. I went over before they arrived and found Henry pacing back and forth with his walking cane in front of the living-room window in anticipation. The girls brought wonderful Japanese food and served Henry like a king. When they sat down, Henry asked them intimate sexual questions that he could somehow get away with. They answered honestly and in a surprisingly straightforward manner. I saw pure joy in his face as he studied the girls' every move.

Around ten, Henry said, "Well, I've got to go rest now." He smiled. "My beauty rest." I helped him upstairs, and on the way he called back down, "If you young ladies insist, you can join me up here."

We heard giggling coming from the girls.

"I think they like me, don'tcha know?" Henry said.

"Sure," I said. "But I don't think you could handle both of them."

He let out a coughing laugh. "Oh, don't bet on it." He lay down, closed his eyes, and drifted off with a slight smile on his face.

BACK AT THE RANCH—literally, since Shangri-La was still a ranch, in appearance, anyway—Larry Samuels was bringing on some new help. The most unusual hand we brought into the fold during this period was Rock Brynner, who became our road manager. He had quite an unusual background. Rock was the son of actor Yul Brynner and actress Virginia Gilmore and had grown up around the Hollywood set with the likes of Liza Minnelli. Then, later, he lived in London before coming to the conclusion that he was a full-blown alcoholic. He stopped drinking, pulled himself together, and subsequently worked as Muhammad Ali's bodyguard.

Rock was an intellectual and what some might consider mild-mannered, not your typical bodyguard type. I enjoyed having him around, because he was incredibly entertaining as well as helpful. Sometimes when he talked to his father on the phone he would put me on for a minute. Yul would ask me in a kind but concerned tone if Rock was doing a good job, maybe because of Rock's dark past. I didn't bother to mention that even though Rock was quite a character, he was still one of the sanest people in our crazy world.

As the days of wine and roses unfolded around us, cocaine became as common as candles. No matter where you turned, somebody was offering better-quality stuff than the next guy. Quaaludes were also all the rage. Doctors prescribed them and Percodan like they were health supplements. One doctor in Malibu would talk you into having an assortment of these meds on hand "just in case." No cautionary advice, only the occasional "Don't get carried away, now." All of this carrying on felt weird around our children, but it was a part of the culture that surrounded us. Sebastian was now going on two years of age, and Dominique no longer treated him like a baby. Our girls, with their friends in the Colony, had a routine of their own going. And with Jacques and Rosemary to help, everything seemed reasonably well covered.

For some people, pot made drinking unnecessary. For others, cocaine made alcohol more desirable to "take the edge off." I didn't drink much regardless, but as time went on, Dominique was finding more comfort from vodka. I flashed back to when we lived in Woodstock and she and our nanny, Nicole, had come home tipsy after drinking a vodka cocktail at the Bear restaurant. She'd thought it was such fun, and relaxing. Now it was progressing to a place of concern. But it's hard to be judgmental about anybody when you're no angel yourself, so you live and let live without recognizing danger up ahead.

IN '76, the Band was booked for a summer tour. One of the dates at the end of June was just up the way at the Santa Barbara County Bowl. It was an afternoon show and a little unusual to be playing in broad daylight. The day turned out to be an extreme scorcher—over one hundred degrees on the stage. Our roadies had to set up fans to keep the amplifiers from overheating, so you can imagine how we felt. After the first song I looked over at the guys, and we were all soaked with sweat. Well, maybe not Garth. He always claimed that he didn't perspire—ever. I'm not sure how, but we played really well while being cooked.

Sometimes extreme circumstances will do that to you. After the show, Dolly Parton came backstage to let us know she really enjoyed the concert. We looked like a bunch of drowned rats smoking cigarettes, so she didn't stay too long.

On this tour we struggled from job to job with Richard's drinking. Half the nights he didn't know if he could sing. By then he was no longer with his wife, Jane, and had taken up with an old girlfriend of Levon's, Cathy Smith, from Toronto. Cathy tried helping Richard keep it together, but she had her own battles with drugs, so this was a relationship with definite pitfalls.

Toward the end of the summer we were booked to play a festival at Steiner Ranch near Austin, Texas. The roads were blocked, and the only way in and out of the festival grounds for the acts was by boat. They had speedboats ripping up and down the river, carrying performers to and fro. The boat bringing us in was flying over the water when Richard decided he wanted to move up to the front. But as he stood up, we hit a wave and the boat pounded down hard and threw Richard backward, snapping his neck badly.

We found a doctor, who told us that Richard had fractured his neck. He could barely move without excruciating pain. We had several more dates booked on our tour and had no idea what we were going to do. Then Rock Brynner came up with a very strange suggestion. He said that when his father was on the road doing the musical *The King and I*, he had developed a serious health issue, and was treated by some Tibetan monks led by Norbu Chen, headquartered not far away in Arlington, Texas. As the story went, Norbu and his associates attended to astronauts who came back from outer space with mental issues. I wasn't exactly clear on how Norbu and his people helped the astronauts get grounded again, but Rock made what they had done for his father sound quite miraculous. It seemed like a long shot, but we were lost, and Richard was in extreme pain.

Rock made a call, and a few hours later Norbu and another monk showed up at the door of our hotel suite. I was expecting men in robes with shaved heads but these guys looked more like FBI agents. Dressed in dark suits with big, clunky shoes, they were direct, almost rude—as if they were on some kind of mission.

Richard was laid out on a flat table in the bedroom, squirming in discomfort. Norbu and his partner approached him on either side of the table. When we asked what they were going to do, they shooed us away like you would an annoying horsefly and closed the door to the bedroom.

"This is very odd," I said to Rock. "I'm concerned."

"It was the same thing with Yul," he replied.

I listened at the bedroom door. First I heard a quiet chanting, then two voices holding certain frequencies, with the tones rubbing against each other.

"This is some weird shit right here," said Rick.

After about an hour, Norbu opened the door. Both monks looked flushed as they rolled down their sleeves and put their jackets back on. Their facial expressions had completely changed from when they'd arrived—now they seemed pleasant and content, calm and respectful. Norbu explained that Richard should be okay to finish the tour, but because he was healing he should be careful not to cause any unnecessary stress to his neck area. In disbelief, I went to Richard, who looked somewhat reinvigorated. "What happened?" I asked. "Are you okay? They say you're going to be able to . . . How do you feel?"

Richard sat up and rubbed the back of his neck. "My neck feels okay," he said, "but I think my eardrums nearly exploded."

"What did they do?" I asked.

"First they both put their hands over me and moved them to different areas of my body. They hummed different notes like they were searching for a sound. Gradually, the humming got louder and louder until I could hardly take it anymore. My eyes started to water, so I closed them to help shield me from the sonic bombardment. Didn't you hear it out there? It was the loudest thing I've ever heard, by far. Finally it got quieter and softer and softer until they stopped. They took my head in their hands and moved it around and around and it didn't hurt. I told them they nearly burst my eardrums."

Norbu smiled. "That was just a tonal vibration. Very strong, but in no way harmful to your hearing."

I helped Richard to his feet carefully, and by the time we made it out to the living room, Norbu and his partner had left. Larry said he gave them a check for their institute and they went on their way. As the guys and I tried to digest what had just happened, we settled for thinking, *If Richard's going to get better, we'll take it.*

THE NEXT FEW days were tough. At a show in Mississippi I kept a keen eye on Richard. He wore a neck brace during the day but removed it when we played. At this point, I wasn't even that worried about his injury; it was the drugs and alcohol that were way out in front, and not just with Richard. We were all skating on thin ice in one way or another.

Even before Richard's accident I had started to contemplate the idea that we might need to get off the road before something really bad happened. One night I spoke to the guys about the possibility of bringing this phase of our journey to a conclusion, that we needed to look out for one another and get out of the line of fire for a while. At every concert we played, packs of destructive influences showed up like they were in the business of helping you drown. It made me paranoid.

Our rock 'n' roll lifestyle was passing the point of no return. The examples of Jimi Hendrix, Janis Joplin, Jim Morrison—and more recently Gram Parsons, Nick Drake, and Tim Buckley—brought home the dangers of the road. We'd heard this story about so many musicians, it was almost part of the ritual. All around us, bands we knew were imploding, trying to live what they thought was the rock 'n' roll high life. We saw them falling by the side of the road, but through a one-way mirror. We saw everything but ourselves.

Somewhere in the middle of this storm, even with my own shortcomings, I felt a hand tap me on the shoulder, reminding me to tread lightly and try to protect my brothers. I kept harping to Levon, to Richard and Rick, about finding some kind of sanctuary where we could stop riding so close to the edge.

At times we lamented, and other times we rejoiced. But somewhere along the way we had lost our unity and our passion to reach higher. Self-destructiveness had become the power that ruled us. How does that happen? Where did that demon come from? Were we too blind to see?

Levon had been my dearest friend in the world. My teacher. The closest thing I ever had to a brother. We had seen it all together and survived the world's madness, but not our own.

When Rick joined the Hawks, we didn't know if he would make the cut. He had talent and looked the part, but he turned out to be a force—a dependable rock who was there for you night and day. How does a spirit like that get broken?

I first met Richard face-to-face when we were seventeen years old. He had been drinking that night and was somewhere between pure joy and deep sadness. He still had that same yearning sound in his voice, which we loved. We always wanted to help Richard, but we didn't know how to help ourselves.

Garth was our in-house professor, and I felt the worst for him. All he wanted to do was make music, invent, and teach. He operated on his own wavelength and never bothered anybody—even, at one unfortunate point, when his house burned down.

I loved these guys beyond words, until it hurt inside. But this beast was wounded, and we were unsure of its recovery. The natural thing was to find a cave, a quiet place to heal, and then—hopefully—return with a vengeance. My instinct was to have a celebration of our music and then get out of the way, get out of the public eye. So I proposed that we go underground and let the dark clouds pass over. Nobody had the answer, but something inside of me said, *You boys gotta get off of this train.*

We'd been playing live and touring for fifteen or sixteen years, so it was a shocking proposition to remove that part of ourselves. But we couldn't keep going out there incapable of doing our best. On any given night, something or somebody would be broken. On some nights we could hit our stride, but more and more it was becoming a painful chore. The best painkiller, of course, is opiates, and heroin had been creeping back under the door for some time now. Larry Samuels talked about it openly and bragged that he had a great connection. I worried that Garth and I had three junkies in our group, plus our so-called manager. Finally I declared, "No more."

We had a meeting at Shangri-La and I suggested that we do a final concert at Winterland in San Francisco, where we had played our first show as the Band.

No one was opposed to the idea. Richard seemed relieved and said, "I need some time anyway, for my neck to heal properly."

"I think we could all use a good time-out for health reasons," Garth added.

Rick said, "I like the idea of doing a special concert to bring this period in our journey to a conclusion."

Levon knew we couldn't continue with our live shows in this state, and was convinced we had to do something. I hoped it would give us the opportunity to regroup and get back to a productive, inspired place.

It was still September, and I thought Thanksgiving would be an appropriate occasion for the show. We agreed that having Ronnie Hawkins and Bob Dylan join us would be a respectful thing to do: they had both played an enormous part in our musical journey, and we appreciated them tremendously.

When I called Bill Graham to discuss the idea of doing our last show where we had started, at Winterland, he was shocked to hear the news. But he agreed it was the proper venue for this momentous occasion, and that we needed to figure out a way to document the event.

Each day that passed, we couldn't help but think of other musical friends to invite. We wanted to make it a musical celebration, something that captured the essence of what we were about. We hoped to have not just artists who were close friends and influences but people who represented the many different musicalities we respected: Eric Clapton for the British blues, Dr. John for the sound of New Orleans, Joni Mitchell, the queen of women singer-songwriters, Muddy Waters as the king influencer of the Chicago blues, and harmonica master Paul Butterfield; then, representing the tradition of Tin Pan Alley,

Neil Diamond; the Belfast Cowboy, Ireland's greatest R&B voice, Van Morrison; Neil Young to represent our Canadian roots; and, of course, Ronnie Hawkins and Bob Dylan.

We went on a mission to track everyone down; Richard reached out to Clapton, Levon got in touch with the Hawk and Muddy, and Rick called Butterfield. I got in touch with Neil Young, Joni, Van, and Neil Diamond. Hearing the idea, they all seemed moved to be part of the show. I asked John Simon to be the musical director. He'd know just what to do all the way around: arrangements, signals, horn section— he had our backs covered. John was thrilled at the idea. I also called Albert and asked if he and Sally would like to come out for the event. The idea of gathering everybody who had played a special part in our past was just what the doctor ordered. Before long, it was becoming bigger than anything we had ever imagined

Filming this event and recording it could add up to a special project if we had the financial support to pull it off. I went for a meeting with Mo Ostin, the president of Warner Bros. Records. Mo had always had an interest in the Band since he wanted to sign us back in 1967. I told him our plan and that I hoped we could figure out a way for the concert soundtrack to be on Warner. The Band only owed Capitol one more record, which would come out before this soundtrack release. Plus, I told Mo, a lot of the guest performers for the show happened to be on his label. He said he was definitely interested in being a part of the project.

I knew we would need someone special to capture this event on film. I didn't want to go the typical "music documentary" route, so I started thinking about directors who had a special relationship with music. Hal Ashby had used music skillfully in some of his movies, like *Harold and Maude*. Same with George Lucas in *American Graffiti* and Francis Ford Coppola in *The Conversation*, and Miloš Forman was definitely a music guy. One name that stood out for me was Martin Scorsese, whom I had met briefly at a screening of *Mean Streets* that Jon Taplin had set up back in '73. His use of music in that film showed he had a powerful connection to it, as did the fact that he'd worked on the Woodstock movie and directed *Taxi Driver*, which featured the last score by the great Bernard Herrmann. I called Jon Taplin, who had produced *Mean Streets*, to see if he could set up a meeting between me and Martin Scorsese.

Jon made arrangements for us to gather a few days later at the Mandarin Restaurant in Beverly Hills. Marty had a dark Vandyke beard that made his eyes quite piercing. He came with his wife, Julia, and Liza Minnelli, who was starring with Robert De Niro in a musical Marty was shooting called *New York, New York*. I brought Dominique and her friend Geneviève Bujold. Jon Taplin introduced everybody. When I told Marty about the Band's final concert event and the artists we were hoping to include, I could see the wheels turning in his head. He made no secret that music played an enormous part in his life.

"We have one basic problem," Marty said. "When you're directing a movie for a studio, you're not allowed to go off and shoot another film at the same time."

I mentioned that we were going to do the concert over the Thanksgiving holiday, if that would be helpful at all. Everybody around the table was hoping there might be a way Marty could do it, but like he said, you can't do two movies at once.

After dinner we decided to stop by the after-hours lounge On the Rox for a nightcap. Lots of friends were there, and the place was hopping. Marty and I talked about Van Morrison's songs, and Joni's, and Muddy Waters, and Bob, until he finally said, "The hell with it. I gotta do it. These are my favorite artists, and the Band—oh my God. I have to do it, and that's it. Fire me. They can fire me. I have to do it."

Jon Taplin lit up like the Fourth of July, and I was over the moon. I had strong feelings about Marty being the right man for this—he had music under his skin. We wanted to have a toast, but Julia and Dominique were the only ones with drinks. A couple of friends in the club asked me if I wanted a "taste," a little cocaine, then somebody came over to shake my hand, palming a little bottle of coke.

Marty looked to be coming down with a cold. He seemed all stuffed up. "Do you think anybody would have any nose spray?" he asked me. "I can hardly breathe."

I took a chance. "A friend just slipped me some coke. That can sometimes clear up your nasal passages."

Without skipping a beat, he answered, "No. I've got that," showing me his own little bottle of coke. "I just need some Afrin or something."

The night ended with Marty asking me and Jon Taplin to come to his office in a couple of days so we could start figuring this out. He had to be discreet so that the studio wouldn't get wind of what he was up to. We had two months of whispering ahead of us before Thanksgiving to put this whole thing together.

WHEN I TOLD Bob about the final concert, he said, "Is this going to be one of those Frank Sinatra retirements where you come back a year later?"

"No," I told him. "The Band has to get off the road. It's become a danger zone, and we're afraid of what might happen." Bob knew from all the car wrecks back in Woodstock and from his time with us on the road that it could be a delicate balance inside the Band keeping things from steaming off the tracks.

I brought Mo Ostin up to speed on the development of the concert and the film, and he said he would put up the seed money for us to record and film the show. Warner would get the soundtrack, and he thought it would be good if we gave Warner Bros. Films the first shot at purchasing the movie and distributing it. It was great finally being in business with Mo, one of the most respected and well-liked executives in the industry.

My excitement in telling the guys about landing Martin Scorsese to make the film went slightly unheard—they didn't have the cinematic passion that I did, and that was okay. It was my responsibility to make this happen as best I could. Sitting up at night putting together pieces of the puzzle for Bill Graham's concert production, and for Marty's filming needs, became my calling. Rock Brynner and I would imagine all kinds of possibilities for our limited budget. One thing I needed to address was what to call this concert, this gathering. Rock and I threw all kinds of ideas against the wall, and the one that stuck was "The Last Waltz." It sounded old and, under these circumstances, new at the same time. It made me want to write a movie theme for the show in the tradition of some of the great Johann Strauss waltzes or "The Third Man Theme." I borrowed an old Gibson harp guitar to compose something in this vein. The instrument had the regular six-string setup and then about twenty other strings that, when tuned properly, vibrated and were sympathetic to certain notes played—a similar concept to some East Indian instruments.

Meanwhile I was hoping Richard's voice would hold up through our next shows at the Palladium in New York City with promoter Ron Delsener. Richard had taken to carrying a bottle of Grand Marnier or Drambuie around with him. He claimed it helped lubricate his throat. The Palladium had formerly been the Academy of Music, where we did the *Rock of Ages* recordings, and one of the shows at the Palladium was going to be broadcast live on the radio, so we needed to be in shape for it.

We were staying at what was then the St. Moritz Hotel on Central Park South and Sixth Avenue, and a time had been set up for Lorne Michaels, the producer of NBC's *Saturday Night Live*, to come by. I was looking forward to meeting him. He was also from Toronto, and his groundbreaking comedy show, now in its second season, was probably the hippest thing on television. When Lorne came up to my suite, I immediately thought he must be the coolest-looking TV producer around, handsome and well dressed, with a sharp sense of humor. We chatted for a few minutes about our Canadian backgrounds and then Lorne got down to business. He had heard that the Band was going into exile after our Thanksgiving show, and before that he wanted us to play *Saturday Night Live*.

"You can host the show, not host the show, play several songs, whatever you want to do," said Lorne. "We really want to make this happen."

I told him we wouldn't want to host the show; we weren't really that funny. He laughed. "Okay, how about this? We'll get a great host for the show and the Band can do four songs—nobody's ever done four songs. How's that sound?"

We shook on it. "I'll tell the guys. Let us know when you've got a date."

He didn't blink. "October thirtieth. The show before the presidential election. Let me go to work on getting the right host."

Everyone said the radio simulcast of our Palladium show that night sounded really good, but our next shows were hit-or-miss. I was looking forward to getting back to LA to feel the grounding of my family and work on the details for "The Last Waltz" concert.

My kids looked fantastic. Alexandra was getting taller and had the brightest smile around. Delphine had a magnificent coloring to her skin. You could see her native heritage when the light hit her just right. Sebastian, being raised on the beach in Malibu, was totally blond. He looked like a miniature beachcomber. Dominique looked thin and a bit tired, though, and I was worried about the way her relationship with alcohol was progressing. She didn't like discussing it and said it was no big deal—she was just having a good time.

Whenever he had a break, Marty would come out to Malibu with Julia and sometimes his assistant, Steven Prince (who played the guy who sells the gun to Travis Bickle in *Taxi Driver*), and we would go over ideas for the show. He said as soon as we chose which songs we would play, he'd need a copy of the lyrics to turn into a shooting script for camera moves and lighting cues. László Kovács was the director of photography on *New York, New York*, and Marty said he was going to ask him to be the DP on *The Last Waltz* too.

We had a meeting with László at Marty's office. He carried himself with a level of confidence that was undeniable. His credits spoke for themselves: *Five Easy Pieces*, *Paper Moon*, *Shampoo*, and many more. "If you're going to do this movie, don't shoot it in sixteen-millimeter, do it in thirty-five," he declared. "It will look so much better."

Marty immediately liked the idea. "Yes. If we can do this in thirty-five, it would look beautiful. It's never been done for a concert before. Can the cameras even shoot that long?"

"You won't know unless you try," said László. "But you have to do it in thirty-five, or it won't live up to these performers."

Marty agreed. "If the cameras melt, the hell with it. We'll know we gave it our best."

He suggested we ask the production designer Boris Leven, who was also working on *New York, New York*, to help us out. Boris was famous for being the man behind the designs of *West Side Story* and *Giant*, James Dean's last movie.

"What will Boris say when we tell him we have no money for sets or design?" I asked.

Marty laughed. "Well, I guess we'll find out."

If everything by the grace of God should come together and we actually ended up with a finished film, I would be credited as producer and Jon Taplin would be executive producer. Jon was coordinating between Bill Graham and Marty's assistant, Steve Prince. Bill was now insisting on serving a full Thanksgiving turkey dinner to the audience before the show. It was a grand gesture, and unique. "But that's hundreds of gallons of gravy!" I joked.

"Don't worry, I'll handle it," said Bill. "We'll have tables with white tablecloths and serve dinner for five thousand. Then the tables will magically disappear and the show will begin."

One day, I stopped into an art gallery in Santa Monica where a couple of collages by the French surrealist artist Georges Hugnet caught my eye. They were works from 1935. One of the images showed a man in a suit in front of a naked woman, with the same woman in a chair watching herself and the man; in the background, an older couple heads in their direction, with the man carrying the woman in his arms. Something about the piece said "Last Waltz" to me, so I purchased both Hugnet collages. I showed the one with the man and naked woman to Bob Cato and asked if he thought it could make an interesting *Last Waltz* poster. This was right up his alley. "Let me at it," he said.

Confiding in Art Linson, my movie producer friend, about the challenges of putting the whole event together became a regular routine. One evening he said, "Well, I can tell you one thing: it sounds unbelievably amazing. And I'm sure not going to miss it." I found some comfort and reassurance in his words, and got up for the next round.

LORNE MICHAELS INFORMED us that he had booked Buck Henry to host our episode of *Saturday Night Live*. I loved the idea—Buck was extraordinarily talented and a terrific guy. Lorne asked if the Band could come to New York for the whole week leading up to the show, that way his team would have the opportunity to come up with something special for our performance.

We showed up to the studio at Rockefeller Center on the Tuesday before the show, and the place was like a beehive—people running around, changing things up, proposing outlandish ideas. We met the cast, who were funny before they even said anything. The place had a wonderfully crazy, out-of-control feel to it, with Lorne somehow holding it all together. John Belushi and Dan Aykroyd were the most musically connected cast members, and throughout the week, while Dan was busy working on skits, John would hang out with us until somebody called his name. Lorne introduced us to Edie Baskin, who was responsible for the great photographs of the cast members and guests. If we were going to do four songs on the show, we needed to find a way to break it up with images. She wanted to do some montages with classic photos of the Band, especially Elliott Landy's shots.

We played through a few songs so they could figure out different possibilities for camera moves. Everybody on the show gathered around while we took a couple requests from Lorne and crew. I told them we weren't going to do "The Weight," to change things up, and that we wanted to try some tunes we could do with the *Saturday Night Live* band's horn section. We ran through "Life Is a Carnival" and it felt like a keeper.

Back at the hotel that night, John Belushi stopped by. I don't think John knew how to turn off his wit, quickness, his impersonations—it was truly mind-boggling. Then, suddenly, he went quiet and pulled me aside. "Who's got the blow?" he whispered. "I mean, you're musicians, right? The musicians always got the cocaine—is what I've been told. Please, don't burst my bubble. The musicians on our show aren't always dependable. Some do, some don't—you know what I mean?

But they're not legends like you guys. They're not in your league. So who's got the blow?"

"Rick said somebody's coming by soon with a delivery," I told him. "Thought he would have been here by now."

John smiled. "Where's Rick? I like him. I gotta talk to Rick."

About a half hour later the delivery still hadn't arrived, and John said he couldn't wait anymore. He asked me under his breath if I could loan him thirty-five bucks for a taxi and a snack. I gave him the money and he thanked me and took off.

Five minutes later, there was a knock on the door. It was Rick's deliveryman, and standing right behind him, smiling, was Belushi. They came in and the guy handed Rick a paper packet. Rick poured out a little bit of coke on the dresser and John said, "Come on, Rick, don't be shy," and Rick poured out a bunch more, laughing. John honked up half of it and said, "I'll keep the money you loaned me for the taxi, but I don't think I'll be needing a snack anymore."

Lorne decided we would do two songs back to back, and after a commercial we would do a third song. He suggested we could close the show with one more. Before we came to New York we had cut a version of "Georgia on My Mind" at Shangri-La that Richard sang beautifully. After the last few years of Richard Nixon's turmoil and then Gerald Ford, our old friend Governor Jimmy Carter felt like a refreshing choice for president, even from the point of view of Canadians like us. We decided to close the show with "Georgia" as a way of offering our best wishes to the governor for the election taking place in only three days.

On Saturday night, everybody was jacked for the live show. This was the third time Buck had hosted, and he looked cool and on his game. The Band were the only newcomers here, and we were definitely feeling some nerves. The energy in the air was explosive—one skit after the other, like clockwork, until John Belushi accidentally cut Buck Henry's head while playing a sword-wielding samurai. Everybody stopped breathing for a moment. After the skit they put a bandage on Buck's forehead. Lorne was not happy with this and Belushi felt terrible. Through the rest of the show, as a running gag, the entire cast wore bandages on their foreheads.

When Buck introduced the Band, he mentioned our upcoming final concert. I think the end of that show was unlike anything they've done since, with the upcoming election and the song "Georgia on my Mind," with the Band's live performances coming to a close, with it being Chevy Chase's last show, and with Buck and his bandaged head. What an experience. We were told later that people watched our performance in a sad and beautiful light. I tried to express my appreciation to Lorne and the gang, but the after party had a bit of a quieter feel to it: everyone knew Buck's injury could have been a lot worse.

We had sent a message to Jimmy Carter that we were doing "Georgia" for him on the show. He won the presidency that week and sent back a thank-you note. I asked him for a copy of the photo we had taken together in 1974 at the governor's mansion, posing in front of the painting of George Washington. To have a copy of that shot, with the now-president of the United States, arms stuck in our T-shirts like George in the painting—that would have been so great. But the response from his office was "No such photo exists." Just shows you shouldn't wait until somebody is president to ask for the funny picture you took with him.

WHEN I GOT back to LA, Marty told me László Kovács had decided it was too much work for him to be director of photography on both *New York, New York* and *The Last Waltz*. He said he would be happy to be one of the cameramen, though. Marty asked Michael Chapman, his DP on *Taxi Driver*, to take over *The Last Waltz*. Michael was in, but he was concerned that the thirty-five-millimeter Panavision cameras weren't designed to run continuously for hours. We'd have to figure out how to reload film and change batteries during the shoot, and because this hadn't been done before, he didn't know if the cameras would overheat. Everything was up in the air, but we had to go for it to find out whether this was a disaster in the making.

We started to set up rehearsals at Shangri-La with some of the guest artists, trying to run over a couple of songs with anybody on our list who might be in our part of the world. Joni Mitchell stopped by and we took on the challenge of figuring out some of her chord changes. We rehearsed very briefly the song Neil Diamond and I had written for *Beautiful Noise*. Neil Young decided he wanted to do a full-on Canadian connection with his song choices, so we ran over Ian & Sylvia's "Four Strong Winds" and his song "Helpless," with its references to our homeland. Van Morrison was in and out of town, and we decided to do his song "Caravan." I had an idea for another tune we could do with him, "Tura Lura Lural," an Irish lullaby. When I told him, he laughed and thought I was crazy. "Sure," he said, "and then we can go right into 'When Irish Eyes Are Smiling.'" So I picked up a guitar, we stepped into one of the bedrooms at Shangri-La, and I sang him a slow, gospel-feeling version of "Tura Lura" with some rare traditional lyrics. The song was in waltz time, something like Ray Charles's "Drown in My Own Tears," written by our friend Henry Glover (whom I then asked to do a horn arrangement for it). Van looked a touch watery-eyed when I finished my version of the song, but maybe he just had a bit of hay fever.

When Bob came by Shangri-La, he thought we should do a couple of tunes from *Planet Waves*, like "Hazel" and "Forever Young," or maybe one of the tracks we used to do when we first hooked up, like "Baby, Let Me Follow You Down" or "I Don't Believe You." We played through a few songs once and left it at that. Afterward we had a little coffee and a snack in the kitchen at Shangri-La, and Bob asked, "What's this filming business everybody's talking about for the concert?"

"We're trying to figure out how to document this event," I told him. "We started out with black-and-white video cameras, then a couple sixteen-millimeter cameras. Then four super-sixteen. Now we're talking about five or six thirty-five-millimeter cameras with Martin Scorsese directing. Nothing like this has ever been attempted before."

Bob stubbed out his cigarette in an ashtray full of butts and said he was already making a movie from the Rolling Thunder Revue tour and didn't know if he wanted to be in two movies. I wasn't surprised about his hesitancy. He was never one to commit.

I said, "Well, they're just going to film the show, and if you don't like your part, we won't use it. Although, how can we not have you be a part of the Band's story?"

Steve Prince called me and said, "László has invited his fellow Hungarian master DP, Vilmos Zsigmond, to be one of the cameramen. Michael Chapman and Marty have also secured Fred Schuler, Bobby Byrne, Michael Watkins, and David Myers—the best handheld guy."

Later that night, while I was writing a new song, a Cajun waltz called "Evangeline," the phone rang. It was Marty, speaking in a low voice: "Hey, Rob. Yeah, it's pretty crazy over here. You know, we're making a movie without a finished script. Anyway, I spoke to Boris Leven, my production designer, about *The Last Waltz*, and he said he'd help us out. That's good. He needs to take a look at Winterland, so he'll go up there and we'll see what he suggests."

I kept sending Marty lyrics of the songs I knew we were going to play so he could make his notes. The problem was that some of our guest artists wouldn't be rehearsing with us until we got to San Francisco a day or two before the show. With these folks we wouldn't know what we were going to play until we met up. But what could you do? Last-Minute Productions for *The Last Waltz*.

At the beginning of November, I took a quick trip up to San Francisco with Jon Taplin and some of our movie people to meet with Bill Graham and look over the venue. Winterland had been an old skating rink (hence the name) and was looking pretty funky these days. Bill was concerned about the appearance of the facade of the upper balcony and thought he would need five thousand dollars out of the budget to fix it. My head was in a whole other space with staging and logistical issues, so I coined the phrase, joking with Bill, "Fuck the facade!" He showed me how the tables for the Thanksgiving dinner would be set up and how they would ship in the food. He suggested having a waltz orchestra during the dinner, so people could get up and dance if they felt inclined. I said, "If we can afford it, I like that idea."

Bill smiled. "Done."

As they checked the place out, Michael Chapman and Steve Prince noted that the floor at Winterland had "give" to it. With the audience moving around and dancing, this would make the cameras unsteady. Jon Taplin knew this would be a major problem for Marty and asked Chapman what to do about the floor. He said, "It's going to take some construction, so I'll have to figure it out."

Bill said he hoped the cameras wouldn't obstruct the view of people in the audience. "We're making a movie here," said Steve. "That's our priority."

"The crowd is *my* priority," Bill answered. "After the artists, of course."

As we were leaving the building, Bill cornered me. "I want my crew, all the people working on this event, to be in tune with your vision. Is there a movie we should watch to inspire us for what you have in mind?"

I didn't know how to respond for a second. At first I thought maybe Michael Powell and Emeric Pressburger's *The Red Shoes*. Then I opted for Jean Cocteau's *The Blood of a Poet*. Bill shook my hand and thanked me as we left. I had no idea what his crew would get out of that extremely bizarre film, but it sounded good.

With ten days left to go Emmett Grogan got in touch, asking if he could put together a poetry reading by Lawrence Ferlinghetti, Michael McClure, and other San Francisco poets for the show, maybe during intermission. Then Marty found out that production on *New York, New York* was going to take a break the week of Thanksgiving—the producer was going to Europe and they needed to get some scenes rewritten. Phew! This was the opportunity we needed for Marty, Boris Leven, and Michael Chapman to go to Winterland and prep the shoot. But when they got there a few days later, Jon Taplin called me sounding concerned: Bill Graham was being very uncooperative. He was saying he didn't want cameras here and didn't want cable running there. Marty got on the phone and was adamant. "We have to secure the setups for the three cameras on the floor, or they'll be shaking all over the place."

I asked, "How do you secure the cameras so they won't move around on that cushiony floor?"

"We're going to have to drill through the floor," he said, "cut it open and send down stabilizing poles to the solid ground."

"You're going to have to call Bill," Jon told me. "I've tried to talk to him, but he's being very tough and won't listen."

I called Bill immediately and told him, in no uncertain terms, that if he didn't agree to everything Marty Scorsese wanted for his filming, I'd pull the plug. "I will cancel this whole event, here and now."

Bill started to explain about the film blocking the view of the fans, and I said, "Bill, stop. Do I have your word on your complete and full cooperation? That you will not interfere in any way with this film production?"

"Mr. Robertson," he said, "you have my word and my complete cooperation. In fact, I've even paid for the 'fucking facade' out of my own pocket." I laughed and thanked him.

I had asked Marty at one of our earlier meetings if we could not have those red and green and blue lights you saw in every rock-concert documentary. "Could we do something much more theatrical with backlighting and amber footlights and spotlights, like in MGM musicals?" I needn't have mentioned it. Marty was already on that page.

Boris Leven, our production designer, was a special man with a special talent. He thought of brilliant design ideas for *The Last Waltz*, but most of them our modest budget couldn't afford. Then he stopped and said, "San Francisco. What do they have here? Of course! The San Francisco Opera." He got access to their storage facility and came upon the set for Verdi's *La Traviata*, and some elegant chandeliers. "This is what we need," he said. Marty thought this completely original for a rock concert, especially one called *The Last Waltz*. They made arrangements for the set to be shipped in while they built a backlight cyc behind the set for different effects and moods. Michael Chapman and Marty were going over the lyrics and shooting script, imagining lights and shadows. They argued about whether my song "The Weight" was Protestant or Catholic, and I couldn't dispute either one of their colorful visions. But I didn't want to confuse things by reminding them of my Jewish and Native heritage.

I talked with Levon, Garth, Richard, and Rick individually about this abstract experiment we were embarking on. Each of the guys, in his own way, expressed to me how he emotionally embraced this finality, this new beginning. We needed to close one door to open another—to die, to be reborn. None of us truly understood where we were headed, but we knew change was inevitable.

When Levon and I got together for a one-on-one, he said in a quiet, brotherly tone, "I know you can't take going out there on the road and us not being on our game, and Lord, neither can I. Maybe if we can have one last stand, it will give us a good look at tomorrow. I'm ready to give it my best shot, so you can damn well count on me."

Between rehearsals at Shangri-La, Rick pulled me into a side room and urged, "Let's get the boys together and size up whether we're ready to come out full force for this Last Waltz."

When we did, Garth said, "This is an opportunity to do what no band I can think of has ever done before. I think we should give it all we've got."

Richard swore to us, "I will not let you down." I looked at Rich with every hope and belief that he would sure as hell stand by his word. Thanks to Rick, this meeting made me feel almost bulletproof, like we could go out there and take on the fucking world.

So we got on an airplane to San Francisco and never looked back.

TWENTY-SEVEN

At the beginning of the week of Thanksgiving, we checked in to the Miyako Hotel in San Francisco. My suite had a Japanese bath in the middle of the living room, but the first thing my eyes searched for was a corner where I could continue writing. There were two songs I hoped to finish in time for the concert—"Evangeline" and "The Last Waltz Theme." I put my guitar by a desk and chair, as far away from the entrance to the room as I could. Playing music—writing—can be a self-conscious feeling in hotel rooms. Am I going to bother anyone? Is anyone going to bother me? Am I going to be too loud? Even more so in this Japanese-themed environment, where some of the areas were separated by what looked like rice-paper sliding doors.

I had purchased a classic original sunburst Stratocaster with no tremolo bar, so that it would stay in tune better. For this occasion, I decided to have my red '59 Strat dipped in bronze like baby shoes. I hadn't taken into account how much heavier it would make the guitar, but it looked and sounded phenomenal.

Our first order of business in San Francisco was to set up a rehearsal schedule with all the guest artists as they got to town. When possible, we would run over songs on the stage at Winterland, but ongoing work on the set, the cyc, the tracks for the cameras, and all the lights often made that impossible. As a backup plan, we had the banquet rooms at two hotels blocked out, with spare equipment floating back and forth.

Larry Samuels, Rock Brynner, and I went to the hall early to see how Marty and the crew were making out. It looked like they were building a city inside this old, weathered skating facility, sawing, hammering, and cutting away, with Bill Graham going with the flow to the best of his ability. Boris Leven showed me where the chandeliers above the stage would go, and mentioned offhandedly that these particular ones had been used in the movie *Gone with the Wind*. I had been a little unsure about the concept of chandeliers, but that fact seemed to make them perfectly appropriate.

Marty was in high spirits seeing this monster come together. You would never believe that in this run-down neighborhood where Winterland was located, they were building one of the most elegant sets ever seen in rock 'n' roll. "They might as well burn this place to the ground when we're done here," Steve Prince remarked. "And there's a possibility we might take care of that for them, because the electric current in this place can't handle all the lighting that's going up."

Michael Chapman nodded. "They're bringing in backup generators."

Rock looked at me, shaking his head as if to say, *This is a disaster waiting to happen*. Jon Taplin was so overwhelmed dealing with the needs of the production that he didn't have time to consider looming catastrophes.

Bill Graham showed me where and how the white-clothed dining tables would be set up. It would look like Rock 'n' Roll's Last Supper. Michael Chapman and Marty were having the carpenters build a big scaffold toward the back of the hall for Vilmos Zsigmond's Panavision camera, which would be filming the master shot of the stage.

When we checked out the backstage and dressing rooms, Bill was anxious to show me what they had put together from the inspiration they'd gleaned from *The Blood of a Poet*. He had the biggest grin on his face as he escorted me into one of the rooms. The walls were covered with plastic noses. A tape played sniffing sounds in the background, and a table in the middle of the room was covered with glass mirrors, razor blades, straws, and other coke-related paraphernalia. He was delighted with his take on Jean Cocteau's surrealism. I found it a bit *too* "on the nose" and embarrassing, but I acted like he had really come away with a vision.

Our rehearsal schedule looked intense and nearly impossible to pull off. All we could do was put our heads down and charge forward. The guys and I congregated in the banquet room of the hotel with Muddy Waters; his piano man, Pinetop Perkins; and guitarist Bob Margolin. Trying to choose what songs to do with Muddy was like visiting a musical candy store. We ran over "Got My Mojo Workin'" and my old fave, "Forty Days and Forty Nights." Soon as we kicked into "Mannish Boy," though, we set the room on fire. It felt like a powder keg getting ready to blow. Levon and Muddy had done some recording together up at Levon's place in Woodstock, where they cut a version of Louis Jordan's old classic "Caldonia." Muddy wanted to do that one, which featured a special vocal interplay between him and Pinetop.

Van Morrison came directly to the hall in San Francisco. We needed to learn his song "Caravan" and run it down with the horn section. John Simon helped us get the arrangement straight by figuring out hand signals to alert us to which sections of the song were coming up next. When we played "Tura Lura Lural," we heard Henry Glover's horn chart for the first time. It needed some adjustments but sounded very soulful. Van was wearing a beige trench coat, like a private eye would wear in a 1940s movie with Robert Mitchum or Humphrey Bogart. I had never seen a rock 'n' roll singer dress like a private eye before and told Van it was a great look. "Really?" He smiled, considering whether he should wear it for the show.

For our full-on Canadian sequence with Neil Young and Joni Mitchell, we started by trying "Acadian Driftwood" with them joining in on the choruses. Then, when Neil sang "Helpless," Joni did a high background vocal that sent shivers through the hall. In the show Joni wasn't going to perform until after Neil, and I didn't want to give away her appearance before that. I asked Marty if we could film Joni from behind the curtain while she sang her part on "Helpless." "Definitely," he said. "We'll have a handheld camera back there."

With Bob, we ripped through three or four songs without hesitation, not a medley, though everything was interconnected. He wanted to do a combination of material from our early days together and *Planet Waves*. I pushed for us to do "Forever Young" and he was completely up for it. We even joked about doing the *Basement Tapes* song "Tiny Montgomery," which went, "You can tell everybody down in ol' Frisco, tell 'em Tiny Montgomery says hello."

We still felt a deep kinship with our old ringmaster, Ronnie Hawkins. We hadn't seen Ron in a while, but he showed up looking spry in his new official uniform: black suit, white straw cowboy hat, red neck scarf, and a black T-shirt with a picture of a hawk on it. Ron hadn't lost a beat with his famous southern expressions. As a young female crew member passed by, he called out, "Hey, you sweet thing, I ain't as good as I once was, but I'm as good once as I ever was."

By the time we got to run over a tune with him, though, he was getting cold feet. With all these big-name performers, he worried he wasn't going to fit in, and he didn't want to embarrass himself. We immediately waved off his uncertainty and told him he was the first one we'd invited to this event; as far as we were concerned, he deserved to be here as much as anybody. He hemmed and hawed, but we wouldn't hear it. The Hawk was our beginning, and if we were going to throw a last waltz, he was going to have a dance.

I HADN'T FOUND time to think about what to wear for the concert, so the day before the show I asked if any of the guys wanted to go clothes shopping. Richard and Rick joined me and we hit a couple of vintage shops. Richard found a loud checkered suit for the occasion, something you might see W. C. Fields wear to a wedding. Rick picked out a vest that fit him to a T. A sharp-looking scarf caught my eye, as well as a George Raft–ish dark suit jacket with a thin pinstripe. Levon said he was just going to wear something that "breathes." It would be getting hot under all those lights, and it was going to be a long night. Garth said he was going to wear a suit because, if you remember, he didn't sweat—ever.

When we got to the hall, the whole set from *La Traviata* was now assembled and looked incredible. It stood big, bold, and beautiful, with a dark red tone to it. Lit from the front and the back, the set could look regal, gothic, theatrical, or invisible, depending on the light from the cyc screen.

Our sound guys had been working furiously in the recording truck parked outside the hall, trying to figure out how to mic this whole extravaganza. Sure, they could get it on tape, but when you turned everything on, would it sound like a big cluttered mess? Recording engineer Elliot Mazer was leading the charge, and Ed Anderson, our sound mixer on the road and head engineer at Shangri-La, was invaluable because he knew our music so well. Other engineers, like Neil Brody and Tim Kramer, also helped organize the live recording. All this had to sync up with the film, so there were many elements to account for and it took a small army. They didn't have the opportunity to get cues and levels on everybody's performance because we were rehearsing in different locations. There was so much left to chance, but you've got to play the hand that's dealt you.

We ran over Bobby "Blue" Bland's song "Further On Up the Road" with Eric Clapton. He also wanted to do one of the songs he had recorded at Shangri-La with Rick and Richard. Every chance I got I would break away for a few minutes to finish writing "The Last Waltz Theme" and "Evangeline." The problem was that with all the work prepping the event and rehearsing with the guests, I didn't have time to properly teach the songs to the other guys.

Still, we were making progress on other fronts. Our horn section was sounding better with each rehearsal. Some of these guys we had played with before, like Tom Malone and Howard Johnson; they were so good, we brought them in from New York. We were also familiar with Jerry Hey and Jim Gordon, Rich Cooper, and Charlie Keagle, because they had played with so many artists we knew. As a sound experiment, we even added Larry Packer on electric violin. John Simon was helping tremendously in bringing together the horn section's arrangements. We were using some of Allen Toussaint's charts, along with Tom Malone's, Howard Johnson's, and Henry Glover's. Our players would have to double on many woods, reeds, and brass.

As I kept handing over song lyrics to Marty, I observed his method of turning each song's words into a shooting script. Besides pointing out specifics in the arrangement of each song and noting particular lyrics, he wrote out camera moves and lighting changes. He had a multitude of little boxes in the margins beside each verse and chorus, filled with drawings of directorial instructions. It looked masterful and precise. He went over this two-hundred-page script meticulously with Michael Chapman, and for the actual show he would call out these instructions over headsets to all the cameramen and lighting people. This wasn't the usual way, where the camera operators wing it and see if it cuts together later. This was serious direction, focused on capturing these performances with control, even if everything was "take one."

The big question, still way up in the air, was, "Will these thirty-five-millimeter cameras endure constant shooting for many hours?" No one knew. We called Panavision and the various camera companies, but no one could guarantee anything because this had never been done before. Marty knew that we couldn't shoot every song because they had to reload film and change batteries. Those breaks might save the cameras from burning out, but it also meant we had to make some choices. We went over the song list for the whole show and decided what we would shoot and when they could reload. Some of the decisions to not film certain songs were painful, but we had to be tough-minded and realistic.

While going over these song lists, it also weighed heavy on me whether or not the guys and I would be able to remember the arrangements for all our guests' songs. With our limited rehearsal time, this was an overwhelming challenge. "That's like twenty new songs to remember, with nothing written out," I said to Marty. "Holy shit! All you can do now is pray."

"Oh yeah, there'll be a lot of praying." He smiled.

AS WE GOT closer to the day, friends and family started arriving in San Francisco. Uncle Natie's kids—my cousins David and Vicki Klegerman—came in from Toronto. When Dominique and my mother arrived, Ronnie called out, "Mama Kosh, is that you, darling? So galled-darn good to see you!" as he gave her a big bear hug. "Have you been taking those pretty pills again? I swear you get better-looking all the time." She couldn't have smiled any wider as the boys and I looked on like proud children.

Day for night, soon we didn't know the difference. Our crew was on duty around the clock leading up to the show. Larry Samuels wore so many hats, he could have been his own parade. When there was something wrong or something that you needed, you called Larry. Some of this could be absorbed by Sandy Castle, a steady hand from Malibu who was part of Neil Young's crew, but he was more of a good-will ambassador than a troubleshooter. In walking this tightrope, we depended so much on the capabilities of Jerry Caskey and Cliff Crumpler, two of our equipment wranglers. They made sure our instruments worked. Easy to take this kind of thing for granted, but these guys put the bullets in the gun.

Finally, morning arrived on Thanksgiving, our D-day. As everything teetered on the edge, Rock Brynner felt the pressure. I could see the worry written all over his face and hunched shoulders. He began pointing out in detail the many things that could go haywire. In that moment I was incapable of listening to words of failure; my obligation was to turn my back on adversity and negativity. Maybe it was blind faith and a certain amount of denial on my part, but I had to be a stone believer—so much of this whole odyssey was my doing. I couldn't get weak at the knees at a time like this, and I had to send Rock on his way until I got to the other side.

The guys and I finally snuck in a quick run-through of "Evangeline" and "The Last Waltz Theme," but it was easy to see our dance card was full. Trying to absorb any additional arrangements, lyrics, or chord changes felt numbing. "We'll see if we feel brave enough during the concert to give these a whirl," I said, while thinking, *But no more demands, no more pressure, if you please.*

A SHORT NAP, thirty minutes, that's all I asked. I couldn't remember if I had slept since we had gotten to San Francisco. I lay down as soon as

I got to the hotel, but I couldn't sleep—not even close. In two hours they would start serving Thanksgiving dinner, and the Berkeley Promenade Orchestra would begin its set of classic waltzes. I wished I had the ability to close my eyes and fall deep asleep for a power nap. Instead, I felt strangely empty inside. Despite all the hubbub and the clamoring of people all around, I felt very much alone. How was this possible? Why was I drifting into a dark place now? I sat up, unsteady and disoriented.

Then I sensed a feeling running through my bones: pure exhaustion. Drained from pushing forward with the help of drugs in place of food and sleep. But man, oh, man, this was not the time to be having a revelation about not getting proper rest and nutrition. I threw myself into the shower and turned it on cold, telling myself, *You gotta pull it together. You've got to rise to the occasion.*

When I got out of the shower, Dominique had come back to the suite. She ordered me some soup, and I tried on some of the clothes I'd bought. With a little food in my stomach and Dominique helping me get my style on, I could feel the blood start to flow again. Then the phone rang—it was almost time to go. I gathered my change of clothes and Dominique said, "Wait a second, you look so pale." She took a brush out of her purse and said, "Close your eyes." She swished the brush over my cheeks and a bit around my face. "There, that's better."

WHEN WE GOT to the stage door at Winterland, Barry Imhoff was standing there with a mile-wide grin. "This is so amazing. Wait till you see." We entered, and Bill Graham came dashing by in a white tuxedo and top hat. He had most of the staff in formalwear as well. After we got settled in our dressing rooms, Bill came in and said, "Let me show you something." He took Rick and me up a back way to the balcony. From there we looked down on the Berkeley Orchestra and hundreds—no, thousands—of people having Thanksgiving dinner. Some couples were waltzing on the open dance floor.

It was spectacular, and Bill couldn't have looked more proud of himself. He rattled off, "Four thousand pounds of turkey, two hundred of them! Three hundred pounds of Nova Scotia salmon, a thousand pounds of potatoes, hundreds of gallons of gravy, and four hundred pounds of pumpkin pie." It sounded like some kind of a world record. On the way back to the dressing area, we stopped into the Cocteau room to see if anybody was putting it to good use. Albert and Sally Grossman were in there with Emmett Grogan and Dominique, all of them laughing at the spectacle. "When the musical guests arrive," said Larry Samuels, "it will be interesting to note who hangs out in here the most."

I saw Marty backstage. He looked anxious but ready. We discussed the spectacular dinner going on, and the dancing. He said there was a sixteen-millimeter camera covering the waltzing, just in case.

In the dressing room, I got in a huddle with the other guys in the Band to get a pulse on how everybody was feeling. Our spirits were soaring, but a focused calmness was most apparent among us. Richard held out his hand to show he wasn't shaking too bad. When his hands trembled a lot, it meant he needed a drink. He nodded. "Looking pretty good on my end." Rick seemed genuinely pumped. He asked me what key a couple of the guests' songs were in, to refresh his memory, but otherwise he was ready and raring. We had certain moves to signal one another, and Levon reminded me to look over at him for certain breaks or endings. Some technical issues were on Garth's mind, and he went through them with one of our road crew; otherwise he appeared quite unfazed by the whole event, but thrilled at the same time.

Marty stood by the side of the stage with a headset on, communicating with all the lighting guys and cameramen. Jon Taplin and Steve Prince were there beside him to help in any way necessary. I was extremely caught up in running all the details of the guest artists' songs through my head, and had to remember that the audience had no idea who was performing tonight besides the Band. Word had crept out that we might have a guest or two, but nothing concrete. How should I properly introduce everyone? Just then Bill Graham came over to us in the wings and said, "Gentlemen, are we ready?" We gave a thumbs-up and took the stage in complete darkness.

When the cameras were rolling and we were in position, I signaled Levon, and he said over his mic through the darkness, "Good evening." The crowd erupted, and we kicked into the guitar intro for "Up on Cripple Creek." When the lights came up, Boris Leven and Marty's brilliant staging looked stupendous. The lighting was warm, natural and cinematic, nothing like a regular rock show. The sound on the stage felt powerful and clear. Levon was knockin' on wood—his drums were punching right through Garth's electric jew's harp sound and my rumbling guitar tone. We were all adjusting to the altitude and finding our footing. I looked over at Rick and Richard, and they were both in the zone. Levon's vocal was strong and authentic, and he did the yodel section at the end of the song with a grit I'd never heard before. Okay. This was it. I let go of the rope and never looked down.

Richard turned to his clavichord and adjusted the vibrato, and we tore through "The Shape I'm In," with Rich in his scotch-plaid suit singing, "Out of nine lives, I've spent seven." Garth played some wild riffs in the solos, and Richard sang with real power—only a bit shaky in a couple of spots, nothing to sweat about. Now we were locked in. Soon as Rick's voice came in on "It Makes No Difference," you knew he was weaving a spell. Following his vocal with guitar harmonics, I saw that he was looking as good as he sounded. That was the first moment I thought about the filming and I hoped that they were capturing the emotion he was sending out. I glanced over at Marty in the wings, and he was in a flurry, talking into his headset and waving pages of the script. I ripped into the solo at the end of the song, with Garth stepping into the spotlight to join me on soprano sax. We ended the tune looking at one another like: *Put that in your pipe and smoke it.*

By the time we got to "Ophelia," the horn section was warmed up and pouring it on. Levon could hardly sing for smiling, the way Garth's horn chart allowed them to go off script and dance around his vocals and my solos. John Simon was the only one smiling more.

Right from the horns' new free-time intro reminiscent of "I Wish

I Was in Dixie," I felt we were ready to take flight. I don't know if I'd ever heard Levon sing and play "The Night They Drove Old Dixie Down" better than on this night. Looking back at him while he was singing a verse, I saw the horns behind him looking like some kind of glorious funeral procession. His truth in that vocal could tear your heart out, and when we hit the final chorus the roar of the crowd felt like it helped us lift the stage a foot higher. It took me back to when I first wrote the song, wanting to come up with something that Levon could sing better than anyone in the world.

As we ended "Dixie," I could see the camera crews scrambling like a pit crew to reload, racing to beat the time before we would kick off the next song. Garth's intro to "Stage Fright" swung like mad, floating over the audience like a wave of invisible birds. Marty had full-on film noir lighting glowing on Rick when he stepped to the mic and started to sing with all the passion of the song's protagonist. His shadow stretched across the piano, and when the amber footlights came up they cast a glow that could give you chills. When the spotlight hit Garth for his solo, I looked back with amazement and realized he was playing the whole solo with his left hand, which I'd never seen him do before.

We played for about an hour and headed off to take a little intermission while the San Francisco poets took over. Emmett Grogan had brought together Lawrence Ferlinghetti, Michael McClure, "Free-wheelin'" Frank Reynolds, and "Sweet William" Fritsch of the Hells Angels, along with Diane di Prima, Robert Duncan, Dave Furano, Steve Gagné, and Lenore Kandel. During the break, I went back to finish writing the bridge in "The Last Waltz Theme" and went over the words for "Evangeline" on cue cards with the guys. We were going to play these songs when we went on again, for better or worse.

I didn't see any of the poetry during the intermission, but somebody told me that Michael McClure recited the introduction to *The Canterbury Tales* in the original Chaucerian English, and then Ferlinghetti did his own interpretation of "The Lord's Prayer." *Wicked,* I thought. *That'll certainly help people digest their turkey dinner.* Our friends and guests gathered backstage, and everybody looked to be in great spirits, thrilled to be here. Ronnie Wood from the Rolling Stones and Ringo Starr were in the dressing room, and I had to stop and think for a moment if we were scheduled to do a song with either of them. It was a sign that I had a little too much going on. I asked them to come out and join us for the finale. Bill Graham informed us that Governor Jerry Brown had been spotted in the audience.

When we went back on to kick off the sets with our guest artists, naturally our first performer had to be our original fearless leader, "the Hawk," Rompin' Ronnie Hawkins. He cast off his nervousness from the rehearsal and took the stage in blazing form, yelling toward Bill Graham, "Big time, Bill. Big time!" We played "Who Do You Love," Bo Diddley's song that we had covered years earlier. I whipped out some of my old Hawks-style guitar playing, and Ronnie growled like a mad dog. In the middle of one of my solos, he took off his hat and fanned my fingers like the guitar was going to catch fire, just as he had done back when I was seventeen.

Next I introduced our old friend Mac Rebennack, otherwise known as Dr. John, the Night Tripper. He was dressed to the nines for the occasion, with a pink bow tie, a frilly shirt, a black jacket with pink flecks, dark shades, and a French beret. He sat down at the piano and said, "Thankfulness to the Band and all the fellas," looking over at the horn section. He sang and played his song "Such a Night" with pure New Orleans gumbo ya-ya, like it was the theme of the evening. The whole vibe on the stage and in the house rejoiced. Our buddy Bobby Charles came out next to pay further tribute to the music of Louisiana, and Dr. John picked up a guitar to join in. Bobby and I had written some additional words to an old Jonnie & Jack bluegrass song called "Down South in New Orleans": "I'm gonna get too loose on Toulouse Street, and kiss all the pretty girls I meet." We gave it a funky rumba treatment—our own special inside joke.

We called out Paul Butterfield to join us on Little Junior Parker's song "Mystery Train," which we had recorded for *Moondog Matinee*. Richard joined Levon on our second set of drums. As we kicked into the rhythm of the song, the stage lights died. At first I thought it was a special effect for the filming, but then I realized there was a problem:

The film crew had blown a circuit and knocked out all the lights except for one spot coming from the back of the house. It looked noirish—and almost on purpose. Butterfield had choked out that train rhythm on his harmonica and blown all the lights out.

When Muddy Waters performed "Mannish Boy," Butterfield held a note through the whole song. He used circular breathing, and you couldn't hear him ever take a breath. I had never seen or heard that before. Muddy took control of the stage like a master, and hammered out, "I'm a full-grown man," right between your eyes. When he sang the line "I'm a rolling stone," you believed every word.

When I glanced over at Marty, he was yelling and waving to get the cameras rolling. Later we learned that there was confusion over the song list, and that they were reloading instead of filming during "Mannish Boy." But fortunately László Kovács had taken off his headset because he couldn't take all of the hollering and he never got the message to reload. He kept shooting and did a slow continuous move-in on Muddy's incredible performance. The gods were on our side.

I was slightly dizzy after Muddy Waters's performance. It took me a moment to gather myself as I stepped to the mic and said . . .

"Play guitar? Eric Clapton."

I had been concerned about how everybody was holding up backstage, waiting for their turn to go on. But Eric slid effortlessly into the beginning of "Further On Up the Road," like he'd just walked in the door. As he was starting to turn up the heat on his Strat, the strap suddenly came off, and his guitar fell into the grip of his left hand. In a split second, I had him covered and took over the solo. I turned up the heat too and stoked the fire for Eric while he shifted into second gear. He came in singing, and this shuffle took flight. He played another solo—and I played another solo. It was like raising the stakes in poker, higher and higher. I flashed back to my guitar slinger showdowns with Roy Buchanan. Finally Eric couldn't hold back anymore, and wailed off into the cosmos like only he can. Touché.

As soon as Neil Young took the stage, I could tell no one at Winterland was feeling better than he was. He made a profoundly touching statement about how proud he was to be onstage with us that night, before we steamed into "Helpless." Right away, his harmonica set the mood and was magnificent. Neil's vocal was so moving on this beautiful Canadian song of remembrance. When Joni Mitchell's high falsetto voice came soaring in from the heavens, I looked up, and I saw people in the audience looking up too, wondering where it was coming from.

Then, when Joni came out and the lights hit her, she seemed to glow in the dark. She was wearing a beautiful Native American necklace, and I was slightly surprised when she walked over and kissed me. She looked thoroughly enchanting as she sang her song "Coyote," and it sounded sexier than ever. Joni's songs might have been the most challenging of the night, with their syncopation and chord structures that kept you on your toes, but we sailed through that one like a cool breeze.

I had to smile when Neil Diamond joined us onstage. In his blue suit and red shirt, he looked like he could have been a member of the Gambino family. The first thing he said was "I'm only going to sing one song, but I'm going to sing it good." I thought it was brave of Neil to not sing one of his well-known hit songs. Instead he chose "Dry Your Eyes," the tune he and I had written together—a cool album track that not too many people were familiar with, although Frank Sinatra did cover it. We started out in a slow march, and it built beautifully. He turned the words into a prayer, like a sermon out of *Elmer Gantry*. Toward the end of the song I heard myself yelling, "Yeah!" Neil was absolutely right when he said he was "going to sing it good."

Then the lights came down, and John Simon sat at the piano. Richard picked up the microphone, and we rolled into the refrain of "Tura Lura Lural." Henry Glover's horn arrangement flowed like a gospel lament, and Richard's voice, of course, simmered on heartbreak. An empty spotlight shone down on the middle of the stage, and just in time for the beginning of the verse, Van Morrison walked into it. This was the way I wanted to introduce him, to not say his name—let the crowd do that. I could see Van had abandoned the idea of wearing his private-eye overcoat. Instead he had chosen a snug-fitting maroon outfit with sequins—something like a trapeze artist might wear. He looked ready for action, but I didn't know yet what he had in mind.

John Simon moved back to his position in front of the horn section, where he could give them direction and give us hand signals. Just a short intro, and then—bam—we slammed into "Caravan." That voice, this tune—we were on an immediate high. With his barrel chest stuck out like Caruso, the veins in Van's neck bulged as he poured on the steam. Hills and valleys, we would build it up and then come back down—the dynamics were like a roller-coaster ride. "Switch on your electric light," he sang, and Levon went "clink" on his cowbell in the nick of time.

In the middle of the song, after Van sang, "So you know it's got soul," I played him some soulful runs. "Yeeeah," he said as he eyed my fingers. We brought it down, quieter and quieter. I glanced over at John Simon, who had his hand in the air like Leonard Bernstein, ready to give the downbeat as we quietly treaded water. Then Van screamed, "TURN IT UP NOW," and we hit ten on the scale. The place went berserk as Van sang out, "Turn up your raa-dio!" He moved across the stage and each time he let out a "turn it up," he kicked his leg in the air or threw his arms over his head. We built and built, and Van kept kicking and pounding his fist in the air until there was nothing left. Finally he dropped the mic to the floor and walked off, still hitting the accents with his hand above his head. Now I understood why he was dressed like an acrobat. He could have never done those kicks in regular clothes. The Flying Kandinsky Brothers would have been proud—but not as proud as me.

RIGHT AFTER WE ended "Acadian Driftwood," with Neil Young and Joni joining us to make six Canucks onstage pining about our country's history, Garth started making amazing sounds. He jabbed from every direction on his keyboards, with monks chanting in the background and possibly a cow mooing. The rest of us left the stage so as to, in the words of the Hawk, "make room for the Phantom of the Opera."

Garth's hair flew above his keyboard like Tchaikovsky on psychedel-
ics. Again we were all reminded that nobody could do what our key-
boardist could.

While we were standing over in the wings, I asked Marty how the
filming was going. "We've had some problems," he said, "but the cameras haven't died yet, so that's a good sign." He smiled through the
lines of concern on his face as the rest of the guys and I headed back
out to launch into the intro of "Chest Fever."

We were feeling loose and riding high, which gave us the confidence to take a shot at playing my new songs, "Evangeline" and "The
Last Waltz Theme." We got through them by a hair's breadth, but I
knew these songs would have a better day to come. By then the show
had been going on for close to four hours, so you'd think the audience
would have been getting a little tired and weak at the knees. But when
I played the introduction to "The Weight," the crowd let out a roar like
they had just arrived. I looked around the stage and none of us seemed
to be fading either. Adrenaline is an amazing drug.

The crowd was still whistling and cheering as I stepped to the mic
and said, "We'd like to bring on one more very good friend of ours."
Bob Dylan walked out and the energy in the air turned electric.

Onstage, we were still figuring out the order of the songs we were
going to do. It was after one in the morning, but Bob still had a bolt of
energy. He looked somewhat like he had when we first hooked up back
in 1965; his red and white polka-dot shirt and black leather jacket were
certainly reminiscent. Under his white fedora he looked almost biblical. We hit "Baby Let Me Follow You Down" like we hadn't missed a
beat since our first tour together. It felt as natural as waking up in the
morning. With Bob, we shifted into a different zone. Our past came
back and we charged forward.

Next we eased into "Hazel," one of the songs Bob wanted to do
from *Planet Waves*. No one in the crowd saw that coming, and the
looks on their faces were almost comical. From where I stood, I could
see that the cameras weren't shooting. Perhaps it was time to reload, I
thought, or maybe the cameras had finally given out.

Then, back to one of our old standbys, "I Don't Believe You." I al-

ways liked playing that guitar riff behind Bob's vocal on this song. Tonight I approached it with a little extra pizzazz on the vibrato. With no
endings on these tunes, we slipped effortlessly from one into the next.

All cameras were now rolling again. I noticed a scuffling over by
the side of the stage, with Bill Graham pointing his finger and yelling
at someone. I wasn't quite aware of what was going on but I guessed
Bob had told his road manager or somebody that he didn't want to
be filmed, or that only a portion of his set could be shot, and Bill was
letting Bob's guy know that if he went anywhere near the cameras he
would break his neck.

When we hit the downbeat of "Forever Young," Levon looked at
Bob to see if he wanted to pick up the tempo. Bob shrugged back like,
Sure, why not? So we glided along, gradually picking up speed until it
felt just right. Bob sang "Forever Young" with such passion, and I tried
to keep up with him, note for note. By this point my hands were growing numb, but it seemed like for every verse Bob sang he nodded at me
to take another solo. For a moment at the end of that song everything
hung suspended in the air. We had to change keys once more before
we slammed back into a reprise of "Baby Let Me Follow You Down,"
and one more time it was 1966 and we were raising hell. Each of the
guys had a jubilant smile on his face like we were reliving the bad old
days all over again. Music should be fun, and by the look on Bob's face
and the faces of everyone in the entire place, we were having nothing
but fun.

When we finished our segment with Bob, almost all the guest performers were crowded in the wings. I told Bob we wanted to end the
show with everybody coming out to join him and Richard singing "I
Shall Be Released."

"Okay," he said. "When? Now?"

I laughed. "Yeah, we're going to do it now."

Everybody came out and gathered around the mics. Ringo sat at
our second drum kit. Ronnie Wood strapped on my other guitar and
joined Eric on that side of the stage with Butterfield as the Hawk hung
back next to Levon.

I pointed at Richard, and he started the piano intro. I joined in on guitar halfway through. Bob took the first verse, and everybody came in on the chorus. Seeing Dr. John and Neil Diamond singing side by side was a sight to behold. Van joined Bob and me on our mic in the chorus. As glorious as the moment was, there was a melancholy to all those voices that ran right through me, especially when Richard came in, singing the last verse in falsetto with Bob. The song took on another meaning in regard to this "last waltz."

At the end of the tune, everybody looked a bit stunned that it was all over. It was impossible to believe, and the audience wasn't going to accept it. As many of the performers left the stage, some just couldn't do it. Levon and Ringo weren't going anywhere yet. They kicked into a funky, feel-good beat, and I put my guitar back on. Eric Clapton, Ron Wood, Neil Young, and Butterfield all started trading licks. Dr. John took over at the piano. Rick, Garth, and I continued our duties as hosts and let the good times roll.

After about ten minutes of jamming from "the band" that's re-nowned for not jamming, I looked over at the side of the stage and saw Stephen Stills standing there. I waved in his direction and offered him my guitar. He came out just in time for the boys to start another groove. Rick gave his bass over to Carl Radle, a terrific musician friend of ours, and he and I slipped backstage to change clothes and catch our breath. I passed Marty on the way. "Is that it?" he joked. "What, no more? It's over already? We still have a few rolls of film left."

I freshened up and changed, feeling elated exhaustion. I was stand-ing in the shower, dressed, retrieving my clothes from the show, when I saw that somebody had stolen one of my shirts. Annie Leibovitz took a shot of me standing in the shower looking dismayed.

Garth and Levon came back to the dressing room. Richard was already there, and the five of us stood there looking at one another in awe. We had just played for close to five hours, going from Joni Mitchell to Muddy Waters, from Neil Young to Neil Diamond, with no major fuckups. Nobody has any real idea of what a feat that is. We saluted one another like we had just pulled off one of the best musical celebrations in rock 'n' roll history. It really, really does not get any better than this.

Dominique and my mother came into the dressing room, followed by all the friends, relatives, and guest performers. Everybody was shaking their heads like we had just won the marathon. Strangely, everyone else looked more tired than the five of us. We hadn't come down yet. Just as we started to lean back and take a deep breath, Bill Graham came banging and barging into the dressing room.

"No one has left," he said. "The audience is out there stomping and cheering. You have to go back out there."

"Go back out there?" I said. "Are you kidding? This show has been going on for five hours, and before that they had a feast and waltzed. Come on—enough!"

"They know this is a once-in-a-lifetime thing, and they're begging for one more," Bill pleaded. "Do it for me. If this is the Band's final concert, for god's sake, give us one more." His voice cracked as he repeated, "The final concert of the Band. Man, that's heartbreaking."

Hearing that "final concert" line got to me. I felt his sadness a hundred times over, but knew I wanted to ride this train into the station with purpose and pride. "Shall we?" I asked the guys. "Maybe we should do 'Don't Do It,' and then maybe they won't 'do it' anymore."

We alerted Marty and his crew that we were going to do one more. "Wait," he told me, grabbing his headset. "Okay, everybody," he said into the mic, "we got one more."

Steve Prince chimed in, "Everybody back to their battle stations. This war's not over yet."

Jon Taplin laughed as he quickly spread the word. "Back on. We're back on."

When we came out again, the roar was deafening. I couldn't believe the crowd still had this much energy. John Simon hustled the horn players back into position and they pulled out the only chart we hadn't used tonight. Larry Samuels alerted the mobile recording truck. "They're doing another one. Hit 'record'!"

"You're still there, huh?" I mumbled into the mic. "We're gonna do one more song, and that's it." Levon looked around the stage at all of us and went, "One. Two. Three. Uh!" He and Rick pounced on the intro like it was the first song of the night. Richard came in, tinkling ivories, with Garth adding sonic wonderment. I crashed down with my guitar riff, and the horns followed with their Allen Toussaint New Orleans punch. When Rick and Levon started singing with that sassy attitude, we were off and running.

Looking back at Garth behind his array of electronics, I thought, *God only made one of those.* Garth joined the Hawks (the last to become a member) under the guise of "music teacher." His family did not want him getting mixed up with rock 'n' roll and "our kind." I didn't blame them. Garth was a teacher, but much more. A sidekick. Part of our street gang. A brother in arms. An inspiration in showing how much a musical instrument has locked inside of it, and how much you can truly get out of it. For me, in particular, I savored Garth for turning me on to the glorious sounds of Anglican choirs, Greek and Arabic sounds with rhythms accompanying hip-rattling belly dancers, classical music maestros and their masterpieces (some through the impeccable touch of Glenn Gould's piano), jazz masters' unique tones and techniques. I couldn't get enough of it, and it broadened my sonic horizons as far as the ear could see. Garth caught me staring at him, and he threw his arms in the air and then down on his keyboards and played a phenomenal lick, laughing.

Richard and I came in singing. "Pleeease, don't do it, dontcha break my heart." He smiled his big-toothed smile at me and dug in on his piano part. Man, oh, man, Rich could break your heart, either with that voice, sounding like it was on the verge of tears at times, or with his deeply sensitive personality. He had such a rich tone. He could sing lower and higher than anybody in the Band, which made us refer to him as our "lead singer." He didn't like that. He didn't like being singled out, for better or worse. We all knew Richard had a special gift when he first joined the Hawks. What put him on top of the heap, though, was his vocal on the song he wrote with Bob, "Tears of Rage," the first cut on our first album, *Music from Big Pink*. That separated the men from the boys. We were awestruck by his power and soulfulness. I think Garth appreciated Richard's piano playing more than anybody. And before Levon came back to join us, when we were making the basement tapes, Richard sat behind the drums. We all messed around playing the drums a little, but Richard became a real drummer on the spot. What happened? Where the hell did that come from? Yesterday he didn't play the drums at all, and today he's a monster. He ended up becoming Levon's favorite drummer. Yep, God only made one of those.

As I tore into the guitar solo on "Don't Do It," Rick pushed me higher with his churning bass part. His support in music and in life was unparalleled in this group. You never even had to look around: Rick had your back come rain or shine. And boy, what an ear! He could hear intricate intonations and parts like he had a dog's super-hearing. He was the king of harmonies in the Band, but not because he studied harmony or read music; it just came perfectly natural to him. It was because of Rick that our vocals became known for their harmonies. For a long time Rick played a fretless bass while singing countermelodies and harmony and killer lead vocals. That's a full-on high-wire act. He had no idea how incredible I thought that was. For him it was just normal. It pissed me off how easy he made it look. He was one of those musicians who could pick up a trombone, a violin, or a pennywhistle and be playing it competently in ten minutes. He evolved into an incredible force in the Band's machine, and I knew God only made one of those. I finished my guitar solo, and Rick nod-ded at me like, *Good work, my brother.*

Breakdown! We all stopped, except Levon. What a beat! What a feel. He sang, "Go down to the river and there I'll be, I'm gonna jump in 'cause you don't care about me"—pure music through every bone in his body. The very first time I ever saw Levon play, when I was fifteen years old, it struck me right then and there: God only made one of those. He was a star already, playing with Ronnie and the Hawks. Five guys from Arkansas, all with remarkable talent, but you couldn't take your eyes off Levon. Ronnie knew it too; he danced in front of him, sang in his direction, and looked to him for musical cues, while Levon played eighth notes on the kick drum, the cymbals, and the snare, with a backbeat on the toms like a locomotion. All the while laughing until everybody joined in. I had never seen anything like it, and still haven't to this day.

When I joined the Hawks as the first Canadian in for the long haul, I hoped that some of Levon's southern magic would rub off on me. The two of us started a brotherhood with a big lock on the door. We let no one in until Rick, Richard, and Garth arrived. They were the goods. They were road warriors we could go to battle with anytime, anywhere. This band was a real band. No slack in the high wire here. Everybody held up his end with plenty to spare. Over the years, Levon and I did a lot of foolish things and probably could have wound up in prison for some of it. In the end, we did a whole lot more beautiful things, and I am honored to have been in his musical grace. He was our leader when we left Ronnie, and I would have followed him into the fires of hell—which I nearly did. In the last couple of years, our brotherhood came into rough times, whether from drugs and alcohol or our own pure madness, and we sure didn't want to see anybody get taken down.

At the end of the chorus on "Don't Do It," we sang out for the last time, "Pleeease, don't break my heart." Levon gave me a nod to go into the solo at the end of the song. I clawed at the strings on my guitar with an anger, with a sadness, with a finality I could hardly stand. In that moment, there was only the five of us in the world. No audience. No celebration. Nobody. Just the sound of the Band ringing in my ears. As I descended back into the signature guitar riff to signal the end of the song, we all locked eyes and crash-landed. Bam—the end.

Each of the guys bowed his head. Levon looked up at me, winked, and waved at this phenomenal audience. My eyes circled the stage, taking in my brothers Garth, Richard, Rick, and Levon. This can't be the final anything. This cannot be the end. What we have can never die, never fade away. We all raised our arms in the air and thanked the crowd for being here with us right to the bitter end. I adjusted the hat on my head, stepped to the microphone with what little strength I had left, and said:

"Good night—Good-bye."

CODA

Nobody wanted to come down—

Many of our guests had hardly got warmed up. They'd just had a taste and needed to play more music. Impromptu sessions were starting up in hotel suites and various locations, but for me, my cup had runneth over. I couldn't play another note. I found myself sitting on the floor against the wall of the hotel banquet room as people came and went in party spirit. Marty joined me on the floor. We didn't need to talk; we just had to remember to breathe.

The Band felt a tremendous sense of relief and accomplishment at having got through the concert *alive* on Thanksgiving Day. To be thankful, pay tribute . . . and celebrate at the same time was good medicine. I don't know if I'd ever felt as proud of our band as I did on that day.

After all those years on the road I'd discovered that, for the most part, things don't just happen. No, it depends on who comes along. And I'd had some doozies come down the pike: geniuses, ruthless individuals, gifted savants, goddesses, master thieves, swamp rats, hit men, hustlers, record-business shysters, and muses. I thought I knew where I wanted to go and what my calling was, but if I hadn't run that red light, or gone downtown on a Tuesday night, or hopped that southbound train—who knows?

A FEW DAYS LATER back home in Malibu, Marty called me sounding pretty jazzed. He said he'd seen some of the footage from the concert and it looked beautiful: the 35mm, the staging, the lighting—all of it had paid off. We had the makings of something special, and now he wanted to film the Band telling stories of our days on the road, so it would be clear what *The Last Waltz* was all about.

I mentioned to Marty that although we'd been able to embrace many different flavors of music in the show, there was still something missing: We never got to pay tribute to gospel or country music. I suggested we shoot my new song "Evangeline" with the exquisite Emmylou Harris and "The Weight" with our favorite gospel group the Staple Singers (who had covered the song themselves). He liked this idea and thought we should shoot it on an MGM soundstage where many of the great Hollywood musicals had been filmed. One of Martin Scorsese's great gifts was how he moved the camera, and this would give him full rein to do his thing.

The guys and I got together the following day to stir up our next move. We all took a deep breath, as if shedding one skin in anticipation of a new one. The Band had an album to complete for Capitol called *Islands*, which would mostly be made up of outtakes and B-sides (an unusual concept at the time). I had some new songs in the works for it as well. We had to deliver this record before *The Last Waltz* concert soundtrack could be released on Warner Bros.

There was also the possibility of doing a suite of new music that would include "The Last Waltz Theme," which I was writing in the tradition of a classic movie theme. Everybody agreed that we'd roll up our sleeves and start recording the following Monday at Shangri-La. Over the weekend I could get a couple of the tunes ironed out. When I got back to the house, I went straight up to my music room, looking forward to organizing the new material. I was fired up, so the lyrics came pretty smoothly.

We'd made a plan to meet at Shangri-La around high noon. I got to the studio early so I could tell the engineer the instrumentation of the first song and what to mic. By midday we were set up for the guys to walk in and sit behind their axes, ready to go. While waiting, I sat at the piano and found a couple of nice breaks and turnarounds for one of the new songs. Our recording engineer asked me to play some guitar so he could get a sound before everybody got there.

A while later, our studio manager, Larry Samuels, walked into the control room and shrugged his shoulders as if to say, "I don't know where they are." I asked him to call each of the guys to see what was happening. In the meantime I wrote out a couple of lyric alternatives, just in case one might sing better than another. When Larry came back he said he couldn't reach anyone, and now it was past 3:30. We all know that in rock 'n' roll the rules are vague and sometimes there aren't any. And sure, there were occasions when somebody didn't show up, but to have all four guys be this late was disturbing.

I knew we would eventually finish all of our commitments. We would get the music recorded to deliver the album we owed Capitol, and we would cut "The Last Waltz Suite" come hell or high water. But waiting there as the sun went down, it finally hit me—what I had been in true denial about: this train we'd been riding for so long was pulling into the station, not just for touring, not just for recording, but for everything. Nobody showed up. Nobody called. And I had to read the writing on the wall.

"THE END OF AN ERA" was how many people referred to the close of 1976. The dreams of the '60s and early '70s had faded and we were ready for a revelation, a revolt, a changing of the guard. The United States, Russia, and China were all testing nuclear weapons. Destruction loomed boldly in the air. Punk rock and hip-hop wanted to give music and culture a good slap in the face. It felt like everyone wanted to break something.

The Band had come to a crossroads. So many mixed emotions leads to confusion—and confusion can lead to self-destruction. The feeling was, if we can't break something else, we'll break ourselves. None of us wanted to destroy the thing we loved, but we didn't know how not to—and we didn't know how to say good-bye.

Still, through all the turbulence, I am left with such a deep appreciation for my journey, this shining path I've traveled being part of the Band—and there will never be another one like it. Such a gift, such talent, such pain, such madness . . . I wouldn't trade it for anything.

A fresh canvas, a new beginning, that's what you wanted, that's what you got, I told myself. I was venturing into the great unknown, quite daunting after having been a member of the Hawks and the Band for the last sixteen years, more than half my life. But I felt a shimmer inside, looking outward to the explorations and challenges that lay ahead: Bring on tomorrow, I want to get some on me. Let's turn the page, let's take the high road, let's break some rules . . . like we did before the revolution.

Dedicated to my family with boundless love:
Alexandra, Delphine, Sebastian, and Dominique
Tim, Rich, Dawn, and Nicholas
Donovan, Angelica, Gabriel, Seraphina, and Dominic
And to the memory of Rosemarie Chrysler Myke

ACKNOWLEDGMENTS

First of all, I want to thank Jared Levine, who has walked through the fire with me writing this book from the beginning.

Kevin Doughten—editor extraordinaire, for his dedication and help getting this manuscript down to a digestible length while never limiting the color of my voice.

Louise Dennys—with deep appreciation for her brilliant eye and intuitive ear, always in search of the soul.

Ryan Harbage—who made this book a reality and has supported its existence every step of the way.

Jim Guerinot—who read the first incarnation, the very long version of this book. He never flinched and even asked for more.

Sam Benjamin—for his enthusiasm and prompting me to dig deeper.

Tricia Boczkowski, Maya Mavjee, Molly Stern, and David Drake—for their fervid support and encouragement.

DG for the writing sanctuary and glory of RS.

LG for a healing hacienda and the ghost of Gary Cooper.

PA for the phantasmic destinations.

JW for offering the hand of experience and perspective.

MS for his friendship and timeless collaborations.

And LA for the love and inspiration.

SPECIAL THANKS TO:

Heather Reisman for her guidance.

Rob Bowman for his historical insight.

Elliott Landy and John Scheele for their photographs, and Bill Scheele for his archival contributions.

Nick and Stephanie.

Art and Fiona.

Much appreciation to Kristin Cochrane and Brad Martin.

Gary Stiffelman, David Jackel, Steve Bing, Charlie Conrad, Christina Brehm, Lesley Anton, Mirena Kim, Jeff Greenberg and the Village, Tomas Hernandez, Michael and Diane Budman, Jim Finley, Bruce Hardin, Jon Friedman, Marty Davis, Chantal Renaud, Jan Haust, Sally Grossman, Mo Ostin, Mark Birkey, Elizabeth Rendfleisch, Jesse Aylen, Linnea Knollmueller, Christopher Brand, Ellen Folan, Rebecca Marsh, Tammy Blake, Julie Cepler, Kelsey Lawrence, Cathy Paine, Matthew Sibiga, Mary Giuliano, Lindsey Reeder, Lynn Henry, Amanda Betts.

And to my dear cousins David Klegerman, Vicki Klegerman.

PHOTOGRAPHY CREDITS

Front endpaper (hardcover only): © Serge Daniloff
Back endpaper (hardcover only): © John Scheele
Page 495: © Elliott Landy

INSERT 1:

All photos pages 1–3: Courtesy of the author
Page 4, top: Courtesy of the author
Page 4, middle: Courtesy of Ronnie Hawkins & Wanda Nagurski
Page 4, bottom: © Serge Daniloff
Page 5, top left: Courtesy of the author
Page 5, top right: Courtesy of Ronnie Hawkins & Wanda Nagurski
Page 5, middle: Courtesy of the author
Page 5, bottom: Getty Images/Michael Ochs Archives
Page 6, top: © W. Eugene Smith/Black Star
Page 6, bottom: © Dale Smith
Page 7: © Daniel Kramer
All photos page 8: Courtesy of the author

INSERT 2:

Page 1, top: © Elliott Landy

Page 1, bottom: © John Scheele

All photos page 2–4: © Elliott Landy

All photos page 5: © John Scheele

Page 6, top: © Barry Feinstein Photography, Inc.

Page 6, middle right: Courtesy of the author

Page 6, middle left: © Barry Feinstein Photography, Inc.

Page 6, bottom: Courtesy of the author

Page 7, top: © John Scheele

Page 7, bottom: © Steve Gladstone, courtesy of Brian Hardin

Page 8, top: © Steve Gladstone, courtesy of Brian Hardin

Page 8, bottom: Courtesy of MGM